THE PRINCESS
AND THE PROPHET

THE
PRINCESS
AND THE
PROPHET

THE SECRET HISTORY OF MAGIC, RACE, AND MOORISH MUSLIMS IN AMERICA

{ JACOB S. DORMAN }

BEACON PRESS
BOSTON

BEACON PRESS
Boston, Massachusetts
www.beacon.org

Beacon Press books
are published under the auspices of
the Unitarian Universalist Association of Congregations.

22 21 20 19   8 7 6 5 4 3 2 1

This book is printed on acid-free paper that meets the uncoated paper
ANSI/NISO specifications for permanence as revised in 1992.

Text design and composition by Kim Arney

COVER: Top: Photos of Eva Brister; bottom: Walter Brister, both from Harry Wilson
and Lloyd F. Nicodemus, *Official Route Book of the Pawnee Bill Wild West Show Presenting
a Complete Chronicle of Interesting Events, Happenings and Valuable Data for the Season
1900. Being the Official Record of the Devious Wanderings of the Troupers En Route with
Pawnee Bill's Historic Wild West* (Newport, KY: Donaldson Lithograph Co., 1900),
81, 83, Circus World Museum, Baraboo, WI. Edges: Strobridge Lithograph Co.; cover
image: Barnum & Bailey: The Wizard Prince of Arabia, 1914, ht2000328, John and
Mable Ringling Museum of Art, Tibbals Circus Collection.

Library of Congress Cataloging-in-Publication Data
Names: Dorman, Jacob S., author.
Title: The princess and the prophet : the secret history of magic, race,
and Moorish Muslims in America / Jacob S. Dorman.
Description: Boston : Beacon Press, 2020. | Includes bibliographical
references and index.
Identifiers: LCCN 2019037408 (print) | LCCN 2019037409 (ebook) |
ISBN 9780807067260 (hardcover) | ISBN 9780807067482 (ebook)
Subjects: LCSH: Black Muslims. | African Americans—Religion. |
Amusements—United States—History.
Classification: LCC BP221 .D67 2020 (print) | LCC BP221 (ebook) |
DDC 297.8/7—dc23
LC record available at https://lccn.loc.gov/2019037408
LC ebook record available at https://lccn.loc.gov/2019037409

For Eli and Abby

CONTENTS

ORGANIC MOSAICS

The imaginative capacity of subordinate groups to reverse and/or negate dominant ideologies is so widespread—if not universal—that it might be considered part and parcel of their standard cultural and religious equipment. . . . Properly understood, any hegemonic ideology contains, within itself, the raw material for contradiction and conflict.

—JAMES C. SCOTT[1]

The world of apocrypha is a world of books made real, which may well be understood and appreciated by readers of Borges, Calvino, Lewis Carroll—or certain of the Sufis. . . . In the world of apocrypha the Images of established religion and canonical texts acquire a kind of mutability, a tendency to drift, to reflect the subjectivities of the (often anonymous) visionaries who sift through fragments in order to produce more fragments—so that texts become fluid organic mosaics with replaceable parts, each bit catching and reflecting a shard of light, like a magpie's hoard. . . . And thus are born the scriptures of heresies, the canons of the gnostics, the fugitive poetics of self-revelation, the rants of the cults of love and light.

—PETER LAMBORN WILSON, a.k.a. Hakim Bey[2]

A wise man once said, "There are no religions which are false, all are true in their own fashion."[3] Religions are socially useful, and true in that they work; they make sense to those who believe in them, and they help those who believe them to make sense of the world. They help explain pain, death and suffering, pleasure and joy, labor

1

and its rewards, sin and its consequences. And so the usefulness of religion doesn't depend on its truthfulness, any more than the usefulness of Alice depends on the accuracy of her Wonderland. The story of the birth of the Moorish Science Temple, and the precursor to the "Black Muslims" of the Nation of Islam, is truly more wonderful than I could have imagined when I set out to tell this tale seventeen years ago. Nor could I have imagined that its central character, Noble Drew Ali, would transform himself so many times in so many death-defying ways. Follow me, then, down a wormhole into the not-so-distant past, and find a cast of characters and a sequence of events all the more extraordinary because they are true.

We are late. All the people in this saga are no more, as are virtually everyone they ever knew. The story I have to tell lies just south of living memory, sticking up here and there like scattered potsherds from an ancient age. It is the product of sifting thousands of brittle circus programs, lithographs, letters, and newspaper pages, their leaden ink on wood pulp turned hard and orange with age so that they crumble at the touch. On occasion a relative few of those broadsheets get filmed, and the results captured with optical character recognition, digitized and bundled into subscriptions sold to great research universities and searchable by the millions of pages per second. In those versions some of the shadows we seek leave furtive tracings, and from them we can begin to piece together trajectories, outlines, the slightest suggestion of a form. If we are lucky, and I have been very lucky, we find photographs, and within the very pores of those faces still more clues and questions emerge. But most of the printed past, even the not-so-distant past, fades from sight and has long since given up the ghost. It is all the harder to find evidence of secret societies, and criminal rackets by their very nature resist exposure; the most secretive actions are seldom committed to paper in the first place. Names carved in stone tend to endure, but in a hubristic age fueled by knowledge, when algorithms stalk our every move, practicing history is humbling and illustrates that what we don't know about the world is vastly greater than what we *do* know.

Taking this journey requires expanding the customary narratives of US history in the Gilded Age and Progressive Eras with wider geographical and topical scopes while also attending to the political racketeering, corruption, and graft that was endemic in big cities in general and Chicago in particular. The end of the nineteenth and beginning of the twentieth centuries featured incredible conflicts between capitalists and workers that bordered on warfare. There were influxes of millions of immigrants, great urban political machines vying for votes and dispensing hundreds of thousands of jobs, and progressive programs to reform the nation and save its soul that revolutionized government, social services, and faith alike. Inventors like Thomas Alva Edison gave the world electrical generators, electric lights, telephones, and moving pictures, while the automobile upended every aspect of life.

With so many new people, new industries, new inventions, new forms of corruption, and new social pressures, the Gilded Age also saw a tremendous series of social revolutions. Thrust together in unfamiliar cities, men and women of all classes and regions tested and tried new gender roles. Earning wages opened up new opportunities and time for leisure. Among migrants to the burgeoning cities, chances to earn wages, live with greater independence, and attend novel entertainments like dance halls led to a late nineteenth-century sexual revolution. These processes, conflicts, and crusades were so great that they over-spilled the nation's borders: during the Gilded Age, the United States conquered, resettled, and ruled American Indian nations, and American industrialists and missionaries alike ventured around the globe, not far behind the consumer goods that spread the American manufacturing empire even beyond where steam ships and steam locomotives could reach.

Religion itself was busy being transformed as well; the Methodist Church mushroomed across a grief-stricken nation after the Civil War, as did an offshoot of Methodism and the Baptist faith known as Holiness, and its offspring, Pentecostalism. The religious revivals of the time affected the cities as much or more than the countryside; great revivalists like Dwight Moody set up shop in American towns such as Chicago. Cities filled up with church spires. Approximately two million Ashkenazi Jews fled persecution in the Russian Empire and found new homes in the United States of America, while the numbers of Muslims in America were very small—even most Lebanese Arabs who immigrated at the end of the nineteenth century were Christians. In the face of the wave of Christian enthusiasm, a counter-stream of occultists peddled alternative faiths, many of which proclaimed the sanctity of the Orient, the Oriental travels of Jesus, or the spiritual wisdom of Tibet, India, and Arabia. Not infrequently, these alternative faiths drew much of their power from sexual energies, tapping into the era's repressed animal spirits and the seemingly endless human appetite for erotic encounter with "the Other," variously construed. There were no "old-time religions" at the turn of the century: these were all new religions, all in flux.

In the Gilded Age, the Orient appealed to Black Americans as an antidote to Western materialism, as a place fantastically strange and wondrously exotic, and as a cultured, heterogeneous repudiation of the sterility and dumb brutality of Jim Crow oppression. Black Americans such as Frederick Douglass visited the pyramids. The Reverend Edward Wilmot Blyden, a minister born in St. Vincent, admired West African Islam from his adopted Liberian home, though he never thought that Islam was superior to Christianity, as some have thought. Rather, he viewed Islam as a kind of intermediate monotheism that was far better than Christianity at winning converts in Africa and might be used by missionaries like himself as a means of bringing followers to the "higher" truths of Christianity. By the end of his life he taught "that Mohammedanism is the form of Christianity best adapted to the Negro race," and that "Islam is the form that Christianity takes in Africa."[4]

In Shakespeare's 1603 masterpiece *The Tragedy of Othello, the Moor of Venice*, literature's most famous Moor vainly pleaded, "Men should be what they seem." Yet many of the most interesting men in the development of "Moorish" American forms of Islam were anything but what they seemed. A London-based Black actor, journalist, political activist, and serial entrepreneur who variously called himself Duse Mohamed and Dusé Mohamed Ali took his first name in honor of the Victorian actress Eleonora Duse and cooked up a preposterous origin story as a Sudanese Egyptian that he plagiarized from a history of Egypt. Though he knew little of Islam and nothing of Arabic, he connected the Black struggle globally with the pro-Ottoman movement in London and the cause of colonized peoples around the world. He portrayed Othello at the Universal Races Congress in 1911, a gathering conceived and organized by the Jewish-born leaders of the Ethical Culture Society, and then used the mailing list from that congress and funding from an English colonial magnate to start the *African Times and Orient Review*. Among the people who worked for that publication was a young Jamaican printer named Marcus Mosiah Garvey, who would go on to adapt many of Duse's pro-business and anti-imperialist ideas to his organization, the Universal Negro Improvement Association. Duse for his part spent some time in America in the 1920s editing Garvey's newspaper, living in Detroit between 1924 and 1926. He helped organize a Central Muslim Society that organized regular Friday prayers, helping to explain the large membership in the Moorish Science Temple in the Motor City. When the foremost practitioner of "Hindu" escape magic, Harry Houdini, died in Detroit in 1926, Duse filled in for him on an interim basis with his own "Oriental" show.[5]

The Black migrations that began with Emancipation, continued with the Exodusters in Kansas in the 1870s, and culminated in the First Great Migration of World War I, saw millions of people search to better their lives by moving from the rural South to the urban South, from the upper South and Gulf Coast to the Midwest and West, and from all points of the compass to Chicago, Detroit, Philadelphia, and New York. But the East never lost its appeal for people of African descent. In the 1920s the Jamaican-born writer Claude McKay wrote the signal novel of the Harlem Renaissance, *Home to Harlem*, from the safe remove of Marseilles, France, and Muslim North Africa. Rather than himself hurrying home to Harlem, McKay bided his time, spending years enjoying the marvelous tolerance of homosexuality, affordable living, and lack of American racism to be found in both places. "In Fez I felt that I was walking all the time on a magic carpet," he remembered. "The maze of souks and bazaars with unfamiliar patterns of wares was like an Oriental fantasy." Liberated from the problems of "colour prejudice," Morocco created a heady sensation for McKay: "Excited and intoxicated and fascinated," with the colorful sights and the "Afro-Oriental bargaining," he remarked, "I went completely native."[6]

In between Blyden, Duse, and McKay, a host of people of African descent constructed their own visions of the Orient, or the "Afro-Asiatic" world, that linked the Near East to Africa and Black Americans. There was no stark separation between the Christian "Holy Land" and more profane depictions of the belly dancers and sword swallowers of the Orient. Rather, such religious formations rode along on the magic carpet of late nineteenth- and early twentieth-century American Orientalism, a diverse ridership including freemasons, "Nobles of the Mystic Shrine," or Shriners, occultists, and exotic "savage" and "barbaric" peoples from World's Fairs and traveling circuses. It was not a multicultural but a *polycultural* and decidedly motley crew that formed dense webs of ever-branching rhizomatic connections rather than bounded racial silos. American Orientalism blurred borders of all kinds and gained much of its

subversive power from its defiance of the norms of Jim Crow segregation at home and racist imperialism abroad.

This book is the first to reveal that, in 1925, a veteran performer
named John Walter Brister took the name "Noble Drew Ali" and
founded the Moorish Science Temple of America, the first American
Muslim mass movement and the progenitor of the Black Muslims of
the Nation of Islam. A secret serpentine path through show business,
imperialism, racism, and religion connects Harry Houdini, Pawnee
Bill, Hindu magicians, and the creation of African American Islam.
The tale of Walter Brister's metamorphosis into Noble Drew Ali has
never been told before because historians have been looking for the
wrong person in the wrong places. A skilled magician who was adept
at making people appear to disappear, Brister faked his own death
prior to his emergence as Noble Drew Ali and has until now been
able to hide his origins by claiming he was born in North Carolina
rather than Kentucky. Yet his impact has been vast. As the first Black
child star on Broadway, and then the founder of the first Muslim
mass movement in America, Walter Brister was incongruously both
the forerunner of the blond tap-dancing cherub Shirley Temple and
of the militant Black Nationalist icon Malcolm X.

At the outset of this project, one thread that I felt I had not ex-
plored thoroughly enough in my prior research on Black Jews, Black
Israelites, Rastafarians, and Black Spiritual churches was Orientalism—that is, the idea of the East in Western culture as seen through
the arts, commerce, and colonialism. It was the Orient, I found, that
was the shared reference point not just for early twentieth-century
Black versions of Judaism, but for Black forms of Islam, conjuring,
and Rastafarianism as well. Yet no one had ever remarked on the overriding Orientalist quality of these practitioners and groups, whose
members wore fezzes, turbans, and headscarves and often lionized
"the East." More than forty years after the late Palestinian American
scholar Edward Said published *Orientalism* in 1978, the notion that
African Americans, as oppressed people, could themselves adopt Orientalism, a discourse of oppressors, still strikes some as exotic, or even
unthinkable—incongruous at best. But Orientalism also contains
oppositional elements, not only oppressive ones. Anarchist author Peter Lamborn Wilson, a follower of Noble Drew Ali, writes of a "heretical culture of resistance within Islam" that has been appropriated
by Western heretics and become part of a "Western culture of resistance." For Wilson, also known by his Moorish name, Hakim Bey,

this mode of appropriation amounts to a cooperative venture among global heretics, artists, rebels, and visionaries. "Romantic perception often deliberately distorts," Wilson writes, "but does so in the interests of freeing the very means of perception from the oppression of consensus and the deadly humdrum of mere accuracy."[7] Taking Black esoteric traditions seriously means allowing for the possibility that their practitioners sometimes were challenging the very structures of perception beyond "the deadly humdrum of mere accuracy" in a time when white-dominated institutions of the humanities, science, politics, and entertainment united behind the outrageous slander that Black people were less than fully human.[8]

As I completed my first book and began the research for my second, I noticed that the literature on Black Muslims was far larger than that on Black Jews, but that it was wedded to the notion of African "retentions," popularized by anthropologist Melville Herskovits, which I felt in the case of Islam as with Judaism was not only misleading but demonstrably false; people do not "retain" their religions and cultures in a linear manner from their ancestors, but reinterpret and reinvent tradition anew in every generation. The dynamism of cultural change in the present is just as surely true of the past; only our myopic faith in our own uniqueness blinds us to this fact. Many scholars have attempted unsuccessfully to demonstrate a link between the Muslim faiths practiced by Americans of African descent in the twentieth century and enslaved Muslims in the Americas before the Civil War. It is not that enslaved African Muslims were not present in North America; they were, though almost all arrived before 1770 except for those who landed in South Carolina in the last decade of the slave trade. Most were men and boys, limiting their abilities to have children or pass Islam to descendants. There were no known Muslim communities among the enslaved here; the only example of Muslims worshipping collectively as opposed to individually comes from a single family who worshiped together on Sapelo Island, Georgia. Moreover, the total number of known enslaved Muslims in North America is little more than fifty. In addition, enslaved Muslims began integrating Christian worldviews into their own in the very first generation. Finally, there was a gap of more than a century between the official cessation of the transatlantic slave trade and the emergence of a community of at least seven thousand Muslims in the Moorish Science Temple of America between 1925 and 1929. When researchers for the Works Progress Administration

scoured the Sea Islands for Muslim customs in the 1930s, all they
could find was the use of Islamic names like "Omar," and the making
of *saraka*, sweet rice cakes, whose name comes from the Arabic word
for charity, *sadaqah*. "There is no indication so far that the African
American Muslims of today inherited Islam from the Muslims of
yesterday," writes historian Sylviane Diouf, who has contributed as
much as anyone to our knowledge of Islam among the enslaved. "The
orthodox Islam brought by the enslaved West Africans has not survived. It has left traces; it has contributed to the culture and history
of the continents; but its conscious practice is no more."[9] Simply put,
by the early twentieth century, those who were descended from enslaved African Muslims were no longer practicing Islam. Then there
is the fact that the Moorish Science Temple when first constituted
did not use the Qur'an like other Muslims, but shared many features
with other Black alternative religions of the period of the Great Migration, including a reverence for occult books published by the De
Laurence Company of Chicago, many of which featured an Orientalist reverence for Arabia, India, and Tibet.

So who were these seven thousand Moors who began identifying as Muslims in the latter half of the 1920s? Like their cousins
the Black Israelites and Rastafarians, I viewed the Moors as a great
example of "polycultural bricolage," the highfalutin term I theorized
in my first book, not as an example of mechanical "retention" of a
putatively pure African past.[10] Instead, individual visionaries create
collages from sacred and profane traditions alike—they "sift through
fragments in order to produce more fragments," forming "fluid organic mosaics with replaceable parts," in the words of Peter Lamborn
Wilson/Hakim Bey.[11]

And so, I followed up on a clue that had gone unnoticed in every
existing account of the Moors: Noble Drew Ali's earliest advertisements proclaimed that he would perform escape magic, freeing himself when bound by rope. The Associated Negro Press also reported
that "in 1915 he was accompanying a Hindu fakir in circus shows
when he decided to start a little order of his own."[12] Maybe, then,
Drew Ali's knowledge of Islam did not come from enslaved Muslim
ancestors, but from images of Islam in popular entertainment such
as circus magic.

Asking what it meant to be a "Moor" around World War I
pointed me toward a wealth of associations with the *Arabian Nights*,
Barbary Coast pirates, Civil War Zouave soldiers, Moorish rebels

fighting the Spanish in the Rif War from 1920 to 1927, and most especially, the circus shows, minstrel shows, medicine shows, magic shows, sideshows, carnivals, and vaudeville stages that presented the "Mystic East" and its entrancing Muslim acrobats, dancers, equestrians, and magicians. I visited twenty-six theatrical, religious, fraternal, and historical archives between 2006 and 2019, in London and fourteen cities in the United States, looking for evidence of Blacks, Arabs, and Muslims in the circus. Eventually, I compiled a database of 14,500 images I shot in the archives or pulled from online newspaper databases, which I annotated and combined with information from dozens of books and articles.

Representations of the Islamic Orient in American and European circuses were actually quite plentiful and easy to find, going back as far as the 1830s. Depictions of Arabia, along with animals with Oriental associations such as camels, were so common in nineteenth-century America that it would be much harder to find a circus *without* some kind of reference to the Mystic East than it would to find one *with* them. Troupes of Arab acrobats from Morocco, Egypt, and Syria started tumbling, twirling rifles, doing trick riding, and forming impressive human pyramids before the Civil War, and became especially plentiful in the golden age of the circus between 1871 and 1915. The Islamic Orient was also one of the most popular subjects of the gigantic spectaculars that served as the impressive opening performances in many circuses.

Black main stage performers have always been rare in American circuses, but Black workers behind the scenes were numerous and could earn a "Zulu ticket" by dressing up as an Arab, a Moor, an Oriental, or a Zulu in these big opening "specs." And American circuses not only displayed Arabs and Moors as Orientals; they pointedly portrayed them as Muslims performing the *hajj* or their daily prayers. In the fertile few decades between the production of nineteenth-century Orientalist knowledge and the disenchantment of the world through the spread of newsreels and the mass travel of the world wars, "colored people" with the right skin tones, knowledge, and acting abilities could play almost anyone from Africa, India, or the Middle East. After all, many US Americans did not know what Indians from the subcontinent looked like: only 8,681 Indians immigrated to the US in the first three decades of the twentieth century. Of those, only 1,040 were estimated to have been Muslim.[13] The repackaging and revaluation of Orientalist knowledge, frequently by

African Americans assuming an Oriental identity themselves, had an unmistakable political spin as a critique of imperialism, materialism, racism, and the West. In contrast to the many derogatory views of Africa and Africans, at a time when Africa was being colonized by European nations, lynching was prevalent, and Black political disenfranchisement was soaring, and in an era before the Great Migration provided mobility, economic opportunities, and greater hope for the masses of Southern Blacks, the Oriental exhibits of circuses, carnivals, and the 1893 World's Fair displayed Islamic people of African descent in a romantic, mysterious, exotic, and mostly favorable light.

I could easily show that America's fascination with Islam in circuses and vaudeville stages was both lengthy and meaningful. But unless I could find a younger version of Noble Drew Ali as a circus performer, few people would care. My first stop on the way to amassing my digital archive was the Circus World Museum and Archive in the bucolic hamlet of Baraboo, Wisconsin, a place of intensely green hills and faded red barns. The museum, which has its own miniature circus including live Bengal tigers, is located along a creek where the Ringling brothers grew up and returned every winter for annual repairs as the snow piled up around the many barns that housed circus animals, ornate wagons, and beautiful costumes. I began by compiling a list of every circus I could find that included Arab acrobats, and then started working through the route books of those circuses. (Route books are a record of the circus season primarily sold to circus performers themselves but frequently available for sale to the public as souvenirs.)

Before long, I found a line drawing from 1899 and a photograph from 1900 from the Pawnee Bill Wild West yearbook of a young Black man, Walter Brister, dressed as a "Hindoo Magician," by the name of Armmah Sotanki. The time period fit perfectly with the little we know of Noble Drew Ali's life before he founded the Moorish Science Temple. By researching the man's given name and his wife's name, as well as their stage name, "Sotanki," I was able to locate Brister in the circus and identify his prior career on Broadway. I even found a letter from him in the collection of the great Harry Houdini, who at the start of his career practiced "Hindoo" magic at the Algerian exhibit on the Midway Plaisance of the Chicago World's Fair of 1893.

In researching the life of Noble Drew Ali, I found many Black entertainers who used the Shriner title "Noble," or who used the name "Drew" or "Ali." How could I be certain that this young man grew into the Prophet Noble Drew Ali? I did not find the definitive clue that I was looking for until I purchased a high-resolution photograph of the Moorish Science Temple's 1928 annual convention from the New York Public Library. It was a photograph that I was familiar with; it even appears on the back of one of the albums of the rapper Mos Def (Yasiin Bey). But I wanted a larger version, a version that would allow me to peer into the very pupils of Noble Drew Ali's eyes. When I enlarged the photograph I could see that Noble Drew Ali had a dark mole on the right side of his nose. When I blew up the picture of Brister and stared at it closely for several minutes, a constellation of darker dots on the right side of his nose merged into a single dark dot exactly where the mole appears in the picture of Noble Drew Ali, taken twenty-eight years later. A microhistorical proof has seldom rested on such microscopic evidence.

Connecting those tiny dots brought much larger issues into focus. The very concept of magic originated in an Orientalist fear of Zoroastrian and later Islamic and Jewish religions, and, to my surprise, Gilded Age and inarguably Orientalist stage magic had played a crucial role in developing sincere and authentic Islamic religions in America, upsetting received wisdom about the alleged separation between the sacred and the profane, commerce and confession, magic and religion, East and West, and the interplay of ancestors versus contemporaries in creating new religious cultures.

But finding the secret show business roots of the founder of the twentieth century's Black Muslims opened even broader questions about America's relationship with Islam, which has been so tortured of late. In my archival research I did not find what either conservatives or liberals would have predicted I would find by investigating Islam in the American past. The late conservative Democrat Samuel P. Huntington and his admirers on the right might claim that Islam and the West are destined to clash, while Edward Said might have argued that the West has always feared Islam and mistreated Muslims. Sure, I could find some anti-Islamic sentiment in the archives, but not any more than the general ambient level of animus that one finds against all minority racial, religious, and ethnic groups in the vitriolic Gilded Age. The voice of a prominent Islamophobe like Holiness preacher John Alexander Dowie, who fought and lost a prayer battle with Indian Muslim Prophet Mirzā Ghulām Ahmad, was more than balanced by the hundreds of thousands of American Nobles of the Mystic Shrine, both Black and white, including Franklin Delano

Roosevelt, William Jennings Bryan, Thurgood Marshall, Harry
Houdini, Harry S. Truman, Earl Warren, John Philip Sousa, and
J. Edgar Hoover, who greeted each other with *salaams* and swore a
"Moslem's oath" to "Allah, the God of Arab, Moslem, and Moham-
med."[14] Even though most Shriners did not think of themselves as
Muslims, and their rituals were complex performances laden with
parody and sarcasm, the investment in Islamic narratives by so many
prominent Americans of many races was at the very least surprising.
Indeed, what I found as I investigated past American attitudes toward Islam was that Americans of all descriptions had once treated
Islam and Muslims with overriding fascination and respect. Americans were surely Orientalist in that they subscribed to romantic and
spurious myths about Muslims and "the East" being essentially and
unalterably different than Christians and "the West." But within that
Orientalism I found a strong strain of positive sentiment toward Islam little mentioned by either Edward Said or his critics.

America's Islamic Orientalism was part of such diverse and
important changes as the rise of commercial leisure and amusement parks, the liberation of women from corsets, the first female
bloomers ("harem pants"), the reimagining of female sexual agency
and desire in Orientalist romance novels and risqué dance performances, the adoption of elements of Moorish architecture in iconic
public buildings like Chicago's Auditorium Building, whose Moorish arches are repeated in the Hollywood Bowl's band shell; and the
use of sumptuous Islamic elements in the new capitalist consumer
palaces of department stores and ornate Orientalist cinema buildings. There is even a good chance that one of the most American
of pastimes, football cheerleading, owes its genesis, its human pyramids, its rifle twirling, and its midriff-baring costumes to the Arab
acrobats who were ubiquitous in American popular entertainment at
the turn of the twentieth century. If you believe that Noble Drew Ali
was divinely inspired, then knowing that he was born in Kentucky
and worked as a musician and a magician before his emergence as a
prophet does not change that assessment, any more than knowing
that Jesus was once a carpenter changes one's position on whether he
was the messiah. On the other hand, I do expect this book to change
the opinions of those who believe that the United States of America
or "the West" is now or has ever been inalterably opposed to Islam.

In sum, this book proposes a radically new explanation of the rise
of Islam among people then known as "Negroes" in the 1920s: rather

than being the direct descendants of antebellum enslaved African Muslims, twentieth-century movements harvested the produce of a century's worth of representations of Islam and the Orient from popular culture. The incredible story I dug up in the archives suggests not just that the United States was actually less Islamophobic a century ago then it is today, but also that ideas of Islam once helped to expand the liberties of all Americans and usher in the sexual, gender, and racial liberation movements of the modern era. In time, perhaps the world will again agree that there is nothing antagonistic about Islam and the United States of America.

Finally, a note on terminology: the term "Black" has much older origins but came into widespread favor with the Black Power movement of the 1960s and 1970s and has never lost its currency; it is the label I use most often in this text. I agree with the Moorish Science Temple that people are not colors but believe that the Blackness of Black people is the result of shared culture, history, and ancestry, not a description of skin color. More importantly, I agree that Black people form a national group, with distinctive and somewhat shared history, ancestry, language, geography, and culture, and so are not merely a racial group like "whites," which is a marker of structural privilege in the context of white supremacy, not a marker of shared culture or even ancestry. Accordingly, I have chosen to capitalize the word "Black," much as some once argued for and achieved the capitalization of the label "negro." One of the merits of the term "Black" is that it is transnational, not limited to North America, but space constraints have forced me to focus on the United States in this book and so I use "Black" interchangeably with "Black American." I do so knowing that not everyone of African descent wanted to be called "Black" in the 1920s or earlier when there was greater colorism among "colored folk" than exists today.

The followers of the Moorish Science Temple of America, the subject of this book, reject the term "Black" and prefer the terms "Moor" and "Moorish American," since they assert that the people known as "Black" are actually part of a nation with roots in Morocco and indigenous America. It is certainly true that Islam has flourished in West Africa for more than a thousand years, and that North African Muslims have long influenced sub-Saharan societies, not only in the heavily Muslim Senegambia region but also in present-day Nigeria, where the name of the Yoruba high god, Olorun, is said to be derived from the Muslim name Allah. So whether or not Black

Americans have genealogical African Muslim ancestors, the notion that the descendants of African slaves are Moors is poetically valid, and certainly infinitely more true than the racist canards about "Negroes" that it opposed. While the historical documentation of the transatlantic slave trade shows that the majority of the ancestors of today's Black people are indeed from sub-Saharan Africa, I also agree with many American Moors that those ancestors are not exclusively African but include people from every continent on earth, including in many cases indigenous Americans.

Since "African American" did not appear in print until the 1960s and was not the most widely accepted label until 1989, I usually avoid the term so as not to be anachronistic or to foreclose the dynamic and political debate by which former "Negroes" came to call themselves African Americans, nearly a century after this book begins. I place the terms "Negro," "colored," and "Afro-American" in quotation marks to indicate that these terms were contested in their own time, and have generally fallen out of use today. Sometimes my sources use descriptors of Blackness such as "The Race," "race man," "race woman," "Asiatics," "Afro-Asiatic," "Ethiopian Americans," or "Moorish Americans," and I employ these terms as well; each has its own distinctive nuance. I leave racist slurs as originally written, so as not to deodorize the savage racism of the past, an essential spur for the rise of Black liberation movements, including an incredible version of Islam with inspirations in circus tents, Wild West shows, vaudeville theaters, Indian magical mendicants, herbal medicines, religious tracts, anti-imperial political movements, and places as diverse as contemporary Africa, ancient Arabia, and old Kentucky.

CHAPTER ONE

OLD KENTUCKY

When I was born, it turned black dark in the daytime.
The people put their hoes down and came out of the fields.

—NOBLE DREW ALI, circa 1926[1]

In 1893, the year of the Chicago World's Fair, Walter Brister spent a lot of time practicing his cornet. He was thirteen years old, but his small size made him seem younger than his age. He practiced his horn daily—he had to. Any brass player would tell you as much. He would notice if he skipped even a single day with his horn, even if the audience did not. But perhaps worst of all, his father, "Professor" John Henry Brister would notice, and there might be hell to pay. "Professor" was a term that certain professionals assumed in that day, whether they were leading a band or selling patent medicines and other tonics to heal whatever might ail you. In any event, Professor J. H. Brister, a medium-brown-skinned man with a gravity-defying mustache waxed horizontally much wider than his face, was leader of what he called the "Woodlawn Wangdoodles" or the "Original Pickaninny Band," which he led in a new Broadway show called *In Old Kentucky*. The show was one of those sentimental musical concoctions set in the Old South demonstrating how much better it was for "the darkies" back in slavery times. It was noxious, but it paid the bills.

Producer Jacob Litt came up with the idea of using a "pickaninny" band and dispatched his general manager, A. W. Dingwall, to find one. Playwright C. T. Dazey wrote a section in the second half of the play featuring the "Woodlawn Wangdoodles," in honor of a famous mansion and stables in Kentucky. The producer created a racist origin story for the band that essentially told the white American public to relax; the novel concept of a Black juvenile band on Broadway would reinforce racist stereotypes of Black servility and primitiveness more than it challenged them. Litt allegedly sent A. W. Dingwall on a tour of the South in search of Black child musicians, winding his way through more than a dozen Southern cities from Charleston to Jackson, Mississippi. Finally, in Jackson, a "loquacious old hotel porter" reported that "Dah was a old hog-raiser 'bout ten miles in de country who used to hab a niggah boy what played a brass horn." This account from the San Francisco *Morning Call* was about as truthful as its horrible rendition of Black speech. The writer must have been a frustrated novelist, as he added no shortage of such flourishes: "'Great oaks from little acorns grow,' thought Dingwall, as he followed the directions of the old man through the woods on horseback." According to the fable, Dingwall rode until he found a "tumble-down log cabin, hidden away in a dismal swamp," the home of one George Washington Johnson. "A picturesque old 'auntie,' in variegated calico, red bandana head-covering and bare feet, timidly responded to the travel-stained stranger's knock at the much battered and hingeless door." Having invented one "uncle" in Jackson, the reporter now invents an "auntie," employing the false "familial" terms of slavery that outlasted the peculiar institution in just such "picturesque" tales as this. In response to Dingwall's asking if there were any colored boys who could play the horn "came the amused and amusing reply, 'Laws amighty, honey, yaas, Dat rascal "Ike" kin jes make dat ole brass horn talk.'"[2] Dingwall found Ike, along with twenty-eight of his "ragamuffin" comrades, who all taught themselves to play the cornet, completely innocent of any formal instruction; truly "magical Negroes," these. In fact, none had ever seen another musical instrument "save a banjo, without which, of course, no Mississippi negro would care to live." The boy's mothers, "the mammies" in this tale, resisted the idea of their sons going on tour initially, but when Dingwall told them how much he would pay, "the popping out of eyes and gaping relaxation of mouths was almost audible." Dingwall took the boys to New York and in only a month "the famous Pickaninny band of 'In Old Kentucky' was the talk of the theater-going public of the metropolis."[3]

Although producer Jacob Litt created this fantastical and deeply racist story about rounding up untutored miniature musicians from the deepest swamps of Mississippi, all of whom had managed to learn to play without lessons, and on one single shared instrument, the actual training and recruitment of Black kid bands took considerably more work, and capitalized on established Black networks of musical instruction in Indianapolis and Cincinnati, not in the Deep South. The pickaninny band debuted during a road tour of Pittsburgh and soon proved to be one of the highlights of "the immediately phenomenal success of this enjoyable play."[4] In the "Negro" community of the day, "colored" juvenile bands were sometimes called "kid bands"; for white audiences, they were called "pickaninny" bands. The Woodlawn Wangdoodles, who were all between the ages of nine and thirteen when they started in 1893, would become the most famous kid band of the 1890s and, by initiating a craze for such bands, it eventually became a legend in the annals of Black entertainment.[5] In much of the show they were adorned in rustic fashion with short pants and broad-brimmed hats, but as the Wangdoodles they were resplendent in red trousers and blue jackets with gold trim forming five horizontal bars up the torso, diagonal gold bars on the forearms. They wore snazzy red caps with shiny black bills and glittering gold brocading. No slave rags these. There were twelve band members and Professor Brister, who played the cornet like his son and also played the role of "Caesar." Walter was so short, he did not even reach the shoulders of most of the other boys in the band. Even when he was a child, there was something about the cast of Walter Brister's eyes set in his handsome, brown-skinned face; it was a composed, contemplative, faraway look that came across even in an 1894 lithograph, just as it would in later photographs after he became an Oriental magician and Muslim prophet. He might have taken some measure of pride in the fact that when the band appeared in *In Old Kentucky*, he was billed as "the youngest bandmaster in the world," on the handsome Strobridge lithograph that promoters pasted on the sides of barns and buildings in each place the band visited.

John (Jack) Powell took over the leadership of the Woodlawn Wangdoodle band around 1898. As the original members outgrew their childhoods, Powell recruited new members by running advertisements for musicians who "must be small," not over five feet four inches in height.[6] The *Indianapolis Freeman*, one of the largest Black publications in the country, explained that "to belong to 'Mistah Pow'l's band of Ol' Kentucky' is in itself most important to the youthful colored lad, and to receive musical instruction at Powell's summer school of band instruction is the prime ambition of all the tender, youthful colored lads of Indianapolis, and it is with regret and sorrow that, as the years go by, they find themselves up against the 'deadline' and are forced to resign in favor of some more youthful and smaller sized aspirant for musical and terpsichorean honors."[7]

Despite its racist origin legend, *In Old Kentucky* was several rungs above the usual sentimental pap on American stages of its day, and found enthusiastic audiences on the way to becoming one of the most popular American plays ever by the First World War.[8] It was the *Hamilton* of its day, but with the longevity of *Cats*, and featured a nostalgic Stephen Foster classic, "My Old Kentucky Home," that achieved musical immortality. It was a show that mixed comedy, pathos, and thrills to tell the story of a woman who rescues a horse from a burning stable, disguises herself as a jockey, and then rides the horse to victory.[9] The plot was actually somewhat adventurous for the time, when American women were actively challenging their social subordination and political disenfranchisement, in that its female protagonist cross-dresses as a man and beats men at a male-dominated sport. The show also had thrills aplenty, including the heroine swinging across a chasm on a rope to escape a burning building. It also had six real racehorses, who galloped upon a mechanical treadmill hidden in the stage floor while a panorama behind them unspooled in the opposite direction; it was quite a mechanical feat then, as it would be now. The show's use of a juvenile "Negro" band was innovative, as were the antics of Brister and his bandmates, "youthful, frolocksome [sic] Afro-Americans," as the *Indianapolis Freeman* put it, "whose acting, playing, dancing, and comic abilities add much to the fun and jollity of this interesting play, and help to preserve admirably the atmosphere of life in Kentucky."[10]

In Old Kentucky debuted in New York on September 11, 1893, overlapping with the final months of the World's Columbian Exposition in Chicago that same year. It was an instantaneous hit. Audiences thrilled to the band of Black children, of all sizes and ages. They saw a member of the band plunk out tunes on a banjo, and watched various exploits including buck dancing—a percussive form of rhythmic dance emphasizing lower body stamps and taps, performed with taps on the shoes—and soft-shoe dancing, a slower, smooth, and graceful form of tap dance performed with or without taps on the shoes. There was something thrilling about seeing a dozen small Black boys playing, dancing, and joking around so adroitly. As one reviewer remarked, "The effect of their music, so good is it, is somewhat unexpected and a little short of startling."[11] True, any supremely talented child dancing and playing music as well as an adult is fascinating to audiences today as in the past, but the Woodlawn Wangdoodles on display in a dramatic comedy about the Old South served a distinctive ideological purpose, telling audiences in effect that the order of the Old South was justified and that things were not so bad for Blacks, including Black slaves. The show business rag the *New York Clipper* wouldn't even call a slave a slave, instead referring to the "pickaninnies" as the "colored attaches of the plantation."[12] As audiences applauded wildly, the show and its juvenile "colored attaches" extended the run by moving to the Academy of Music near Union Square starting in October, where the "musical pickaninnies" received curtain call after curtain call. The scene featuring the juvenile band, purportedly an illustration of "plantation life" in the Old South, was singled out by almost all reviewers as one of the highlights of the show. This scene, with "the darkies' own picnic," took up the majority of the second half, and audiences responded with "roars of laughter and cheers" and multiple standing ovations. "Walter Brister as drum major scored a great hit with a lightning manipulation of his baton," one New York reviewer wrote. "The band blows for all it is worth, and its music is full of stir and vigor."[13]

Brister may have been small but he was mighty, and he rapidly emerged as not just the bandleader, but a star. "Master Walter Brister, the phenomenal colored lad only 13 years of age, excites increasing wonder by his remarkable ability on the cornet, nightly playing selections of his own composition," wrote a newspaper from White Plains, New York. Critics called the band's rendition of John Philip Sousa marches and exhibitions of buck dancing "remarkable."[14] At Christmas time in 1893, Brister's bandmates presented him with the gift of a cornet, indicating both that they had some money in their pockets and that they recognized their bandmaster's importance to their own success.[15] Two weeks later, as the holidays came and went, business remained strong. The management gave away a bronze statuette of young Brister as a souvenir. Brister was fourteen years old, and already immortalized.[16]

The New York engagement stretched to ten weeks by Christmas of 1893 and was still drawing large audiences, thanks to its melodramatic scenes and "the novelty and merit" of its pickaninny band.[17] *In Old Kentucky* played until the end of February in New York and then hit the road, drawing large crowds in Kansas City in March. A year later, the *Kansas City American Citizen* announced that "the famous Wangdoodle pickaninny band made such a hit in the musical world [that] pickaninny bands are in demand all over the country."[18] By December of 1895 there were fourteen nostalgic song-and-dance shows about the antebellum South imitating the success of *In Old Kentucky*, using "pickaninny bands" and frequently named after a Southern state or a river; among them were *In Old Tennessee*, *Down in Dixie*, and *On the Mississippi*. All of these shows were so similar that it seemed as if they had been written by the same person, "who probably had one object in view: the Pickaninny Band," according to the *Herald* of Leavenworth, Kansas. "We are getting tired of the pickaninny business," the *Herald* wrote, although not so tired that the writer did not propose the need for another show about the "Afro American" experience, this one to be called "In Kansas."[19] Between 1894 and 1899 the *In Old Kentucky* company crossed the pond four times and played London and the English provinces, as well as Edinburgh, Scotland. In Edinburgh one reviewer wrote that Master Brister could give the rest of the company instruction "in animation."[20] "America, it is said, has no literature of her own," he continued. "She has her melodrama," before snootily noting that audience members in the cheap seats seemed particularly appreciative of all the explosions and histrionics.[21]

By presenting the "Old South" and slave plantations without African American adults, melodramatic shows like *In Old Kentucky* presented a peculiar view of the peculiar institution. They omitted most of the enslaved workforce and depicted Black children removed from Black families, playing into long-held assumptions of Black families as dysfunctional. The levity and gaiety of the pickaninny scenes salved the guilty consciences of white audiences by presenting slavery as, well, fun. Four years after it opened, *In Old Kentucky* was still going strong, and the pickaninny brass band was, "as usual, the tremendous hit of the piece" when they played in Los Angeles. The band, which had now grown from a dozen to seventeen "darkies" who "'are not colored but were born that way[,]' keep things humming with a vigor and solid joy that is worth going miles to see," in the estimation of the reviewer for the *Los Angeles Times*. The pickaninny band's plantation scene received roars of laughter, cheers, and numerous ovations, as "the little niggers played jokes on each other, fought and furnished forty kinds of fun."[22] By this time, Walter Brister would have been closing in on eighteen years old, if he was not eighteen already. And though he was still the star of the second half of the show, capable of bringing down the house on any given night with his cornet or his baton, the days when he could believably play a "pickaninny" were numbered, if they were not already past, as he approached maturity. Moreover, making a living by inhabiting so many lies must have exacted their own psychic punishment on Brister and the other performers, who were likewise standing on the cusp of manhood at the brink of a new century. Yet, each night they took the stage they were still mired in the tar of the slave past, making white people laugh with hijinks that probably felt old when they had begun the charade in 1893 let alone after five additional years on the road with the show.

The Wangdoodles began their tour near the very peak of lynching in America. Lynching accelerated as a tool of political violence in the South after the Civil War, as the Ku Klux Klan, called "the military wing of the Democratic Party," employed lynching to take the right to vote away from Black Americans and to drive off white Republican allies. Initially, in the 1880s, lynch mobs killed more whites than Blacks, peaking at around 160 in 1884. But the numbers of Blacks lynched surpassed whites in 1886 and spiked to 161 killed in 1892, averaging 111 a year in the 1890s, 79 a year in the 1900s, 57 annually in the 1910s, and 28 a year in the 1920s.[23] Beginning in 1892, the year three of her friends were lynched in Memphis, journalist Ida B. Wells led a public campaign exposing the fact that lynching was a tool of economic and political terrorism; most Black men who were lynched were not even accused of sexual violence, let alone guilty of it. Wells advocated armed self-defense for Black people, writing, "One had better die fighting against injustice than to die like a dog or a rat in a trap." She campaigned tirelessly for an end to the barbaric practice of lynching, saying it was uncivilized and unworthy of an allegedly Christian country.[24] In the 1890s, allegedly "Progressive" reformers advocated expanding racial segregation in all areas of life, a racist system given official sanction by the Supreme Court's infamous 1896 *Plessy v. Ferguson* ruling. But despite the best efforts of Wells, other Black activists, and both Black and white liberal politicians, Southern white Democrat segregationists held so much sway that the US Congress never passed an anti-lynching bill, even during the administration of Franklin Delano Roosevelt.

How could Walter Brister and the rest of the Woodlawn Wangdoodles break out of the vicious cycle of dehumanizing and historically falsifying racial stereotypes in a climate of racist terrorism, a destructive cycle that their own success had fortified? The Woodland Wangdoodles broke new ground for Black performers of all ages. Before their success, perhaps as few as a half-dozen Black children had ever even crossed the threshold of a theater's stage door, according to the *Indianapolis Freeman*. But by 1910, the *Freeman* guessed that as many as five thousand colored actors were seeking fame in the limelight.[25] Walter Brister, as the smallest of the original Wangdoodles, helped to initiate a whole new genre of entertainment—the singing and dancing child star. Walter Brister was the Black Shirley Temple before she was Shirley Temple, let alone Shirley Temple Black.

For a production whose depiction of slavery times in "Old Kentucky" was such a bold-faced lie, it is ironic that the original band director, J. H. Brister, and the original star, Walter Brister, were actually from Kentucky, just across the river from Cincinnati. In the summer of 1898, just before Jack Powell replaced the elder Brister as bandleader, the two Bristers and the rest of *In Old Kentucky*'s pickaninny band visited the Bristers' hometown of Carlisle, Kentucky, to play for "a colored pic-nic." They were traveling from Carlisle to Cincinnati on a summer tour following a European one, and were planning to rejoin the theatrical cast for the coming season.[26] The 1880 census recorded that Walter Brister was born in Carlisle, Kentucky, around 1879. His father, John Henry Brister, was thirty-six years old and made his living as a carpenter before traveling the world with *In Old Kentucky*. Walter's mother, Lucy Conway Brister, was a twenty-three-year-old housekeeper, and his older sister, Magdalena, was nine. Demonstrating the vagaries of racial classification was the fact that the census enumerator listed Walter and his father as B for "Black" but Lucy and Magdalene as "Mu" for "Mulatto." Everyone in the family had been born in Kentucky. At the bottom of the cluster of Bristers was little Walter, his age listed with a single vertical line: one. Great oaks from little acorns grow, indeed. Brister would one day make his living producing mango trees from seeds before the astonished faces of paying audiences, and his signal contribution of replanting Islam on American shores was even more consequential and more mysterious.[27]

CHAPTER TWO

ORIENTAL MAGIC

Human beings are magical. Bios and Logos. Words made flesh, muscle and bone animated by hope and desire, belief materialized in deeds, deeds which crystallize our actualities.

—SYLVIA WYNTER, 1995[1]

In the year 610 CE, a forty-year-old merchant from the Arabian city of Mecca withdrew to a cave for a period of solitary prayer and meditation. There he received a revelation from the angel Gabriel that came to him with such force that he at first thought he was being attacked by a *jinni*. Now a prophet, Muhammad, peace be upon him, began preaching his revelations, teachings that formed the basis of the religion of Islam and its holy text, the Qur'an. Islamic histories teach that the Prophet fled with his followers from Mecca to Yathrib (later known as Medina) in 622, then after a period of warfare against the Meccans returned victoriously eight years later with ten thousand followers. The faith of Islam that Muhammad founded accepted the validity if not the divinity of earlier prophets like Moses and Jesus and rested on five pillars: *shahada*, the profession that "there is no god but Allah, and Muhammad is the messenger of Allah"; *salat*, the regular observance of the five daily prayers; *zakah*, the regular giving of alms for the needy; *sawm*, primarily ritual fasting during the month of Ramadan, but also fasting for repentance and ascetic purposes; and the performance of the *hajj*, or pilgrimage to Mecca, at least once in a lifetime. The Prophet accepted followers without bias toward the color of their skin; "race" was a concept that had not been created yet, but among his first followers and the first *muezzin* to call Muslims to prayer was Bilal ibn Rabah, born a slave of African origins and emancipated by the Prophet Muhammad.

Soon, most of the people of the Arabian Peninsula had converted to the new faith and spread it to the Somali coast within the lifetime of the Prophet, who died in 632. Between 639 and 642, Muslim armies from the Arabian Peninsula, led by commander 'Amr ibn al-'As, conquered Byzantine Egypt. By 661 the first four Muslim rulers, or caliphs, controlled an empire from Tripoli in the west to Iraq and Persia in the east. Outside the Arabian Peninsula, relatively few of the inhabitants of Muslim-controlled lands actually converted to Islam initially. For the majority, conversion did not come swiftly, "by the sword"; in fact, Muslim rulers usually made few attempts to convert the inhabitants of conquered lands. Rather, Islam spread gradually, by prestige, as Muslim traders and rulers attracted converts by their example of discipline, prosperity, and upright living. By the eighth century, Muslims had evolved into three major factions: Sunnis, Shi'ites, and Kharijites. Sunnis recognized the first four caliphs as the Prophet Muhammad's rightful successors, whereas Shi'ites believed that Islamic leadership ought to be traced only through the fourth caliph, the Prophet's son-in-law Alī ibn Abī Tālib and his wife, Fatima. The much smaller sect of Kharijites, who emerged from Muslim Berber resistance to the rule of the Arab caliphs and were strongest in North Africa, taught that leadership in Islam should be based not on descent but on piety and knowledge.[2]

The empire spread under the subsequent Umayyad caliphs, who traced their lineage to a cousin of the Prophet; by 690, Muslim Arabs had successfully subdued the migratory Imazighen (Berber) tribes across North Africa as far as the Atlantic, and their naval supremacy in the Mediterranean forced the Byzantines to withdraw from their remaining positions along the African coast. In 711 CE, Arab and Imazighen warriors began the conquest of the Iberian Peninsula, and completed the defeat of the Spanish Catholics by 732 CE. By 750, Muslim lands stretched from the Iberian Peninsula, or Al-Andalus, to the Indus River of northern India in the east. When North African Imazighen pastoralists who traded across the Sahara desert with sub-Saharan Africans converted to Islam, they introduced the faith to the Sudanese kingdom of ancient Ghana by 990 and soon established trade routes to the Senegambian region south of the Senegal River in the occipital bulge of the African continent, closest to North

America. There they established Muslim sections in local capitals and taught Kharijite Islam, though as in other places, for centuries the only practitioners were merchants and other elites. Meanwhile, in the Muslim north, the Andalusian Jewish community flourished under Umayyad rule, adopting Arabic and gaining exposure to Arabic and Greek works of philosophy, philology, rationalism, theology, arts, medicine, and science. Jews refer to the period from the Umayyad conquest to the Moorish conquests as the "Golden Age" of Jewish history. Under Muslim rule, Al-Andalus boasted one of the most culturally advanced and religiously tolerant civilizations in all of Europe.

By 1076 the *al-murābiṭūn* ("those who are garrisoned") or Almoravids, based in the Western Sahara, launched a *jihād* to purify West African Islam, seeking to defeat non-Muslim Sudanese Blacks and conquer Koumbi Saleh, the capital of ancient Ghana and the largest city in the Sahel region south of the Sahara's trading routes. Successful in this quest, they ranged north and conquered the Muslim states of the Iberian Peninsula by 1110, beginning the Moorish rule of Spain and Portugal under the Almoravids and their successors, the *al-Muwaḥḥidūn* ("those who attest the unity of God"), or Almohads. These were the famous Moors, or, in Shakespeare's day, the "Blackamoors," whose origins were in Africa and whose skin tones ranged from tawny olive to dark brown or "black." Jews who had suffered centuries of persecution in Christian Europe welcomed the Moorish invaders, and fought side by side with them in religiously mixed armies in the cities of Seville, Granada, Málaga, and Toledo. But the new Moorish conquerors also disrupted the prior religious peace. An Arabic-speaking Jew born in Córdoba named Abū 'Imran Mūsā ibn Maymūn ibn 'Ubayd Allāh, also known by his Hebrew name Moses Ben Maimon (1135–1204), fled his native Córdoba to escape anti-Jewish prejudice that came with the Almohad invasion, settling first in Fez, Morocco, and then Cairo, Egypt. He went on to systematize the faith and teachings of modern Judaism, becoming known as Moses Maimonides, or the Rambam, while also serving in Cairo as a physician to the Muslim sultan Saladin, the liberator of the holy city of Jerusalem from the Christian Crusaders in 1187. At their principal city of Gharnāṭah, or Granada, the Moorish sultans built spectacular buildings like the fabulous, geometrically ornamented sultan's palace the Alhambra, along with its fortress, the Alcazaba, and the sultan's summer palace, the Generalife. Moorish rule lasted through the long, arduous Reconquista of Spain between 1212 and 1492 that led to the expulsion of Moors and Jews from Spain and their resettlement in places as diverse as Holland, Brazil, North Africa, and the Ottoman Empire, but the memory of Muslim Andalusia as an exceptional if brief period of religious amity and cultural achievement lingered for centuries.

🦅   🦅   🦅

Unlike Christianity, Islam has not thought of magic and astrology as antithetical to religion, but as an integral part of a unified field of both worldly and supernaturally directed activity including faith, prayer, almsgiving, study of holy scripture, and the other tenets and practices we customarily recognize as "religious." Nonetheless, Islamic jurisprudence has considered magic to be a real and potent threat and forbade certain forms of supernatural manipulation on penalty of death.[3] "We can think of Islam as having originated in a world of magic," Michael Muhammad Knight writes, a world in which not only Muslims but neighboring seventh-century CE Jews, Christians, and Zoroastrians widely used charms and practiced astrology and divination.[4] The Qur'an's designation of *sihr* is often translated as "magic" or "sorcery," but it is actually far more expansive, including not only astrology, the harnessing of spirits, and even juggling and sleight-of-hand tricks, but also, as Knight writes, "the use of drugs and perfumes to confuse people, the charismatic seduction of crowds, and causing divisions between people through slander and spreading rumors."[5] Even bewitching poetry could be considered *sihr*.[6] The Qur'an condemns using *jinn* or spirits for evil or as an illegitimate source of divine knowledge, and the text also contains long discussions of *jinn*, soothsayers, and supernatural topics such as King Solomon's magical powers, including his ability to command *jinn*, control the wind, and speak the language of birds. Following the Islamic conquests of Alexandria and North Africa, Muslim rulers in the ninth century sponsored the translation of foreign sciences into Arabic, which introduced ancient Greek and Syriac texts on magic, divination, and alchemy into Islamic societies.[7]

Most evidence of magical practices in Muslim sources comes from the medieval period, in the twelfth century and later. Islamic history is replete with magical practices among elites as well as common folk including the widespread use of protective magical items such as blue beads or the "hand of Fatima," with its outward curving thumb and little finger, named after the youngest daughter of the Prophet Muhammad and wife of his cousin Ali. There are stories of Muslim rulers who rode into battle with the blessing of astrologers or while wearing magical garments to protect against injury. And an extensive body of medieval Islamic texts discusses what we would call magical practices, including grimoires, or manuals, giving detailed instructions for both divination and magic. In the twelfth century, Sufi scholar Ahmad ibn Ali al-Buni expounded on the hidden and magical qualities of Allah's ninety-nine names and gave instructions on activating their supernatural powers using talismans and amulets—efforts that got him condemned for witchcraft by fourteenth-century historian Ibn Khaldun but praised as a great saint and mystic by Sufi biographers.[8]

Wherever Islam spread, it left amulets containing verses of the Qur'an considered to have magical properties. The Arab ancestors of Muslims had worn rocks around their neck for magical protection and worshipped at the site of the Kaaba, a black rock that was a pilgrimage site for Arabs in Mecca. Muslims added verses from the Qur'an to these amulets, and Islamic talismans composed of Qur'anic verses written on pieces of parchment and frequently worn around the neck were thought to hold great magical protective powers among Muslims and their non-Muslim neighbors alike wherever Islam spread, including West Africa. As Scottish explorer Mungo Park testified of Senegambian Muslims, whom he observed in the 1790s, they as well as their neighbors "consider the art of writing as bordering on magic; and it is not in the doctrines of the prophet, but in the arts of the magician, that their confidence is placed."[9] Some of the few African Muslims enslaved in mainland North America were known to have been able to inscribe *suras* from the Qur'an, a continuation of this venerable Islamic practice of manufacturing protective amulets, perhaps the most widespread example of Islamic magical *sihr*.

In the Christian world, in contrast, the concept of magic is a relic of Greek stigma against Persian Zoroastrianism and later Christian opposition to Islamic sorcerers—in other words, it is an artifact of the longitudinal schism between "East" and "West" that bifurcates the discourse of Orientalism. As Edward Said wrote in his influential if controversial 1978 book, an Orientalist is first an academic who teaches, writes, or studies the Orient. Second, Orientalism is a style of thought based on a distinction between "the Orient" and "the Occident," a binary opposition that is blurs all distinctions between vastly different epochs and material conditions and denies the shared humanity of Easterners and Westerners. Third, in its modern stage, "Orientalism is a Western style for dominating, restructuring, and having authority over the Orient."[10] The word "magic" comes from the Greek *mageía*, which referred to Zoroastrian priests during a period in the third century BCE when Persian religious influence in Greece was strong but stigmatized and feared. Nonetheless, the great Greek philosophers Pythagoras, Democritus, and Plato were all said to have learned *mageía* from Persian sources.[11] But though he may have studied *mageía*, Plato (428/27 BCE–348/47 BCE) also was the first philosopher in classical Greece to make an invidious distinction between religion and magic that echoes through modern scholarship and popular understandings alike. Unlike base, mechanistic magic, religion (*eusebeía*) as pictured by Plato was a devout, pious, and selfless faith in gods so far above the human plane as to be beyond reproach.[12]

Christianity's greatest theologians followed Plato in condemning magic and superstition to a blasphemous order below religion, and added the twist that magic and Greco-Roman divination were actually demonic. Augustine (354 CE–430 CE) wrote that Egyptian sorcerers were bested by Moses's superior magic when he transformed his staff into a snake because they relied on demons, which were less powerful than the angels under the control of the Hebrew god.[13] Thomas Aquinas (ca. 1225–ca. 1274) agreed with Augustine that magic was superstitious and demonic, and added that even unconscious acts might create a tacit pact with demons. He also responded to another threat from the East—not Persian Zorastrianism this time as in Greek days, but the Islamic use of talismans composed of Arabic phrases from the Qur'ān, which he considered superstitions, lumping them with fortune-telling and astrology. Aquinas permitted amulets and incantations for healing as long as they used texts from the Christian scriptures and no symbols other than the cross.[14] Thus Aquinas extended the modern separation between religion and magic along the fault line of familiar "Western" and unfamiliar "Eastern" symbols and sacred texts. The threatening Eastern religion had shifted over the centuries from Zoroastrianism to Islam, but the Orientalist divide at the heart of Western thought about the sacred and the profane, and between divinity and demonology, endured and led to later centuries' conceptions of "white" and "black" magic.

The 1453 Muslim Ottomans' conquest of Constantinople, capital of the Byzantine Empire, led to an exodus of scholars and Greek texts westward throughout Europe, which fed a new hunger for rediscovering classical texts. The conquest also coincided with Johannes Gutenberg's invention of a printing press using movable type in 1455, which made printed books widely accessible for the first time. These developments amplified and spread the "humanism" that over the prior century had turned to classical Greek and Roman texts for models of how to organize society and reform religion, reaching beyond received Catholic teachings and sparking the Renaissance. In Italy and elsewhere in Europe, people with humanistic training began to dominate professions requiring literacy, such as state bureaucracies. The new androcentric "humanism," and its methods of close textual analysis, opened up alternatives to blind obedience to Church authorities and also provided a powerful new means of studying sacred writ, methods that would not only impact the Catholic church but also Protestant strongholds like Geneva, where John Calvin endorsed his own humanist school.

One might say that in terms of religion and science, a funny thing happened on the way to decorum. The Renaissance, the Enlightenment, and their celebration of arts, sciences, and humanism should not be mistaken for hostility to magic and the occult. In fact it is more accurate to say that occultism spurred the development of science, and that early scientists were often occultists as well. Just when it might seem that magical thinking, rituals, practices, and traditions would go extinct with the blossoming of arts and sciences in the European Renaissance and early modern period, magic exploded in popularity. As Theodor Adorno and Max Horkheimer wrote in *Dialectic of Enlightenment*, the triumph of rational thinking strangely spurred its opposite: "Myth is already enlightenment, and enlightenment reverts to mythology."[15] Much of the blossoming of interest in the occult during the Renaissance and Enlightenment occurred because of the discovery of texts preserved in Islamic repositories that purported to reveal secrets of earlier eras, principally the *Corpus Hermeticum*. As French classical scholar Isaac Casaubon demonstrated using close textual analysis as long ago as 1614, the *Hermetica* were a series of Neoplatonic dialogues of mixed Greek, Roman, Egyptian, Jewish, and early Christian elements concerning philosophy, astrology, and alchemy written in Greece in the first few centuries of the common era. They claimed an even more ancient origin—ancient Egypt—and were attributed to an Egyptian priest known as Hermes Trismegistus, roughly contemporary to Moses and sometimes identified with him.[16] The *Hermetica* were full of ideas that might sound strange to contemporary readers but had deep roots in Gnosticism and other countercurrents of heretical and mystical thought. For instance, the *Hermetica* claimed that the world was created not by God but by a demiurge, and that the truth of biblical scriptures was inverted from their plainest meaning. They bore the influence of a strong strain of Persian Manichaeism as well, which claimed that supernatural forces of good and evil were locked in an eternal struggle, a battle that could explain both.[17] In the late fifteenth century, Neoplatonist priest Marsilio Ficino, director of the Platonic Academy in Florence, the leading scholarly body of the Renaissance, translated the Hermetic texts into Latin and credulously accepted their origin legend as being from ancient Egypt. His contemporary Lodovico Lazzarelli and others contributed more works to the *Hermetica*, including some translated from Arabic, Coptic, Armenian, and other Near Eastern languages. Ficino used hermetic texts to create a system of "natural magic" whereby magicians attempted to harness the astrological power of the stars by using music, hymns, and plants. He took pains to distinguish his system of "spiritual magic" from the "demonic magic" of the European medieval period. By suggesting that human beings could effect changes in nature, hermetic magic created a new worldview that spurred scientific investigation and suggested that people had some of the abilities to manipulate the natural world that had previously been widely thought of among Christians as the sole prerogative of God.[18]

This was far from the first time the *Hermetica* had been debated and discussed; Augustine had argued against them in the *City of God*, even, but by translating the texts into Latin and eventually various common tongues, Renaissance scholars transformed the hermetic texts into a powerful influence on European thought. Hermeticism soon influenced explorations of alchemy, astrology, mysticism, occultism, and magical spells. Perhaps even more significantly, alchemical experimentation produced early scientific breakthroughs, and such titans of scientific empiricism and the Enlightenment as Sir Isaac Newton, Robert Boyle, and John Locke embraced various combinations of magic, mysticism, and alchemy.[19]

Jewish mysticism and magic, which itself had been influenced by Hermeticism in the first centuries of the Christian era, also had a major and lasting impact on wider esotericism. Influenced by their neighbors as well as by an intense desire to hasten the coming of the messiah in light of persistent persecution, Jews of the Middle Ages and later centuries developed their own intricate form of mysticism, called Kabbalah, which became a key element of both Jewish and non-Jewish forms of effective magic. While devotees usually studied Kabbalah for mystical enlightenment, it also was believed to have the magical ability to effect changes in the world, and those who knew the names and numbers of Kabbalah's seventy-two angels could call on them for assistance.[20]

A contemporary of Ficino's named Giovanni Pico della Mirandola (1463–1494) was largely responsible for introducing Jewish mysticism into Renaissance occultism, where it flourished. A young nobleman who began to study canon law at ten, Pico met Ficino in Florence and studied Hebrew, Arabic, and Kabbalah with several Jewish scholars. Excited by the similarities between Hermeticism and Kabbalah, Pico created a Christian synthesis of the two he called "Cabala." He claimed that Ficino's "natural magic" was weak without the addition of Cabala as it did not aspire beyond the realm of the earth and stars, whereas Cabala invoked supernatural beings and the divine power of the supreme God. Pico asserted that no magician could perform magic of any real power without knowledge of Hebrew and Cabala. Pico's Cabala also entered widespread circulation among Hermetic occult circles, so much so that historian Frances Yates spoke of a "Renaissance Hermetic-Cabalist tradition."[21] Elements of Cabala entered freemasonry in the eighteenth century, and Cabalistic books like the grimoire *The Sixth and Seventh Books of Moses* became widely distributed and influential not only in Europe and its diaspora but among Africans and their descendants in the Americas as well.[22]

🦅   🦅   🦅

Despite the popularity of Cabala among Christians, the Protestant Reformation accelerated the official disavowal of magic among Protestant thinkers who rejected practices deemed magical and therefore spurious such as exorcism and the transubstantiation of the blood and body of Jesus into the wine and wafers of the

Catholic mass.[23] Moreover, they reasserted a belief found in both Platonic and early Jewish thought in a distant God far above the human plane. For English geographer Charles T. Middleton, writing during the American Revolution, magic was "a mere relick of popery funk deep in the minds of the ignorant and credulous."[24] For Protestant theologians, unlike Jewish, Catholic, and Muslim predecessors, any human attempt to compel divine forces through magical spells and incantations was not just blasphemous; it was also ineffective.[25] For Protestants, there was now a bright line between valid and invalid ways of accessing the supernatural. As Middleton wrote, "It is not poverty and nastiness that makes a witch, nor age nor wrinkles, not yet a revengeful eye or malicious tongue, but it is craft and cunning and imposture . . . practiced to the detriment of truth and religion."[26]

The Protestant Reformation and the Thirty Years' War between Catholic and Protestant states brought another set of supposedly secret texts to the fore outlining an alleged secret society that gathered under the sign of the Rosy Cross, or the Rosicrucians, as they came to be known in the competing books that debated their existence. Between 1614 and 1616 there appeared three publications most likely emanating from Tübingen, near Stuttgart in southwest Germany, describing a secret Order of the Rosy Cross, although it is unclear whether such an order existed or was merely an elaborate fiction. To say that they were the Dan Brown novels of their day fails to acknowledge how indebted his novels are to those older texts. The idea of a secret society that took the Rose and Cross, the emblem of Protestant England, as its standard arose in the context of religious strife between Catholics and Protestants during the reigns of Holy Roman Emperor Rudolf II of Prague, a great patron of artists, scientists, and alchemists, and Frederick V of Heidelberg, a Protestant ally of Great Britain.[27] Whether or not the brothers of the Rosy Cross ever existed, the combination of social, scientific, and mystical experimentation that came to be known as Rosicrucianism became one of the key building blocks of freemasonry as it emerged in Scotland during the seventeenth century and spread throughout Europe and the Americas in the eighteenth.[28]

The tumultuous years of the Protestant Reformation of the sixteenth century and the Thirty Years' War from 1618 to 1648 also brought a spasm of witch hunting to Europe and Anglophone America, resulting in the deaths of around forty thousand accused witches and wizards, mostly women, and the torturing of many more.[29] Folk magic had long existed in Europe as it did in the rest of the world, but the spread of magical practices through elite humanistic circles during and after the Renaissance prompted the Catholic church's official commendation of witchcraft as the work of the devil and instigated the first early modern witch trials in the second half of the fifteenth century. Protestant reformers in England battled not only with "popish" elements of Roman Catholicism but with entrenched conjuring and magical practices in villages whose practitioners drew more on oral traditions than on the elite body of Hermetic and Renaissance magic that coalesced in Italy and among scholars working in Latin in London. Reginald Scot in London and Jean Prevost in Lyon, France, each published the first texts describing magic tricks and prestidigitation in 1584, and their texts remain influential among stage magicians to this day. They argued against the persecution of alleged witches and exposed the secrets of conjurers and magicians in an effort to demonstrate that their tricks were the result of practice, mechanical devices, misdirection, psychological manipulation, and sleight of hand, not supernatural abilities.[30]

Though British historian Keith Thomas pictured magic declining by about 1700 in advance of the abolishment of English antiwitchcraft laws in 1735, subsequent scholars have documented magic's stubborn persistence not as a forerunner to modernity but a fellow traveler that inspired new forms of knowledge from chemistry to abstract expressionism. What changed in this revisionist view, according to Hildred Geertz, was not the decline of magical practices but the emergence of the category of magic as fully distinct from religion.[31] Magical practices seemed to thrive in particular among often socially marginal people such as women, working people, and people of African descent, as the great English historian E. P. Thompson noted in another rejoinder to Thomas.[32]

With the passing of the European witch hunts, and the rise of a new capitalist world order, nineteenth-century entertainers were free to commercialize the effects that witches, wizards, and conjurers once used to convince viewers of their supernatural abilities. In fact, freed from the potential death sentence that a witchcraft accusation once imposed, many such entertainers cultivated an aura of preternatural ability to enhance their charismatic personas. In the Golden Age of Magic in the late nineteenth and early twentieth centuries, magicians frequently pictured themselves with devils and imps to underline their association with the dark arts, finding that their gate receipts increased with a faint hint of sulfur. In the eighteenth century, fairground conjurers in Europe turned magic into a performance art, and the Italian Chevalier Pinetti brought magic into theaters for the first time in the 1780s. French watchmaker Jean-Eugène Robert-Houdin (1805–1871) was so influential in the development of stage magic that he is commonly referred to as the "father" of modern magic; he separated the new performance craft from the old ways of witches and fairground grifters by pioneering the upper-class "gentlemanly style" of stage magic, performing in a costume of white tie, top hat, and tails. His Viennese contemporary, Johann Nepomuk Hofzinser (1806–1875), pioneered the use of card tricks and ingenious mechanical devices. In an era of strict cultural hierarchies, Robert-Houdin, Hofzinser, and the many who imitated them took magic out of the streets and brought it into the finest theaters in full evening dress. It was, not incidentally, the uniform of European upper-crust elites in an era of direct imperial rule over people of color worldwide.

🐦 🐦 🐦

Islam remained the faith only of a small number of West African nobles and traders for its first five hundred years in West Africa, from about 1000 to 1500 CE. In the thirteenth and fourteenth centuries it spread with Mande-speaking merchants during the rise of the kingdom of Mali. But most Mande speakers did not become Muslims. In the fourteenth century, Hausa merchants between the middle Niger River and Lake Chad adopted Islam, but once again most Hausa peasants did not convert to Islam until far later. Similarly, in the fifteenth century, Islam spread in the Wolof Empire, especially among the nobility. At first, then, Islam in sub-Saharan Africa was practiced by peoples of the Sahel, the grassland just south of the Sahara, and small numbers of merchant and political elites in trading towns above the jungle region of equatorial Africa. No Muslim city became more famous than Timbuktu, a southern Saharan Desert trading town in the Empire of Mali boasting three famous mosques that became a center of Islamic learning and was conquered sequentially by the Tuaregs, the Songhai, and the Moors.

The slave trade destabilized West African states, as wars of enslavement fed captives into the maw of both the Arab slave trade and the transatlantic slave trade. The Qur'an sanctioned slavery, and roughly eleven million Africans were enslaved in the Arab slave trade to serve in Muslim harems, households, and armies.[33] As unpleasant as captivity and enslavement was in West African societies and in the Islamic world of North Africa and the Middle East, such slaves were still considered people. They often occupied positions of status and authority within such societies, and functioned within many African households as almost members of the family. The trade in slaves as chattel—that is, as things—was a unique and vicious feature of the European-directed trade of African slaves to the Americas. The transatlantic slave system began in the fifteenth century with Portuguese traders along the coast of Africa and accelerated as the sugar industries of Brazil and the Caribbean demanded and consumed laborers in subsequent centuries. African captives in the Atlantic slave trade were usually marched overland by foot, sometimes hundreds or even thousands of miles, where they were held at the coast in stockades or forts and loaded on board European and American vessels. Men and women were separated, stripped of all clothing, and packed into the stinking holds of cramped ships for voyages that lasted sixty-eight days on average. Death and disease were common; bodies of the dead were thrown overboard. Some of the more desperate and stoic threw themselves overboard into the cold Atlantic as well, preferring death to the watery hell of pestilential slave ships. Sharks commonly trailed the ships attracted by the scent of human effluent and the possibility of an easy meal. Revolts on the slave ships were common, and some of these revolts, including the famous seizure of the *Amistad*, involved African Muslims, who instigated many other slave uprisings in the Americas.

The scale of the transatlantic slave trade and the death toll en route were enormous. Although the precise numbers are disputed, the most thorough study has estimated that of the 12.5 to 15.4 million African captives who began the Middle Passage, between 1.82 and 2.24 million perished along the way. Conditions on board slave ships were hellacious, but conditions in the cane fields were perhaps even more deadly. Overseers in the cane fields commonly worked slaves to death, or slaves frequently succumbed to disease and malnutrition as slavers often found it was less expensive to replenish their slaves with fresh imports than to provide the rest, nutrition, and medical care necessary to keep slaves alive. Reproductive family structures proved difficult to form and maintain as 64.5 percent of the Africans brought to the Americas were male, and 22.3 percent were children.

Historian Patrick Manning has argued that the colonial societies of the so-called New World were only economically viable because of the unpaid labor of the many millions of Africans who died far from their natal homes, while European cities filled up with cathedrals and other monuments built with the riches extracted from Black bodies in the killing fields of the Americas.[34] It was perhaps the largest, deadliest, and most inhumane racket in human history.

When trying to understand how African cultures did and did not transfer to the Americas, it is essential to remember that North America was one of the smaller importers of slaves in the New World: twelve and a half times as many captives landed in Brazil (4.86 million) as in mainland North America (less than 389,000). Even and especially the small islands of the Caribbean dwarfed the United States in terms of their appetite for human beings: the British Caribbean was the landing place of 2.32 million African captives; the French Caribbean took 1.12 million; the Spanish Americas, both in the Caribbean and the mainland, claimed another 1.29 million enslaved Africans. The North American mainland directly imported even fewer African captives than did the small Dutch territories of Surinam, Curaçao, and Guiana, with 444,728, although these numbers do not reflect African-born slaves imported to the North American colonies after "seasoning" in the Caribbean.[35] As historians Michael Gomez, Sylviane Diouf, Allan Austin, and Paul Lovejoy have argued, Muslims formed an identifiable and distinct subgroup of slaves at a higher proportion on the North American mainland than anywhere else in the Americas. But almost no Muslims arrived after 1770, except for those who landed in South Carolina in the last decade of the trade.[36]

It was only with Connecticut resident Eli Whitney's invention of the cotton gin in 1793 and the subsequent movement of the slave system from the depleted soil of the upper South to the richer soil of the Deep South's frontier that American slavery exploded. But soon thereafter, to the great consternation of slaveholders, the British and then the US governments banned the importation of slaves. The cotton fields of the lower South thus slaked their thirst for workers not with African-born captives but almost entirely with slaves born in the upper South and then torn from the breasts of kith and kin and sold "down the river" to the great entrepôt of human misery in the slave pens and auction blocks of New Orleans.[37]

❧   ❧   ❧

The slave trades fueled the expansion of Islamic states in West Africa, both as resisters and collaborators. West African Islam would become far more popular with a series of jihads that brought efforts to purify Islam from North Africa southward across the caravan routes of the Sahara to the kingdoms of the Senegambia. In the seventeenth century, a Moorish *marabout* (holy man) named Nasir al-Din waged a successful jihad to purify Islam in the kingdoms of the Senegambian river valleys and met little resistance. Al-Din imposed Islamic religious law and condemned the transatlantic slave trade. He died in 1674 and his movement was defeated with the help of the French in 1677, sending many of his Muslim followers into captivity in the transatlantic slave trade.[38] The eighteenth century saw Islam expand in the states of Bundu, Futa Jallon, and Futa Toro along the Senegal River, creating cleric-led governments and, by the end of the century, overwhelmingly Muslim societies. In the nineteenth century, Islam started to become even more popular among Senegambians as a form of opposition to the arbitrary rule of the aristocracy, while the Muslim theocratic warlords of Senegambian city-states waged war to enslave their non-Muslim neighbors, raising massive slave armies to capture more slaves and sending approximately half a million Senegambians into the sorrows of the Middle Passage between 1711 and 1810.[39]

The largest expansion of West African Islam came just as Britain banned the Atlantic slave trade in 1814 and as the British and French used the pretext of suppressing the slave trade to expand their grip on the African coast. From 1805 to 1812, the Fulani philosopher, scholar, mystic, and revolutionary Uthman dan Fodio (1754–1817) waged a jihad in Futa Toro and Futa Jallon, where Hausa leaders had banned conversion to Islam and the wearing of Muslim garments. The jihads created a new Muslim state in Hausaland, in what is now northern Nigeria and northern Senegal, and created a superstate of twenty million people, making Islam the dominant faith from coast to coast along the savannah south of the Sahara, all the way from the Senegambia in the west to the modern state of Sudan in the east. In part because of this era of warfare, there were so many Muslim captives sent to Brazil that Rio de Janeiro bookshops sold copies of the Qur'an, Brazil boasted literate and learned African-born Muslim clerics, Brazilian Muslim slaves were known to proselytize their Christian fellows, and in 1835 secret societies of Muslims banded together and created an armed slave rebellion in the Brazilian state of Bahia.[40]

The West African jihads continued with the efforts of al-Hajj Umar ibn Sa'id al-Futi Tal (c. 1794–1864), a renowned Tijaniyyah Sufi mystic and military commander from Futa Toro who waged a war in the mid-nineteenth century to purify Islam, capture slaves, and convert more West Africans to the faith. By 1854 he had conquered all of the upper Senegal Valley, including the Muslim states of Bundu, Futa Jallon, Futa Toro, and Hamdullahi, as well as the Bambara states of Segu and Kaarta, comprising much of contemporary Mali, Senegal, and Guinea, and enforcing a strict form of Islamic orthodoxy. By the end of the nineteenth century, Islam was not only a venerable and worthy opponent of Christian Europe and deeply rooted in West Africa but was part of a worldwide movement of resistance to European imperialism. To be Muslim was to be part of a global civilization of undeniable antiquity and racial liberalism. Africans and their descendants in the West could admire and emulate those qualities, whether or not they knew of direct Muslim ancestors.[41]

When Europeans traveled to Africa, or Africans by the tens of millions were transported in chains on ships to the Americas, their respective concepts of magic traveled with them. The often violent expansion of Europeans and their networks of traders and missionaries into African, American, and Asian lands through both trade and conquest brought Christians into contact with diverse religious systems, practices, and pantheons they were quick to castigate and suppress as magical and demonic. In the minds of Europeans, the practice of "magic" typified peoples as disparate as Persian Zoroastrians, Arabian Muslims, and West Africans of all descriptions. But African so-called pagan or pantheistic religions, with their many "witch-doctors," their spirit possession, their use of charms, herbs, and divination, their animation of the natural world, and their secret societies, fit especially well into European notions of both witchcraft and magic, despite the fact that they had little to do with Zoroastrianism, Hermeticism, or Cabala. In 1777, an English observer wrote of West Africa that "many other strange maxims prevail among the

Negroes of these nations; and to their superstitious notions may be added, the great faith they have in magicians and sorcerers."[42] Practicing malevolent magic or witchcraft, alongside crimes such as adultery and murder, could get Africans enslaved by their neighbors and sent to the Americas in European vessels, helping spread African magical systems to the Western hemisphere. English anthropologist E. E. Evans-Pritchard wrote that every member of the Azande group he studied, save for small children, "whether old or young, whether man or woman, is to some extent a magician," since there existed such a thorough complex of witchcraft, oracles, and magic for such a wide variety of activities.[43]

Africans and their descendants in the Americas brought and developed elaborate systems of propitiating intricate pantheons of gods in praise, prayer, and direct action, both to help and to harm. These systems developed into practices of conjure or hoodoo in North America, hoodoo or voodoo in New Orleans and the Gulf Coast, *vodou* in Haiti, and other African-influenced religions in Haiti, Cuba, and elsewhere in the Americas. Euro-Americans (and many Christian Blacks) may have castigated African elements of African American religious practices, but they were wise to fear conjurers' knowledge of poisons and ability to wreak revenge even on white slaveholders. Belief in conjurers' powers was so strong among fellow slaves and free Blacks alike that they often played integral roles in slave rebellions and revolts. The Haitian Revolution was the most successful slave revolt in the Americas, and started with a *vodou* ceremony in 1791. In his autobiography, the great abolitionist Frederick Douglass described how a root given him for protection by a conjurer named Sandy allowed him to fight back against the slave driver Covey and to experience "a glorious resurrection, from the tomb of slavery, [to] the heaven of freedom."[44] Denmark Vesey conspired with a conjurer known as Gullah Jack to lead a slave revolt that was squelched in Charleston, South Carolina, in 1822. Nat Turner led a bloody slave revolt in 1831 and rejected conjure but followed mystical visions and dreams.[45] Nor were magical practices limited to Southern Blacks, before or after slavery: as historian Paul Harvey writes of the South in the nineteenth and twentieth centuries, "conjure and Christianity were in theory antithetical but in practice complementary," and variations of magical practices perceived as African attracted both Black and white believers.[46] While we may be wise to distinguish between African and "Afro American" religions such as *vodou* and

Santeria—with their elaborate pantheons, mythologies, worship rituals, sacrificial systems, and social hierarchies—and the more fragmentary magical practices for healing and harming, slaveholders and later Christians both white and Black made no such distinctions; for them any practice that invoked supernatural powers having anything to do with Africa were pagan, magical, spurious, blasphemous, and evidence of a damning lack of civilization that demanded correction by way of colonization and Christian evangelization.[47] European traders and missionaries viewed African religions as "magical," but so did African Americans who practiced African-descended religions in the Americas. One former slave from Georgia told a Works Progress Administration folklorist that "Africa was a land a' magic power since de beginnin' a' history." As scholar Yvonne Chireau notes, this association between Africa and magical power became widespread and characteristic of African American supernatural practices.[48]

🦅   🦅   🦅

Modern capitalism transformed life in the eighteenth and nineteenth centuries, uprooted peasant societies globally, created sprawling factory-filled and soot-choked cities in rapidly industrializing urban cores, enslaved millions of Africans and their descendants in the Americas, colonized millions more people globally, disenchanted the natural world with scientific and technical accomplishments, and transformed older mercantile colonies into imperial regimes for the extraction of the raw materials that fed metropolitan factories. Supernatural magic was one of the many peasant traditions that interfered with capitalist labor discipline worldwide. In this context, the degree to which people allegedly practiced magic became a potent index of their primitiveness and a powerful indictment of their readiness for self-rule and civilization. Whether in China, Burma, Laos, India, Madagascar, South Africa, Egypt, the Arabian Peninsula, Palestine, Persia, Angola, Benin, Quoja (modern-day Sierra Leone), or the Congo, eighteenth-century European geographers described the existence of magical rituals as spurious and ridiculous. According to English geographer Charles T. Middleton, "magical" rituals were benighted practices "which mankind naturally follow who are not acquainted with physics, history, and true religion."[49] European Protestants came to see the rest of the world's peoples as magical and hence uncivilized.

Prophet Noble Drew Ali would teach that race was a fiction, and that the only race was the human race. Today, most scholars would agree with him. Europeans of the nineteenth century invented their own scientific theories of race that in retrospect seem not just as spurious as witchcraft but, in truth, far less sophisticated. In the mid-eighteenth century, Swedish botanist Carl Linnaeus (1707–1778) published his *Systema Naturae*, a taxonomy of more than four thousand animals and seven thousand plants of genus and species names using the "binomial" method that is still employed today. Although the only member of the species *Homo sapiens* that he examined was himself, that small sample size did not prevent him from dividing all of humanity into four groups: Europeans, American Indians, Asians, and Africans. If dividing the world up into so few groups seemed crude, the "Prince of Botanists" compounded his folly by assigning each group essential qualities. For example, Europeans were sanguine, brawny, gentle, and inventive, while Africans were phlegmatic, crafty, indolent, and negligent.[50] Johann Blumenbach (1752–1840), a German professor of medicine at the University of Göttingen, amassed a large collection of human skulls and proposed that all of humankind could be divided into five races that linked Linnaeus's divisions to specific geographic sub-regions: Caucasian, Mongolian, Ethiopian, American, and Malay. He chose the Caucasus Mountains as the ancestral homeland of Europeans for no more consequential reason than that he was enamored with the skull in his collection of a woman from the Caucasus, believing that its appealing, rounded shape made it the most beautiful skull in his possession. A subsequent trip to the Caucasus region confirmed for him the beauty of its people, and the utterly fallacious myth of the "Caucasian race" was born. The foremost scientific racist was Comte Joseph-Arthur de Gobineau, who published his *Essay on the Inequality of Human Races* in the decade before the American Civil War, and divided all human beings into three races, labeled by colors: white, yellow, and black. Like English philosopher Herbert Spencer (1820–1903), who originated the idea of the "survival of the fittest" that Charles Darwin would make famous, de Gobineau believed that Europeans' success in subjugating much of the globe could be explained by their alleged genetic superiority.

European Americans were avid consumers of this self-flattering new racial science, such as it was, and soon got into the game of producing it themselves. Samuel George Morton (1799–1851) was a doctor from Philadelphia who collected over a thousand human skulls, and used them to argue that different races had different brain sizes and hence intelligence levels. Morton stopped up the openings in his skulls with wax and filled the craniums with white peppercorns and lead shot in order to measure their volume, discovering, he claimed, that "Caucasians" had the largest heads.[51] Few would ever seriously propose that bigger people are more intelligent than smaller people, but Morton's enterprise, and that of many imitators, cloaked a core belief in white supremacy with the confirming rituals of a new form of scientific witchcraft—a form of what contemporary historian Karen E. Fields calls "racecraft." When E. E. Evans-Pritchard, the greatest chronicler of magic in Africa, asked why his subjects "do not perceive the futility of their magic," he came up with twenty-two explanations, many of which could as easily explain the persistence of racism. Racism became part of natal and seldom-questioned "readymade patterns of belief which have the weight of tradition behind them," as Evans-Pritchard described witchcraft among the Azande.[52] An interest in the witchcraft of Africans and other peoples of color not only drove the new racecraft, but witchcraft and scientific racism shared similar qualities: both used reason to operate in an irrational manner by using "confirming rituals" that were ignored if they contradicted the preconceived correct answer. For the crazed phrenologists filling skulls with peppercorns, the results of their experiments could be set aside if they contradicted their larger racist worldview. It was an outlook as impervious to contradictory evidence as the hull of a European slave ship was indifferent to the crashing of waves or the screams of its suffering cargo.[53]

But magic and racism were not the only traditions influencing the development of theatrical magic over the course of the nineteenth century. Equally as important, and braided inextricably with the other two strands, was the long European tradition of dividing the world into East and West, each with its own essential unchanging qualities. The work of early Orientalists presented the East as a place of faded grandeur and dazzling antiquity. European Orientalists were not only active at the same time as the expansion of European colonial empires, but in many cases they were themselves either missionaries or colonial officials who played active roles in the expansion of those empires. Academic Orientalism began in the eighteenth century, following the expansion of European trading companies in the seventeenth century. French translations of ancient Vedic manuscripts rocked Europeans in the middle of the eighteenth century, who had to admit that their ancestors were not the only ones who had made history. British Orientalists soon followed, as Great Britain unified its three Indian territories by 1774 and scholars studied Sanskrit and codified Indian history, law, literature, music, and flora and fauna, inspiring generations of Orientalists to come.[54] Napoleon's 1798–1799 campaign to occupy Egypt and Syria was partly inspired by his study of European histories of the Orient, and his determination to conquer India was informed by the writings of British Orientalist Sir William "Oriental" Jones. Napoleon spurred the development of Orientalism even further when he brought a large retinue of scholars trailing the French army to Egypt, whose job was to bridge the cultural gap between the French occupiers and Egyptian locals and to create the enormous, richly illustrated, oversized twenty-three-volume encyclopedia of Egypt published between 1809 and 1828 that fueled the nineteenth century's fascination with all things Egyptian.[55] Imperialism thus joined magic and race as one of the key ideas linking the Orient and the Occident.

🦁   🦁   🦁

The dichotomy between magical "primitives" and capitalist "moderns" was so firmly etched in the nineteenth-century imagination that Karl Marx could effectively cast doubt on capitalism by blurring such categories. In 1848 he wrote that modern bourgeois capitalism had "conjured up such gigantic means of production and of exchange, that it is like the sorcerer who is no longer able to control the powers of the netherworld whom he has called up by his spells."[56] Capitalist modernity was born of the rationalist attempt to master the natural world through science and the abstemious effort to make money multiply through intellectual abstraction, capitalization in corporations, and long-distance exchange. But the inventions, cities, wars, and new social forms that capitalism produced were so new, violent, vast, and difficult to comprehend that they seemed to introduce ever greater forms of mystification, not less. The nineteenth century's bloom of occult traditions with allegedly ancient origins and often fanciful documentation were part of a larger pattern during the Industrial Revolution: amid all the social upheaval, migration, and labor strife, Victorians hungered for new traditions of spuriously ancient provenance, even when, as in the case of Scottish tartan kilts, they had to make those traditions up out of whole cloth.[57] Whether those traditions were the dozens of new varieties of fraternal lodges where everyone from punters to princes spent their evenings, or new forms of pomp and circumstance surrounding state functions in Europe and the Americas, new nationalist movements with invented ancient pasts, or new religions inspired by old legends, uprooted Victorians were so eager to find deeper connections that many did not closely interrogate those intrepid cultural entrepreneurs who sought to satisfy a hunger for authenticity, historical identity, anti-modern spirituality, or contemporary social connection. Amid the upheaval of slavery, colonialism, and industrial capitalism, it was magic, whether "primitive" or "civilized," that resisted the onward march of progress, suggested there were still-dark lands where the newly discovered laws of science might warp, and injected performing magicians into the heart of allegedly rational modernity who were capable of inducing childlike wonder among workers who spent their days producing the modern world.

The occult's association with radical causes such as feminism and socialism slowed its growth in England after the repression that followed the French Revolution of 1793, but it continued to spread as the First Industrial Revolution gave way to the Second and steam power supplanted stream power. Magic was supposed to fade away along with other forms of irrationality in the face of the march of science, capitalism, and evangelical efforts to spread European Christianity, civilization, and colonialism. Oxford University anthropologist Edward Burnett Tylor, the "father of anthropology," published his landmark volume *Primitive Culture* in 1871 and proclaimed that magic was a barbarous "survival" from the past, and belonged "in its main principle to the lowest known stages of civilization, and the lower races, who have not partaken largely of the education of the world, still maintain its vigor."[58] His successor James G. Frazer documented thousands of magical practices outside Europe and similarly depicted magic as a primitive version of science, one stage on the step toward higher forms of religion, an atavism that would inevitably atrophy.[59] Frazer included a vast array of examples from every documented culture on earth, from the Aztecs to the Zulus, and counseled his readers not to scorn so-called savage and barbarous cultures since the achievements of civilization were built upon their accomplishments.[60]

The spread of capitalist modernity facilitated the growth of leisure industries in Europe and America that multiplied opportunities to create spectacles filled with magic, whether of the top-hat-and-tails variety or the turbaned Indian fakirs in circus sideshows presenting tricks once only known to European travelers, colonial agents, missionaries, or corporate emissaries who had toured the British colonies. Those brown-skinned avatars of the Mystic East, including numerous Europeans and Americans who tinted their faces with walnut juice and billed themselves with Chinese, Indian, or Arabian names in order to increase their magical mystiques, commodified the idea that the mysterious Orient hid people and places immune to the laws of nature as codified in Cambridge, England, or Cambridge, Massachusetts.

The Victorian era's occult religious movements, especially the variant of Indian religion known as "Theosophy," presented Indian, Buddhist, and other "Eastern" ideas. Likewise, its stage magicians performed a wide variety of Oriental magic in European and American theaters, marking a very literal return of what colonialism had repressed. Travelers to British colonial India had long marveled at the feats of the fakirs who lay on beds of nails, walked on hot coals, charmed snakes from baskets, ate glass, made mango trees appear to grow and bear fruit instantaneously, and made boys disappear inside wicker baskets. Now, European and American magicians began performing such tricks in theaters, circus sideshows, and amusement parks, usually wrapping their heads in turbans, decking themselves in Oriental finery, and using the mystique of the Far East to entrance Western audiences. The first stage magician's journal published in America called itself "the Mahatma," and was filled with learned disquisitions and exposés on the workings of "Oriental" magicians of all kinds.[61] One American magician who started performing "Hindoo magic" at Chicago's World Columbian Exposition of 1893 later made a name for himself by converting escape magic, transforming it from the ropes of fairground fakirs to the manufactured locks and chains of the twentieth century, reaching back a hundred years to borrow the name of the "father" of stage magic, a name that also conjured up "Hindoo" magic. He called himself "Harry Houdini."

And so, by the time Walter Brister started practicing magic on the cusp of the twentieth century, both "traditional" magic and its stage variants had become traditions that undermined their own story of cultural evolution and modern scientific progress, and illustrated instead the uncomfortable kinship and deep connection between East and West, brown and white, colonized and colonizers, and mysticism and modernity. But stage magic was not merely derivative of "real" magic or religion; Oriental stage magic and the ersatz knowledge of the Orient that it produced actually helped to spread Black American adoption of Islam after World War I. Scholars may have theorized that there was an unalterable distinction between the grandeur of religion and the mendaciousness of magic, or that the magic of colonized people was a marker of their backwardness, but the doubly Orientalist discourse of "Oriental magic" became a crucial conduit in the evolution of American Islamic faiths. It seems paradoxical, yet this doubly counterfeit, doubly Orientalist activity of "Oriental" or "Hindoo" stage magic at the turn of the twentieth century could help produce genuine and heartfelt religious identification with one of the most venerable and populous monotheistic religions on earth. Like most things it inherited, the not-very-United States of America would transform magic, combining disparate sources from various continents, and make it dance to a bolder syncopated and fascinating rhythm.

CHAPTER THREE

MUSLIM MASONS

To me there is nothing so simple, nothing so impressive, nothing so devout, as a Muhammedan standing in the presence of his God. There is a childlike faith, a manly trust, a sincere belief evinced and experienced by these believers, that never seems to predominate in any other form of religion.

—F. HOPKINSON SMITH, 1892[1]

The same year that Walter Brister began leading the "pickaninny" band in the hijinks and strained merrymaking of *In Old Kentucky* on Broadway, a very different vision of the Black past was unfurling in Chicago, one that presented a facsimile of the Muslim world complete with dozens of performers who were "Negroes" in American terms. Chicago's World's Columbian Exposition of 1893 drew twenty-seven million admissions during the six months it was open between May and October, a figure that was equivalent to one-quarter of the residents of the United States—although many of those were repeat visitors. Crowds thronged to see the "White City" of dazzling white neoclassical plaster-covered buildings dedicated to areas of industry and human endeavor, to stroll the crowded Midway Plaisance, and to take in the boat parades on the man-made lagoon surrounding the ornate buildings on the shores of oceanic Lake Michigan. Visitors viewed the neoclassical statues dedicated to industry and other virtues, and stood in line to admire the vistas from the world's first Ferris wheel, a gargantuan contraption with compartments as big as street cars that hoisted fairgoers two hundred and sixty feet in the air. America's greatest landscape architect, Frederick Law Olmsted, the designer of New York's Central Park and San Francisco's Golden Gate Park, planned the fairgrounds in Chicago's Jackson Park, complete with lagoons and canals designed to set off the fair's buildings and provide room for boat races and pleasure boating. A select group of the nation's leading architects designed impressive neoclassical buildings arranged like overdecorated white wedding cakes around Olmsted's central lagoon.

To the west, past the various rings of the main fairgrounds, was the rowdy and populist pleasure ground of the Midway Plaisance. The Midway connecting Jackson Park, on the lake, with Washington Park, to the west, was a strip of land about one mile long and eight hundred feet wide, containing 1,440 concessions, three-quarters of which were owned or operated by a few of the 1,650 foreigners who took part as salesmen, musicians, or "natives."[2] The official guide to the Midway claimed that if its attractions were stretched in a straight line they would extend more than six miles, and the US Customs Office estimated that visitors to the Midway spent over $7 million on its attractions—mostly in 10- and 25-cent increments.[3] Observer Frank H. Smith deemed the concourse a "Human Kaleidoscope," featuring representatives of every country in the world, "both civilian and barbarian," all following their vocations and "mingling together as a happy family," a truly wonderful sight that was at times bordering on pandemonium but "withal producing a happy sensation of enjoyment nowhere else experienced."[4] Groups of Inuits sweated in their fur coats in the summer heat, while ornately costumed Balinese dancers shimmied and Norwegian Laplanders tended their overheated reindeer. There were two Irish exhibits, a sprawling German village, a Viennese village, and Turkish, Egyptian, and Algerian concessions, among many others, from a Swiss Village to a "Dahomeyan Village" with Africans performing music and dances. Despite various historians' claims to the contrary, there was no rhyme or reason to where these peoples were located, aside from a clustering of some of the representatives of Muslim countries, which occupied a prominent place close to the fairground at the center of the strip.[5]

Far from being a didactic display that demonstrated the superiority of the West, the Midway was a chaotic and confusing pleasure zone that blurred categorical distinctions between East and West, familiar and foreign, and created a human kaleidoscope that tumbled together diverse peoples in a disorienting and dazzling array. "There have been other world's fairs," an observer for the *Daily Inter Ocean* opined, "but there never before was a Midway—a spot where the lines of longitude and the parallels of latitude were tangled together like a skein of silk after a kitten's play; where the occident and the orient were mixed in the most gigantic amusement potpourri the world has ever seen." It all "combined to give a polyglot effect, confusing, but in the main pleasing."[6]

The many Muslim exhibitions became the Midway's most popular sights, and together they lent the Midway an Islamic Orientalist flavor.[7] The Algerian and Tunisian Village, the Persian Palace, the Street in Cairo, the Moorish Palace, and the Turkish Theater displayed Oriental finery, Islamic arts, and most scandalously, gyrating, dancing women in loose-fitting costumes. Nor did the Islamic entertainments stop with the Midway itself; outside the Midway, Buffalo Bill's Wild West Show featured the Hassan Ben Ali troupe of Moroccan acrobats and one whirling dervish, with eight accompanying veiled wives, while a group of Syrian horsemen and camel riders—dubiously billed as Bedouins—encamped on a nearby baseball field until they found space at the edge of the Midway to demonstrate their impressive riding skills as the "Wild East Show."[8]

The Street in Cairo was the most popular exhibition of the Midway, and was consistently thronged with visitors.[9] The street presented a picturesque, Oriental façade, with gaily colored buildings painted grayish yellow and striped with muted tones of green and red, and with overhanging second-story window casements enclosed in latticework, bringing to mind the enclosed harem spaces of Cairo even if there were only 11 women among the more than 175 performers in the Egyptian Village. Numerous visitors remarked that it felt as if they were transported to Cairo itself, with the brightly colored buildings and people, the brilliant rugs and tapestries for sale, the groups of men puffing on water pipes, the crowds of noisy children, and the big, plodding, smelly animals.[10] Twenty donkeys, seven camels, and assorted snakes and monkeys formed the Street's menagerie, all imported from Alexandria, Egypt, along with their human handlers.[11] Clowns managed to get laughs with slapstick antics, slapping each other in the face, fighting duels with monkeys, and telling jokes. Roaming groups of swordsmen, wrestlers, and musicians performed for tips while jugglers and small boys executed acrobatic flips. Magicians roamed the streets, making objects disappear from audience members' hands and reappear in their ears. Snake charmers, magicians, and fortune-tellers charged an extra admission into their tents scattered throughout the Egyptian exhibition.

By intention, the colorfulness and exoticness of the costumes of Muslim lands and the hundreds of native performers lent this slice of Chicago the air of a Middle Eastern bazaar, with numerous performers vying for the attention and coins of passersby and drumming up business in many languages. Sideshow barkers and food vendors shouted over the din of the thousands of jostling visitors enticed by strange-smelling foods, fine teas, and foreign wares. One journalist attested that everyone visited the Midway Plaisance, "and what a picture that road down the center presented." Regardless of the day of the week, one met people "of all nations, all stations, all classes and all dressed in holiday attire." At a time when American clothing was generally quite drab, the visitors from Islamic countries presented a riot of color and exotic dress. There were Turks in European costume, with red fezzes, and Turks in all the glory of rich silk turbans, purple silk mantles, and yellow silk trousers; Arabs in long, pale, tan-colored robes, embroidered in gold, and in long silk robes, covered with gold lace.[12] As the official guide to the Midway described the Egyptian exhibit, only a few steps from the crowded roadway the visitor found him- or herself in a busy thoroughfare in "ancient Egypt," where the architecture, the surroundings, and the people were "as far removed from anything American as could well be imagined." The narrow bending street offered Oriental buildings, picturesque shops, and quaint overhanging upper stories. Curiosity seekers crowded the shop windows facing the street, and olive-skinned Egyptians, fair-skinned Greeks, and sable-hued Sudanese mingled with the visitors all around. "There is merry laughter on all sides," one visitor observed, "and for a few minutes at least you are lost to all consciousness of being in that extremely modern city called Chicago."[13] In other words, the Midway created a dizzying collapse of time, space, and even racial hierarchies. Contemporaries could understand themselves not just to be traveling to another place, but also to be traveling back in time, to "ancient Egypt," apart from the modernity of Chicago. The Street in Cairo even had a display devoted to the time of the Pharaohs, complete with mummies.[14]

The sacred as well as the profane was on display at the Street in Cairo: the muezzin issued a call to prayer several times a day from the mosque's minaret, and spectators were allowed to watch prayers from the gallery. Likewise, visitors watched an imam instruct the boys in daily lessons in the Qur'ān and Arabic penmanship. A performer played the role of "Gamal El Din El Yahbi," a "Mohammedan of the time" who was said to own a stately house in the middle of the street and who ostentatiously demonstrated the hospitality of the Muslim world for quizzical American passersby.[15]

Denton J. Snider, an independent Hegelian scholar from St. Louis, wrote about the Midway as an expression of specifically Islamic culture. "The Greek spirit in its best form still rules largely in the Exposition proper; but in the Plaisance it is Allah, who is supereminent, Allah Akbar, with Mohammed as his prophet," he commented. "So the student is led to have a desperate grapple with Allah, if he is going to grasp this World's Fair. The Allah of Mohammed is the one God, in whom all individuals are one, or must make themselves one by an act of Will, which is resignation." Snider classified the Hebrew Bible, and consequently Judaism, Christianity, *and* Islam, as Oriental, and viewed the Orient and its alleged "idea of lapse" as a necessary counterbalance to Occidental obsessions with ascent and progress: "We have to keep and lay to heart this Oriental contribution to our Western world; very necessary indeed is it, a great corrective of our one-sidedness and egoism."[16] At Chicago's Midway, the Muslim East came west.

🍂   🍂   🍂

One of the most consequential events at the Chicago World's Fair in terms of its lasting impact on American culture was the transmission of the rituals of the Shriners to Americans of African descent. Well-known New York thespian William J. "Billy" Florence and a prominent Masonic and "devoted Arabic" scholar, Dr. Walter M. Fleming, founded the Shriners, or the Ancient Arabic Order of the Nobles of the Mystic Shrine for North America, in 1872.[17] No secret society had been more deeply immersed in the mythology and magical legends of the Islamic Orient. Although not properly speaking a Masonic organization, the Shriners were only open to those who had achieved the highest degrees of freemasonry. The Nobles of the Mystic Shrine called themselves the "playground of freemasonry" and sought to embody a spirit of Oriental decadence and frivolity, balanced by charitable works. The order took off in 1878 when the founders hired Albert Rawson, an Orientalist expert and friend of Theosophist Madame Blavatsky, and determined to "decorate it with all the mysticism of the Orient" and "a certain degree of mystery."[18]

Mocking the solemnity of the Western Orientalist quest for authenticity in the East and the absurdities of fraternal regalia and hullabaloo, the Shriners created an intentionally fraudulent legend linking their secret order back to Ali, the son-in-law of the Prophet Muhammad, and the city of Mecca in 644. The silly miniature vehicles that fez-wearing Nobles rode in their parades invited their audiences to release their Westernized workaday woes and enjoy a carefree, absurd Orientalist spectacle.[19]

Intent on having a good time, supporting charitable projects, and enjoying the fleshpots of Egypt as literally as possible, the fake North American Nobles seldom took their own legends very seriously. Even their own historians speak of the liberties taken with their genesis story. "The placing of the origin of this Order at Mecca is a fancy of the imagination which historians in general have a license to claim use of," one Shriner historian wrote in 1906, referring to the rites of the order as a "compilation of facts and fancies which subsequently were handed out to a waiting and anxious constituency."[20] The Shriners' fancies had a distinctly Orientalist flavor, describing Muslim lands with exotic and erotic language, as in the following passage:

> Looking backward toward the home of the Order, we find the Brotherhood in Egypt flourishing and fruitful in good works, as beautiful as are the queenly palms which wave their feathery arms in the soft airs that crinkle the surface of the lordly Nile into rippling lines of loveliest corrugations, or cast their cooling shadows upon the star-eyed daughters of Egypt.[21]

This kind of Orientalist fantasy was so overwrought that it did not disguise its air of winking, and slightly salacious, irreverence, which fit with the air of droll irony that became part of American masculine culture in the wake of the horror of the Civil War.[22] The order's costumes also embodied Western Orientalist ideas of the East. The Nobles wore rich costumes "of Eastern character," made of silk and brocaded velvet "of Oriental intensity of color," topped with a fez. According to the Shriners, the wearing of the fez originated from the time when the Crusades interrupted the *hajj* to Mecca around 960 CE, and "Mohammedans west of the Nile" journeyed to the city of Fez in Morocco instead.[23] Shriner myths were loosely based in Islamic history, but included many inaccuracies. As a center of Islamic learning, Fez has long been a destination for travelers searching for knowledge (*talab al'ilm*). Jerusalem was sometimes used as a *hajj* destination when Muslims have been unable to visit Mecca, but Fez never served a similar purpose.[24]

As historian Susan Nance explains, the Shriners' rites were not a simple mockery of Islam but were part of a late nineteenth-century masculine burlesque of reverence, and satirized the feminizing influence of Theosophists and other Western admirers of Eastern spirituality. "Like many popular arts and amusements in the nineteenth century the Shrine ritual could be all things to all men," she writes. "Whether an initiate sought relief from the seriousness of Masonry, a humorous interpretation of exotic travel narratives, or just a lighthearted elite fraternal experience, whether they despised the Muslim Arabia, romanticized it, or were indifferent to it, they could all find their own meaning in the tricks and skits of the Muslim Shrine."[25]

In the Islamic Orient, all roads lead not to Rome but to Mecca, and the Shriners appropriately began with "Mecca Temple" in New York City on September 26, 1872. It would be four years before they expanded, but when they did they swept across the land, littering America with a strange poetry of Arabic-named shrines. In 1876, the year that a disputed presidential election led to the withdrawal of Federal troops from the South and the end of Reconstruction, Shriners founded "Damascus Temple" in Rochester, New York; "Mt. Sinai" in Montpelier, Vermont; and "Al Koran" in Cleveland, Ohio. The year of the Compromise of 1877 brought the "Oriental Temple" to Troy, New York, and similarly Orientally named temples in Cincinnati, the Northeast, and the Midwest.[26] The Nobles spread to the West Coast in 1883 with the opening of "Islam Temple" in San Francisco, but the center of the movement remained the East Coast and Midwest, where there were four or five new temples almost every year of the 1880s, with names like Osman, Jerusalem, Palestine, El Kahir, Moolah, and Abdallah. There were also a spate of ancient Egyptian names, such as Osiris, Rameses, and Isis. The Alhambra lodge landed in Chattanooga, Tennessee, and residents of Fargo, North Dakota, cavorted at "El Zagal." The year 1890 witnessed the Battle of Wounded Knee, the last major battle and massacre of Indian peoples by US soldiers, while in other parts of the West, men playing Muslims founded "El Kalah" in Salt Lake City and "El Katif" in Spokane. By the end of the year there were 16,980 Shriners nationwide and new chapters in Erie, Pennsylvania, and Birmingham, Alabama, with many more to follow.[27]

By the time the World's Columbian Exposition opened in 1893 there were sixty-three shrines nationwide, with almost 23,000 members, and by the time it closed there were four more chapters.[28] The Shriners continued expanding at this breakneck pace for the next many decades, and by the time they published their official *History of the Imperial Council* in 1921, there were a total of 154 chapters, at a time when the country as a whole had only fifty-eight metropolitan areas. They sported such exotic Oriental names as Bedouin, Arabia, Kazim, Salaam, Luxor, Cairo, Alcazar, and perhaps strangest of all, Jackson, Mississippi's "Wahabi," founded on July 12, 1911. Notably, they all remained in the continental United States, except for places where large numbers of US citizens sojourned for commercial reasons: Honolulu, Winnipeg, Mexico City, London, Ontario, and Panama.

Unlike other streams of freemasonry, which started in Scotland and embellished upon legends drawn from Central Europe, the Shriners were a distinctively American version of freemasonry that drew on romantic Orientalist legends at a time when America itself was bursting onto the world's stage as a major industrial, cultural, military, and colonial power, while simultaneously suppressing Americans of African descent through new systems of segregation and disenfranchisement. There is no simple correlation between Shrinerdom and the new imperialism, however. Through subversive laughter and ribald parodies of Islam, some of the country's most prominent men ridiculed the Victorian hypocrisies of their own society, using the carefree, potent, and appealing mythology of the Muslim East.

🦅   🦅   🦅

The Midway's Muslim diaspora in general and its Street in Cairo in particular contained all the elements of Egyptology and romantic Orientalism that were the stock-in-trade of the Shriners. Chicago's Medinah Temple of the Nobles of the Mystic Shrine cosponsored the Turkish mosque; the sultan of Turkey, Abdul Hamid, was the other cosponsor. Hamid had intended to provide a place on the fairgrounds where Muslims might worship without molestation, but the Shriners had more lighthearted ideas. Medinah Shrine sent invitations to shrines across the country, and representatives from New York, Milwaukee, Indianapolis, Cedar Rapids, and Grand Rapids attended, two thousand strong. All the Shriners wore bright red fezzes emblazoned with a crescent moon, and they included a contingent of an Arab guard, dressed in Zouave fashion with fezes, vests, and baggy pantaloons, followed by the two hundred members of the Turkish delegation, wearing fezzes or gorgeous silk turbans. A large number of Syrian riders from the "Wild East Show," dressed as turbaned Bedouins astride camels and magnificent Arabian horses, provided additional interest. Together, the Turkish villagers and the visiting Shriners paraded all the way from the Exposition train station, through the length of the Midway Plaisance, and into the Turkish village.[29] One woman, observing the Shriners' and Turks' parade, remarked that the Turks looked just like Americans. When told that most of the "Turks" *were* indeed Americans, the disappointed woman told her husband that the foreigners were frauds.[30] When the parade reached the mosque, the "real Turks"—most of whom were Jews—took off their slippers and fell to their knees in prayer, while the Shriners rushed in with their shoes on as spectators. After the muezzin, Osin Bey, issued the "weird prayer with something of the sweetness of a yoddle in its intonation," the Turkish drum corps beat out a frenzied crescendo. The Shriner band, caught up in what it thought was the spirit of the moment, kicked into high gear, as one of the Turkish officials tried and failed to hush the band, playing popular numbers such as "the Bowery," and "Ta-ra-ra Boom-de-ay." The Turks prayed, foreheads to the ground as the Shriners from Moslem Temple in Detroit and the others watched. At the end of the Nobles' visit to the Shriner-Ottoman mosque on the Midway, the floors had to be scrubbed of all the mud the enthusiastic if culturally insensitive fez-wearing American pseudo-Muslims had tramped into the building.[31] Many Shriners seemed to treat this solemn ceremony as a huge joke, which was more or less the modus operandi of the Shriners in general, and struck some onlookers as sacrilegious and terribly offensive. The Greek supervisor of the Egyptian mummy display barred Shriners that afternoon since they were so rowdy and disrespectful.[32] Still, the fact that there was a functioning mosque at an exposition dedicated to the memory of Christopher Columbus, who allegedly hated the "infidel Saracen," struck some as deliciously ironic.

Shriners were not only largely ignorant of the religious practices of Muslims; the "American Turks" were also unaware of political divisions among denizens of the Ottoman Empire. One American Shriner got himself in trouble when trying to gain admission to a restricted portion of the Egyptian exhibition by displaying a Shriner badge with a scimitar, two tiger claws, the head of the Sphinx, and the star of the Orient. The Egyptians saw the symbol as signifying allegiance with the Turkish Ottomans and became hopping mad to the point that the Shriner began to fear for his safety. He wondered, "Where was the link in the Mystic Shrine that made brethren of these men of the East?" according to his friend's account. "Certainly there must be a 'degree' beyond the one brought back by the late 'Billy' Florence," the founder of the Nobles of the Mystic Shrine.[33]

If the Shriners were the "playground of Masonry," then the ersatz Islamic Orient of the World's Fair was a veritable playground for Shriners. So it is particularly appropriate that the World's Fair was the place where Shriners passed on the twenty-one-year-old traditions of the "Ancient Arabic Order" to Black freemasons. The key figure in this transmission was a Black attorney from Chicago named John George Jones, who was born on September 18, 1849, in Ithaca, New York. At the age of seven his family moved to Chicago, and when Jones came of age he studied law under the tutelage of W. W. O'Brien, a noted criminal attorney. Jones passed the bar in the state of Illinois in 1881, became a law partner to Ida B. Wells's future husband, Ferdinand Barnett, and later was elected to the state legislature from Chicago. At the time, Jones was the leader of Chicago's small Afro-American community, "the central figure around which the lesser lights gathered."[34] He was a man of considerable eloquence and organizational acumen whose unyielding opposition to racial discrimination earned him the nickname "Indignation" Jones. His rejection of segregation in any form led him to oppose the founding of a Negro YMCA in 1889, and also the establishment of Provident Hospital for "Negroes" in 1891. Jones also became a vociferous critic of Booker T. Washington, the "Wizard of Tuskegee," and the most powerful Black man in the country at the time. When prominent doctor Dan Williams remarked that "Negroes" were fond of secret societies and bright regalia, Jones called a meeting to censure Williams for defaming the race as frivolous since the implication was that Blacks spent too much time and money on fraternal activities that could have been better spent uplifting "the Race." But ironically, there was no one more important to the multiplication and mutation of Black Masonic regalia than "Indignation" Jones himself.[35]

Prince Hall was a former slave who joined a masonic lodge of British soldiers in 1775 and then formed the first Masonic lodge for men of African descent after the war, becoming the founder of

Black freemasonry. A century after Prince Hall, John George Jones became a prominent member of Chicago's Prince Hall Masonic lodge, rising to the rank of Deputy Grand Master in 1875. In 1887, however, he began to stray from Prince Hall orthodoxy, finding himself suspended and then reinstated in the same year on the charge of ignoring the orders of a Masonic court.[36] Around 1890 he began representing himself as the "Sovereign Grand Commander of the United Supreme Council of the Southern and Western Masonic Jurisdiction, United States of America" and began petitioning the Shriners' "Grand Council of Arabia," seeking to be initiated into the Shrine and to be vested with the power to organize Shrine Temples in the United States.

On June 1, 1893, Jones got his wish when a delegation in town for a Shriner convention timed to coincide with the World's Fair conferred the degree of Ancient Arabic Order of the Nobles of the Mystic Shrine on Jones in impressive ceremonies at Chicago's eighteen-story Masonic Hall. Along with the initiation, the Shriners gave Jones the power and authority to confer the degree of the Mystic Shriner, to found temples, to create Grand Imperial Councils, and to call himself Imperial Potentate of the Imperial Grand Council in the United States of America. The head of the Shriner delegation called himself "Noble Rofelt Pasha, Deputy of the Shriners' Grand Council of Arabia," and he was assisted by three others, who likewise claimed to be from the Islamic Orient.[37] According to one of Jones's successors, the others were "S. Hussein of Syria, Turkey, Amel Kadar of Palestine, Turkey, and A. B. Belot of the north of Africa, while representing their various countries at the Chicago World's Fair."[38] The following day, Jones convened thirteen members of the local Prince Hall Masons in Chicago, just as thirteen white Masons had met in New York to form the Mystic Shrine twenty-one years previously, and together Jones and his associates founded the Black version of the Shriners, beginning appropriately enough with "Palestine Temple."[39] They followed that up before the end of the year with "Mecca Temple" in Washington, DC, "Jerusalem Temple" in Baltimore, Maryland, "Medina Temple" in New York, "Pyramid Temple" in Philadelphia, and "Persian Temple" in Indianapolis, thus mapping ancient Egypt, the Orient, and the holy cities of the Islamic world onto some of the major Black American cities of the late nineteenth century.

The white Shriners noted the advent of a "colored" group as early as 1894, when their Imperial Potentate, Thomas J. Hudson, reported the existence of "organizations of our colored fellow citizens, who have pirated our title almost verbatim."[40] Prince Hall Shrine historian Joseph Walkes concludes that a member of the white Shrine "was directly involved with Jones and his organizing the Prince Hall Shrine."[41] Despite protests from some white Shriners in succeeding decades, others continued to supply their Black counterparts with regalia and meeting places.

Black Shriners faced dissension from within and without from the beginning, when a rival named Milton F. Fields emerged and began conferring the mysteries of the Mystic Shrine on fellow "colored" Masons. With the order split between a "Jones Faction" and a "Fields Faction," Jones lost a bid for reelection as Imperial Potentate in 1895 and organized a rival Supreme Council.[42] In 1897 Prince Hall Shrinerdom became further fragmented when ornery John George Jones began expelling members en masse. In order to quell dissension between what had become three separate Black Shriner organizations, representatives of three of the first temples met in December of 1900 and formed the Imperial Council of the Ancient *Egyptian* (emphasis added) Arabic Order Nobles of the Mystic Shrine of North and South America and Its Jurisdictions. By placing "Egyptian" in their name, the Black Shriners were distinguishing themselves from the white organization with a reference to Africa that connoted both the contemporary Egypt of the Ottoman Empire and the ancient glories of the pharaohs that had long played a central role in Masonic legend.[43] The Prince Hall Shrine's founder, old "Indignation" Jones, got himself expelled from "regular" Prince Hall Masonry in 1903 for setting up a fraudulent Grand Lodge of Illinois without approval from legitimate Prince Hall organizations, and spent the remainder of his life until his death in 1914 feuding with other Black Masons.[44]

Prince Hall Shrine temples had spread rapidly, from twenty-five in 1895 to sixty-one in 1899. As with the white Shriners, the Black Shriners' choice of temple names reflected their fascination with Islam and the Muslim Orient. There were temples named Allah, Sahara, Koran, Medina, Arabia, Mecca, Palestine, and Mosslem (*sic*). Of the thirty-two temples on the roster for the annual convention in 1909, only Birmingham's "St. Joseph Temple" and Oklahoma City's "Great Western Temple" lacked identifiably Arabic or Oriental names.[45]

African Americans interpreted the Orientalist myth at the heart of Shrinerdom differently than their white peers, just as Joanna

Brooks has argued that African Americans developed their own in-terpretations of freemasonry in general.[46] Whereas the white Shrin-ers tended to treat their origin legend as an elaborate joke, Black Shriners took a more reverent approach. As the decades progressed and Black Shriners started to come under attack from their white counterparts, they became even more deeply invested in their ori-gin legend, which they used to argue that white Shriners were the ones who lacked authority to practice the ritual of the Mystic Shrine. Black Shriners used their origin story to distinguish themselves from white Shriners, arguing that they had received the ritual directly from the mysterious Noble Rofelt Pasha and the "Grand Council of Ara-bia."[47] In a speech given at the establishment of Jerusalem Temple at Baltimore, Maryland, in September of 1893, John G. Jones claimed that "the Ancient Arabic Order of Nobles of the Mystic Shrine of Masonry is possibly the most profound of all the mysteries of Ma-sonry, for its origins bears internal evidence of its existence soon after the creation of the world." Likewise, Jones emphasized the uplifting and morally edifying nature of the order's ceremonies and principles, which promised to unite men, to teach "solemn and important les-sons of truth and justice for all," and to promote "the evangelization of man and the promotion and practice of Christian faith."[48]

Blacks and whites also related to the Orient very differently in the era known as the "nadir" for Black Americans, when lynching and Jim Crow segregation attained a new ferocity. The most common attitude in white Shrine literature is one of overwrought reverence for Islam and the Orient. However, it was not uncommon for white Shriners to associate Arabs with Africans and to connect both with denigrating stereotypes of Black Americans. In one illustration for a function of the white Islam Temple in San Francisco, California, an elephant threatens an "Arab," drawn with the cartoonish buggy eyes and exaggerated lips, both tropes of American racist caricatures of Black people.[49]

In contrast, Black Shriners used the mystique of the Orient to ad-vance the cause of the uplift and progress of "the race." At the twelfth annual session of the Imperial Council of the Black Shriners, held in Detroit in 1910, Imperial Potentate Jacob F. Wright melded the vocabulary of Islam into the language of the Exodus narrative, por-traying Detroit as an oasis in the Michigan "desert." "Many years ago," he said, "there lived in the minds of a people, who had for years been driven by hard task-masters, that somewhere on the northern

boundary of our country situated between two lakes, was the gateway to a country of human liberty," he began, employing the poetic
language of Black American spirituals that turned the South into
Egypt and the North into a metaphorical Promised Land. Then he
superimposed the Holy Land of Islam on top of the Holy Land of
Judaism, Christianity, and the Spirituals: "Many struggled in vain
for this Mecca," Potentate Wright continued, "but to many others
the dream became a living reality." For Black Americans living in
an age of Southern horrors, the struggles for the "Mecca" of Detroit
were very current. The warm reception "our caravan of the faithful"
received there made "each pilgrim" feel that "life is worth living in
Detroit."[50] As Shriners, Black men were metaphorical pilgrims to
the Mecca of the North, living Judeo-Christian and Islamic mythology simultaneously.

   "Negro" Shriners consciously used the language of uplift to describe the mission of their organization, which, Imperial Potentate
Eugene Phillips stated in Atlantic City in 1911, "means so much for
the advancement and uplift of our race." Conversely, the factional-
ism among Prince Hall Shriners was a "retardation not only of the
progress of our order but of the race as well."[51] In 1913 Phillips, addressing a gathering in Indianapolis, defined the work of the Order
as allaying the suffering of humanity, "which is so wretched and so
sadly in need of love." The duty of members was never to "lull their
conscience to sleep while there is one soul suffering from the injustice
of his brother, whether that brother be black or white." Rather, they
should "give a cool drop of water of encouragement to every effendi,
oh yes, to every man, be he Seyyid or be he Fellah whenever he needs
our assistance as he journeys by the oases of our desert." Phillips continued, at full gallop, "Illustrious Sons of the Desert, the day is now
here upon us and about us when we must confer and consult for the
good of the race to which we have the honour to belong." Rather than
simply making merry in Indianapolis, the gathering was a time to
"consecrate . . . the solution of the great questions of Justice and Righteousness of the Unity of Allah and the Brotherhood of Man." And
all of this was to be done to glorify Christ, in the "Spirit of that lowly
One, the Man of Sorrows."[52]

   For Black Americans not only was the African-ness of Moorish
and Islamic peoples a source of pride, but the foreignness of the Orientalist rituals of the Mystic Shrine provided a lifeline outside the
racism of American shores. As Masonic historian Joseph C. Walkes

explains, some of the motivation for the creation of the Shriners "came from the need of African-Americans to be recognized outside of their own communities, and such recognition coming from a 'Grand Council of Arabia,' from a mysterious foreign land, perhaps was the spark."[53] For Black Americans, the Mystic Shrine was a way of staking a claim to the world's most ancient mythology while also building fictive ties to a global imagined community of Shriners, Masons, and Muslims.

Freemasonry contained many references to both Israel and Egypt. Yet the main referent for the initiation rituals of both branches of the Mystic Shrine was not Judaism or Christianity but Islam. The rites of the Nobles of the Mystic Shrine became an important inspiration for the rise of Black Muslim sects in the United States because the rites were suffused with Islamic legends, myths, and passwords. The opening words of the Shriner ceremonial explaining their initiation rites were: "My friends or Nobles of the Mystic Shrine, the order with which you have become united was founded by Mohammed and has as its background the trackless desert of Arabia and the fearless, devoted, and barbaric Arab."[54] All initiates were made to "cross the hot sands," which represented the perilous journey of the first Muslim pilgrims to Mecca. Initiates promised to "worship at the Shrine of Islam" and cleanse themselves in a pool meant to signify the Well of Zem Zem (or, alternatively, Zamzam), where Islamic tradition teaches that Hagar and her son Ishmael quenched their thirst when they were expelled from Abraham's tent. Initiates gave a "Grand Salaam" and bow in imitation of Muslim prayer, and they kissed a representation of the Kaaba, the black stone that is the focal point of the annual Muslim pilgrimage to Mecca.[55] Black and white Shriners alike swore on both a Bible and a Qur'an in their ceremonies, and taught reverence for the Qur'an and the Prophet Muhammad, who they claimed was the founder of their secret society. "The Koran is the unique history of our founder Mohammed," Shriners of all races learned upon initiation.

> The work is absolutely unique in its origin and in its preservation, upon the authenticity of which no one has ever been able to cast a serious doubt. The Koran is the actual text as dictated by Mohammed himself, day by day and month by month, during his lifetime. It is the reflection of this master-mind, sometimes inartistic and self-contradictory, more often inspiring and lyrical, and always filled with great ideas which stand out as a whole.[56]

In sum, the heart of the secret ritual of the Shriners was Islamic history and Islamic ritual. As they explained themselves, "Our whole ritualistic system is based upon these kindly attributes [such as refinement, education, and moral integrity] together with an unflinching faith in Allah." One part of the initiation was intended "to teach you to always renounce the wiles and evils of the world and promise to ever worship at the Shrine of Islam, where the air is rich with the wisdom of Allah."[57] Shriners swore a "Moslem's oath" to "Allah, the God of Arab, Moslem, and Mohammed," and they used "Moslem Greetings" such as "Es Salamu Aleikum" (Peace be with you) and "Aleikum Es Salaam" (With you in Peace).[58]

In their ceremonies, Shriners professed reverence for the Holy Prophet, the Holy Qur'an, and the holy city of Mecca; they reenacted Islamic history; they spoke Arabic phrases; and they identified not simply *with* Arabs, but *as* Arabs. In the lecture given to initiates upon their entry into the order, the speaker referred to those present as "we, as true Arabs."[59] Intense theatrical rituals, some of which the Shriners designated as "sacred," performed a kind of magical alchemy; in part by disorienting and frightening initiates, the Nobles became fictive Muslims in a theatrical Arabia. The initiation lecture proclaims, "This city in which you now stand is the Holy City of Islam . . . situated in the Desert of Arabia."[60] Shriners both Black and white luxuriated in this Islamic Orientalist role-playing. "You have made the road clear for the journey of your camels," the Black Imperial Potentate told his charges in 1909. "I find it an easy task to ride through the Desert of burning sand to an Oasis of success."[61] Nobles of the Mystic Shrine of all races imagined themselves into a global community of Muslims stretching back chronologically to the sixth century and spatially across the chasm of oceans to the Islamic-majority countries of the mysterious Orient.

🦅   🦅   🦅

African American Masons, Shriners, Elks, Knights of Pythias, and others played vitally important roles in the civic and social lives of Black communities in the twentieth century, especially as the seedbed of political organizing and new alternative religions. As African Americans moved north in the Great Migration, and as West Indians joined them in places such as Harlem, Cleveland, Philadelphia, Chicago, and Detroit, they formed dozens of benevolent, insurance, and fraternal associations to go along with new mainline churches, storefront churches, social clubs, political clubs, athletic clubs, and literary societies. For example, freemasonry and its derivative secret societies played a central role in the social life of Harlem in the twenties, second only to the church among Black organizations in terms of members and influence. The Elks, Prince Hall Masons, and Odd Fellows all had several thousand members, and there were dozens of secret societies that battled each other for legitimacy and members.[62]

Fraternal organizations came under fire in the Black press for spending most of their funds on regalia and conventions, and offering little tangible benefit to the community. Some even argued that they retarded the progress of "the race" by diverting energy and time that could have been used for more constructive purposes. Yet there is evidence that secret societies played an important role in "Negro" political life in the twenties and in future decades. Lodge meetings provided not only fellowship but opportunities to develop skills in public speaking, politicking, and parliamentary procedure. Lodges provided safe spaces in which to air racial grievances and imagine a future of greater economic justice. One Harlem lodge member explained:

> The reason these fraternal meetings last so long into the night is that all week the colored man, in his job under a white man, has had little things that make him mad and that he can't talk out loud about. These things pile up inside of him. And when he gets on the fraternity floor among his own folks at the meeting, that just biles out of him in laying down the law and asserting his rights to his own brethren. It's his turn to tell other folks where they get off. And how he does tell 'em.[63]

Lodges constituted a Black public sphere that provided more privacy than churches and thus allowed for even franker discussion of the slings and arrows suffered at the hands of whites. The meetings were governed by laws, and the men who gathered there asserted their rights as liberal subjects in the context of a wider society that frequently fell short of the ideals of equality penned by the Masonic Founding Fathers of the United States. Historian Margaret Jacob has argued that European Masonic lodges were laboratories of democracy, where people living underneath repressive autocratic regimes of the eighteenth century learned skills critical to participation in a democratic society. It is quite possible that secret societies and other clubs played an equivalent role among Black Americans, training members in oratory, parliamentary procedure, and voting in times and places where the punishment for Blacks voting could be death.[64]

While the mainstreams of both "regular" Masons and Prince Hall Masons have tended to be bourgeois and conformist, composed primarily of professional members, at their margins their religious dimensions have been more pronounced. Masonic lodges may have helped to create Black citizens and liberal subjects, but viewing Black freemasonry as primarily bourgeois obscures a dense thicket of political dissent and religious energies connected to freemasonry that has flourished among the Black working class. Because of its highly developed secret rituals, its alluring promise of hidden knowledge, and its custodianship of ancient mysteries, freemasonry cultivated religious belief and inspired the formation of numerous religious sects. Whereas the history of the establishment African American "Prince Hall" Freemasonry is well documented, the story of the dozens of alternative forms of Black freemasonry is much less well known. These various forms of alternative freemasonry not only served Black men and women of lower classes and statuses, but they also were more commonly interracial in composition and invoked the transnationalism of the oppressed, throwing their lots not with the European colonial powers but with the colonized nations of the global South. Finally, alternative African American freemasonry was critical to the development of a sympathetic form of Black Orientalism that helped to generate many of the alternative African American religions of the twentieth century, from the Black Israelism of Bishop William Saunders Crowdy and Rabbi Wentworth Arthur Matthew to the Black Spiritual church of Father George W. Hurley and the Black Islam of Noble Drew Ali and the Honorable Elijah Muhammad.

The refusal of most white Masons to recognize their Black Prince Hall counterparts encouraged the mushrooming of religious sects from the soil of Prince Hall Freemasonry. Non–Prince Hall Black Masons asserted their own claims to legitimacy, for example, by deflecting challenges to their legitimacy back upon their Prince Hall accusers, arguing that the Prince Hall lodges were themselves irregular. Much of the literature written by Prince Hall Masons either defends the legitimacy of their own Masonic charter and its lineage from Prince Hall himself, or attacks those purveyors of "bogus," "clandestine," or "spurious" African American Masonry.[65] "Recognized" or "standard" Prince Hall Masons were eager to condemn those they considered illegitimate, partly in an effort to gain legitimacy in the eyes of the wider Masonic world. In 1925 the *New York World* announced a "vigorous campaign" to out illegitimate Masonic bodies on the part of standard Prince Hall Masons, "who seemed to think the public had been unintentionally given the false impression that all negro Masonic lodges are bogus."[66] The Prince Hall Masons contended that one's Masonic legitimacy was not determined by race, and made that argument in part by emphasizing the questionable legitimacy of many lodges of foreign origins.

The grandfather of many of the unrecognized Prince Hall lodges was none other than the founder and first Imperial Potentate of the Black Shriners, John G. Jones, who began to organize unauthorized lodges in New York City with Associate Bishop Jesse B. Thornton after his expulsion from a standard Prince Hall lodge in 1903.[67] Lacking the central controls that put a check on doctrinal and ritual innovation among Prince Hall Masons, alternative freemasons, both Black and white, were free to innovate and mutate, driven by charisma, opportunity, or the marketplace. The central charges raised by Prince Hall Masons against the others was that unscrupulous people were selling the secrets of the order as a moneymaking venture. In some "spurious" lodges, the officers of the association ran the organization as a racket and simply divided up a percentage of the lodge's earnings among themselves.

The multiplication of Black Masonic organizations led to general confusion and great consternation among Prince Hall Masons, who admitted that even well-meaning people could be confused about which organization was "genuine" and which was "spurious." Indeed, "unrecognized" African American Masons sometimes even used the name Prince Hall, as when they used the terms "Prince Hall Origin," "Prince Hall Affiliation," and "Prince Hall Descent."[68] Oregon Prince Hall Grand Master Fred Hartman predicted in 1946 that "if his branch of the Fraternity did not take unofficial action to stem the tide, those 'unrecognized' bodies would eventually overwhelm the Prince Hall institution."[69] Eight years later, Prince Hall Masonic historian Harry Williamson concluded "that 'overwhelming' is rapidly progressing."[70] There were eighteen "unrecognized" African American Masonic organizations in New York City in 1954, and two of them together had more members than all of the "legitimate" Prince Hall bodies. All told, there were four times more alternative Black Masons in New York than "standard" Prince Hall Masons.[71]

Statewide, the situation was even more chaotic, as the world of clandestine Prince Hall lodges was prone to infighting and fragmentation: former partners Jones and Thornton were even said to have expelled each other from the same Grand Lodge. In a world in which Prince Hall Masons recognized the authority of only one Grand Lodge, there were an astounding fourteen competing Grand Lodges of "Negro" Masons in New York State alone by 1954, claiming a total of over sixty affiliated lodges. Texas had about twenty African American masons who all styled themselves the Grand Master of the state. Nationwide, there were at least ninety non-standard Prince Hall Black Masonic organizations by the mid-twentieth century.[72]

Often arguments about Masonic legitimacy spilled into the dockets of the public courts, and Black Shriner legal battles to protect their rights to observe their rituals paved the way for landmark civil rights cases later at midcentury. In two pathbreaking cases, the US Supreme Court overturned state courts' rulings barring Blacks from practicing fraternalism. In 1912's *Creswill v. Grand Lodge Knights of Pythias of Georgia* and 1929's *Ancient Egyptian Arabic Order of Nobles of the Mystic Shrine v. Michaux*, the highest court in the land ruled that white Masons had abrogated their copyright and trademark rights by not defending them. The rulings confirmed the viability of using the courts to seek redress for violations of "Negro" civil rights, a strategy that would become central to the Black freedom struggle in the postwar era.[73]

In 1914, the year after "Professor Drew" founded Newark's Canaanite Temple, Noble W. O. Murphy of Medina Temple No. 19, New York, remarked on the splinter groups, or "spurious lodges," being formed around the country, and suggested that the Prince Hall Shriners take some action to eradicate them.[74] Prince Hall Masons may not have accepted or liked the fact that freemasonry was permeating this alternative and somewhat shadowy alternative religious sphere, but there was little that they could do about it.

{ CHAPTER FOUR }

IMPERIAL INFERNO

If this crime of silence, this infernal desire of the well-to-do
to crush out of sight this awful suffering, is persisted in, do
not think that you will rest in security. If you well-to-do
people do not listen—will not wake up—you do not know
but that a bomb may be thrown in your midst here. . . . A
desperate man, feeling in himself all the injustice that is
inflicted on his fellows, will kill—will destroy.

—THOMAS J. MORGAN, 1893[1]

The labor strife that was brewing during the World's Columbian Exposition, with its 25,000-person Labor Congress, burst out into the open as soon as the fair closed. The thousands of working people who built the towering plaster-and-lathe fair buildings found themselves out of work just as the nation confronted the worst economic depression it had ever known, another of the cyclical depressions that plagued the country in its boom-and-bust Gilded Age. The trouble had started in February of 1893 when the Philadelphia and Reading Railroad collapsed, followed by the failure of the National Cordage Company in May. When the US Treasury's gold reserves dipped below $100 million, investors feared that the nation would go off the gold standard for its currency, and rushed to withdraw their deposits from banks. Thirty steel companies, fifty railroads, four thousand banks, and fourteen thousand other businesses failed, most by the end of 1893. The following year witnessed more than 1,300 strikes against factories, mines, and railroads, as unemployment reached 20 percent and many of the two and a half million unemployed rode the rails as hobos in search of work. The suffering was nearly as bad as the misery of the Great Depression.

With the close of the fair, the Panic of 1893, and the widespread strikes and job losses, armies of homeless, hungry, and desperate people were everywhere in Chicago, carpeting the stoops and sidewalks "like the frogs in the Egyptian plague," according to crusading British journalist William Stead.[2] Saloonkeepers did their part by providing tens of thousands of their customers with free or extremely cheap vittles along with their grog, while the city's aldermen converted City Hall into a vast homeless shelter. Visitors there found a "pavement of human bodies," and the stench from so many unwashed and destitute people created a foul odor that was worse than Chicago's famously odiferous stockyards. It was said that one in ten faced starvation. Those who staved it off only did so by stealing food to survive.

Faced with suffering on such a horrific scale, on November 12, 1893, journalist Stead convened a meeting to discuss the crisis in the Central Music Hall, "thronged by men and women of all grades, races, sects and conditions," including both respectable matrons and corporate titans sitting next to notorious madams, anarchists, and socialists.[3] With his fiery rhetoric, his condemnation of the rich and comfortable, and his extolling of the saloonkeepers and madams who at least provided food and lodging for tens of thousands of the dispossessed, Stead reminded those assembled of a Hebrew prophet, with his fiery rhetoric, thick red beard, and blazing blue eyes. After Stead sat down, socialist Tommy Morgan stood up, directly addressed the "well-to-do people," and called for someone to "blow [them] out with dynamite" if they did not heed Stead's warnings and provide relief for the suffering of the indigent. Jeers and cheers alike greeted Morgan's inflammatory remarks, forcing Stead to plead with others "to defer to another occasion the thunders and threatening of dynamite."[4] Only three months later, Stead published a 450-page jeremiad entitled *If Christ Came to Chicago!* with a frontispiece picture of a vengeful Christ driving the money changers from the temple in ancient Jerusalem. Only Stead replaced the faces of the money changers on the cover with recognizable portraits of some of the city's wealthiest and most prominent corporate and political leaders. The phrase "instant bestseller" does not do the book justice: the tome sold seventy thousand copies on its first day alone, and spurred the creation of a new "Civic Federation of Chicago," composed of the Windy City's wealthiest elites and most prominent reformers, such as hotel magnate Bertha Palmer and settlement house pioneer Jane Addams.

The American political and economic system teetered on its axis following the fair, and that axis was a lot shakier than the massive steel rod that turned the now-dismantled Ferris wheel. The federal government suspended silver purchases in order to preserve its dwindling supply of gold, which harmed Western silver-producing states and drove several decades of Populist agitation among farmers and others who found their flawed champion in Oklahoman William Jennings Bryan. Bryan argued that the nation should back its currency with silver and famously asked not to be crucified on a "cross of gold." But the bombastic Populist lost three presidential races as the Democratic Party's candidate and was forever crucified as the Cowardly Lion (rhymes with "William Jennings Bryan") in L. Frank Baum's classic 1900 parable *The Wonderful Wizard of Oz*, each of whose characters may have been meant to represent a different interest group in the strife that was tearing America apart.[5]

In the spring of 1894, Ohioan Jacob S. Coxey led an "army" of hundreds of the unemployed on a grand symbolic march to the nation's capital, where President Cleveland refused their demand for a federal program to put the unemployed to work building roads, an idea that would be resuscitated with Franklin Delano Roosevelt's Works Progress Administration the next time the nation ran into a great depression. A young radical named Eugene Debs organized the workers in the company town of the Pullman railroad car manufacturing company, just south of the abandoned Exposition grounds, toilers who called themselves "the white slaves of Pullman." They formed a railway union open only to white workers and started a strike that paralyzed rail traffic in the Chicago area and much of the nation from May through July. In Chicago, mobs of youths and the unemployed used the opportunity to destroy property and vent their frustrations against the wealthy. Soldiers riding train cowcatchers fired into crowds of desperate, angry workers blocking railroad tracks, and shot down thirty-four people over the course of two weeks of clashes. The police threw Debs in jail and he came out a committed socialist. He went on to help found the radical union the Industrial Workers of the World in 1905 along with socialist and labor leader "Big Bill" Haywood, anarchist Emma Goldman, and many others. Debs ran for president five times as the candidate of the Socialist Party, the last time managing to win almost a million votes despite the fact that he was then imprisoned in the Atlanta Federal Penitentiary.

In the midst of all the bedlam of 1894, "fire fiends" put the plaster-and-lathe White City to the torch in July, and thousands of Chicagoans gathered in Jackson Park to watch the blaze light up the sky. The *Chicago Tribune* reported that the crowds celebrated the spectacle and did not mourn the passing of the fair that had entertained so many but also contributed to the labor unrest and massive economic inequality that had thrown the city and the nation into such a tailspin. It was "a grand, glorious ending" to the most "splendid [and] beautiful thing Chicago had ever created," said one of the leading papers of a city long familiar with the regenerative potential of destructive fires.[6] As the nation struggled with massive unemployment and militant strikes, Chicago's elite Civic Federation waged war on the big open gambling "hells" on Clark Street and drove them out of business or underground by the end of 1894.

The economic depression that the nation faced in the quarter century after 1893, and especially at its nadir during the four years after the fair went up in flames, was not so easily vanquished. This was not just an economic crisis; it quickly became an existential one as well. "It is probably safe to say that in no civilized country in this century, not actually in the throes of war or open insurrection, has society been so disorganized as it was in the United States during the first half of 1894; never was human life held so cheap; never did the constituted authorities appear so incompetent to enforce respect for the law," wrote H. P. Robinson, editor of the trade rag *Railroad Age*, judging the crisis of the 1890s more critical and more menacing than any since the Civil War. "It is not surprising that the events of those days should have awakened in many quarters grave misgivings as to the stability of our form of government, and serious doubts as to the adequacy of our present political conditions."[7] Many agreed that the nation's very survival was at stake.

Leading minds came to find a culprit for the country's economic crisis that at first blush must have seemed strange: the very manufacturing dynamos celebrated and even worshipped in those towering plaster temples of the White City were in a sense the culprits causing the country's economic woes. If there were not enough Americans with money to buy all the things US industrial workers could now produce, the country would just have to find more consumers overseas. The United States of America could pull itself out of the economic doldrums, these sages argued, and stave off a workers' revolution, if it could only convince more people outside America to buy its goods. The best candidates to become American consumers were those populous brown peoples of Asia, Africa, and Latin America who happened to be represented mostly on the carnivalesque and distinctly Oriental Midway, not the palatial Manufacturers' Hall of the Greco-Roman Court of Honor. Europeans had their own manufacturers and their own colonial territories where they could market their goods; the US had no colonies or overseas territories outside the contiguous and recently reunited states. But not all European empires were created equal; in particular, the Spanish empire had seen better days, and also controlled valuable colonies both in the Western hemisphere and in Asia. And so, when Cuba waged a war of independence against its Spanish overlords in 1898, and a US ship blew up in Havana harbor, likely of a faulty boiler, the US seized upon the explosion as a pretext to declare war on Spain, help the Cubans to victory, steam across the Pacific claiming islands and atolls along the way to be used for coaling stations, and join the Filipino rebellion against Spain with the addled and ultimately erroneous reasoning that the Philippines could become a gateway to the lucrative Chinese market. Once ensconced in the Filipinos' best fortified positions, the US made peace with the Spaniards and waged a brutal war against the Filipinos themselves, which incensed Mark Twain, president of the American Anti-Imperialist League, as positively un-American. Both fascinated by his age's new industrial inventions and completely hapless in business, Twain was nothing if not a creature of the nineteenth century and accurately perceived but dimly understood the economic and political rackets driving the new twentieth-century imperial expansion.

In other words, it was not the Columbian Exposition of 1893 that convinced American elites to get into what Twain called the "European game" of overseas imperialism, and it certainly was not the fault of the millions who watched African drumming, Hindu and Arabian magicians, Islamic educational instruction, or Balinese dance on the Midway, let alone the thousands who got stoned out of their gourds on German alcohol and Egyptian hashish before taking in the views from the towering Ferris wheel or tethered hot air balloon. It certainly was not the fault of the millions of workers who starved, struck, accepted reduced paychecks, manned barricades, and faced down armed soldiers and Pinkerton guards in the tumultuous 1890s. The United States' political and corporate elites were determined to master the colonial project and stave off a workers' revolution, no matter that Twain, like former president Grover Cleveland, derided the whole enterprise of taking over other people's countries by force as un-American, an exploitative racket that allocated the spoils of imperialism to elites at the expense of the masses of workers, soldiers, and the colonized themselves. Workers were not hypnotized by the world's fair into supporting overseas imperialism by the mystifying hegemony of the elites; just the opposite: it was the White City's collapse in an inferno of arson, labor militancy, and nationwide financial panic that convinced American corporate and foreign policy elites that they needed to enlarge American economic markets or risk the end of their power and the possible collapse of the nation as they knew it.

Even though greater numbers of prominent Americans joined Twain's anti-imperialist organization than spoke in favor of imperial expansion, the press had a field day with the military victories overseas, and much of the American public came to support the adventure, knowing on some level that they had lost the ability to control the state, if they ever were able to do so. "Afro American" troops played crucial roles in the fighting both in Cuba and the Philippines, and the Democrats' candidate, William Jennings Bryan, staked his candidacy on the silver standard and lost to William McKinley in both 1896 and 1900. Bryan was a staunch opponent of American overseas imperialism in the later election, and yet voters preferred stability and President McKinley. Then, in 1901, a foreign-born anarchist assassin slew the president at the Buffalo Pan-American Exposition, seemingly confirming every fear about the radicalism of workers, anarchists, and immigrants at a fair designed to celebrate the country's newfound hemispheric ambitions.

Theodore Roosevelt had become New York City police commissioner in 1895 in response to the exposure of the rackets of pimps, gamblers, police, and politicians that oversaw that city's Tenderloin District, then vaulted to fame as the swashbuckling "Rough Rider" hero of the Battle of San Juan Hill in the Cuban phase of the War of 1898.[8] With McKinley's assassination, Vice President Roosevelt took office and put the American imperial expansion into overdrive both in Asia and in the Caribbean, which he endeavored to turn into an "American lake" with his foreign policy of backroom deals and gunships sent to dictate other nations' economic policies. Here again was a racket: a state-run operation that used military power to accumulate cheap bananas and other economic advantages for American corporations and consumers without respect for the well-being of foreign workers or the fairness or democracy of foreign states. Roosevelt won election in 1904 and stolid Ohioan William Howard Taft delivered Bryan his third and final presidential defeat in the election of 1908. In sum, American voters roundly ratified the imperial adventure that began with a suspicious explosion in Havana harbor—or at least, white American males did so, the only people who could vote in most of the country since women still could not vote at all and male "Negroes" and other people of color were by then mostly disenfranchised.

American imperialism influenced American culture industries in interesting and sometimes unexpected ways. On the one hand, circuses drew millions of viewers to patriotic spectacles restaging the exploits of American forces in Cuba and China, complete with reproductions of warships that moved on wheels across the sawdust rings of the big tops. More surprisingly, the war led to a surplus of brass instruments cast off from military bands, which made such secondhand instruments affordable for the masses and allowed them to land in the hands of Black musicians in places such as the Colored Waifs' Home for Boys in New Orleans, where a boy named Louis Armstrong learned to play the cornet after he was arrested in 1910 at nine years old for being a "dangerous and suspicious character." On May 31, 1913, the *New Orleans Times-Picayune* recorded that an eleven-year-old Armstrong led the parade of sixteen "little black imps" in honor of Federal Decoration Day, now called Memorial Day. Armstrong got his start playing patriotic music in a patriotic parade, but Black children, in their blackness, could always be compared to imps, those diminutive demons so often pictured on the shoulders of magicians in the white-tie-and-tails imperial era of Euro-American magic. The comparison to the original pickaninny band of *In Old Kentucky* and its original cornet-playing, pint-sized bandmaster Walter Brister must have been obvious to many, since by then *In Old Kentucky* had become the most popular American play of all time, spawned dozens of imitators, and had already been made into a movie—which was only the first of four film versions released between 1909 and 1935. (The last one featured Native American comedy star Will Rogers and the great African American dancer Bill "Bojangles" Robinson. Robinson, another inheritor of Walter

Brister's legacy as the first Black child star on the Great White Way, appeared in other films with tap-dancing waif Shirley Temple.)[9]

The expansion of American military power overseas also facilitated travel opportunities for American entertainers, including circuses and individual "Afro-Americans," who started to travel across the Pacific to Hawaii and Australia as steamer travel across that great ocean became commonplace. Blacks of the era found themselves on the horns of a dilemma: they were often agents of US military power and representatives of the nation abroad, and yet as Black people they endured disenfranchisement and third-class citizenship that made their situation much like that of the people of color in American and European colonies. This dilemma was all the more acute for Black entertainers who made their livings representing colonized people, like Walter Brister.

CHAPTER FIVE

HINDOO MAGIC

Oh, East is East and West is West, and never the twain shall meet,
Till Earth and Sky stand presently at God's great Judgment Seat;
But there is neither East nor West, Border, nor Breed, nor Birth,
When two strong men stand face to face, though they come from the
ends of the earth!

—RUDYARD KIPLING, "The Ballad of East and West," 1889[1]

The Pawnee Bill Wild West Show covered the thirty miles on the Pennsylvania Railroad from Perth Amboy to Princeton, New Jersey, on Sunday, May 14, 1899. The heaving steam locomotive made the short trek in good time, grunting and spewing steam theatrically as it wheezed its way through the spring countryside with the entire contents of a Wild West Show loaded onto specially constructed freight cars and passenger compartments behind its coal-fired black boilers. The train deposited Pawnee Bill's men, women, and animals at a large empty lot on Cottage Street in the college town of Princeton, New Jersey, and a crowd of locals came just to watch the wondrous spectacle of hundreds of men and women unloading their possessions, erecting the grandstands, and stretching the canvas over the viewing area. They created an outdoor arena about as big as one side of a football stadium, in which the uppermost seat was no more than perhaps twenty rows high. The arena was big enough to seat around fourteen thousand spectators at a time, without a bad seat in the house. The weather was fair and the excitement was palpable among the crowds of local kids, men, and women watching the horses, cowboys, and various people of color, many in Western dress or native costumes. Others were "Buffalo Soldiers" wearing dashing navy blue uniforms with shiny brass buttons, Black veterans of the Tenth Cavalry Regiment of the US Army that had seen action fighting Indians on the Western plains, Spaniards in Cuba, and Filipinos in the Philippines.

The show was led by Major G. W. Lillie, "White Chief of the Pawnee and Hero of Oklahoma," a frontiersman and former Pawnee Indian teacher and interpreter who wore a broad-brimmed hat over his wavy, shoulder-length chestnut brown hair, much like his show business mentor, Buffalo Bill Cody. He was joined by his wife, Miss May Lillie, the world-class horseback shot, herself a native of Pennsylvania and a graduate of the elite Smith College for women in Northampton, Massachusetts. In addition, there were cowboys like John M. Murphy, a.k.a. "Wild Horse Jack," a former Rough Rider who had fought with Teddy Roosevelt in Cuba, and the "King of the Cowboys" Heck Quinn, whose mustache was so bushy it entered a room before he did and whose very name sounded like cussing. There were also six Cheyenne Indian men, seven Sioux men, four Sioux women, and three Sioux children, as well as their interpreter. In addition to showing off their equestrian skills, some Indians performed the "Ghost Dance," a phenomenon that started with a Northern Paiute prophet named Wovoka outside Virginia City, Nevada, in 1889 and swept across Indian communities of North America. As adopted by the Lakota Sioux, the Ghost Dance was a circle dance performed for five days, thought to be able to renew the earth, wash away evil, and remove all whites and their livestock from the land. "They told the people they could dance a new world into being," in the words of Miniconjou Lakota Sioux chief Lame Deer.

> There would be landslides, earthquakes, and big winds. Hills would pile up on each other. The earth would roll up like a carpet with all the white man's ugly things—the stinking new animals, sheep and pigs, the fences, the telegraph poles, the mines and factories. Underneath would be the wonderful old-new world as it had been before the white fat-takers came. . . . The white men will be rolled up, disappear, go back to their own continent.[2]

Much as corporations figured out how to commodify dissent after the 1960s, Wild West shows turned the Ghost Dance into entertainment for the very people the dance sought to eliminate from North America. But the true meaning of the ceremony could not have been lost on all of the people of color who lived with the Indians day in and day out. These avatars of the western frontier did very well for themselves in the east; business in New Jersey had been "phenomenal."[3] But Wild West shows did more than simply depict the West, as if that could ever be a simple task in itself; they also portrayed the "East" and a heterodox world outside of the boundaries of the United States, boundaries that were themselves rapidly expanding.

The following morning, Monday, May 15, 1899, dawned another fair spring day. The cooks for the show were up before dawn to prepare hundreds of cups of coffee and enough breakfast foods to feed an army in the show's canvas mess tent. The masses of performers and laborers were so numerous it took fifteen waiters to serve them. Among the hungry that day were performers with names like Mexican Rufus, cowboys Shin Hegley and Tex Smith, Cheyenne Indians Big Man, Deafy, Medicine Horse, and Texan, and Arabian acrobats Sarapon, Abdala, Side, and Ambark Ali. In the stables where hundreds of horses were penned, the smell of coffee mingled with the pungent aroma of manure and the sweet smell of animal feed as grooms forked hay and alfalfa for the animals' morning meal and began the process of saddling the steeds for their riders. The canvas men had already hitched horse teams to great ropes and pounded giant stakes into the ground with precisely timed blows of heavy sledges to raise the 600-foot-square arena canopy, the 100-by-220-foot horse tent, the 90-by-50-foot dressing tent, and the annex tent.

Somewhere in the midst of all this activity strode a "Hindoo Wonder Worker" named Armmah Sotanki. Since this was a parade day, he would have already been in costume by the time he made it from his bunk to the mess tent, perhaps exchanging a word with the Arab acrobats known as "the Ali's." Sotanki was a good-looking young man, with a steady, almost hypnotic cast to his eyes. He was young in 1899, about twenty years old. His costume consisted of an ornate, satin-like tunic that was brocaded at the neck and breast pocket and covered with stripes and circular decorations. It was finished off with a long string of beads that he doubled over four times to create five loops from his belly button to his clavicle, and he topped his head with a long stretch of cloth that he wrapped into a turban. The artist who drew his picture drew a long mustache with upturned ends over the corners of his mouth, but that mustache was likely either a prop or simply a flight of fancy, as Sotanki could grow no such mustache, at least not at that young age; his photograph the following year shows not much more than a shadow gracing his upper lip.

Here with Pawnee Bill, Armmah Sotanki led his own troupe. His barouche—a small horse-drawn carriage—even led the parade, coming right behind the bugler and in front of the bandwagon and everyone else. It may have been called a Wild West show, but there were so many acts from Asia and Arabia that the posters the show's advance men pasted all over the buildings along the route would soon start billing it as a Wild East show instead. Sotanki was what you would call a "fakir," in its original sense. The word is pronounced fa-keer', with the accent on the last syllable. It comes from the Arabic *faqīr*, meaning "poor man." The *Oxford English Dictionary* defines fakir to mean "properly an indigent person, but specially applied to a Mahommedan religious mendicant, and then loosely, and inaccurately, to Hindu devotees and naked ascetics." In the United States the word was used to denote a faker, especially one who sold small goods and patent medicines. Erroneous or not, the word has evolved to contain both meanings. Fakirs were both the men who followed Pawnee Bill's show selling medicinal potions of dubious efficacy, and they were also "Hindoo" magicians like Armmah Sotanki. The word itself had spread from Muslim religious beggars to Hindu devotees. Sotanki himself would traverse this continuum between "Hindoo" and "Mohammedan," but that journey was still many years ahead of him when he sat there in his carriage with his fellow "Hindoos" at the end of the Pawnee Bill parade, winding its way off the lot on Cottage Street in Princeton that fair spring day in 1899.

With its long string of dozens of costumed riders astride impressive horses, the parade line unspooled itself like an exotic millipede before the disbelieving eyes of the townspeople and the knots of children who had gathered to watch. This was no ordinary parade: everyone in the show was readying themselves for battle as much as for display. For fifty years, the students and townspeople of sleepy Princeton, New Jersey, had decreed that no circus parade was allowed to pass the campus of the august college. Princeton was laid out in such a way that it was impossible to parade through the town without passing the college twice—going and returning. From the Civil War until the Spanish-American War, what started as a local custom had become an unwritten law. Against the urging of the town fathers, who feared violence if the show attempted to parade, Pawnee

Bill, the "Hero of Oklahoma," determined to proceed. He had faced more fearsome foes in the real Wild West; on that day, he and his fellow performers would attempt to open Princeton as a market for tented shows, by force if necessary.[4]

From his perch on the barouche at the head of the parade, just behind the bugler, Armmah Sotanki could see the bandwagon trailing him, full of eleven Italian musicians in dressy uniforms with brass buttons, under the baton of Nicola Olivieri, a bespectacled young fellow with neatly parted hair plastered on his forehead, and a perfectly waxed and upturned handlebar mustache. Next came Pawnee Bill himself, in his wide-brimmed hat with his flowing brown locks, looking extravagantly and romantically Western, like one of the Three Musketeers in buckskin clothing. The line of the parade stretched for blocks and included "about 120 mounted people" in colorful costumes—cowboys in large hats and fringed shirts, Indians in war paint and feathers, lady riders riding sidesaddle in long Victorian dresses, Russian Cossacks in dark uniforms, Mexican vaqueros, Argentinian gauchos, and Arab "Bedouin" riders with keffiyeh-covered heads and flowing white robes, among many others.

Children and other spectators took in the spectacle and ran alongside, but as the parade reached downtown, Armmah Sotanki could plainly see from his perch that there was trouble brewing ahead. The music of the bandwagon coming down Nassau Street could be heard just when Princeton students were streaming outdoors to go from the first morning lecture to the second. Drawn by the music, around six or seven hundred of them joined the Princeton townspeople who were massed on Nassau Street not far from the college. Newspaper accounts pieced together after the fact reported the total at seven hundred, but the show's chronicler, who was actually there but had more reason to exaggerate, estimated twice as many. Regardless, Pawnee Bill's crew was badly outnumbered.

The crowd of Princetonians assembled in front of the college, completely blocking the street. All of Pawnee Bill's performers steeled themselves for a fight as they approached the mass of rowdy students. But something remarkable happened when the parade reached the roadblock of Princeton tigers: first the bugler arrived, and the students let the bugler through. Then Armmah Sotanki and his fellow "Hindoos" Miss Arkorskieah, Arjailey, and Armeto approached, followed by the bandwagon, and the students let the emissaries of the Orient and the makers of music pass, unmolested. It was as if

Sotanki's Eastern dress had commanded students bent on trouble to become docile, almost hypnotized by an Orientalist Jedi mind trick. Princeton was then, as it is now, an institution that celebrated the merit of academic Orientalism, and it is telling that students set on mischief let the emissaries of the East pass. But when Pawnee Bill approached someone threw a firecracker under his horse. The firecracker exploded with a bang, and it was off to the races. First Pawnee Bill's frightened horse charged through the crowd, and then the other riders raced through the gap that Bill's horse had created. May Lillie and her fellow lady riders galloped their horses through the gap riding sidesaddle, and then the Arabs came at full speed and the Indians zipped through with their horses and stagecoach. "It soon looked like it was a race course instead of a street parade," a member of Pawnee Bill's outfit reported.[5] For expert horsemen and -women, galloping horses through a mass of college students, even extremely entitled college students, did not pose much of a challenge. The only mishap was that one horse harnessed to a team of horses slipped, fell, and was dragged a considerable distance.

The Princeton students' faces were crestfallen when they realized they would not be able to stop the parade, and they went to work to halt it upon its return. They laid in stores of rotten vegetables and entire crates of eggs, either bought or stolen from the six grocers lining Nassau Street, which faced the college.[6] Those who could not get their hands on rotten food tore up chunks of turf from Princeton's famously verdant lawns; others stockpiled rocks, determined to stop the parade at all costs. Three members of Pawnee Bill's advance crew were mingling among the milling crowds, and when they saw the students making preparations for war, they warned the members of the Wild West Show to be ready to defend themselves. The parade attempted to avoid the throng now massed in front of the post office about a block and a half from the entrance to the campus by heading north abruptly into John Lane, dodging the throng on Nassau Street, but the crowd saw what the show was trying to do and swooped down on the parade with a fusillade of eggs, potatoes, clods of turf, and firecrackers.[7] Many of the eggs missed their marks, and instead comically splattered their friends on the other side of the street, but horses and riders alike got pelted nonetheless. Cowboys and Indians responded by charging the students and whipping them with their bullwhips, which proved to be the turning point. "Stung by the whips and bruised by the riders riding into them, the students became ugly," and started throwing rocks.[8] "The aim of the students was good, and the scene was exciting," according to the *New York Times*.[9] Pawnee Bill's frontiersmen let loose on the crowds of students in a manner that betrayed a fundamentally different attitude toward personal injury and the law than those operative in our own time. The Argentinian and Mexican gauchos used their bolas, leather straps with leaden weights at either end, with great effect against the crowd, while the cowboys and Indians used their whips and charged the crowd, trampling those who could not get out of the way. Some performers drew their pistols and fired live rounds over the students' heads or intentionally burned students' faces with the muzzle flashes from blank cartridges. Irate cowboys and gauchos lassoed college students and dragged them over the washboard streets like poor little lambs who had lost their way, as Princeton's rivals in New Haven would later sing of themselves.

From the barouche, Sotanki had an unobstructed view of the cowboys and Indians ramming the crowd of stone-throwing elite white students with their horses and lashing them with rawhide whips normally used for driving herds of cattle on the Western plains. He watched as Wild Horse Jack, wearing a thick, dark mustache under his broad-brimmed hat, charged his horse into the crowd. Jack and the other expert riders easily controlled their horses, pushing the students back from Nassau Street and forcing them to flee backward, tripping over themselves, as their fellow students rained a hailstorm of vegetables, eggs, and rocks down upon the mounted riders. Sotanki could see the fabric-covered heads of the Ali Brothers, in their flowing robes on their beautiful Arabian steeds, take the fight to students who resisted. Circuses and Wild West shows had been importing these horses for decades along with their Arabian riders, most from Morocco, the ancient home of the fabled Moors. The Ali Brothers that day included Charles Lewis, a white high diver, acrobat, and horseman who was known in the show as Charles Lewis Ali. As the Ali Brothers drove their wild-eyed mounts back and forth, their hooves clattering over the paving stones, and the Indians, cowboys, gauchos, and other mounted riders lashed the elite white students with whips, lassos, and bolas. Hundreds of hollering, panicking students sought refuge in the shops and side streets off Nassau Street, and others flooded in retreat back over the lawns that minutes earlier they had torn up for fusillades. What had started as a college prank went from farce to tragedy: a Princeton student was trampled by a pony and badly injured, and a local "colored" man, Edward Dimon, had his skull fractured when he was kicked by a horse. Many students, and many mounted riders, were injured in the fray. Sotanki saw blood spilled everywhere. According to the show's own route-book compiler, H. G. Wilson, the performers "drove them back into the college campus, whipped for the first time in Princeton's existence by a traveling exhibition company, and licked good."[10]

Armmah Sotanki would have seen all this mayhem, whether he dismounted from his carriage and took part in the ruckus or not, and the capability of people of color, including the Arabian Ali Brothers, to defend themselves from one of the most concentrated pools of privileged, wealthy white Anglo-Saxon Protestants could not have failed to make an impression on the young "Hindoo Wonder Worker." The riot only ended when the giant bandwagon, with its four-horse team, barreled down the street, clearing the way of whatever students remained.[11]

Afterward, the streets and lawns of some of the residences were so transformed, no doubt littered with debris, pieces of clothing, and pools of blood, that "one could imagine you were looking at the results of the San Juan Hill battle laying everywhere," in the words of the Pawnee Bill Wild West Show's chronicler. But this was a multiracial San Juan Hill battle of a different kind. The show's official account singled out "the work of" performers such as McCullum, Stoneman, Taylor, Murphy, and Tex Smith along with Mexican Jo, the Ali Brothers, and the Indians—"in fact, all of them, can not be commended too highly." In other words, Mexicans, Arabs, Indians with whips, and Argentinian gauchos slinging bolas were fighting side by side with white whip-wielding American cowboys against the most elite white male students in the country. The skirmish pitted "about 120 mounted people" against hundreds of students, "who, though supposed to represent some of the best families," in the words of Pawnee Bill's scribe, "supposed to have qualities that only culture, refinement and education can develop, resort to some of the most brutal acts to accomplish their ends, such as cutting one of our horses, a dumb brute unable to defend himself."[12] The trampled Black townsman was left unconscious and near death, while many students were bloodied and bruised, some with lacerations from whips wielded by the Indians.

The Princeton students earned themselves a severe reprimand from the college president, Francis Landey Patton, who condemned the attack on the parade and strictly forbade the students from attending the show. Some townsfolk pledged they would not go either, in solidarity with the students, but many students attended anyway and received a lecture from Pawnee Bill and Miss May; such was the irresistible thrill and the power of tented traveling shows in an era when they were the premier theatrical spectacles in the land. "The Princeton Riot," as it became known, was reported by the Associated Press and made headlines nationwide, some of which betray what might appear to contemporary readers as a curious lack of concern with the rawhide- and pistol-whipping of townspeople and Ivy League college students by a motley crew of mounted athletes and former soldiers from around the world, including many foreigners and indigenous people who would have been considered people of color then as now. Far from being embarrassed or ashamed of their actions, the Pawnee Bill show chronicled the event blow by blow while the *Los Angeles Herald* proclaimed "Cowboys Show Good Temper in Failing to Resort to the Use of Clubs."[13]

If Armmah Sotanki learned something that dramatic day, it was not simply that it was a bad idea for a bunch of Ivy League students who were merely paper tigers to try and mess with a bunch of cowboys, Indians, Buffalo soldiers, and other rough-hewn frontiersmen and -women. He also would have learned that wearing a turban and representing the brown-skinned Orient actually could spare one from harassment, remembering how the seas parted for his carriage as if he were Moses only to engulf the others performers behind him. Being Oriental, or at least appearing as such, allowed Armmah Sotanki and his group of "Hindoo Wonder Workers" to pass unmolested through the ill-tempered crowd, while the cowboys, Indians, and vaqueros had no such luck. As "Afro-Americans" would discover, if they did not already know, wearing a turban and representing the East allowed one the privileges of sitting in the best railway car instead of the Jim Crow car, spared them the brunt of racist violence, and gave them a claim to an ancient Asiatic identity that was older than the conflict between cowboys and Indians, let alone the conflict pitting cowboys and Indians against Ivy League students. Whether Sotanki was aware of it or not, to be an "Ali" meant being part of a Muslim identity linking one to an exalted lineage tracing back to the son-in-law of the Prophet Muhammad. To be an Oriental "fakir" meant to be part of a Muslim-inflected Indian identity older and more venerable than the United States of America itself.

Armmah Sotanki's own identity was something of a mystery in 1899, but the following year, when he signed on for another tour with Pawnee Bill, that mystery was solved. This time, just before the turn of the century, rather than a line drawing of Sotanki the souvenir route book printed a photograph of a "colored" young man, and underneath the photograph the letterpress print left a clue imprinted into the thick cotton paper in capitalized black ink: "The Sotankis, Hindoo Fakirs. WALTER BRISTER."[14]

Above his searching eyes arched two delicate eyebrows, and between them lay a long nose with wide, rounded nostrils and full lips. Not insignificantly, Sotanki's skin was brown, and his features were those of someone of sub-Saharan African ancestry. When he was not in his costume he would be recognized as "Black," or "Negro," "colored," or "Afro-American," and discriminated against by white folks accordingly. But underneath the turban, and at a time when most Americans had no idea how people from the Indian subcontinent looked, Sotanki was no longer "Afro-American," and no longer had to play the humiliating role of a musical "pickaninny." He was now a foreigner, a magician, and a master of esoteric mysteries.

CHAPTER SIX

WHITE TOPS

The wit of the clown was highly original, and being directed principally against the negroes, was highly relished and vociferously applauded.

—ANONYMOUS, Topeka, Kansas, 1867[1]

In 1893, the year that the Columbian Exposition and the show *In Old Kentucky* both opened, the Sells Brothers Circus had trumpeted the coming of "Hassan Ben Ali's Moorish Caravan Arabian Nights' Entertainment and Spectacular Pilgrimage to Mecca," as the "Orientally Splendid and Weirdly Romantic Spectacular Pilgrimage to Mecca. Introducing the Only Berber and Bedouin Tribal Caravan of Moorish Barbarians and Warriors." The circus covered the sides of barns and buildings across America with gorgeous full-color lithographs depicting a colorful caravan winding past a desert oasis with camels carrying litters topped by Islam's crescent moon. There were white-robed soldiers on noble Arabian stallions, women with veils, and men wearing colorful turbans, headscarves, curly-toed blue Moroccan slippers, and capacious robes. The whole procession was led by four men with dark skin and Black African features representing Moors, and there were also olive-skinned maidens and swarthy, bearded men.[2]

The poster was one of thirty the Sells Brothers plastered across the country to announce its North American tour and their headliner, Hassan Ben Ali. Another featured a picture of ten men wearing fezzes forming a human tower while other men in fezzes twirled guns, juggled swords, and performed flips, all in front of an ornate Moroccan courtyard with a two-story arcade, jagged crenellations on the fortified walls, and a minaret in the background. Its text read: "A Whole Amazing Sahara Desert Circus. Wild Berber and Bedouin Moors in Strange and Prodigious Illustrations of Ability and Strength." Other posters featured pictures of camel or elephant races, although more traditional circus fare such as acrobats, horse races, and trapeze artists were more commonly the pictorial subject of the posters, whose masthead remained constant: "Sells Brothers, Roman Hippodrome, 3 Ring Circus, Two Elevated Stages, 5 Continent Menagerie, Imperial Japanese Troupe, Combined with Hassan Ben Ali's Moorish Caravan Arabian Nights' Entertainment and Spectacular Pilgrimage to Mecca."[3] The Hassan Ben Ali posters demonstrate that his show did not just depict the common Orientalist tropes of harem girls, fakirs, and fierce mounted warriors, but made an attraction out of Islam itself, and its *hajj*, or the "Orientally Splendid and Weirdly Romantic Spectacular Pilgrimage to Mecca." Indeed, Islamic Orientalist pageantry and visions of Oriental grandeur, opulence, and otherness were stock elements of European and American circuses in the late nineteenth and early twentieth centuries.

T he contemporary circus originated with exhibitions of trick horse riding in 1760s England, and the centrifugal force needed to keep a standing rider on the back of a cantering horse determined the dimensions of the circus ring. The growth and spread of the circus, like the spread of freemasonry, was coterminous with both the Enlightenment and the spread of European empires into Asian, Muslim, and African lands. Riders on horseback raced around the circus ring, sometimes pantomiming patriotic scenes from cavalry battles, as wars, revolutions, and real cavalry charges circled and transformed the globe. The equestrian circus spread to France by 1772 and John Bill Ricketts began the first American circus with horses and clowning in Philadelphia in 1792, where it found favor with President George Washington, himself an avid horseman.[4] That was also the year that the French Revolution spawned several decades of wars around the globe between France, Britain, Austro-Hungary, and Russia, contributing to the decline of the Spanish and Portuguese empires, the rise of the Russian and British empires, the Haitian Revolution of 1791–1804, the Simon Bolivar–inspired Latin American revolutions of 1808 to 1826, and the unification of the countries of Italy in 1861 and Germany in 1871. The circus's equestrian art form came to harness the exponentially greater power of the iron horses that pulled ever-increasing amounts of cargo across the country's growing network of railroad tracks. There were unsatisfactory experiments with circus travel by rail beginning in 1856, but railroad circuses only took off with the cessation of the Civil War and the standardization and exponential growth of railroad tracks that followed. In America, the golden age of the circus from 1871 to 1915 was facilitated not only by the consolidation and growth of the US nation-state, but also (as with the nation itself) by the power of railroads, which the circus harnessed to multiply its size, grandeur, and geographical reach.

Orientalist depictions of Asian and Muslim subjects featured prominently in the circus parades that wound their way through American cities and towns when the first traveling tented circuses appeared, as early as 1825. In the decades that followed, circus parades with richly ornamented and carved wagons dazzled Americans, announcing the arrival of the tented spectacles. In 1848, one of the very first accounts of an American circus parade noted that Il Signor Germani, "the great rider of Italy," would appear "representing the Hindoo Miracles of an East India juggler, attired in the exact costume and caste of his tribe, with an Orrery [sic] of Golden Globes and Sacred Daggers, the Sacred Vase of Destiny and Fated Bullet."[5] Throughout the nineteenth and early twentieth centuries, typical circus parades included an "Asia Wagon," with carved representations of Asian peoples on its sides, and sometimes an "Africa Wagon," which included representations of North African Arabs along with those of sub-Saharan Africans, helping to construct a continental image of Africa in the minds of all Americans that comingled Muslim and non-Muslim African peoples.[6] Across America, in small towns and large cities alike, the American circus provided a constant and colorful stream of images of human otherness. In addition to representations of the United States, Russia, and Great Britain, a typical Barnum & Bailey Circus parade from 1916 included a cage with four horses and six "Orientals," a "Tableaux India," and five Arab boys in their "own wardrobe" riding horses.[7]

Few things could have seemed more exotic or more exciting in Gilded Age America than visions of multihued, brightly colored, bedecked and bedazzled, alluring and forbidden "Moorish," "Bedouin," "Persian," "Arab," "Indian," or "Egyptian" wonders, from exotic animals to fierce Bedouin warriors and seductive, veiled harem beauties.

The tales of the *Arabian Nights* featured prominently in these depictions: the Sells Brothers Circus later combined with the Hagenbeck-Wallace and 4-Paw circuses and put together a show called "The Pageant of Persia: The Glorious Origins of the Arabian Nights," whose poster featured a white-bearded ruler surrounded by a comely courtesan and a wild menagerie of colorfully attired attendants and animals. This image was the source for a later image on the poster of the Al. G. Barnes Circus, called "Persia and the Pageant of Peking," which then made the leap around 1916 to the Barnum & Bailey Circus as "Persia, or the Pageants of the Thousand and One Nights: The Most Gorgeous Oriental Display Ever Seen in Any Land Since the World Began." Later—perhaps when this show had worn thin—the Barnum & Bailey Circus featured five different posters of the "Supreme Pageant of Aladdin and His Wonderful Lamp," which was always depicted along with images of Chinese processions, illustrating the mixed-up quality of American Orientalism and its willingness to fuse the Near and Far Easts.[8]

Exotic animals were even more prevalent than exotic humans in the circus. In the golden age of the circus almost every show had both camels and dromedaries; in 1875 the European Circus had advertised an "Oriental Music Car Drawn by Egyptian Camels" with a picture of a dozen musicians in turbans towed by a team of a dozen camels wearing blankets covered in Islamic stars and crescent moons. In the early twentieth century the Ringling Bros. had a "Camel Corps," with a team of sixteen camels pulling an Egypt float decorated with Sphinxes and dark-skinned people in front of pyramids; the Forepaugh-Sells Circus had a similar Egypt wagon pulled by eight camels in 1911.[9]

Occasionally the circus veered into the realm of the scientific, such as the time in 1895 when Barnum & Bailey's Greatest Show on Earth staged the "Great Ethnological Congress," which displayed humans representing exotic cultures next to cages of exotic animals in the "Spacious and Colossal Menagerie Tent." The circus freak show, with its fat ladies and fleshless men, its giants, midgets, piebald "Negroes," and Siamese twins, had always capitalized on human morphological differences, just as its exotic animals were kinds of animal freaks: the massive lions, the long-necked giraffes, and the hump-backed camels gained their appeal partly from their freakish deviation from domesticated beasts of burden familiar to Americans in both urban and rural settings. Barnum & Bailey's Ethnological

A photo of Walter Brister as "Armmah Sotanki," a "Hindoo Magician," used for the Pawnee Bill Wild West Show and the John
Robinson Circus 1900–1902. At the right distance from the page
one may be able to see the dark mole on the right side of his nose,
below the corner of his right eye, halfway between that point and
the tip of his nose.

The first annual convention of the Moorish Science Temple of America, Chicago, 1928. Prophet Noble Drew Ali is standing in white and making the Masonic Sign of Fidelity, right hand over the heart. Notice the prominent mole on the right side of his nose, and how it has grown over time. Seated next to the Prophet is his first wife, Eva Alexander Brister, wearing a Moorish Adept sash.

BUFFALO BILL'S
WILD WEST AND CONGRESS OF
ROUGH RIDERS
OF THE WORLD

A GROUP OF RIFFIAN ARAB HORSEMEN

Buffalo Bill's Congress of Rough Riders of the World featured Arab equestrians performing jaw-dropping feats on the world's finest horses. At the beginning of the nineteenth century, English breeders bred Arabian stallions with English mares to produce thoroughbred racehorses.

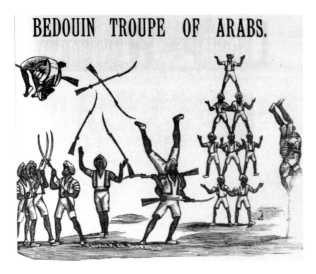

BEDOUIN TROUPE OF ARABS.

An 1886 ad for the Abdallah Ben Said "Bedouin Troupe of Arabs," showing their tumbling, leaping, rifle twirling, and pyramid building. The Said troupe featured four Hadjis who had made the pilgrimage to Mecca, three Ali's, and at least two acrobats who would go on to lead their own troupes, including Ambark Ali and Hassan Ben Ali.

A lithograph for the Barnum & Bailey Circus showing one of the many troupes of Arab acrobats and equestrians that were a mainstay of American and European circuses at the end of the nineteenth century.

THE ORIGINAL PICKANINNY BAND, ORGANIZED BY PROF. **J.H.BRISTER** ESPECIALLY FOR "**IN OLD KENTUCKY**" AND DIRECTED BY MASTER **WALTER BRISTER**, THE YOUNGEST BANDMASTER IN THE WORLD.

The Woodlawn Wangdoodles, the Black juvenile band that starred in the hit Broadway show *In Old Kentucky* starting in 1893. Note diminutive bandleader Walter Brister holding a cornet.

The horse race scene from the show *In Old Kentucky*, which used real racehorses galloping on a mechanical treadmill. Note the Black jockeys and the Black boys capering on the side.

Three boys who performed as part of the Street in Cairo exhibit at the 1893 World's Columbian Exposition Midway. Many of the Arab and Muslim performers would have been considered Black in American racial terms.

Harry Houdini, c. 1899. Houdini transformed the escape magic of Hindu fakirs by using chains and locks instead of ropes. In this, his cabinet escape, and in his East Indian Needle Trick, he updated staples of Hindu magic for American audiences.

8488. Cairo Streets, Midway Plaisance, World's Fair, Chicago.

A stereograph of the Street in Cairo, the most popular exhibit of the 1893 Midway.

"Fire Fiends" put the torch to the White City of the 1893 Columbian Exposition amidst economic and social turmoil following the close of the fair and the Panic of 1893.

Gordon W. Lillie, a.k.a. Pawnee Bill, the "Hero of Oklahoma," and his sharpshooting wife, May.

An illustration of the Princeton Riot, May 15, 1899.

The five Ali Brothers, members of the Pawnee Bill Wild West Show of 1899, and a typical group of Arab acrobats and equestrians commonly found in American and European circuses near the turn of the twentieth century.

A lithograph for the Hassan Ben Ali group showing some of the daring human pyramids, tumbling, and rifle twirling that Arab acrobats used to dazzle American fans during the Gilded Age and Progressive Eras.

Congress incorporated the new label of "ethnology" into a longer history of freak show spectacles, in the context of a world that was being thoroughly colonized by European powers. One might even argue that by exhibiting people representing imperial possessions, the circus helped to normalize colonization for Americans and Europeans alike.

The circus was a quintessentially populist art form, and it found audiences among all sectors, races, genders, and classes in nineteenth- and early twentieth-century America. Even before the intensification of Jim Crow in the 1890s, Black audiences frequently sat in segregated seating areas, but there is also evidence that segregation was sometimes enforced less rigidly in the slightly disreputable setting of the circus tent. "Everybody went—all classes, ages, colors and conditions," wrote Hiram Fuller in 1858, describing a circus in Newport, Rhode Island. "There were as many as five thousand people there, all mixed up with the most democratic indiscrimination— Fifth Avenue belles sitting on narrow boards . . . alongside of Irish chambermaids and colored people of all sizes and sexes."[10] Many Southern states passed Jim Crow statutes mandating segregation at the circus relatively late, not until the middle of the twentieth century's second decade.[11]

African Americans were a sought-after audience for traveling tented shows. Traveling circuses tended to follow the harvest cycle throughout rural America, when field hands would have had a little bit of money to spend on leisure, and no place had a greater density of circuses and traveling minstrel shows than Mississippi during the cotton harvest. In the words of a performer with the Silas Green minstrel company, Mississippi "isn't a large state, but it's one of your greatest cotton states and has a great Race population of real show-going people."[12] During harvesttime in 1925, Mississippi boasted an astounding convergence of seven Black minstrel shows, one white minstrel show, and two major circuses, the Sparks Brothers and the Ringling Bros. Barnum & Bailey Circus. In other words, the circus's version of Orientalist spectacle and Arabian delights undoubtedly reached Americans of all genders, races, and classes, including "race" men and women

Noble Drew Ali was not the only one who created African identities for "Afro-Americans." The circus was in the business of exhibiting and commercially exploiting human difference, with a healthy dose of humbug and little regard for ethnological accuracy. In so doing, it provided venues in which "Afro-Americans" could make a living by impersonating Africans—performing and commodifying racial difference. In the 1890s at least four performers claimed to be Africans or African princes—two of whom were circus performers, one of whom was a lecturer, and another of whom was a singer and musician. For example, a man calling himself "Jave Tip O'Tip, the Zulu Prince" appeared in Yazoo City, Mississippi, in September of 1891, claiming to be a "native African of the fearless Zulu tribe" trying to raise money to help assist three sisters attending school in Washington, DC. The following month he turned up in St. Louis, and gave his name as "Jave Tip-O-Tip, Victoria Flosse, Zulu, Dungan Omish, son of King Cetowa Totowa," although he also answered to the more prosaic alias of Mr. Dempsey Powers. He sang the well-known Gospel hymn "Come to Jesus" with improvised "African" words. Only a week later, however, the *Kansas City American Citizen* reported that the Zulu prince was a "first class fraud" and a South Carolinian who "learned of Africa from a showman." The *Race Problem* paper of St. Louis reported that Tip-O-Tip had been employed by P. T. Barnum's circus to play a "Zulu youth," and that "so well did he learn his part that he concluded he was 'just from Africa' sure enough." Despite the paper's assertion that he knew "no more about African customs and habits than an unlettered rustic does about Blackstone's Commentaries," Tip-O-Tip enrolled in Central Tennessee State College in Nashville, and gave a lecture as a visiting speaker in July of 1892 on "the habits and customs of his people." But according to the *Detroit Plaindealer*, things truly fell apart for the erstwhile African the following month when he was exposed in Covington, Kentucky, and accused of being "a scurrilous thief, robber, and assassin." Another man, claiming to be "the real Zulu chief, Mata Mon Zaro," accused Tip-O-Tip of being "an Arabian, assuming the nationality of an African." "Zaro" was convinced that his rival's performances had thwarted his own success as a lecturer, and said "were he to meet him again on his route, he would smack him so that he would feel and know the Zulu's power." As Zaro's accusations indicate, there was money to be made on the lecture circuit by performing as an African, and Tip-O-Tip's story shows that performances of African-ness in the circus could cross over into lecture and performance circuits in Black churches and colleges.[13]

The most successful "African" circus performer may have been Prince Oskazuma, who was referred to as "the well-known copper-colored African" and "the African prince and warrior." He toured with the Sells and Renfrow Circus in 1893, then retired to join a company of singers, and by the turn of the century had joined up with Buffalo Bill Cody's Wild West Show, where he was billed as an "African Warrior, Lecturer, Mimic, Fire Fiend." Another alleged Zulu illustrates how intertwined these performances of Africanity were with circus performances. Orlando Gibson, who went by the name Boneo Moskego and sang hymns in an "African language," also performed various feats of strength and courage, such as walking on broken glass, putting a rope in his mouth and defying the strongest men in the audience to pull it out, lifting a man with his teeth, and putting a glass of water in his hand and defying six of the strongest men in the house to prevent him from drinking.[14] Gibson's performance combined elements associated with various racial groups who met under the circus big top: singing like that associated with "colored" minstrels, walking on glass like Islamic "Hindoo" fakirs, and feats of strength associated with circus strongmen of all nationalities, feats that Walter Brister would also perform to establish his preternatural abilities when he presented himself as Noble Drew Ali, the Muslim prophet.

In addition to "African princes," which satiated a certain fascination with royalty and nobility among "savage" and Oriental peoples, Barnum & Bailey's circus also featured degrading images of Africans, such as "a tribe of savages from the wilds of Darkest Africa," and the famous "Zip," representing the "missing link" between apes and humans. Barnum had displayed a Black person as a "missing link" called the "What Is It?" as early as 1860, thereby profiting from the social Darwinist idea that people of recent African descent were less evolved than Europeans and that a proto-human ancestor might be alive in the dim recesses of the "Dark Continent." William Henry Johnson, a microcephalic Black American from New Jersey with a steeply sloping forehead and a pointy shaved head, wearing in a furry suit and carrying a staff, inhabited the role of Zip from at least 1865, when he was photographed by famous Civil War photographer Mathew Brady, until his death in 1926. In 1922, after Johnson, as Zip, put on a show of speaking "native Zulu" for newspaper editors and being frightened of flashbulbs, a reporter caught up with him on the sidewalk. "Great life, this wildman stuff," he remarked. "I was in a crap game last night with the guy who took my photograph. I won. He lost. He ought to be the wild one."[15] As historian Robert Bogdan explains, Johnson operated in a freak show world where "the outsider was held in contempt. Life was about tricking the rube, and making money."[16] Johnson may have been embodying a racist role, but he was also, in his own modest way, one of the most famous Black performers of his era: he had posed for a photographer who had also photographed Abraham Lincoln, and had performed for over a hundred million people over the course of his long career. The circus allowed Black Americans to not only impersonate Africans but to make good money doing so.

☙   ☙   ☙

Not bound by any scientific scruples, committed only to spectacle, wonder, and the marvelous, the circus and its allied arts were willing to combine anything that sparkled and dazzled, whether it was Persia and Peking or India and Arabia. If the spectacle they presented was only a fraction as gorgeous and opulent as the posters they left behind, they would have been impressive to behold. Barnum & Bailey produced one particularly beautiful series of posters in 1914, when the circus was still exhibiting the "savage Africans" and the "missing link" in its freak show. These posters announced Barnum & Bailey's "New Big Indo-Arabic Spectacle / The Wizard Prince of Arabia" with a poster featuring dozens of bejeweled and costumed "Indian" and "Arabic" girls dancing with shapely legs half-cocked in what looks to be a can-can, framed by elephants and palm trees and bookended by capering clowns in the style of the Italian commedia dell'arte. The caption promised "Dazzling, Dancing Scene in the Magical, Mighty, Wordless Play, Combining the Weird Wizardry of India and Arabia, in Opulent, Oriental Grandeur." A reporter for the New York Times caught the show and described the opening spectacle as a pantomime and ballet telling the story of "Abdallah, Wizard Prince of Arabia, who after many wonderful adventures won the hand of Princess Ahloe Ssaran, daughter of the mighty King Babar, whose magic city and palace were the wonder of all India."[17] In contrast to the circus's degrading depictions of Black people, the Indian "Wizard Prince of Arabia" represented racial others in favorable, if stereotypical, terms. "The city and palace of King Babar were represented with gorgeous scenery high upon a stage constructed at the east end of the arena," the Times wrote. Leading down from the palace front were spacious steps, by which members of the ballet, courtiers, and ladies descended to a low platform that covered almost the entire palace garden. Here the ballet company danced in long, sinuous lines, and the leading actors in their resplendent costumes strutted before the audience. It was as if a bizarre fever dream of a Bollywood production roamed American cities and hinterlands underneath circus big tops during the late nineteenth and early twentieth centuries, spreading professed "weird" and "strange" visions of Oriental opulence and grandeur, taking Americans along on an "Orientally Splendid and Weirdly Romantic Spectacular Pilgrimage to Mecca."[18]

While Black Americans frequently worked behind the scenes or on the bandstands at America's circuses, there were relatively few roles open to Black performers in the circuses themselves. Until the rise of Black minstrel performers at the end of the nineteenth century, even most blackface performers were white. In the 1890s, however, the new fad of combining Black and white performers in "mixed minstrelsy" provided a transition to the primacy of Black minstrel performers in the new century. On occasion these "mixed minstrel" troupes included performances of ethnicities other than the stock racist caricatures of Black rubes that peopled most minstrel shows. Sometimes such companies presented Black Americans portraying African, Arab, or even Japanese characters.

Especially popular among Black minstrel performances were absurd caricatures of Africans, commonly using the referents of "Dahomey" and "Zulu." These portrayals gained popularity following the exhibition of a "Dahomeyan Village" at the World's Columbian Exposition in Chicago in 1893. The leading comedy team of Bert Williams and George Walker, who called themselves "the two real coons," starred in a show called *The Sons of Ham* in New York in 1901, which included hits such as "My Little Zulu Babe," "In My Castle on the River Nile," and "The Phrenologist Coon." Williams and Walker were known for a kind of "coon song" that was less offensive than the normal fare of fried chicken snafus or watermelon capers. "In My Castle on the River Nile" boasted music by J. Rosamond Johnson and lyrics by Robert Cole and James Weldon Johnson, the future head of the NAACP and brother of Rosamond. "The Phrenologist Coon" was a witty send-up of the racist science of phrenology, which had attempted to determine character and intellectual traits by skull shape.[19]

Often, "mixed minstrel" shows exhibited Arabs, or "Moorish-Bedouin Arabs," performing feats commonly associated with the circus. Likewise, another white minstrel show proprietor named Al. G. Field put a company of "genuine negroes" and "Arabs" on the road in the fall of 1894, beginning in Columbus, Ohio, with ambitions to conduct national and international tours. Dubbed "The Al. G. Field Real Negro Minstrels and Troupe of Arabs," the show joined together performers representing Arabs with "colored" singers recruited from an actual Charleston camp meeting, along with other ethnographically minded depictions of Southern Black life. "The show will not be of the old style of negro minstrelsy," the newspaper announced. "To introduce scenes peculiar to the South will be the aim of the management." Yet, old minstrelsy or new, the show still featured slapstick firemen, comedic watermelon scenes, and gauzy representations of the plantation South in slavery time.[20]

Likewise, in 1895, white minstrel impresario William S. Cleveland put together a minstrel show boasting white minstrels, "genuine colored" minstrels, Japanese contortionists, jugglers and gymnasts, and fifteen "Moorish-Bedouin Arab" acrobats, tumblers, musicians, and equilibrists performing skills commonly associated with the circus. Just as circuses staged elaborate parades to announce their arrival in a new location, the "All Nations" minstrel show staged an elaborate parade, showing off their "Moorish-Bedouin Arab" performers in all their Oriental finery. Cleveland claimed that his was the only minstrel company with an internationalist "All Nations" theme, but the performance certainly echoed the Barnum Circus's "Ethnological Congress" as well as the ethnographic spectacles of the world's fairs. Interestingly, while Cleveland billed his Arab performers as "Moorish-Bedouin Arabs," clearly stressing their Blackness as "Moors," newspaper accounts of the show labeled them simply "Arabs," indicating that ragtime Americans readily accepted Black people as Arabs.[21]

We remember minstrelsy as a white-on-black crime, but Blacks also got into the act of impersonating themselves and others. Ernest Hogan was a Black minstrel star and pioneer of "vaudevillized" minstrelsy who in 1896 penned the ironic hit that made fun of white racist ignorance, "All Coons Look Alike to Me." Hogan often performed in companies that included specialists in the impersonation of European and Asian national groups. In 1902 Hogan appeared in Honolulu, Hawaii, with a Black performer impersonating a Jewish real estate speculator. In the words of the local Hawaiian paper, "[Henry 'Hen'] Wise as a black face Hebrew was fairly good, there being a straining at some points, but with all a careful representation of the anxious real estate man."[22] In 1906 Hogan toured the East and the Midwest with a show he produced and starred in called *Rufus Rastus*, and among his understudies were several character actors who excelled at stereotypical comedic depictions of non-Blacks. The cast included Harry Fiddler, "the Man of Many Faces," who at times pulled down the corners of his eyes in an Asian impersonation, and Tom Logan, who was equally at home with straight roles and "grotesque character work, such as Chinese, Italian, Dutch, Jew, and other impersonations."[23]

Similarly, Archie Jones and John Baptiste Verdun were two "character comedians" from New Orleans who specialized in impersonating Jewish characters. In 1910 the Florida Blossom Minstrels staged an elaborate comedic skit called "B. Grabbenheimer's African Colony," in which Verdun, in the title role of "the Jewish immigration agent," created his colony with the help of a cast of characters that included "Toody Roosevelt" and "Doctor Kill M. Quick." The plot summary does not survive, but presumably the skit made fun of Jews, the safari-loving former president, and the many plans for Black colonization of Africa that began with the founding of the American Colonization Society in 1807 and peaked with the efforts of the Episcopal reverend Alexander Crummell, who lived in Liberia from 1853 to 1872, and the plans of A.M.E. Bishop Henry McNeal Turner, who led two boatloads of emigrants to Liberia in the 1890s.[24]

Between 1910 and 1914, the same Verdun appeared with Allen's Minstrels in a skit called "The Jew and the Coon," which no doubt gave a politically incorrect view of what would later come to be called "Black-Jewish relations."[25] To be sure, by far the most common act of racial imposture on the minstrel stage was the performance of ignorant, absurd "coon" caricatures. But the Black "authentic" minstrels that began to dominate the minstrel stage in the age of ragtime also signified on other ethnicities, holding up Jews, Chinese, Italians, and others to the sort of ridicule commonly dealt out to Americans of African descent. Impersonating the Yiddish-inflected speech of European Jews was a distinct performance genre among Black religious figures as well as entertainers. Just as some Black performers made money by impersonating "African princes," some Black Israelites, such as "Rabbi Warien Roberson," would do the same in interwar New York by asking for contributions from Jews of European origins while impersonating their Yiddish-inflected speech and mannerisms.[26]

Sometimes Black minstrel and tent show performers did not simply portray people from other parts of the world but actually had opportunities to travel the world themselves. Tented minstrelsy provided global mobility for Black musicians, and it was not uncommon for Black performers to travel to Sydney, Australia, in the 1890s. Sometimes they ranged much farther afield: Pearl Moppin, a "Hoop Roller and Trombonist" from Kansas City, Missouri, spent two years between 1912 and 1914 touring through the Hawaiian Islands, Fiji, Samoa, New Zealand, Tasmania, Australia, Ceylon, India, Persia, Arabia, Somaliland, Abyssinia, Palestine, Egypt, Crete, Sicily, Italy, Corsica, Sardinia, Morocco, France, Spain, Portugal, England, and Ireland.[27] It may have been the height of Jim Crow and lynch law in the American South, and many Black Americans may have been tied to sharecropping the land and suffering racist violence, but for the few talented Black performers able to escape and earn a living on the popular performance circuit, it was a small world after all.

The Orient itself was so heterodox, colorful, and exotic in American eyes that it was sometimes described as a circus itself, as when the leading Black newspaper the *Chicago Defender* wrote in 1922, "The life that ebbs and flows along some of the streets of Cairo is like nothing so much as a circus parade back home." Circuses had employed the people, animals, and aura of the Islamic Orient for so long that now the Islamic Orient could be explained as such. What stood out most to the *Defender*'s observer was the tremendous diversity of people, animals, and things in the busy Cairo streets: "Deliberate camels move along, brightly dressed riders perched upon them or with suspended cars in which are veiled damsels, while drummers thunder their rhythm and fife blowers emit their shrill notes," wrote the *Defender*. "Snake charmers pass along with their bags of snakes; magicians perform in some nook; bullock carts and laden donkeys compete for space with shining limousines."[28]

For Black Americans, the Orient represented a subversive heterogeneity and stood as a rebuke to the sterile segregation of the American Jim Crow system. In an article titled "All Races Found in Cairo City: Great Metropolis on River Nile Is Now Very Cultured," the *Defender* reported:

> Cairo is a living kaleidoscope; its colored fragments are tumbled into place not merely from east and west, but from north and south as well. White-robed Bedouin, ill-clad fellah, shiny-black Soudanese

and Central African Negro, swarthy Turk, Persian, Hindu, Mongolian, dusky Moor, Italian, Greek, Armenian and the white folk from Europe, America and their antipodes—all are jumbled together in Cairo, their various tongues making a babel that can hardly be duplicated at any other spot on earth."[29]

By asserting that Cairo was "cultured" in addition to being racially heterogeneous, the *Chicago Defender* was implicitly rebuking racist Americans who asserted that racial mixing was a symptom of a society not having attained an advanced level of civilization. Implicitly, the Orient's heterodoxy stood as a wonderful reminder for Black Americans of how bizarre, juvenile, rude, and uncultured the Jim Crow segregation system truly was. Images of the Orient suggested not simply the marvelously strange but hinted at the potential for radically different ways of ordering society.

Black Americans who attended the circus, then, would have seen Africans denigrated and degraded while Arabs, Muslims, and subcontinental Indians were stereotyped and celebrated. Given that the "missing link" was obviously specious, a melancholy spectacle of a Black man in a monkey suit, the notion that Black Americans could have been descended from noble, romantic, dashing, and dangerous dark-skinned African Muslim Moors was far less insulting and indeed far more plausible than many of the other anthropological ideas circulating in the popular culture of the Age of Empire.

CHAPTER SEVEN

DEATH DANCE

*I may now add that civilization is a process in the service
of Eros, whose purpose is to combine single human individuals, and after that families, then races, peoples and nations, into one great unity, the unity of mankind. . . . The
meaning of the evolution of civilization is no longer obscure
to us. It must present the struggle between Eros and Death,
between the instinct of life amid the instinct of destruction,
as it works itself out in the human species.*

—SIGMUND FREUD, 1930[1]

Walter Brister's last known performance in the "pickaninny
band" of Old Kentucky was at Chicago's Grand Theater in
January of 1897, and his first known performance as Armmah Sotanki was on May 14, 1898, at Wonderland in New York City, alongside a fat women's bicycle tournament captained by "Big Alice" and
a lecture by J. H. Burtram, who falsely claimed to be a survivor of
the explosion on the USS *Maine* that sparked the spread of the US
empire overseas. From there Sotanki and his companion Armatoo
played Heck's Wonder World, a vaudeville theater in Cincinnati,
alongside a plantation comedy featuring a pickaninny band like the
one that he himself had pioneered. He was billed as "a star attraction . . . the great Sotanki and his companion Armatoo. These are
genuine high priests of Oriental magic." Sotanki, the "East Indian
high priest," appeared with an entire company of "Hindoo jugglers,
fakirs, and wonder workers," and performed the famous Indian basket trick, making a boy disappear into a basket. Indian magicians

also frequently performed juggling as a kind of magic, and sometimes were called jugglers. Not only did Sotanki present himself as a religious figure, but his ads promised that his act could not be explained except through the teachings of Theosophy.

By the week of November 29, 1898, Sotanki & Armatoo shared the Heck's stage with an even more accomplished Black Oriental magician named Prince Ishmael, who boasted an even more impressive set of magical skills and was proficient at sleight of hand. He was able to make a mango tree grow in front of the eyes of an audience, hatch live chickens from eggs, and make burned ribbons whole. Prince Ishmael also cloaked himself in the mystery of Oriental religions, with references to Islam, Buddhism, and Hinduism. He was "Ishmael, the renowned priest of Buddha—a Hindoo juggler." As we have already seen, juggling seemed a type of magic, a form of *sihr* in Islamic terms, and Muslim mendicants in India could be called jugglers, magicians, or fakirs. Later, Walter Brister would profess a reverence for Buddha much like that of Prince Ishmael when Brister became the Prophet Noble Drew Ali. We can trace some of Walter Brister's movements during the winter months because letters he wrote to various theaters' booking agents that November ended up in the personal collection of the famous magician and escape artist, Harry Houdini. Houdini, born Ehrich Weisz, was an avid collector of magical materials and a historian of the magical arts who amassed a large collection of letters, books, devices, and sundry materials relating to magic and its practitioners. At some point in his career he acquired two letters from Armmah Sotanki on Sotanki's ornate personal stationary. Dated November 21 and November 23, 1898, Sotanki was writing to arrange a booking at the Wonderland Musee of Toledo, Ohio, while he was two weeks into a three-week engagement at Heck's Wonder World. His stationary boasted that his group, billed "The Royal Hindoo Wonder Workers," was "Endorsed by Herrman, The Great, the Napoleon of Necromancers," one of the leading magicians of the day, a master of mystery as famous in the 1890s as Charlie Chaplin was in the new medium of cinema twenty years later.[2]

On Christmas of 1898, Brister was back with the company of *In Old Kentucky* for a two-week engagement, playing the role of Caesar that his father had pioneered in 1893 in New York. It was Walter's last known performance with the pathbreaking Southern musical. He was now free at last of that phenomenally successful but intrinsically demeaning show. By March of 1899, Sotanki's ten-person troupe of royal "Ashantee fakirs" were playing Austin and Stone's Museum in Boston, and that summer Sotanki went on tour with Pawnee Bill's show, where he took part in the Princeton Riot.[3]

But of even greater consequence in Walter Brister's professional and personal career was the fact that the following summer, while on another tour with Pawnee Bill, he married a member of the Sotanki troupe. Eva Alexander was the daughter of Arthur Alexander and Rebecca Garrett, born just across the river from Cincinnati in Kentucky. She was a vivacious, pretty girl, and was attracted to the theater at a young age. Her first marriage ended in divorce; she was twenty-three the second time she married, to a West African named James Hammond on August 26, 1898, in Manhattan, New York City.[4] Her time in New York overlapped with Brister's performances as Sotanki in the Big Apple, so she may have already been performing as a Sotanki then; she was certainly a member of the troupe by the following summer. Her second husband soon died, and she took as her third husband John Walter Brister, the former bandleader of *In Old Kentucky* now working as the magician Armmah Sotanki, on August 18, 1900, in Cincinnati, Ohio. The ceremony had a presiding "minister of the Gospel," Reverend J. O. Burney, meaning that theirs was a Christian wedding. On their marriage certificate the groom listed his profession as "musician," while she listed hers as "magician." At the time of their marriage, Eva lived at 574 W. Sixth Street in downtown Cincinnati, Ohio, while John Walter lived just on the other side of the Ohio River in Covington, Kentucky, less than two miles away. It appears that the Brister family based itself in Cincinnati even during the time they were performing and touring with *In Old Kentucky*, since Walter's father, John Henry, listed himself as a music teacher in Cincinnati city directories in 1895 and 1898.

The 1900 route book for Brister's second season with Pawnee Bill included two studio portraits. On the right, "The Sotankis, Hindoo Fakirs, WALTER BRISTER." And on the left, a beautiful studio portrait of a lovely African American young woman with the caption: "The Sotankis, Hindoo Fakirs." Then: "MRS. E. BRISTER."[5] Like her biblical progenitor Eve, whose narrative was also inextricably linked to a serpent, her renown in many ways would surpass that of her husband after she started dancing with a giant python.[6]

After his second tour with Pawnee Bill, when the show slugged it out with Princeton students, Sotanki found work in March of 1900 as "one of the cleverest wonder workers of the far east," in the words

of the *Boston Herald*, leading a group of "Ashantee fakirs" in a series of magic tricks, the most impressive of which was the mango
tree trick, the most famous trick in the genre of magical acts that
gained the name "Hindoo magic" in homage to the Indian necromancers who plied their trade for the benefit of anyone who would
pay.[7] Members of the audience jostling each other for a better view
at the Pawnee Bill sideshow or viewing the performance from the
comfort of a theater seat would see Armmah Sotanki produce a large
mango pit, a turban wrapped above his delicate features and slight
frame, his hypnotic gaze seemingly focused beyond or through the
audience and perfectly balanced on some distant Eastern horizon
knowable only to him and his crew of Oriental confederates. The pit
of a mango, scraped of its clinging yellow-orange flesh and dried, appears to be off-white in color and fit perfectly into the concave cavity
of the palm of his hand, like a long razorback mussel shell. Producing
the mango pit with a flourish, Sotanki held the strange seed in the air
for the audience to slake its curiosity about these two odd Oriental
curios: mango and man.[8]

As "Armmah Sotanki," Walter Brister presented many tricks
once presented by Prince Ishmael, the Black "Hindoo" magician with
whom he shared a bill in Cincinnati when just starting out in 1898.
They were also tricks that were explained by "Professor" Samri S.
Baldwin, who called himself "the White Mahatma" and published
a manual of Hindoo magic in 1895 called, *The Secrets of Mahatma
Land Explained: Teaching and Explaining the Performances of the Most
Celebrated Oriental Mystery Makers and Magicians in All Parts of the
World*. Baldwin posed for his portrait wearing an Indian *kurta* and
pyjama with a large piece of cloth wrapped over these like a sari, with
a turban loosely wrapped on his head and curved Moroccan slippers
on his feet. He and his wife, Kitty, advertised themselves as "High
Class Entertainers" who were on their fifth world tour "with the
queerest, quaintest, most bewildering and fascinating entertainment
ever presented to the public." Yet even though Hindoo magic was
exotic, it was still morally upright—"clean, pure, high class and extremely attractive in every particular," according to alleged testimonials from five thousand clergymen.[9] Baldwin traveled from Egypt
and Zululand to India, Ceylon, and beyond, documenting the fakirs
and magicians he met along the way and explaining their tricks when
he could—which he was not always able to do. A Muslim fakir in
India confounded him with an amazing series of feats in which he

somehow switched his right and left shoes, caused them to shrink and expand, and stole his socks right off his feet, all in daylight when Baldwin was sober, as he made sure to tell his readers.

The mango tree trick, on the other hand, was simpler to explain, even though the illusion it produced was quite wonderful: the fakir planted a mango pit in a small pile of earth, watered the earth, covered the mound with a cloth, and then a tree appeared to grow. Covering the twig, then sapling, with the cloth at intervals, the fakir enticed a mango tree to grow two or three feet tall, more or less in front of the audience's very eyes. Then it would flower and bear fruit, which the fakir shared with audience members as souvenirs. One day in India, Baldwin asked a fakir, "Why do you always bring forth the Mango tree? Why do you not sometimes vary your performance by producing a young palm, or a tea plant, or a banyan tree? If you grow for me a little apple or oak tree I will give you ten rupees." The fakir refused, saying "Nay, *Sahib*, cannot do. Mango tree the only one can make." Baldwin explained that fakirs used a mango pit because the twigs, branches, and leaves of the mango tree are tough and leathery, and could be rolled up and fit into a pocket or small space without showing creasing on the upper surfaces. By reading Baldwin's book, or being taught by a fellow performer, Armmah Sotanki could have learned that the first iteration of the mango tree, a small sapling as much as thirteen inches tall, could be rolled up and concealed inside the mango pit itself. By unrolling the plant a few inches at a time, the fakir could create the illusion that the sapling was growing, and when a bigger plant was needed, the assistant could pass a larger plant, folded and concealed inside the cloth that was laid over the sapling at intervals.[10]

Another of Sotanki's tricks was the basket mystery, another staple of Hindoo fakirs. "Almost every traveler in India and the East has witnessed one form or another of the celebrated basket trick," according to the White Mahatma. "Very nearly every band of Fakeers produce this basket illusion."[11] There were many variations, but in the most common one the fakir bound a child or small woman with rope and netting and placed him or her standing inside a basket. The basket was oval shaped, and about four feet long, like a slightly flattened egg laid on its side. The magician threw a sheet over both the assistant and the basket, and the assistant gradually descended into the basket. Then the cover was placed over the sheet on top of the basket, and the fakir made a show of incantations, muttering, and

mummery. He intoned appropriate Eastern incantations: "Abraca-
dabra!" and so forth. He thwacked the basket four or five times with
a stick, shouted to the confederate in the basket, and the confederate
shouted back. The fakir then removed the lid but left the sheet in
place so that the audience could not see inside the basket, and the
magician jumped up and down all over the basket, seemingly on top
of the assistant. Now came the most dangerous part of the trick:
the fakir took a sword and passed it through the basket rapidly in
many different locations. Finally, to the audience's amazement, the
magician produced the assistant from among the crowd itself: the
assistant has defied the laws of time and space and traveled out of
the confining coffin-like basket and into the world, unfettered. Of
course, all it took to pull off this illusion was a blindfold that partially obscured the face of the assistant, a flexible assistant capable
of untying the rope and netting and wrapping him- or herself into
a ring shape inside of the basket, the steady hand of the magician in
thrusting the sword where it wouldn't hurt the assistant inside the
basket, and a confederate who looked enough like the person in the
basket that the audience would believe that two people were actually
one and the same.

The Sotanki troupe traveled and performed constantly between
1898 and 1913, and there is a solitary reference to a Princess Sotanki
performance in 1921 as well. Show business required the couple to be
apart from time to time. In 1903 Walter was back in Cincinnati, using the local offices of the theatrical rag *Billboard* as a mail forwarding
address, but Eva Sotanki was using the New York mail forwarding
address of the *New York Clipper*, the premier show business journal for vaudeville and tented shows. Walter listed himself as a musician in 1905 and 1909 in the Cincinnati city directory. From 1900
through January of 1909, Eva, as "Princess Sotanki," was also receiving her mail in Cincinnati. By November of 1912 Princess Sotanki
was receiving letters in Indianapolis, and in 1913 she was managing
a theater in Paducah, Kentucky, an Ohio River town about three
hundred miles west of Cincinnati. At holiday time that year she was
entertaining out-of-town guests with her mother in her hometown
of Cincinnati.

As "the Sotankis," the Bristers advertised their services through
the offices of the *Clipper*.[12] They performed in Oriental costumes and
invented Oriental identities in museums like Heck's Wonder World
in Cincinnati, where they played as "Sotanki's group of Oriental

jugglers" in April of 1901, and in Pawnee Bill's Wild West Show the same year.[13] Pawnee Bill's sideshow concert featured a mix of African American, Orientalist, and other arts, beginning with an exhibition of buck-and-wing dancing and a blackface comedian. Next came a monologue comedian, a sketch team, and a female singer, Mademoiselle A. Monk. One Mademoiselle Zelda performed a dance, and the Sotankis did magic as "Hindoo Fakirs." Next came Clippel, the contortionist. A group of Jubilee Singers, the Georgia Minstrels, followed the contortionist, singing spirituals in the mode of the famous Fisk Jubilee Singers. The Georgia Minstrels were Elmer Beardsley, Alphonso Grey, William Davis, William Jordan, and Charles Goins, five extremely dark-skinned Black gentlemen in white pants, dark jackets, vests, and straw boaters perched on the back of their heads. The show's photographer shot them in front of a sideshow banner depicting well-dressed Black cakewalkers, unsmiling, hands held stiffly at their sides. Next, the Australian Boomerang Throwers, dark brown–skinned aborigines who made their wooden projectiles swoop and spin for the amazed audience two years before the Wright Brothers used similar airfoils for winged human flight.

In other words, the Bristers, also known as the Sotankis, developed their Oriental disguises amid an extraordinary display of Black and Oriental acts. Oriental and Islamic "greenface" was not in opposition to blackface so much as it was in partnership with it; impersonations of Muslims emerged with blackface and perhaps from it. As "Armmah Sotanki," Brister billed his troupe in 1900 as the "Royal Ashantee Fakirs," and himself as "one of the cleverest wonder workers of the East," thereby mixing a reference to the Ashanti people of the Gold Coast with the Orientalist "Hindoo" Magic, and he performed on the same bill as the Golden Gate Quartet, the famous Black Jubilee song presenters.[14] Brister had gone from one show exhibiting buck-and-wing dancing, *In Old Kentucky*, to another show, Pawnee Bill's, that exhibited blackface comedians, jubilee singers, and buck-and-wing dancing alongside belly dancing and boomerang throwing. Pawnee Bill and his mentor Buffalo Bill were not simply creating an idea of the West; their theatrical performances were also very clearly constructing the East and Blackness as well. By exhibiting so many "Afro-American" acts alongside Eastern ones, the two Western "Bills" helped associate Blacks and the East in popular consciousness. Racism overlaid Orientalism but it never overwrote it entirely, while for African American performers Orientalism afforded them opportunities to inhabit a rich, ancient, and enticing imaginary, the mystical world of fakirs, snake charmers, magic carpets, and belly dancers. In the following season of 1902 the Sotankis left the Pawnee Bill Show for the John Robinson Circus, and a Hindoo magician with a Sikh name, Ishar Singh Sundhoo, took their place. The Sotankis were on to bigger and better things.

But first they had to survive one of the worst circus accidents in history, the tornado and fire that destroyed the big top of the John Robinson Circus on Thursday, May 22, 1902. The day opened with lovely summer weather and good-sized audiences on a lot in the middle of the Allegheny Mountains at Ridgway, Pennsylvania. But that night at 8:45 p.m., a hurricane-force gust of wind picked up the sideshow tent where the Sotankis performed and blew it into the big top tent in the middle of a performance. The spectators jumped out of their seats and ran underneath the sidewalls to get away from the danger of being struck by a pole or trapped underneath the heavy canvas of the big top. The tornado howled for ten minutes, eventually blowing candelabra into the canvas and setting the big top on fire, creating a spectacle even more amazing than anything the circus could have created intentionally. The John Robinson press agent, Harry "Punch" Wheeler, wrote, "And herein ensued the most costly, brilliant and dazzling scene ever witnessed on any show grounds." From what was at first a small blaze, "the angry wind fanned into an enormous bonfire, lighting up the Allegheny mountains for miles, creating a genuine gorgeous realistic spectacle." Miraculously, the menagerie had already been cleared and not a single circus or audience member was injured. As the assembled throng watched the yellow-orange flames illuminate the mountains, a drenching rainstorm came and put out the flames, their salvation seemingly heaven sent. The show weathered the worst disaster in its history, did not skip a beat, and played its next two engagements in Clearfield, Pennsylvania, the following day. Two months later it would survive a second direct hit by a tornado, with a packed big top tent and a drenching downpour.[15]

In the John Robinson show, Princess Sotanki began her career not just as an Oriental magician's assistant, as she had been when she and her husband appeared together, but as a headlining performer in her own right, taking part in the incredible dance between humans and animals that has always been an integral part of the circus. Six days after the big top conflagration and two days after the birth of three new Bengal tigers, the same day that "Tom, the sad elephant" was sent away, some of the railway men were playing pinochle when the entire cage train, filled with elephants, tigers, and all manner of exotic animals, started downhill on its own. It ran for miles, and miles, and miles, all those elephants and exotic animals enjoying a slow, relaxing slide without the noise of the engine or the clumsy interferences of their human handlers. The train ran for eight miles before "the big elephant flagged the station of Homer, thinking we were going to stop there for next stand."[16] Apparently elephants not only remembered people; they could remember previous circus stops as well. In any event, a switch engineer finally captured the runaway train and brought it back up the hill to where the rest of the circus was waiting in Indiana, Pennsylvania.

It seems preposterous that a person would work an animal as powerful and dangerous as a lion inside the tight confines of a circus ring, let alone an entire den of lions or tigers, each weighing four hundred pounds or more and equipped with massive claws and fearsome fangs. One flick of the leonine wrist, one casual tilt of the head and snap at the jugular, and the lion tamer would disappear as surely as a mouse snared by a housecat. Yet taming lions was exactly what Mrs. Eva Brister did as "Princess Sotanki" with the John Robinson Circus in 1902. Her picture that year was the same as the one that ran the prior year in the Pawnee Bill route book, only now her title was "Hindoo Lion Tamer."[17] There had been a few African American wild animal trainers before Princess Sotanki, including Moses "Eph" Thompson, who once found himself sleeping underneath the girth of a slumbering lion one cold and besotted night when he ended up in the lion's cage instead of his own bed, but Princess Sotanki was undoubtedly the first Black woman to be a lion tamer. Like other "Negroes," she had to hide her identity underneath an Oriental disguise to work with lions, but tame lions she did.

The Sotankis continued to receive letters through the *New York Clipper* mail service in 1903 and 1904, and in 1905 "Sotanki's Hindoo Wonder Workers" performed with Miss Leah May, a seven-foot, seven-inch giantess, as well as a fat girl, Powell's Minstrel Maids, Zolta, queen of the trapeze, Punch and Judy, and Trixie and the snakes at Austin and Stone's museum in Boston. By the summer of 1907 the Sotankis were back with Pawnee Bill, only now Princess Sotanki received top billing: the partnership of the Bristers and their employees was now called "Princess Sotanki's Troupe." After the outdoor season closed, Princess Sotanki's Royal Hindu Wonder Workers, (now "Hindus," no longer "Hindoos") "this troupe from the land of wonder-workers," appeared in December of 1907 at Lubin's Theater in Baltimore; the following year they were back with Pawnee Bill's Wild East during the outdoor season and in Boston at Austin and Stone's in the winter. The Princess worked with seven "Hindus" in 1908 and introduced a new act that would become her calling card, "The Sacred Indian Snake Dance." Harold G. Moran of Cincinnati was their agent, and he booked the Sotanki "Hindus" through the Casino Vaudeville Circuit and other vaudeville houses west of the Mississippi River.

And so, two "colored" Americans named Walter and Eva Brister made their living for more than two decades representing Hindu magicians, traveling all over the country, dodging tornadoes and flying sideshow tents at times, filling slots in vaudeville theaters at others, making mango trees grow and flexible people disappear, sometimes taming lions, wrangling snakes, or working other "wonders," and representing the majestic, mystical, magical Orient. It was all good preparation in its own way for even bigger things to come. Whether it was making a mango tree grow in front of people's eyes, or making a person seemingly vanish and reappear, Walter Brister as Armmah Sotanki and his wife, Eva, as Princess Sotanki mastered skills that would come in handy later in life. Mighty trees would surely grow, if not from acorns then from mangos.[18]

🐘   🐘   🐘

Eva Sotanki's star eclipsed her husband's, and she began to receive top billing over him starting in 1903. In October 1908, Harold G. Moran began booking Princess Sotanki, then with Pawnee Bill, throughout the Casino circuit and other Western vaudeville houses in a new act called "The Sacred Indian Snake Dance."[19] The Princess danced hypnotically with a large serpent and then mimed being bitten by the snake and pretended to die in front of her transfixed audience. She was now known as a "snake dancer and Hindu magician." Trading on tropes of the Orient established over a century of performance in both Europe and America, her act, sometimes called "the Hindu Dance of Death," was "preceded by that peculiar, weird music known as the snake charming music, noted for its solemnity and monotony—drums much in evidence," according to the *Indianapolis Freeman*.[20] The princess made a glittering and alluring entrance: "She comes on, dazzling, in a bespangled costume. She shines and sparkles all over, enough to charm any kind of 'varmint,' including men." While the reviewer did not mention any movements of the torso, her use of bells and the slow movements she circumscribed, as well as her loose-fitting and alluring costume, certainly fit within Western representations of "Oriental" dance made famous by the belly dancers of World's Fairs and Expositions: "Slowly she reels about the stage to the music of the orchestra, accompanied by bells in each of her own hands. Some don't see the significance of it all until she stops and drags forth a huge reptile: it is now plain enough. The audience admires the woman's nerve, but with no thought of a desire to exchange places with her; not a man, woman or child." With the production of the snake, the alluring spectacle of the princess's dance is given a note of danger, and a heightened layer of eroticism: "She fondles her great snake, pressing it to her bosom, and other forms of endearment." But this transgressive display of serpentine love led to an instant punishment whose sexual overtones could not have been lost on the audience members:

> Finally she pretends to be bitten; gives a piercing scream which has the ring of reality. The audience shudders. Then comes the death scene, which is so artistically done that it is good to see. Her death agony has the appearance of the real thing. No laughs at this masterful presentation. The stupefied audience does not know whether to keep silent in contemplation or applaud the artist for her fine work. The curtain rings down.[21]

It mattered little that pythons don't bite their prey, or that snake-handlers needed few qualifications other than remembering to feed their serpents before performances and being able to stomach handling the muscular reptiles; Sotanki was playing on a deeper register of the soul, what her contemporaries and their descendants would come to call "the psyche." In Princess Sotanki's "Hindoo Dance of Death," the death drive of Thanatos triumphed over the life instinct of Eros, leaving audiences so variously titillated, stunned, and contemplative that they did not know how to respond. One late Victorian who might have found words for Sotanki's performance was Sigmund Freud, but he would not propose the death drive until

1920, a dozen years after Sotanki first acted out the tug of war between Eros and Thanatos with sequins, a snake, and a hip shake.[22]

Sometimes a pipe is not a pipe and a snake is not just a snake; perhaps there was something undeniably erotic about watching a beautiful woman coiled in the muscular girth of a giant serpent, not simply a phallic symbol in psychological terms but also the animal with which the Hebrew God tempted Eve and then Adam in the story of the Garden of Eden, a story that would have been instantly familiar to the biblically literate audiences of the early twentieth century. Whatever the associations, snake handling started with men but became dominated by women by the turn of the twentieth century, often in some state of exotic dress that challenged Victorian standards of propriety and traded on Orientalist stereotypes of foreign women of color as alluring and promiscuous.[23]

Princess Sotanki cut quite a striking figure with her Oriental garb, her sequined costume, and her enormous boa constrictor in a 1913 promotional photo, dressed in the manner of the Salome dancer Maud Allan, who had become such a sensation following the 1893 and 1904 World's Fairs and the debut of the Oscar Wilde–Richard Strauss opera *Salome* in 1905. Princess Sotanki chose a sequined, dazzling boat-necked dress with a head scarf resting on top of black, straightened hair, a diaphanous shawl that reached her ankles, and a sequined bodice that looked like nothing so much as glittering, bare breasts with enlarged dark shiny areolas, much like the bodice that Maud Allan wore in her American debut as Salome in 1908. An apron of what look like pearls attached below Sotanki's chest and dangled over her midriff, hanging to her knees, again like Allan's costume. She even had a similar hairstyle and headdress as Allan. Sotanki wore bangles on each arm, which she held away from herself with a slight inflection to each wrist, like an Indian dancer at rest but about to move. It was a costume that would have moved, sounded, and glittered as she moved and swayed. She rested her weight on one leg, jutting her left hip to the side, while her right knee was slightly bent, her feet flat on the floor and her right foot turned out, her posture suggesting that of an Indian dancer in the *abhanga* pose. The newspaper reproduced her skin tone as light brown, lighter than the photos from her circus days and well within the shades to be found on the Indian subcontinent, as if she had used the cosmetic skin bleaches that had become so popular among "colored" folks by then.

But without a doubt the pièce de résistance of her costume and her act was her giant serpent. Maud Allan's movements had been described as "serpentine," while Princess Sotanki used the real thing. Sotanki posed her snake winding its massive girth around her body, with a striking quadruple S curve up the front of its mistress's abdomen, the lemon-shaped head resting suggestively between the almost comically oversized, double-sequined "breasts" that lay on top of her own chest, a phallic arrow between the double bull's-eye erogenous zones of her bodice. That picture ran in a Savannah, Georgia, newspaper. The ad called Sotanki's performance "one of the Greatest Acts in Vaudeville, 'The Sacred Snake Dance of Death,' as it is danced in East India with a large Boa Constrictor Snake," and advertised Savannah's Star Theatre as the "Finest and Largest Theatre in the South for Colored People Only."[24] Sotanki's burlesque of the Orient helped construct the idea of the Orient for race men and women in a Blacks-only Jim Crow theater, and in many other vaudeville theaters across the country.

In 1913, when Princess Sotanki began a successful stint as amusement director of the Crown Garden Theater in Paducah, Kentucky, located on the Ohio River's sinuous border with Illinois, 180 miles southeast of St. Louis, she packed the theater nightly with a varied assortment of vaudeville acts. An inveterate performer herself, she ingratiated herself to the performers by always paying them promptly on Saturday nights, which made them "feel like giving her the best performance they can," the *Indianapolis Freeman* noted. "All acts going south would do well to get in communication with the princess."[25] But the princess probably had too much of the taste of the road herself to settle in one place for very long; in any case, by May of 1914 she was appearing at the Pekin Theater, not far up the Ohio River in Cincinnati. The princess thrilled the crowds with her faux Hindu dance of faux death. As we shall see, she had already faked death for real, just the prior month.

In an era when white magicians commonly took Chinese names, grew out queues, and used makeup and costumes to appear as obviously false "Asians," Princess Sotanki's "Negro" phenotype did not hinder her career as a show business "Indian." The Black audiences who caught her hypnotizing show might not have been taken in anyway; to be a fake Hindoo was part of the artifice of the performance, in the vein of the stage's fourth-wall convention. But it is entirely possible that she was able to convince her audiences that she was indeed from foreign shores. "A wonderful little lady is Princess Sotanki," wrote one credulous or just good-humored reviewer for the *Indianapolis Freeman*. "It has been her privilege to have the most varied and most wonderful career of any colored performer before the public." She had allegedly traveled the world over, and given exhibitions with her husband, a "Hindustan." The reviewer reported that she had lived among the peoples of the Far East, and that "the Syrians insist she is one of them. She has their features, their language and that different personality that belongs to foreigners." In addition to learning French in France, she was also at home in India, where she had allegedly lived and learned magic, snake charming, and lore. "She has what she calls the reading gift—delving into the future—that occult science about which there is so much dispute."[26]

By 1912 Eva Brister as Princess Sotanki was billing herself as "the biggest Novelty Act in colored vaudeville," and "the only Lady Hindoo Magician in [the] world today doing this Star Act." She came to be recognized as something of a trailblazer for Black artists. "Princess Sotanki offered the Crown patrons something new and novel," wrote reviewer Tim Owsley in the *Freeman*.

> After one witnesses the act of Princess Sotanki he is thoroughly convinced that the colored actor or actress offers just as much in the legitimate way of entertaining as his white brother or sister actor or actress. The Princess' feat of levitation, suspending the body of a young lady in mid-air, without the aid of a mechanical or human device, held the audience spellbound. Her closing number was a feature within itself, known as the "Dance of Death," which she executed with a real live snake twenty feet long and about six inches in diameter. Princess Sotanki's act is exciting, entertaining and pleasing.[27]

Princess Sotanki was not just an Orientalist snake dancer, but she was a magician, presenting the famous "levitating lady" illusion, which actually did depend on a hidden mechanical device. There were other African Americans performing "Hindoo Magic," but Princess Sotanki was the only woman to do so. And perhaps it was her gender that explains why her star eclipsed that of her husband, "Armmah

Sotanki," after 1903. After Princess Sotanki assumed top billing, her husband faded into the background of the Hindoo/Hindu troupe that facilitated her performances.

Walter Brister, who played Armmah Sotanki from 1899 until at least 1902, pinged the radar a few times, enough for us to know that he resumed his musical career, but this time as a sideman, not as the cornetist/bandmaster of his youth in *In Old Kentucky*. Touring musicians and vaudeville and minstrel show performers would often say hello to friends or request letters from them by posting brief updates in newspapers like the *Indianapolis Freeman*. In one such communication, on December 29, 1906, we learn that Lunford Davis and his band were "still meeting with good success in the South." Davis sent "regards to P.G. Lowery, Walter Brister, Ted Redman, E.L. Banks and other friends."[28] Lowery was the most famous Black bandmaster of the day, a talent broker who once employed more than four hundred musicians, a conductor who led the Ringling Bros. Barnum & Bailey sideshow band, and a teacher who inspired and trained many of the musicians who would pioneer jazz music. That Davis, who played with the venerable Black-owned minstrel show *Silas Green from New Orleans*, even mentioned Brister in the same breath as Lowery testifies to Brister's place in the upper echelon of professional "colored" entertainers of his day.

Walter Brister traveled as part of the Princess Sotanki troupe for at least some of its wanderings, but Eva and Walter's dual show business careers also likely required them to be apart for stretches of time. Brister made his home in Chicago starting in 1906.[29] Six years later, he was back playing in a Southern musical not unlike the one that made him famous in the 1890s. He appeared at Chicago's famous and ornate Grand Theater in *Southland*, with words and music by Sidney Perrin, produced by Sam L. Tuck. The conductor was the famous Joe Jordan, who had collaborated with Ernest Hogan of "All Coons Look Alike to Me" fame, worked with jazz bandleader James Reese Europe, and been the director of the house band at Bob Motts's famous Pekin Theater in Chicago. He even wrote the song "Salome's Dance" for the most famous Black Salome dancer of all, Aida Overton Walker, wife of Bert Williams's partner, George Walker.[30] Brister was clearly part of Black entertainment communities in the early years of the twentieth century, just as he had been before he became "Armmah Sotanki," when he played in the pickaninny band of *In Old Kentucky* and helped define the new thing called the child star.

The next two times Walter Brister surfaces in the historical record are perplexing, and frankly difficult to explain—mysterious, even. In November of 1912, six months after Brister started in the Chicago company of *Southland*, George Slaughter published a mysterious review of a Princess Sotanki performance in Louisville, Kentucky: "Princess Sotanki gets them in a big way with her mammoth snake, when she does the sacred dance of death," he began, relatively routinely. But then he dropped a bombshell announcement of great import not just for the princess, but for American history as well. "This will be [the] last week of the princess' stage career, as she will retire for life. She is the prospective bride of a successful magnate of Asbury Park, N.J. We will see the little princess in the future assisting in managing business affairs in the interest of her husband's enterprise, as her past stage career will be of great benefit to him."[31]

There are a number of things that are askew about this notice. The most glaring of them is the fact that Princess Sotanki was still married to Walter Brister; the other is that the Princess did not leave the stage. But what is even more interesting is that Asbury Park is in the vicinity of Newark, New Jersey, where an Islamic lodge known as the Canaanite Temple is said to have appeared in 1913. Could this planned business enterprise Slaughter referred to have been the forerunner of the Moorish Science Temple? By communicating so openly such a patently false story, was Slaughter even announcing the new scheme to the friends who knew Princess Sotanki's real identity as Eva Brister, Walter's wife?

The story took another twist two years later, on April 25, 1914, when the following notice appeared in the *Freeman*:

> Walter Brister, the cornet player, died Wednesday 8th, at his late residence 3532 Federal street [Chicago], after a short illness. His wife, Princess Sotanki, the Oriental dancer and snake charmer, on hearing of her husband's illness, hurried to his bedside from Indianapolis, where she had been appearing, and nursed him until he died.[32]

There was a death certificate filed with Cook County that matched the story in the newspaper, but given the Sotankis' histories of magical deception and wonder working, their expertise at making people disappear into a basket or float in midair, was Brister dead or was this merely a more elaborate "Dance of Death," that would allow

Walter Brister/Armmah Sotanki to escape a tight spot in Chicago and reinvent himself once again?

Princess Sotanki did not stop her dance of death, at least not yet. Like her husband, she was part of a community of performers of color who plied their trades on the vaudeville and circus circuits and communicated with each other through the pages of the trade newspapers. On January 2, 1915, George Barrett, a veteran of the venerable Fisk University Jubilee Singers, placed a message in the newspapers read by Black show-business people, reading: "Mr. George Barrett sends regards to Princess Sotanki and says, 'Hello, Drew, look out for Ali Mona he's got some juggling act.'"[33] There was someone named Drew who was part of Princess Sotanki's troupe in 1915, and he was in the same line of work as a juggler named Ali Mona. Was this the man who would become Noble Drew Ali, and was he the Walter Brister who officially died in 1914? Eva Brister's association with Walter survived his fictional demise, but their marriage did not last. Now officially a widow for the second time, Eva remarried a Black laborer named Adam Allen in Cincinnati on July 7, 1919. There was no minister this time, just a justice of the peace. The groom was fifty-one; the bride, forty-two. On the marriage certificate she listed her profession as "snake charmer." The final record of her performing as Princess Sotanki, the death-defying python-wielding Salome dancer, came two years later, in 1921, four years before the establishment of the Moorish Science Temple.[34]

Not only was Princess Sotanki "dying" every night on stage, but Black theatrical entertainment was suffering as well. The migration of millions of Blacks to Northern cities degraded the old circuits that tented minstrel shows and circuses followed in the South. Moreover, art forms tailored for small communities in the South had to adapt to cater to the new booming Black Metropolises of the North. The most talented performers left to seek fame up north, like Blues singers Bessie and Clara Smith, who both sang in tented shows down South before becoming stars. The invention of phonographs made individuals money, but put thousands of bands out of business. More fundamentally, the phonograph fundamentally altered the music that bands played, and in a very real sense, what "Negro" music was. Counterintuitively, the music that Black people listened to became *less*, not *more* diverse, as they made the spatial and epochal treks from Victorianism to modernity, and as technology changed from sheet music and bands to recorded music and 78 records.

In the earlier era, before the Great Migration, it would have been standard practice for "colored" circus and minstrel show bands to play selections from European symphonies, and for American band music to present the latest and most "ragged" "rags," the most coun- trified "coon shouters," and the most down-home blues women. Their performances typically fell between goofy "old-time comedians" and minstrel "plantation melodies," performed at full voice in the half cir- cle on the banjo and "bones" (a pair of clappers like castanets played like spoons against the hands and legs). J. C. O'Brien's famous Geor- gia Minstrels offers a good example of this wild musical heterogene- ity. At the start of World War I, they featured two bands, one drum corps, and one steam calliope, one of those ungainly steam-powered mobile organs whose often-dissonant tone was the signature sound of the circus, prized because they were so loud they could attract customers from miles around. There had been a handful of Black calliope players in circuses, but the J. C. O'Brien calliope produced no ordinary callithump: "Mr. Mancy Williams keeps them walking dogie when he plays the Blues on the steam calliope," the *Freeman* noted, referring to the Black popular dance Walkin' the Dog.[34] The number one band "played all the latest marches and overtures," in- cluding the William Tell Overture, "Flowers of Italy," and "Poet and Peasant," combining European symphonic overtures with standard minstrel fare. The band also played "The Boogie Man Rag," "The Memphis Blues," and all the latest popular blues hits.[36]

Before the shift, Black Southerners experienced musical het- erotopias. Afterward, audiences and market forces segregated mu- sical tastes and products. Black orchestras formed in the North that played a full range of European and American classical music, and Harlem's James Reese Europe formed the first jazz orchestra, but those groups were not well supported compared with the small groups of musicians who could squeeze into an apartment or a small urban club and squeeze out tunes on a compact upright piano. Even the mobile and highly adaptable circus tent was too cumbersome for the limited open spaces of most cities.

Likewise, the new era saw a decline in the multitude of acts, from slack wire walkers to jugglers to monologists and dog and pony shows, acts that filled up the slots between the music in the old tented extravaganzas. Many of these acts had come through minstrelsy and the circus; their hokey vibe was at odds with the newly modern times. The tented shows' aesthetics were unruly and undisciplined, loosely governed if they were governed at all by rules of flimflam, sequined Eros, death-driving and Thanatos-defying spectacle, over-the-top ballyhoo, outrageous humor, and plain old countrified silliness. Those aspects, like the Blues, whose aesthetics were so stylized and compact that they could travel from the backcountry South to the uptown North and from the Victorian age to this strange, sleek new motorized thing called modernity, made the voyage; they were often mislabeled as relics of the "authentic" folk and not as the rather recent innovations of commercialized popular entertainment. But in their new setting they were shorn of all their performative contexts, like crystalline blue jewels hacked out of a heavily ornamented Gilded Age crown.

Not only that, but circuses and medicine shows no longer carried the educational pretensions they once did. The new regimen of recorded sound and images fundamentally altered how people in developed countries like the United States viewed the racial and cultural "others" beyond their boundaries. Americans no longer went to the circus to learn about anthropology, and as a result, as newsreels brought India, Africa, and the Islamic Orient to light in the darkened spaces of cinemas, circus depictions of racial "others" became less ethnographic, and more abstract, much as the advent of photography forced painters to became less realistic and also more abstract both stylistically and in terms of subject matter.

The small but tight-knit group of Black "Hindoo" magicians suffered as a result of all of these transitions. Prince Ali Mona, the "juggler" a.k.a. magician whom George Barrett told "Drew" to look out for, wrote to the *Freeman* from J. C. O'Brien's Famous Georgia Minstrels No. 1 in 1915, saying that the show "is still a headliner in tent minstrels, regardless of the fact some of our best people have left for other fields." Ethnological impersonations—of Hottentots and Hindus alike—were still a part of the tented shows, but there is also evidence of concern beyond the fact that the show had been losing some of its top talent. Like the Sotankis, Prince Ali Mona depicted his magic as "Hindu," and they were all part of a sociable community of "colored" "Hindu" magicians who kept up with each other and

performed "Oriental" magic for one another, as seen in this update
that Ali Mona posted to the wide readership of the *Freeman*:

> Prince Ali Mona, the high caste Hindu entertainer, was guest of
> Prince Haze Ali K Ally, the Calcutta Fakir, and Prof. Wm. Brock-
> son, the southern marvel, at Helena, Ark. A delicious dinner was
> served with wit, repartee and beautiful feats of Oriental magic. A
> very pleasant afternoon was spent in the discussion of [the] future
> of magic and colored magicians. Prince Ali Mona sends regards to
> Harris & Miner.[37]

Prince Ali Mona, Haze Ali K. Ally, William Brockson, the Sotankis, and the mysterious man named Drew in Sotanki's company
were all Black magicians who presented "Hindu" or "Hindoo" magic
at about the time when the Canaanite temple in New Jersey first appeared and a decade before Brister as Noble Drew Ali launched the
Moorish Science Temple. This community of "Oriental" magicians
all faced a dwindling market for their services. Together, they could
have been allies—or, more pointedly, enemies—for Noble Drew Ali,
especially as his enterprises grew increasingly lucrative.

Who were the members of the community of Black "Oriental"
and "Hindu" magicians named "Drew" or "Ali" in the decade before
"Noble Drew Ali" burst on the scene in Detroit with the Moorish
Science Temple, performing feats of strength and escape magic for
his awed followers? There is truly a haze around the performer calling himself "Prince Haze Ali K. Ally," whose notices only turn up in
the first half of 1915. He advertised himself as a "Hindoo Wonder
Worker" based in Memphis in January of that year, and Prince Ali
Mona sent him regards in March. He hosted the summit of Oriental magicians in April, calling himself "the Calcutta Fakir," and
Ali Mona requested that he get in touch in May.[38] Prince Ali Mona,
"the high class Hindoo entertainer," or "the high class magician and
fire king," had a much longer record, much of the time as part of the
venerable Black minstrel show *Silas Green from New Orleans*, which
was owned and operated by Eph Williams, who was one of only two
documented Black circus owners before he started operating the
tented minstrel show. Like the Sotankis, Ali Mona performed the
Indian basket trick, but combined it with a trick known as the sedan
chair, whereby George Barrett's wife, Emma, was made to disappear
from the basket and appear in the empty chair, a trick "in which no

doubles are used," according to one account. "Prince Ali Mona, the high class Hindoo entertainer, is getting columns of applause with his Oriental magic and incomprehensible fire-eating act," the *Indianapolis Freeman* reported. Ali Mona received high praise for his performances and updated his show to feature "all the latest Hindoo magic," including at one point the "Asrah illusion" and "a very unique opening."[39]

Remembering that George Barrett wrote, "Hello, Drew, look out for Ali Mona he's got some juggling act," we can see that juggling was part of Ali Mona's performance of "Oriental" mysticism. The *Freeman*'s report of Ali Mona's juggling act called it "an Oriental mystical offering," and noted that "his juggling of sharp butcher knives while blindfolded showed great skill."[40] Like Noble Drew Ali, who escaped from ropes in the early years of the Moorish Science Temple, Ali Mona also was an escape artist, performing Houdini-like feats nightly such as throwing off a straitjacket, handcuffs, ropes, and chains.

Ali Mona performed with a "juggling jester and slack wire artist" named E. Alfred Drew in the Silas Green show. Drew, who initially used the name E. Alfred Drew Marlowe, worked in the biggest Black-operated tented minstrel shows of his day from 1909 to 1921, including Silas Green, J. C. O'Brien's Georgia Minstrels, and F. S. Walcott's Rabbit Foot Minstrels. These were "colored" shows that catered to "colored" audiences. As a frequent contributor to the "Stage Notes" section of the *Indianapolis Freeman*, E. Alfred Drew was an important chronicler of the world of tented minstrels and the social networks forged among the professional entertainers who made their livings on such circuits. Drew started as a baritone player in the band and also worked as an "eccentric juggler" and slack wire artist in Billy Kersands's minstrel show in 1909, then married in Lake Charles, Louisiana, and formed a troupe with his wife called "the Juggling Drews (Viola and E.A.)." Though their show business partnership doesn't seem to have lasted very long, he gained recognition as "E. Alfred Drew, the Juggling Jester, the boy who keeps things moving, [who is] also holding them spellbound with his slack wire act."[41] For a short while he performed with "S. B. Mancuso's Famous Southern Fun Makers," which featured a "pickaninny band" like the kind made famous by *In Old Kentucky* before Walter Brister began to blunt racist stereotypes with Orientalist ones, performing as Armmah Sotanki.[42]

In September of 1910, E. Alfred Drew posted to the *Freeman* that he would like to hear from "Chas. B. Drew, magician."[43] He worked with George Barrett, veteran of the Fisk Jubilee Singers, in 1914, and also reached out to "Leon, the Magician," a famous Black magician. Another team of "Hindoo" magicians on the Western Vaudeville Association circuit in 1915 was "The Rajahs," otherwise known as Vena and J. A. Downing.[44] "Rajah" was also the name used by "Prince Joveddah de Rajah," the "only Hindu telepathy act in America" in 1918, as well as by a belly dancer, Princess Rajah, or Princess Rajah Sultana. In other words, Walter and Eva Brister were part of a small circle of Black peers who practiced magic, including Hindoo magic, some of whom were also known as "Drew" or "Ali." His eventual choice of the name "Noble Drew Ali" had ample precedent.

But things were getting harder and harder for this small community of Black Oriental magicians. In December of 1921, an article on "the present situation of the colored performer" in *Billboard* lamented that "a few years ago it was customary to find a colored act on almost every vaudeville bill. What causes led to the discontinuance of the practice have not been disclosed. No doubt the reasons seemed sufficient to the powers concerned."[45] There were still a few "colored" acts among the top acts on the Keith, Orpheum, and Western vaudeville circuits, including James Weldon Johnson's brother Rosamond Johnson, composer in 1900 of "Lift Every Voice and Sing," the "Negro National Anthem." Princess Sotanki still was represented by the Theater Owners Booking Association, the main Black vaudeville booking association covering a huge territory from Philadelphia to San Antonio and Chicago to Tampa, Florida, along with blues singer Clara Smith, magician E. Alfred Drew, Thomas Cole, Butter Beans and Susie, Dounveer and Butterball, Prince and Princess Mysteria, and Williams and Williams. So Blacks were still working in vaudeville, but fewer of them were able to make it on the theatrical circuit at the dawn of the Jazz Age. There were fewer good answers to the plaintive question that E. Alfred Drew asked in his 1914 poem "Where Will We Go?"

Sing a song of summer,
Pocket full of dough,
Season was a hummer
Now where will we go?
'Ere the winter passes

Any place will do,
Just so they serve big glasses
And a piping bowl of stew.[46]

Even if US markets for Black vaudeville were contracting at the end of World War I, European ones were expanding. "The success of the American Negro in Europe is apparent from the press comment upon some of the acts," *Billboard* noted in 1921. "Negro artists are so plentiful in Paris as to have justified the opening of several business enterprises that cater almost exclusively to their trade."[47] Indeed, Walter and Eva Brister toured France in 1905, and a French photographer produced at least two postcards of Eva as Princess Sotanki. In one she reclines on her hip and elbow, looking like the cat that swallowed the canary, in the classic Orientalist pose of the odalisque or the opium smoker, a hip down posture that was the origins of the slang term "hipster."[48] She was said to have the reading gift of seeing the future, and she was no doubt able to see that the crisis in tented entertainment presented by the Great Migration created an even greater opportunity for those able to represent the Mystic East. Only a fool would underestimate the power and embodied brilliance of her performance in the dance of death she brought to life onstage, or the one she may have wrought offstage in real life.

CHAPTER EIGHT

PROFESSOR DREW

*According to all true and divine records of the human race
there is no negro, black or colored race attached to the human family, because all of the inhabitants of Africa were
and are of the human race, descendants of the ancient Canaanite nation from the holy land of Canaan.*

—PROPHET NOBLE DREW ALI, 1927[1]

What drives a man to fake his own death? It is a question worth
pondering. To fake one's own death is perhaps the most extreme form of social deception there is, far greater than merely assuming an alias, or pretending to be someone else. To fake one's
death, to erase one's existence, to live on beyond the grave, must be, in
a sense, the most self-destructive and yet strangely liberating action
a person can take. To attend one's own funeral, to free one's self of
debts, and to choose another identity; all of these are the prerogative
of the undead who walk among us. Someone does not take such a
radical step lightly; typically, one might surmise, a man who fakes
his own death is only a few steps ahead of someone who intends to
do him in for real. The reasons why someone might wish a man dead
are no doubt varied, but in 1914 debts owed and husbands cuckolded
were probably pretty high on that list. Walter Brister was a cornet
sideman with a short list of gigs that actually made the newspapers—I could find only a single reference to him playing cornet after
his childhood star turn on Broadway, and that was in a 1912 production of the show *Southland*, staged in Chicago. His wife's absence—in
1914, she was in Indianapolis performing as Princess Sotanki—his

own profession's lack of a regular paycheck, and its proximity to the underworld elements who haunted nightclubs where Black musicians played in Chicago all would have given him ample opportunity to get into trouble, whether related to finances or females. The fact that he later took four wives simultaneously would suggest that he did indeed have a thing for the ladies, and he certainly proved later on that he could navigate the gangster-infested waters of Chicago's South Side politics. But all this is mere speculation. We don't know why Walter Brister faked his own death; we simply know that he did from photographic proof that he survived and became Noble Drew Ali in 1925.

The few friends who might be able to shed light on his circumstances, fellow Black musicians and performers in the vaudeville era who sent him greetings via the entertainment columns of Black newspapers, have long since gone to their own graves. But something drove Brister to fake his death; his wife, Eva, was part of the plan, and the body that went into the ground in the bucolic Black-owned Lincoln Cemetery on the far South Side of Chicago on April 10, 1914, did not belong to John Walter Brister. So the question is, Whose body was it? Was there a body at all in the casket that Eva Brister buried with the help of undertaker R. W. Green, or merely a few bags of sand? Since an official would have had to pronounce Brister dead for a death certificate to be produced, Eva would have had to either bribe a doctor and an undertaker for a phony death certificate and burial certificate or, more likely, present another stiff as her husband. We know that Walter Brister survived because Noble Drew Ali in his photographs not only looks like Brister from his 1900 photographs in the role of Armmah Sotanki, but in both sets of photos he has a prominent mole on the same spot on the lower right side of his nose.

Immediately after he officially died in Chicago, John Walter Brister took up housekeeping in Newark at 181 Warren Street, either living with Thomas Drew, or living *as* Thomas Drew, as his advertisements and draft records indicate. The original Thomas Drew was either Brister's half brother or, more likely, his full brother. Thomas was eight years younger than Walter, and they shared a mother, Lucy Caldwell, who married the carpenter-turned bandleader John Henry Brister in Kentucky before his musical career took the family first to Cincinnati and then to New York City, where father and son starred together in *In Old Kentucky* beginning in 1893, when John Walter (he seldom used his given first name) was about fifteen and his younger brother Thomas would have been about seven. The hit show hit the road and somewhere along the line the elder Bristers' marriage hit the rocks—and according to the 1900 census, one "Lucy" had remarried a longshoreman in Norfolk, Virginia, named James Drew, and bore two children with him in 1898 and 1899. In 1900 this Lucy was living with James, the two young children, and Thomas, James Drew's now-adopted fourteen-year-old son, in Norfolk. Since I have not uncovered a marriage certificate for Lucy and James Drew, I cannot say for certain that this Lucy was the same as Lucy Caldwell Brister. But all the pieces fit together, and if she was the same Lucy, it would explain why Walter Brister took Thomas Drew's name: they shared a mother. By 1903, John Henry Brister had remarried as well, and passed away—his next wife, Grace, listed herself as J. H. Brister's widow in the Cincinnati city directory, just above Walter's listing. Walter, who was twenty-three in 1900, married the beautiful Eva Hammond that year in Hamilton County, Ohio, on a summer day of August 18, when Thomas was only fourteen and living in Norfolk.[2] In sum, in 1900, John Walter Brister was a very different person than his likely younger brother, Thomas (Brister) Drew; but by 1915 or so John Walter Brister was impersonating the man who was probably his younger sibling and presenting himself as "Professor Drew, the Egyptian Adept." It is possible that no matter what caused Thomas Drew's death, Walter could take Thomas's place in Newark because Thomas had taken his own place under the sod of Lincoln Cemetery. Walter cheated death, pulling off the greatest magic trick of all.

🦅   🦅   🦅

Barbershops are sacred spaces. In barbershops, clippers lop and fans circle. Men gather and tell tales, share gripes, exchange barbed jokes, and trade in some of the everyday abuses and hostilities of everyday life for their own space where friends and strangers can gather and recalibrate their basic humanity amid the aromatic smells of shaving cream and pomades. If this is true of barbershops in general, it was even more true of Black barbershops at the beginning of the twentieth century. Black communities in the North were extremely overcrowded, due to the racism that prevented residents from finding cheaper, more spacious living quarters outside the few neighborhoods open to Black settlement in Northern cities. And the barbershops in these communities were one of the few gathering places available to

African American migrants recently separated from homes and extended communities down South. They were also refuges from the racism "Negroes" experienced on the job or on the street. Blacks had developed their own elaborate versions of freemasonry dating back to the American Revolution, but barbershops, more so than official lodges, were one of the prime places where the people W. E. B. Du Bois called "black folk" developed that more informal kind of secret knowledge and fellowship that he termed "the freemasonry of the race." Thinking of barbershops as Black-dominated alternative public spaces makes it easier to see how a religion that taught an alternative version of Black history and sacred history could be born in the place where hair littered the floor and voices, tall tales, political speech, and laughter filled the air.

The last living follower of Noble Drew Ali reported that in 1913, the man who would eventually call himself Noble Drew Ali organized what became the Canaanite Temple in a barbershop in Newark, New Jersey.[3] But there is no definitive record showing that the temple's founding occurred in 1913, the year Princess Sotanki was supposed to have moved to Asbury Park, New Jersey, and married a wealthy magnate, or the following year, the year Princess Sotanki allegedly buried her husband, Walter Brister. We do not know if the Bristers relocated to New Jersey because Walter's little brother Thomas Drew was there, or if Drew's presence so close to Asbury Park was an unforeseen coincidence. In any case, Brister used his brother Thomas Drew's name when he registered for the draft, although some followers relate that his name was Timothy, not Thomas. James Walker, the last survivor of the Newark group, remembered in a 1981 interview that he first met the Muslim prophet who went by the name Drew at the "Dixion" Barbershop on Newark's Warren Street in 1913, just before the Great War started. This was undoubtedly the barbershop of Samuel Dixon, a barber who owned a barbershop at 174 Warren Street and lived at 181 Warren Street.[4] In those days, Walker reported, the barbershop was "the neighborhood social center," as the men known as Negroes had no place to meet and no money, either. At the time Drew had no steady job, but worked part-time, like many Black men struggling to make ends meet in Northern cities.

Sometime in this period, Brister started to advertise himself as "Professor Drew," a healer and spiritual teacher. He distributed a card that started off with the simple, declarative statement: "I am a Moslem." "Professor Drew is a man who was born with Divine power," the card read. "He was taught by the Adepts of Egypt." Drew claimed to have the secret to destroying tuberculosis or cancer of the lungs in ten to thirty days. He also promised to be able to destroy stomach cancer, gout, rheumatism, lumbago, heart trouble, "female diseases," and other serious afflictions. But healing was only part of Professor Drew's expertise. "I also give Divine instructions and interpret the Bible from Genesis to Revelations," the card read. But even more spectacularly, he had secret knowledge "for all who desire to know more about Jesus the Christ," claiming to know about the eighteen years of Christ's life that are missing in the Bible. He held office hours in the morning and the evenings each day at the home he shared with the barber Samuel Dixon at 181 Warren Street, in the heart of the Central Ward with its small but growing population of about four thousand Black Americans.[5]

With the outbreak of World War I and the opening up of wartime jobs to "Negroes," Walker and Drew both found work at the Submarine Boat Corporation on Eighteenth Avenue in Newark. The group that used to convene at the barbershop could not do so as frequently, since most of the men were now working ten or twelve hours a day, but they met in the shop on the weekends. The group expanded as war jobs in Newark continued to attract Black migrants. These members of the largest wave of Black migration since the end of slavery outgrew the barbershop, and in May of 1916 they established a meeting place they called the "Canaanite Temple" over a saloon at Rutgers Street and Twelfth Avenue, half a mile closer to the Passaic River. Drew was the main preacher, and in former member Walker's recollection, he preached from the Bible that "we came out of the Holy Land of Canaan, we were a Holy people and, we was not Negroes, Colored peoples, and, Christianity was not the religion of our people and, we were not Christians but Muslim."[6]

The war also brought a mandatory draft, and on September 12, 1918, the man who called himself Thomas Drew reported to a local school and registered for the armed services, giving his address as 181 Warren Street, the same place he listed for his "office hours" as "Professor Drew, the Egyptian Adept Student." He was of medium height with a medium build, black hair, and dark eyes. The muscles of his forearms were badly burned, the inspector noted. He listed his birthday as January 8, 1886, and his nearest relative was an uncle, Ambros Drew, of Norfolk, Virginia.[7] Drew had ample opportunity to volunteer for the war and, like most Americans, did not do so. He only registered when compelled to do so in the third wave of registrations, when the upper limit of the age range of the draft was expanded from thirty to forty-five. In any case, Drew was entitled to an industrial deferment as an industrial war worker, and was therefore not at risk of being conscripted.[8]

Samuel Dixon, the barber whose shop bore his name, was a Christian preacher on the side, and though he started out as Drew's assistant, they had words over Drew's claim that the proper religion of people then known as "Negroes" was Islam, not Christianity. In 1919, Dixon wrested control of the temple from Drew, who told census takers the following year that he was now a street preacher, having left his congregation above the saloon behind.[9] But although he lost his congregation, Drew remained in Newark and worked at least some of the time alongside Walker, perhaps as late as 1922.[10] Given that within a few years Professor Drew would be charging a week's wages or more for healing services to patrons, it would seem unlikely that this same person would have been willing to work an assembly line job so long. Yet during the war, the very nature of the work protected its workers from the draft. And then there is the fact that it took several years for Brister to start presenting himself as Professor Drew, and so maybe having a steady paycheck was helpful while he was putting his act together, or when rebounding from one of his three convictions as Thomas Drew for practicing medicine without a license.

The savagery of submarine warfare in the Atlantic choked off European immigration during the First World War, and labor recruiters scoured the South for Black workers, promising good jobs at fair wages in attractive quarters like Harlem, New York City, and the South Side of Chicago, just as the boll weevil beetle devastated Southern cotton crops, and after decades of racist violence and segregation had made many Blacks long to improve their lives elsewhere. However, what migrants discovered when they arrived were overcrowded, overpriced, and disease-ridden quarters, as well as a scarcity of medical doctors and hospitals to attend to the burgeoning numbers of new residents. Black healers, root doctors, and conjure men and women stepped in to fill the void with all kinds of remedies, many of which were already familiar to transplanted Southerners both from traditions of using healing herbs stretching back to African ancestors, and from the medicine shows that crisscrossed rural America in the nineteenth century, providing entertainment and elixirs in equal measure. These folk healers' self-assured advertisements filled Black newspapers' back pages, while stories of their numerous arrests for practicing medicine without licenses filled the front pages.

Thomas Drew suffered his first known arrest in 1916 in Harlem, for fortune-telling and practicing medicine without a license, and served five months of an eighteen-month sentence for the first charge, after which he was released before Christmas, having promised to settle his court fees in cash. He was back in the coils of the law again in 1920, when he was still working out of 181 Warren Street in Newark, where he saw patients for a variety of medical ailments, presenting himself as an "Egyptian Adept Student," and as a mysterious "Moslem" gifted with divine powers. Under dim light, from an inner office behind a waiting room where four Black customers waited, Drew prayed, "Allah! Allah! Disperse these ailments!" He testified that he cured by using waters, oils, and the laying on of hands, and that he had special healing powers thanks to his horoscope and birth date of January 8. He instructed a patient to keep quiet during the healing or risk dispersing "the Divine influence," and to take five deep breaths and exhale over his shoulder to "dispel the evil influence." As Professor Drew, Walter Brister's stock of medicines consisted of a large amount of liquids that smelled of sassafras and a lot of bottles filled with salts, according to one skeptical reporter for the *Newark Evening News*. His clients were mostly but not exclusively "Negroes," and they were spread across every big city on the East Coast. Drew received large sums from some; he charged one "colored" woman nine dollars for the first of a series of treatments for heart disease, approximately what a typical Black woman of the time made in a week of domestic service.

He charged another Black patient, Harlem resident Alice Hopkins, twenty-one dollars to cure her degenerative eye disease. Hopkins claimed in sworn court testimony that Drew had hypnotized her by waving his handkerchief slowly in front of her face, and then relieved her of a valuable bracelet, although Drew was never tried for the alleged theft. Hopkins's blindness only worsened. "I have cured and I have proof of it, the living proof," Drew boasted, claiming that he had even raised a man from the grave in Elizabeth, New Jersey, according to the *Newark Evening News*. "Before people can be cured they must trust in their God and believe in me," Drew told the court.

"And bring a little cash," the lawyer who was paid to represent him quipped, to which Drew nodded solemnly, either missing the jab from his own attorney or choosing to ignore it. By implying that his own client was a crook, his lawyer might have been trying to spare him a much longer sentence as an insane person. Indeed, the prosecution questioned Drew's sanity when he claimed to be divine and therefore refused to take an oath. The judge called a forty-five-minute recess so that Drew could undergo an examination by a white physician, who declared him not only sane but quite shrewd. Given the choice of risking a criminal conviction or going to the insane asylum, Drew chose to demonstrate his sanity and take his chances with the criminal trial. He testified under oath, and was found guilty of practicing medicine without a license. "Professor Drew" was arrested for the same charge once again in New York in December of 1923, when he claimed to be a "divine healing teacher" but failed to satisfy a patient he treated for tuberculosis. In retrospect, these run-ins with the law were bumps in the road, not the end of the line, for the Muslim man of mystery.[11]

🕊   🕊   🕊

"Professor Drew" was only one of many Black medicine men in the greater New York area before and after World War I who identified as "Moslems" and sold cures in the long tradition of "Afro-American" conjure, magical root work, and mystical occult "science." Some, like Drew and Prince Ali Mona, had backgrounds performing as emissaries of the Mystic East in the many tented shows that toured America at the turn of the century. As the Great Migration disturbed those circuits of commercial entertainment, Prince Ali Mona turned to crystal gazing, a time-honored Western occult practice with allegedly Oriental roots; the authorities in Springfield, Ohio, took a dim view when they arrested him in 1922.[12]

Even if Prince Ali Mona could not tell what the future held for colored practitioners of Oriental magic when he convened a gathering of fellow "Negro" Oriental magicians in 1915, by 1922 he was telling the future at one of the destination points of the Great Migration. What we can tell from Ali Mona's choices and those of the other African Americans who performed as Hindoo magicians between the turn of the century and World War II was that they were not alone in presenting themselves as Hindus. They were part of networks of

Black performers who corresponded with one another and knew one another. They were part of even longer traditions of representing the Mystic East in magic and religion and performing a specific genre of Hindoo—and, to a lesser extent, Arabic—magic that was a Western reproduction of feats European travelers witnessed in Muslim India. But for Black performers and audiences, the Mystic East carried different associations and different political possibilities than it did for white performers and audiences. Namely, when Black performers represented the East they were not simply representing "the Other"; they were also, implicitly, representing Black people themselves. Over the course of the 1920s, the forms of Black embodiment of Orientalist identities pioneered for circus sideshows, Midways of fairs, and vaudeville stages expanded into the new "colored" quarters of Northern cities. As one observer wrote in the Black-owned *New York Amsterdam News*, Harlem's streets were "full of turbaned 'wise men'" telling fortunes and selling herbs and roots.[13] That Prince Ali Mona was arrested for crystal gazing at the beginning of the Jazz Age suggests that as "Negroes" migrated to Northern cities, and as Black acts fell off the vaudeville circuits, and as "coon shouters" gave way to blues and jazz crooners, the "colored" magicians who had made a living on the tented show circuit began to turn instead to service the spiritual and healing needs of large populations of Americans of Arican descent now concentrated in the urban North.

🐦   🐦   🐦

Orientalist images were common in Black culture of the 1920s, as they were in American culture more generally. Harlem's Unique Colony Circle of America held an Oriental Costume Ball in 1926, much as Oriental balls were common in New York City's white society.[14] Rudolph Valentino's *Sheik* movies were hits in Harlem's theaters, and Harlem slang transformed young male hipsters into fashionable "sheiks." The sheik's female equivalent was the "sheba," in honor of the biblical Queen of Sheba, ruler of Ethiopia and lover of King Solomon. Orientalism was a major theme of early films, with seventeen movies with "sheik" in their titles and nine more featuring sheiks in their plots in the 1920s alone, along with such Orientalist fare as *Cleopatra* (1917), *Salome* (1918), *One Arabian Night* (1920), *Kismet* (1920), *The Slim Princess* (1915), and three film versions of the hit play *The Garden of Allah*. Frequently such films played in movie theaters designed to mimic the grandeur of Oriental palaces, such as the stunning Oriental Theater in Chicago, which opened in 1926, or the equally opulent Fox Theater in Atlanta, opened in 1929, which featured Moorish ornamentation and a mosque-like minaret.

Popular songs distributed through sheet music featured their own slew of Islamic Orientalist imagery. Tin Pan Alley tunesmiths Harry B. Smith, Frances Wheeler, and Ted Snyder wrote the famous "Sheik of Araby" in 1921 to accompany the hit Rudolph Valentino film *The Sheik*, and the song achieved such fame that it became an early New Orleans jazz standard, recorded by such stars as Fats Waller and Louis Armstrong. It even made it into the novel *The Great Gatsby*. But "The Sheik of Araby" was just the tip of the Orientalist sandstorm that blew through European and American popular culture at the beginning of the twentieth century, with scores of songs that made nodding references to Allah and Islam but that fixated on the Islamic Orient as dreamlike, and its women as sexually alluring. A song like "My Lily of the Nile," published by the indefatigable impresario and future congressman Sol Bloom in 1902, illustrates this obsession that arose from the popularity of the Islamic exhibits on the 1893 Midway and in later festivals and fairgrounds: "In the town of Bun-gel-boo, on the river Nile so blue, Where the lotus lilies idly nod and dream . . ." Stand-alone popular songs were not the only form of entertainment fixated on these tropes; musical revues and silent films also featured Orientalist songs; sometimes, as with the musical play *Algeria*, Orientalism provided the central theme. The legendary songwriter Irving Berlin released "Araby" in 1915 with a memorable couplet that commented on the tropes of the craze: "Tonight I'm dreaming of Araby, That's where my dreams seem to carry me / Where everything is Oriental; / And everyone is sentimental." The theme was continued in popular song through the teens and twenties, but the Western obsession with forbidden Islamic sexuality, complete with a kinky longing to surrender imperial power in the Oriental boudoir, was perhaps never expressed so clearly as in 1926's "That Night in Araby": "Oh! what that one night meant, why did I ever leave your tent? Child of the Orient? I'm dreaming of that night of love with you in Araby. . . . Your harem eyes just made a slave of me."[15]

Images of the Orient appeared from the funny pages to the editorial pages of Black newspapers. In the mid-twenties, a "colored" performer named Joe Downing went by the name Joveddah de Raja and dispensed "words of Oriental comfort and wisdom" on a New York radio

station.[16] Many contemporary accounts of Harlem note the large number of mystics plying their trades: "Black art flourishes in Harlem—
and elsewhere in New York," Winthrop D. Lane wrote in 1925.
"Egyptian seers uncover hidden knowledge, Indian fortune-tellers reveal the future, sorcerers perform their mysteries. Feats of witchcraft
are done daily. A towel for a turban and a smart manner are enough
to transform any Harlem colored man into a dispenser of magic to his
profit."[17] There were storefront shops dedicated to selling candles, incense, powders, books, and other spiritual supplies, and every stationary store in Harlem carried a selection of dream and mystery books,
many of which used Orientalist themes, such as the *Oriental Dream
Book, with interpretations of all dreams as vouched for by the Orientals,
Gypsies, witches, Egyptians, augors, astrologers, magi, fortune-tellers, soothsayers, prophets, seers and wise men of ancient and modern times*, by C.
B. Case, published in Chicago in 1916.[18]

Professor Drew, who proclaimed himself to be a Muslim, was
only one of many self-proclaimed "Professors of Oriental and African Mystic Science" in Harlem who constructed the Black Orient
and the Black self in one motion by writing themselves into this romantic Orientalist imaginary. Advertisements in the era's *New York
Amsterdam News* reveal dozens of Oriental Scientists, including Professor J. Du Jaja, "A Mohammedan Scientist," of the Asia and Africa
Remedy Company, Professor S. Indoo of African Science, "Native of
Nigeria," and Professor Eyo, "A Mohammedan scientist and Oriental Occultism [sic], Native of Africa just arrived." The famous Harlem magician Herman Rucker also freely used Orientalist imagery
in his autobiography, which boasted of fantastical feats in Africa and
the Orient before he became a magical sensation in New York.[19]

It is an open question as to how these men were received among
their Black peers. Did most people view them as fakes and frauds, or
did most view them credulously as representatives of Oriental faiths
and dimly understood, faraway lands? There is evidence of both positions, with the elite discourse of the newspapers and editorialists
commonly ridiculing the street mystics, whom they depicted as sexual deviants and charlatans. Yet the omnipresent advertisements of
the mystics testify to the fact that they had large and loyal followings
who relied on their fortune-telling and healing services.

These figures called themselves scientists because a scientist, in
Black speech, was a religious master, a person learned in secret magical religious practices.[20] They were also scientists because scientists

held cultural, quasi-magical powers in the 1920s, when physics and chemistry were beginning to tear back the veil of the universe and expose its fundamental laws. As one advertisement put it, "Science and Oriental is great wonder."[21] But they also were scientists because they were pushing the frontiers of human knowledge, in the spiritual realm rather than the material one. In the words of Aubrey Browser's *Negro Times*, spiritualists "are groping after truth just as the most advanced scientists are doing, and they may uncover some aspects of the subject which the wisest have not as yet been able to reduce to understandable formulation."[22]

In marked contrast to the aversion to Africa in respectable "colored" society, many of these men claimed to be from Africa, and it was common to advertise one's proximity to Africa—it was a bonus if either the scientist or his incense had "just arrived" from Africa.[23] Yet these street scientists expanded hoodoo's identification with Africa as the source of magic, adding another category called "the Orient" that often overlapped with "Africa." India was the key constituent of this Oriental imaginary, but African Islam also featured prominently in the advertisements, and China made a few appearances as well. Sometimes the ads mixed India and Africa, as in the case of "S. Indoo [Hindu] of African Science," or "Professor Domingo, the Hindu Occulist [*sic*] and Healer from Kano West Africa." As scholar Carolyn Morrow Long notes, the image of the Hindu swami was ubiquitous in Black spiritual advertisements and products as a symbol of occult knowledge. An investigator among Southern "Negroes" in the late thirties and early forties discovered the common belief that occult knowledge and spiritual products originated with Hindus, and of course the Sotankis and their fellow Black Oriental magicians had long made a living by representing "Hindoo" magic.[24]

The newspaper advertisements of these healers, mystics, and self-proclaimed scientists show that they were deeply concerned with the contemporary conversation about what it meant to be civilized, but redirected it using Orientalism. One prominent example was the self-proclaimed magician and alchemist who variously went by the names Professor Akpan Aga, Professor Akpandac, Dr. B. Grant, and Alla Gui Barn. His advertisements pictured him in either a fez or a turban and claimed he was a native of Africa and a "Professor of African and Oriental Occultism, Psychic Science, White and Black Magic, etc." Aga's many identities contradicted each other, yet that does not make his message any less interesting. In December of 1922 his advertisements began appearing in Harlem newspapers as "Professor Akpan Aga, Wonderful Magician and Spiritualist by Alchemy and Fire."

By January he was calling himself Professor Akpandac, and had a confederate named Dr. B. Grant. Those early advertisements pictured him in a turban, and preached about Jesus, mixing commerce and evangelism in a manner common to many religious entrepreneurs. By February he had moved to 129th Street and was calling himself "Alla Gui Barn, Professor Akpandac." To match his new Islamic identity, he appeared in his advertisement wearing a fez, concluding the ad copy with "Allah Be Praised!" The month of March saw a return of the turban, but the fez advertisements came back in April and May. Aga/Akpandac/Barn was not finished transforming himself, however. In August he began calling himself Professor Edeteffiong, Professor of African and Oriental Occultism, Psychic Science, White and Black Magic, Etc. Native of Africa. Advice Given—Egyptian and African Formulae Used." Edeteffiong became "Professor Edet. Effiong" in September, October, and November, but he also used the old fez picture in an advertisement for the "Peamanda Co.," which sold "Oriental Incense."

His advertisements disappeared from Harlem newspapers only to reappear in 1925 through 1929 as Edet Effiong or Effiong Offiong, of the Nigeria Remedy Company, Dealer in Roots and Herbs. In this final incarnation, he dropped all references to Christianity. Now he wore a turban with Bedouin robes and claimed to be a "Mohammedan Master of Stricter African Science."[25] Perhaps he switched names so often to escape prosecution—it was not uncommon for healers to be sued for selling remedies that did not work as promised, or arrested for practicing medicine without a license, as happened to Professor Drew. Aga-Akpandac-Barn-Effiong-Offiong's luck finally ran out when he was arrested for interstate mail fraud for selling an Indianapolis man a powder guaranteed to return anything that had been lost, from a lover to a cow. Another customer was a prisoner who had bought a powder that was said to be able to spring him free from jail. At the end of the day, Aga's "Oriental and African Science" looked a lot like Southern hoodoo remedies.[26] More likely than not, Aga/ Akpanandac, etc. was the same person as Professor Akpan Essien, "a mystery healer of the Mohammedan cult," who was arrested and jailed in Washington, DC, in August of 1923 on charges of practicing medicine without a license. If that was the cause, then his given name was not Aga or Akpandac or Effiong, but Thomas Williams.[27]

Yet the obvious fraudulence of Professor Akpandac's self-presentation does not mean that Black Orientalists were not sincerely challenging the racism of the white discourse of civilization with the more complex claims of a version of Orientalism that placed "Afro-American" origins in the Muslim East. It would be a mistake, in other words, to disregard the ideas of someone who exchanged identities so freely. The Bible in general and the life of Jesus in particular provided the lens through which many Americans viewed the Orient. Professor Drew also sold a booklet for a dollar containing secret knowledge of "eighteen years of Christ life that is silent to your Holy Bible for all those who desire to know more about Jesus, the Christ," a version of Levi Dowling's *The Aquarian Gospel of Jesus the Christ* that Drew would make one of the foundational texts of his *Holy Koran of the Moorish Science Temple*. Like Drew, and his later persona, Noble Drew Ali, Akpandac preached a version of this text that taught that Oriental mysteries were the source of Jesus's powers, and that Christianity had cribbed its dogma from Eastern mythology. Akpandac explained:

> When the statement is made that Christ was a Master, it means, literally speaking, that Christ was Master of Himself, educated and trod the path, receiving the instruction of the Masters in India and the Orient. This is a well-known fact and is also a matter of record that Christ did belong to the ancient school of India.[28]

According to Aga and other professors of mystic science, the Orient was the source of otherworldly powers, a reservoir of mysteries and magic that was superior to, and generative of, the religions of the West.

Aga and other mystic scientists like Professor Drew depicted the Oriental East as the necessary counterpart to the materialistic West, a message that had particular resonance given the disheartening spectacle of World War I's mechanized warfare and the life experience of Black migrants who had left homes in mostly rural states and settled in cities in the industrialized North. Aga's ads argued that humans had learned to control the material world through Western technology, but must turn to "the ancient occult mysteries of Africa and India" in order to gain spiritual wisdom. There were many variations on this theme of Western materialism versus "Oriental" spirituality among the several dozen mystic healers who advertised in Harlem newspapers. A man who called himself Amadu, "the Mohammedan scientist dealing in religious incense," wrote that the modern materialist "commercializes everything and is blind to hidden Spiritual truths. . . . To Africa and the Orient, therefore, we must turn if we desire to benefit from these archaic truths."[29] Another motivation for embracing the Orient could be distancing oneself from Africa and the legacies of American slavery.

But as numerous as the Mohammedan scientists were, and as profitable as selling root tonics and hoodoo charms and powders could be, it was a risky business that carried with it the constant threat of arrest and imprisonment for practicing medicine without a license. Religious figures and leaders of secret fraternal societies, on the other hand, enjoyed more immunity from prosecution. Just when Newark's Professor Thomas Drew went to jail for his last arrest in December of 1923, another figure came to prominence who would provide the trailblazing model for the founding of an Islamic religious organization rooted in Black culture, a man who would become Drew's teacher in things both Muslim and Masonic.

As scholar Patrick Bowen has demonstrated, the figure who was most widely known as "Abdul Hamid Suleiman" first called himself "Dr. Prince de Solomon," and seems to have started as a Baptist preacher who addressed the Maryland Colored Baptist Convention in 1906 as "Rev. Dr. P.D. Solomon."[30] Three years later he gave a speech in New York, and in 1910 the census listed him as a lodger in Harlem who was single and forty-six years old, and allegedly was an African who had made the voyage to the United States in 1908. In 1913 he got in trouble and was thrust back into the newspapers for threatening to murder his wife, Lulu, who refused to return to their home unless he was jailed. Not surprisingly, by the time the 1920 census rolled around he was single again, but was now living in Mercer, Pennsylvania, only thirty miles from the steel mill town of Youngstown, Ohio, where he organized the first "Mecca Medina Temple of A.F. & A.M." (Ancient Free and Accepted Masons) on July 15, 1920. His cofounder was the Reverend Robert B. Mount, with whom he had associated since at least 1909.[31]

After a period as a rabbi in one of many Black Israelite movements, during which time he called himself "Solomon," he Arabicized his name to "Suleiman" and taught Oriental languages in Harlem while attempting to convert Blacks to Islam in the years following World War I, first concentrating on Black freemasons and Shriners and then expanding his scope to focus on all "Negro" New Yorkers.[32] Suleiman spoke as an advocate of "Mohammedan Masonry" at a dinner in April of 1922 attended by Marcus Garvey supporters John Edward Bruce, Duse Mohamed Ali, and noted Harlem bibliophile Arturo Schomburg. The "Abdul Hamid Suleiman," who spoke at that Harlem Masonic dinner with many prominent Garveyites in attendance in April of 1922 was "a walking encyclopedia on things Masonic," in the words of Garvey's *Negro World* newspaper.[33] By then, Suleiman lived in Harlem and claimed to be Sudanese, much like Garvey's mentor, Duse Mohamed Ali. His chosen name was a reference to Sultan Abdul Hamid II of the Ottoman Empire, who ruled from 1876 until the Young Turk Revolution of 1908, and garnered much sympathy from Duse Mohamed Ali and other Black opponents of European imperialism.

Patrick Bowen has mustered sources, if not definitive proof, suggesting that Suleiman gained a following among Drew's former followers in Newark's Canaanite Temple in the year 1923, when *Smart Set*, the highbrow literary magazine that was the first to publish F. Scott Fitzgerald, reported that "Moslem groups have been started in New Jersey, one of them at Newark, where a mosque has been established. From there the Islamic missionaries will move upon the South."[34] The core of Suleiman's teaching was that Islam opposed racism and permitted genuine brotherhood between all people, an approach that appealed to African Americans living under the oppressive conditions of Jim Crow segregation.

Some accounts say that one "Dr. Suleiman" was Professor Drew's teacher and that Drew ventured to Chicago only after Suleiman went to jail, which seems likely since Drew incorporated many important elements from the Nobles of the Mystic Shrine, with their secret Islamic initiation ritual. In addition to reverence for Islam, he shared the title used for members, "Noble," and the fez. Indeed, Suleiman did in fact go to jail: by the summer of 1923 he had mustered a few hundred followers between Harlem and Newark, but he was soon arrested and convicted of the rape of the thirteen-year-old daughter of one of his members—after he spent nine consecutive nights with his members' children. He served a prison sentence and returned to Harlem as a fortune-teller in 1927, a few years after Drew's Moorish Temple of Science had gained seven thousand members and became the first Muslim mass movement in America, and watched a Black man who called himself "Sufi Abdul Hamid" obtain even greater notoriety in Harlem as a leader of boycotts of white, Jewish-run Harlem businesses that refused to hire Black workers. Wearing a turban and cape and spouting anti-Jewish rhetoric, the second Hamid, born Eugene Brown, got himself labeled "the Black Hitler of Harlem" for his anti-Jewish invective hurled from stepladders during his boycotts. Sulieman passed away on July 30, 1934, but he lived long enough to see the success of varieties of his vision of Muslim Masonry in both the Moorish Science Temple and its successor group, the Nation of Islam, also known as the "Black Muslims."[35]

🦅   🦅   🦅

The political dimension of identifying as Muslim is what gave force to the first Black Muslim movements, whether in an inchoate form—reading the fine print of the mystic scientists of the Harlem Renaissance—or, in more explicit terms, in the publications of Marcus Garvey's Black Nationalist movement. Marcus Mosiah Garvey (1887–1940) was a Jamaican printer whose interest in Pan-African Black solidarity was awakened by witnessing the suffering of people of African descent who had settled in Central America during the building of the Panama Canal. He lived in London from 1912 to 1914, during which time he sought out the Black Nationalist journalist Duse Mohamed Ali and published in Ali's *African Times and Orient Review*. Upon Garvey's return to Jamaica in 1914 he founded the Universal Negro Improvement Association (UNIA), and sailed for the United States in March 1916 intending to raise funds for a school in the West Indies modeled on Booker T. Washington's Tuskegee Institute.

Moving to New York, where he worked as a printer and was influenced by the great West Indian orator Hubert Harrison, Harlem's stepladder Socrates who turned New York intersections into open-air universities, Garvey electrified crowds with his stirring oratory and an electrifying vision of international Black solidarity. He founded another chapter of the UNIA in Harlem in 1917, and it rapidly spread throughout the United States and around the world, attracting as many as two million followers and readers of its periodical, the *Negro World*. Garvey's old mentor, Duse, came to New York in October of 1921 and began to edit and write for the paper, infusing it with much of the same belief in anticolonialism, anti-imperialism, and independent Black commercial enterprise that had characterized his previous publication in London. Meanwhile, the Rif War in Morocco from 1921 to 1926 brought Morocco to newfound prominence, and infused Moorish identity with revolutionary street credibility, as Berber guerrillas fought French and Spanish troops in northern Morocco, a conflict that was widely covered by the *Negro World*.[36]

The Garvey movement not only continued and amplified Duse's influence, but also that of Reverend Edward Wilmot Blyden, who more than anyone had popularized the notion of Islam as a religion uniquely opposed to racism, and hence well suited to African peoples. Garvey was a fan of Blyden's stirring prose, as was Garvey's mentor, Harrison. John Edward Bruce, the former American correspondent for Duse's *African Times and Orient Review*, had actually been a personal friend of Blyden's, was a mentor of Harrison's, contributed to the *Negro World*, and was a leading figure in the UNIA.[37] It was no accident that the Garvey movement fostered a revival of interest in Islam's status as a Black religion; in 1923, the *Negro World* published an article by UNIA secretary general Robert L. Poston called "The Cross or the Crescent," debating whether Christianity or Islam was more appropriate for Black people and commending Muslim antipathy toward the "arrogant European." The *Negro World* published a similar article, "Crescent or Cross," the following year, as well as sympathetic treatments of Islam such as Bruce's speech linking Islam to anticolonial struggle in Africa, and Indian Muslim Ahmadiyya missionary Mufti Muhammad Sadiq's address to the Harlem chapter of the UNIA. (The Ahmadiyya Muslims were followers of Prophet Mirzā Ghulām Ahmad [1835–1908], a religious leader from northern India whose devotees actively evangelized in India, West Africa, the US, and elsewhere.) For Garveyites, Islam's potential to fight white racism and imperialism was an intrinsic part of its appeal. "With Millions of Moslems the World Over, Pressure Can Be Brought to Solve the Race Question," read part of the subhead of the "Crescent or Cross" article by Jamaican UNIA leader J. A. O'Meally. The Ahmadiyya movement, searching for African American converts to Islam in Chicago and other American cities, reprinted the article approvingly. The possibility that "El Islam" might become "the religion of the Negro" "is an awful nightmare to the white man," causing him to live "in fear and trembling," O'Meally wrote, because Islam teaches its followers to be "manly, self-respecting, charitable and ambitious." Malcolm X's father was a member of the Garvey movement, and in language that foreshadowed Malcolm's critique of the Christian-led nonviolent civil rights movement by more than forty years, O'Meally claimed that unlike a Black Christian, who waits for "the good white man to restore him his rights, the follower of the prophet is always ready to draw his sword in defense of sacred right and honor." Like Blyden, O'Meally observed that "Islam knows nothing of segregation or discrimination," and set no limit on Black religious or political advancement. Islam's anticolonial appeal had been winning it tens of millions of converts in recent decades on the African continent, and Islam had begun to make inroads in America as well, with over one hundred conversions to Islam in three months of 1923 alone.[38] For O'Meally, the spread of "El Islam cannot help but benefit the U.N.I.A." for both were preparing for an ultimate racial conflict between Black people worldwide and white racists and imperialists.

The same year, the Ahmadiyya Muslim missionaries in Chicago amplified the same message by running an article claiming that Islam was "the real solution of the Negro question." Addressing the reader with "Dear American Negro," and a hearty "Assalam-o-Alaikum. Peace be with you and the mercy of Allah," the Muslim missionaries wrote that "the Christian profiteers brought you out of your native lands of African and in Christianizing you made you forget the language of your forefathers—which were Islam and Arabic." But Christianity had proven to be "no good," a failure. "Christianity cannot bring real brotherhood to the nations. So, now leave it alone. And join Islam, the real faith of Universal Brotherhood." The Ahmadis promoted their "School of Islam and the Arabic Language," and invited all to join and "be blessed." The message, which was so resonant with Black Nationalist critiques of racism both present and past, found a receptive audience among the people then called "Negroes." One Garveyite was said to rise at the end of almost every Ahmadiyya meeting in Chicago in these years and declare that he was "glad that somebody was finally teaching the black man's religion in America." The Garvey movement did not create the interest in Islam among Black Americans, and Garvey himself or the UNIA's committee on religion never endorsed conversion to Islam, but the movement helped to bring together like-minded Islam-loving people and spread the idea that Islam was indeed "the black man's religion," and a potent weapon in the global fight against white supremacy.[39]

🦅   🦅   🦅

Back in his Newark days before the war, Thomas Drew had claimed special knowledge of the life of Jesus Christ, and used this knowledge to attract patients and followers. But apparently denying Christianity altogether went too far for the congregation that met first in the barbershop and then in the temple above the saloon. Nonetheless, the Canaanite Temple taught Drew that he could attract followers, create a society, found a meeting place, and begin to influence his followers as "a man born with Divine power" who was, he declared, "a Moslem." Perhaps he could not go all the way from fellow line worker and barbershop regular to prophet in one go, but he would take the lessons he learned in the small Black community in Newark and as a fortune-teller and root doctor in New York and apply them a few years later on another stage: Chicago. By continuing his healing and sale of medicinal roots, while also denying "Negro" racial identity and adding a clarion call to Black people to "return" to Islam, the religion of their "Moorish" ancestors, Drew harnessed pro-Muslim Black Nationalist ideology developed by Blyden, Duse, and the Garvey movement, used familiar Shriner regalia and rituals like Suleiman, repackaged Orientalist esoteric publications of De Laurence and the root work of countless African American hoodoo doctors, and awed audiences with Houdini-like "Hindoo" escape magic honed during his days as the sideshow magician "Armmah Sotanki," much like other magicians who called themselves "Drew" or "Ali." This potent and compelling combination would demonstrate Drew's spiritual powers and spark a religious revolution. It was a beachhead that opened the way for even larger waves of Black conversion to Islam in decades to come.

CHAPTER NINE

CHICAGO RACKETS

Listen, don't you get the idea I'm one of those goddamn radicals. Don't get the idea I'm knocking the American system. . . . My rackets are run on strictly American lines and they're going to stay that way. This American system of ours, call it Americanism, call it capitalism, call it what you like, gives to each and every one of us a great opportunity if we only seize it with both hands and make the most of it.

—AL CAPONE, 1929[1]

At eight o'clock on the evening of March 14, 1929, Claude D. Greene, business manager of the Moorish Science Temple of America, was murdered on the second floor of the stately Moorish Revival brick community center known as Unity Hall at 3140 S. Indiana Avenue in Chicago. He was found in a pool of blood with a gunshot wound and four deep knife gashes in his neck and stomach, crumpled over on his knees, as if he had been begging for his life when he was killed. The wound in his abdomen was so deep that it partially disemboweled him, while the bullet either entered his heart or went behind his ear, according to conflicting accounts.[2] The murder was "one of the most atrocious ever committed on the Southside," according to the *Baltimore Afro-American*.[3] Police hastened to the home of the Prophet Noble Drew Ali, the leader of the Moorish Science Temple, a few blocks away, where a feast was in progress with members of the "slaying crew" who had done the deed, according to the testimony of Unity Hall's janitor. The man known as "Noble Drew Ali" was arrested, along with forty members of his Moorish

Science Temple. In the coming weeks, the police hauled in just about every member of his organization they encountered. The Moors were easy to spot, as the women wore red turbans and the men sported beards and red fezzes. The murder of Claude Greene was the beginning of the end of Noble Drew Ali's reign. He himself would be dead four months later, although the mechanism by which the Grim Reaper collected the Islamic prophet is still disputed.

It was the slaying, and the spectacularly violent nature of the killing, that turned Chicago's South Side power brokers against Noble Drew Ali and the Moors and foreshadowed numerous violent clashes between the police and the Moors in subsequent years. Coming as it did exactly a month after the infamous Saint Valentine's Day Massacre, when gangsters affiliated with South Side don Al Capone machine-gunned rivals from the Irish North Side "Bugs" Moran gang, the Greene murder brought unsavory associations with the gangland killings then transfixing and horrifying Chicago and the world. "The latest approved methods of murder were employed," publisher Robert Abbott's *Chicago Defender* editorialized acidly, "all of which gives one the impression that, in murder, as in other things, we are getting more like white folks every day." Abbott's paper did not intend the comparison as a compliment. "We need no Al Capone and Moran gangs," the *Defender* continued. "We can get along well without hired murder gangs and even those powers behind the throne that pay the bills. If this Moorish order will breed this sort of occupation it should be disbanded. We have enough to contend with besides adding such crimes as this to our already crowded list."[4]

And yet until the violent events on the eve of the Ides of March in 1929, the Moors had received only positive coverage in the newspapers, and their leader was received with diplomatic courtesy by public officials ranging from the postmaster to Chicago's Black politicians to the governor of Illinois. "President Ali teaches fundamental principles which are desired for civilization, such as obedience to law, respect and loyalty to government, tolerance and unity," the *Defender* had remarked approvingly only nine months before Greene met his violent end. The group's many successful businesses exemplified the Booker T. Washingtonian emphasis on collective economic enterprise endorsed by every important "Negro" leader of the day, and showed that "the members of the Moorish temple and their leader have a sound economic program and are blazing the trail and marking the pathway over which our posterity may travel unhampered and unafraid," as the *Defender* wrote eight months before Greene's slaying.[5] But after the murder, and a violent clash between the Moors and the police that left two officers dead the following September, the Moorish Science Temple of America was investigated and denounced as a "racket," like the many rackets that defined both economic and political life in 1920s Chicago. The *Defender* thundered "Stamp Out This Tribe!" in the bold type of a front-page editorial on September 28, 1929.[6] The Moorish Science Temple splintered into warring factions after the Prophet's death on July 20, 1929, but its numbers actually grew; in death Noble Drew Ali was a less divisive figure than he had been in life. Understanding how the public's perception of the Moors fell so far so fast requires knowledge of the shadowy matrix of corporate, political, and criminal rackets that ruled Prohibition-era Chicago during the corrupt rule of its buffoonish mayor, William Hale "Big Bill" Thompson.

🦅   🦅   🦅

The Chicago to which Walter Brister returned around 1924, now under the name of "Noble Drew Ali," was a very different place than the one he left when he faked his death and buried his natal identity under the sod of the Lincoln cemetery for "Negroes" on the South Side in 1914. Of course, people who we would today call African American were a part of Chicago's history from the very start. Allegedly, the local Potawatomi Indians used to say that the first white man to settle at Chickagou was a Black man. His name was Jean Baptiste Point du Sable, a handsome, well-educated, free-born Haitian born to a white French father and a Haitian mother of African descent. In the 1770s he established the first Creole settlement on the western shores of Lake Michigan with his Potawatomi Indian wife at the place where a river emptied into the vast lake, a place where wild garlic bloomed and sometimes rotted, giving "Chickagou" its name and a distinctive stench in the summer months. Early Chicago was a multiracial place long after du Sable and his Indian wife left for Missouri. An English visitor in 1830 wrote that Chicago was full of "rogues of every description, white, black, brown, and red . . . half-breeds, quarter-breeds and men of no breed at all."[7] Later, Chicago's Christian reformers—and they were legion—saw this promiscuous intermingling of races and classes as a problem. In what was typical progressive fashion, they sought to impose order—both racial, occupational, and sexual—on the fractious city. When Chicago rebuilt after Mrs. O'Leary's cow allegedly started the Great Fire of 1871, police pressure pushed the red-light district into the small majority-Black neighborhood, a strip three blocks by fifteen blocks that survived the fire and contained only 2,500 Black residents before the gamblers and whores of the burned-out red-light district joined them. When another fire struck the new Black red-light district in 1874, burning out gamblers, pimps, prostitutes, *and* "Negroes," various clergymen extolled the fire as an act of divine retribution for sin. Most of the Black community shifted south, to the narrow strip of land south of the city's downtown Loop between Twelfth and Seventy-First Streets, roughly bounded by Wentworth on the west and Cottage Grove on the east, a zone that became known as the "Black Belt" of the South Side and remains the center of Black Chicago to the present day, even as Black folk have spread to the West Side and far beyond the limited boundaries of the original "South Side."

In the years between the Columbian Exposition and the First World War, Chicago's Black community remained relatively small. Most jobs available to Black men and women were in service trades; they mainly worked in domestic service, although about 20 percent of Black men worked as porters on the famous Pullman "palace cars" then being manufactured in George Pullman's company town just south of the South Side. In 1910 Chicago's Black population stood at 44,103, and these older migrants thought of themselves as among the proudest and most well-qualified members of "the Race," a migration of "the Talented Tenth," as they called themselves; a "colored" elite focused on the progress of their people and the "uplift" of their less fortunate brethren.

But many "Negroes" chose or were forced into occupations that were less than savory; at the time of the Columbian Exposition, when Chicago relaxed prosecutions of vice to cater to the millions of out-of-town visitors who descended on its bordellos and hotels, a Black woman named Vina Fields ran the largest brothel in the city, where during the fair, sixty "colored" and "mulatto" "sporting women" served an exclusively white clientele. In a letter to the reformer William Stead, Fields expressed the view that her profession was merely helping society to learn the facts of life:

> The present state of affairs results from the want of proper knowledge regarding self. When cultivation of self is made universal, a

better condition is possible, and not until then. The cause for prostitution will continue until it is made honorable for the sexes to seek knowledge of self and their duties toward each other. The most important things of human life ought to never make an honest educated man or woman blush. It is ignorance that causes shame and all this distress. Let the causes of life and common things be more understood and the greater things will take care of themselves, in private matters between man and woman the same as in other things.[8]

Like Paschal Beverly Randolph (1825–1875), the multiracial Black occultist whose books offered frank advice on the benefits of simultaneous orgasm, allegedly learned from Arab Bedouins, Fields pitched her trade as a commonsense solution to society's ignorance and nonsensical shame about all things sexual. Fields managed to attain a position of widespread respect, despite the official illegality of her profession.

Vina Fields was not alone. At the beginning of the new century, a majority of the employees of Chicago's gambling "resorts" were "colored" men, women, and children, and some of the most notorious houses of ill repute were located in the Black Belt.[9] The vice district in the city's First Ward was known as "the Levee," and in 1910 the Chicago Vice Commission estimated that the district contained 1,020 brothels employing 1,880 pimps and madams, with 4,000 prostitutes. Together, they generated approximately $60 million in income and a profit half as large. One reason profits were not even higher was the endemic corruption that diverted millions of dollars to Chicago's police, politicians, and public servants of all ranks from clerks to bailiffs to judges and aldermen. In Chicago, as in many American cities of the day, the criminal underworld and the establishment mixed as promiscuously as the bribes from city contractors and kickbacks from gambling and prostitution "resorts" that sloshed around in such great quantities in the coffers of big-city politicians. In Chicago's Levee—again, as in many big American cities—the illicit activities of the red-light district became integrated into local political machines. "Often the local political club was a social center where pimps and politicians hung out, gambled, and plotted political strategy," Mark H. Haller, the preeminent historian of Chicago's organized crime, writes. "There was, in short, an overlap between the political organizations and the economic activities of the districts."[10]

In Chicago at the turn of the century, the Irish dominated the worlds of gambling, policing, and politics, and often fused all three, as in the example of Billy Skidmore, a leading gambler and political operative, or the long and ignominious careers of aldermen Michael "Hinky Dink" Kenna, who earned his nickname because of his small stature, and his partner "Bathhouse" John Coughlin, who earned his because he started out as a masseur in the steam-and-smoke-filled rooms of a bathhouse. On top of his political duties, Kenna operated a saloon in the First Ward, while the flashy-dressing, gregarious Coughlin was a well-known gambling operator long before he entered public office, and never saw the need to give up the sporting life. From 1892 until the early 1940s, at any time either Hinky Dink or Bathhouse John or both served on the Chicago City Council, from which perch they oversaw and profited from vice in the notorious Levee District. Their lieutenant, Tom McGinnis, ran gambling for the two crooked aldermen, and associated with figures such as John "Mushmouth" Johnson, the Black owner of one of the largest gambling resorts in the Levee, who also was a political operative and delivered votes for the Democratic machine of Mayor Carter Harrison IV.

As colorful as such characters and their nicknames were, the trades they supported were not the kinds that most parents wanted their children to experience firsthand. Yet Blacks could not escape living among the gamblers, drunks, and streetwalkers of the underworld; one Chicago vice commission described Negro families moving into successive neighborhoods "just ahead of the prostitutes," only to watch as the oldest profession in the world colonized each new Black neighborhood.[11] The tonier "Negro" areas resisted this invasion as best as they could, but in the second reign of underworld-connected Republican mayor "Big Bill" Thompson from 1927 to 1931, even they succumbed to waves of streetwalkers and "policy bankers" (gambling bookies) brazenly plying their trades in the open.[12] The effect was to turn the South Side into "a district of high lights and deep shadows which is equaled in few cities," Junius Boyd Wood, a Chicago journalist, disapprovingly wrote.[13]

When a new and energetic police superintendent unleashed a raid on Mushmouth Johnson's gambling den in the Levee in 1901, the fifty-nine men arrested amused themselves by singing "My Old Kentucky Home" as they were hauled off to jail, in a boisterous demonstration of lack of concern for what they knew to be their temporary legal limbo.[14] It was the song that had inspired *In Old Kentucky*; an

1898 Chicago performance had been one of Walter Brister's last appearances in the show before trading his cornet for a turban and becoming a Hindu magician. In these days before recorded music became widespread, Black musicians found plentiful opportunities to play in the gambling dens and brothels that dotted the South Side. The chief booker for Black musicians at the turn of the century was James L. "Daddy" Love, who ran a musical talent booking agency out of his barbershop filled with lithographs and photos of many of the leading "colored" entertainers. His shop was the "theatrical and sporting headquarters" for Black entertainers, and surely a place that a young trumpeter who was new in town would have visited in his search of work. Daddy Love demanded decorous and respectable conduct in his shop; it was a place that "children and wives can go" and be "just as safe from being insulted as much so as if they were attending church."[15] Other musical hangouts were far less salubrious: the place for Black musicians to see, be seen, and more importantly be heard in Chicago at the turn of the century was flamboyant "Negro" underworld tycoon John Weston "Pony" Moore's gambling and prostitution den, the "Hotel de Moore" on Twenty-First Street, which featured thirty elegant rooms, billiards and pool tables, a roulette wheel, live music, and prostitutes working around the clock. The flashy Moore, who adorned himself with jewels and liked to change outfits every hour, enjoyed the company of musicians, and his club became the most popular place for members of Black theatrical shows to stop and a popular after-hours club that entertained revelers with music from nine a.m. until eleven a.m. many nights. Like all owners of similar Chicago "resorts," Moore protected his enterprise by paying off both police and politicians.[16]

The brothels would remain operating in the open in the majority-Black "Levee" district until a march of twelve thousand Christians and Civic Federation types struck in 1909. Mayor Harrison finally shut the Levee down in 1914, which ended up redistributing brothels all over the city. The switch from grander to humbler brothels could not have been good for musicians, who would now have fewer opportunities to play, and those would entail more modest venues that only supported smaller bands or even just solo piano players. Perhaps even more damaging to the musical trade was the growing popularity of moving pictures at the expense of musical comedies and stock companies such as the one that once churned out an astonishing number of new musical plays at Bob Motts's Pekin Theater on the South Side.[17]

The year 1914 brought the Great War, the closing up of Chicago's wide-open town, and the faked death of Walter Brister. The good times were no longer rolling, and it was a good time to get out of town.

🦗   🦗   🦗

Mobsters like Johnny Torrio and Al Capone and their allies among the largely Jewish and Catholic immigrants and children of immigrants dominated illegal enterprises in the years before and after the First World War. These criminals started with graft, gambling, and prostitution when the authorities pushed the oldest profession in the world underground in 1914, and only later turned to bootlegging and became known as "the alky mob" with the triumph in 1920 of native-born Protestant reformers' decades-long effort to prohibit alcohol.[18] Capone was the mediagenic and highly quotable face of the famous "Chicago Outfit" that had its heyday during Prohibition from 1925 and 1930, but the Outfit was actually a loose federation among four partners: Capone, his older brother Ralph, their cousin Frank Nitti, and the pear-shaped Polish-born Jewish pimp Jack (a.k.a. Jake) "Greasy Thumb" Guzik, who was actually the dominant partner thanks to his greater age, experience, and intelligence. Greasy Thumb gained his nickname as the mob's bagman for payoffs to Chicago's police and politicians, which he oversaw from his customary post at St. Hubert's Old English Grill and Chophouse, strategically situated between City Hall and police headquarters.[19] Mark Haller has argued that the very term "organized crime" distorts what were in fact loose and nonhierarchical partnerships created in the main by businessmen who mixed legitimate and illegitimate enterprises. Instead of "organized crime," he has proposed "illegal enterprise" as the best way of describing the matrix of illicit business and political ties that came together in places like Prohibition-era Chicago. Indeed, one did not have to look very hard to find examples of licit and illicit business tactics fusing in the place that acquired the name "Murder City" in the 1920s because of its frequent and spectacular homicides. Chicago's unions and employers alike hired "sluggers" to enforce discipline, bomb rivals' homes, and otherwise intimidate and battle foes. Between 1913 and 1917, assassins hired by William Randolph Hearst's *Chicago American* and the McCormick family's *Chicago Tribune* killed twenty-seven people who either worked for the rival paper or were unlucky enough to be caught reading it.[20] Capone was unusually violent and mediagenic, but held no monopoly on violence in Murder City.

The notorious Capone himself was in part a product of the city's overlapping political and criminal establishments. Torrio brought his cousin Capone to Chicago from Brooklyn in 1921, where Capone had already established himself in a syndicate of Neapolitan crooks who specialized in gambling, pimping, and extortion. Torrio himself came to Chicago in 1910 at the behest of a brothel owner in the Levee named "Big Jim" Colosimo. But Big Jim's mentor was none other than alderman "Bathhouse" John Coughlin, who hired Big Jim as one of his precinct captains and kickback collectors.[21] In 1911, Black gambler Jacob "Mont" Tennes was rumored to have spent $20,000 on Mayor Carter Harrison IV's election campaign; the next decade, Republican mayor William Hale "Big Bill" Thompson, known as "the friend of the Negro," acted as a staunch ally of the local criminal-political syndicate, and in fact was a member of the Sportsmen's Club of America, a group of Chicago gamblers who formed his earliest base of support when he was first elected to public office in 1915. In 1916, state's attorney Maclay Hoyne raided the Sportsmen's Club of America, whose members included Tennes, Colosimo, Jimmy Mondi (a Colosimo lieutenant), and various slot machine manufacturers, and charged that Thompson was using the club to collect graft payments from gamblers, saloonkeepers, pimps, and criminals.[22] Thompson allegedly accepted approximately $250,000 in campaign contributions from Capone in 1927, as well as the muscle of about a thousand of Capone's thugs who threatened the opposition and turned out the vote for Big Bill.[23]

Though opposed by Black reformers and their white allies, who blamed the Thompson machine for the spread of organized crime in "colored" neighborhoods, Thompson also received the loyal assistance of Oscar DePriest, the political "King of the Black Belt," who was a staunch Thompson ally as an alderman from the Second Ward, backed by the South Side millionaire George Harding and Congressman Martin B. Madden. DePriest was indicted though not convicted in 1916 and again in 1928 for allowing gambling houses and brothels to operate and bribing police to look the other way. DePriest allegedly was also a silent partner in gambler Henry "Teenan" Jones's Tammany Club. If that was true, then DePriest, like many Chicago pols before him, was not just taking kickbacks from gamblers, but actually owned a piece of the action.[24] When in 1916 the city shut down the South Side's Panama Club, an interracial "black and tan" club that featured risqué entertainment and served as a front for prostitution, the owner Isadore Levin bribed City Hall and got it reopened. It helped that his attorney was a law partner of one of Mayor Thompson's principal advisers. But Alderman DePriest did not object to such establishments in his ward; he argued instead that the club should be reopened because it provided employment for sixty Black workers. One of DePriest's political supporters ran his Hobnob Club so openly that the rattle of chips could be heard from the sidewalk below. Of course, such cozy relationships between politicians and vice operatives did not sit well with everyone. "The race is being exploited for the sake of men in politics who are a disgrace to their own race," one critic wrote.[25]

With a weak or nonexistent merit system for government jobs, Chicago politicians practiced unadulterated spoils politics at the beginning of the twentieth century, and at least three major factions vied to pack their supporters into an astounding number of government jobs. In 1926, the mayor's office controlled a city budget of $200 million and twenty thousand jobs. The Sanitary District had a budget of $42 million and a payroll of as many as three thousand employees. Cook County had a budget of more than $34 million and thousands of jobs. The sprawling parks system was administered by three units, each controlling millions more dollars and thousands more jobs. The governor of Illinois in turn controlled twenty thousand additional jobs and millions of dollars in payroll.

Chicago's political swamp was no doubt almost as old as its marshy origins, but the modern master of spoils politics was William Lorimer, the "Blond Boss" of Chicago, a congressman who won election to the Senate in 1909, only to be unseated the following year when Illinois state representatives admitted they had taken thousands of dollars of bribes to vote for him, before senators were directly elected by popular vote. Though conventional in appearance, Lorimer's influence was "sinister and terrifying," according to his contemporary, University of Chicago political scientist Carroll Hill Wooddy. He was contemptuous of any suggestion of political reform, and built a nearly impregnable political machine by protecting vice and gambling, by buying and stealing votes, and by appealing to a largely foreign-born and poorly educated constituency with demagogic and entertaining oratory on trumped-up issues. His rivals felt they had to match Lorimer, and the politics of early twentieth-century Chicago descended into a quagmire of spoils politics and demagoguery. Even after Lorimer temporarily retreated from politics following his 1910 unseating, his acolytes carried forward his sleazy standard of spoils politics, bogus demagoguery, and collusion with organized crime.[26]

So when Lorimer acolyte, former gridiron star, and cowboy mayor William Hale "Big Bill" Thompson came to power in 1915 with a program of spellbinding oratory, corruption, and buffoonery, he formed the most potent of three Republican political machines in Illinois by allying with former Lorimer henchman Frederick "the Poor Swede" Lundin, who had become a millionaire by hawking patent medicines. The rival machines were the alliance between Illinois attorney general Edward J. Brundage and US senator Medill McCormick, and yet another alliance led by US senator and former governor Charles Deneen.[27] Of these three camps, Deneen was the sole individual known to be not just virtuous, but a reformer and a "bulwark of civic righteousness," in the words of University of Chicago Professor Wooddy, although by the 1920s his was also the weakest of the three combinations, perhaps not coincidentally. And even Deneen, who was said to have the charisma of a mud turtle, was willing to partner with tainted figures like gangster "Diamond Joe" Esposito. Governor Len Small, for his part, was a Lorimer swamp creature who came to power as a candidate of the Thompson-Lundin City Hall machine and then created an administration that "for waste, mismanagement, inefficiency, intrigue, manipulation, and downright disregard of the public interest has few parallels in the history of the United States," in Wooddy's estimation.[28]

Mayor Thompson, "the Friend of the Negro," commanded the Black vote in the Second and Third Wards. Second Ward alderman Louis B. Anderson, who came to Chicago for the Columbian Exposition of 1893 and became a protégé of pioneering politico Ed Wright, represented the Second Ward on the City Council for many years, and served as Mayor Thompson's floor leader in that body, with the enthusiastic support of the *Chicago Defender*. Thompson's "friendship" brought rewards for a select few "Negroes," and exploitation and neglect for the rest. In a city becoming famous for its gangsters, Chicago's politicians were undoubtedly its wealthiest and most successful racketeers. As the *Evening Post* noted, "It is with the people's money that the political machines . . . are able to impose upon the people forms of government which are more profitable to the politicians than they are serviceable to the public."[29] In Chicago, life was cheap, justice was not blind, and so-called Negroes were forced to live in neighborhoods studded with brothels and gambling dens where police protection was unreliable, public servants were on the take, and crimes large and small were rampant and committed brazenly. A reformer would not have to look far to find things to condemn and correct on the South Side.

{ CHAPTER TEN }

BLACK MECCA

It is to the cities the negroes are flocking. The small towns and the farms possess little attraction for them and it is to the greater market for the negro's only permanent commodity, his vote, he hurries, and there remains as long as the police will permit him.

—*LOUISVILLE COURIER-JOURNAL*, 1903[1]

In the decades after Christian theologians and propagandists loudly pounded their chests and proclaimed the superiority of Christianity and Western civilization at the Chicago World's Fair, Chicago had come close to imploding, and its shortcomings, its attempts at reform, and its illegal enterprises could all be laid squarely at the feet of Christians, and at times, their Jewish allies. Chicago was fertile ground on which to continue the critique of the West begun in 1893 on the Midway and in the Parliament of Religions, and to explore alternatives to both Christianity and Judaism alike, whether they be spiritualist, esoteric, Islamic, or all at once. Writing in 1945, sociologists Horace Cayton and St. Clair Drake commented that "the Negro shares all the glorious hopes of the West, all of its anxieties, its corruptions, its psychological maladies. To the extent he realizes that his hopes are hopeless, he will embrace Communism or Fascism, or whatever other ideological rejection is offered."[2] Islam became just such an ideological objection for hundreds and then thousands of Black Americans, both in 1925 when Noble Drew Ali founded the Moorish Science Temple, and three decades later when the prison conversion of a charismatic felon named Malcolm Little brought the teachings of a successor group to millions.

Black life in Chicago changed radically and forever with the Great Migration during the years of World War I, when Northern industrialists and Black newspapers like the *Chicago Defender* advertised the economic and social opportunities in Chicago and other Northern cities, and Southern Blacks responded by migrating North by the hundreds of thousands. Chicago alone saw its Black population jump by 51,500 souls between 1916 and 1918, and the Black Belt swelled to the bursting point. Almost 125,000 more "colored folks" arrived in Chicago in the 1920s, mostly from points along the web of railroads feeding into the city from the Deep South in the cotton-growing regions of Louisiana, Mississippi, Alabama, and Georgia, reversing the forced flow from North to South their enslaved ancestors had made after Eli Whitney invented the cotton gin.[3] Perhaps with some degree of selective memory, Chicago's "Old Settlers" frequently recalled that in the years before World War I when Blacks made up less than 2 percent of the total population, they faced little overt racism. One recalled that in 1912, "colored folks" worked in downtown department stores and whites patronized "Negro" doctors and professionals; likewise, Black customers could dine and be served with courtesy at any restaurant they could afford. Black and white children frequently played together without incident in antediluvian Chicago.

But with the doubling and then quadrupling of the Black population with the flood of Southern migrants between 1910 and 1930, Chicago's precarious racial truce shattered. Discriminated against at every turn, Blacks took some of the hardest and dirtiest jobs in Chicago's stockyards and factories, creating friction with the Irish, Slavic, and other European immigrants who held such jobs. Their search for housing forced them into the checkerboard of European ethnic neighborhoods around the overcrowded, narrow Black Belt. Whites responded with organized violence, and white terrorists, frequently paid by local "neighborhood improvement associations," targeted Blacks who had moved into white neighborhoods or white real estate agents who had sold them homes. These terrorists bombed fifty-eight homes of Blacks or white real estate agents who sold to Blacks between July of 1917 and March of 1921, killing at least two Black residents in the process. In local slang, these bombs—sticks of dynamite from mining suppliers, hand grenades from military sources, and crude explosives made of black powder—were "pineapples" tossed by thugs known as "gorillas," and they turned Black lives upside down. Even doyens of Chicago's Black elite like Jesse Binga, founder of the largest Black-owned bank in America, were not safe from the violence; his home was bombed multiple times. On average, there was a racist bombing in Chicago once every twenty days between 1917 and 1921, and the bombings lasted until 1924, at which point whites turned to the subtler mechanism of restrictive covenants written into property deeds barring sale to "Negroes."[4]

With a large population and relative wealth but without an effective and unbiased criminal justice system, let alone basic police protection, the city's crime skyrocketed both before and during the influx of the Great Migration, as both petty crimes like stripping pipes from houses and major felonies like murder, assault and battery, and arson all increased.[5] As early as 1903, one account labeled Chicago "the Mecca of Black Criminals," and reported that "Negro" criminals from both the Midwest and the South were heading there to seek their fortunes, preying on Black as well as white victims.[6] The teenaged poet Langston Hughes spent the summers of 1917 and 1918 living with his mother next to the elevated tracks of the commuter rail lines in the Black Belt, and described a vibrant neighborhood that was full of life but seething with poverty, space constraints, organized crime, and racism. South State Street "was in its glory then," he wrote, a teeming "Negro" street with crowded theaters, restaurants, and cabarets. "And excitement from noon to noon. Midnight was like day." The neighborhood was both crowded and heterogeneous. "The street was full of workers and gamblers, prostitutes and pimps, church folk and sinners," Hughes recalled. The pressure on the available housing was extreme, with so many people coming and so few apartment owners willing to rent to "colored" tenants. The shortage of supply in the face of incredible demand made rents in Black sections of cities such as Harlem and the South Side among the highest in their respective cities, but often no amount of money could buy "Negroes" adequate housing. "For neither love nor money could you find a decent place to live," Hughes wrote. Indeed, in those years vacancies were nearly nonexistent, and in 1917 the Chicago Urban League found that only 50 out of 664 Black applicants had successfully found housing.[7]

And although the do-gooders had done good and removed many if not all of the brothels from the Levee district, the historical pattern of the Black Belt overlapping with Chicago's red-light district, along with the general lack of city services and police protection in the Black community, made it the perfect incubator for vice. "Profiteers, thugs, and gangsters were coming into their own," Hughes wrote. It did not take long for the bookish teenager, who had his nose buried in works by Nietzsche at the time, to learn how whiteness and power worked on the streets of Chicago. His first week in town he ventured outside the Black Belt to find out what the city looked like, and "was set upon and beaten by a group of white boys, who said they didn't allow niggers in that neighborhood. I came home with both eyes blacked and a swollen jaw."[8] Indeed, the Irish neighborhoods west of Wentworth Avenue were known to be so hostile to Blacks that "colored folks" were effectively barred from walking there, let alone finding housing.

Roving bands of white hoodlums made life miserable for Blacks unlucky enough to wander outside the confines of the Black Belt, but Black Chicagoans demonstrated that they would fight back when attacked. When whites attacked Blacks in East St. Louis in July of 1917, a "colored" Chicago lawyer urged locals "Negroes" to arm themselves, and the years of the massive Black influx saw many violent skirmishes between white and Black youth gangs. When Chicago erupted in five days of race riots in 1919 resulting in thirty-eight deaths, five hundred injuries, and more than a thousand people left homeless, it was not hard to believe that Chicago was in the grips of a race war, not just a battle over decent housing. Blacks condemned the fighting but were proud that "Negroes" had fought back, defended Black neighborhoods, and even taken the fight to surrounding white areas. In an era of violent struggle including the Russian Revolution and the First World War, this generation of "Afro-Americans" called themselves "New Negroes" and exhibited a determination to fight back and defend their communities from attack.

🦅   🦅   🦅

Of course a lot of the fighting that "Negroes" did in this era was with each other, as the "Old Settlers" who had been in the city since the decade of the World's Fair fought a losing battle to control the "colored" community's social standards against the tens of thousands of Southerners who rapidly outnumbered them. As the Great Migration filled the South Side to overflowing, some of the first to leave if they could were Old Settlers, who complained loudly and bitterly about the newcomers. The migrants frequently scandalized the Old Settlers' standards of respectability, which the latter viewed as vital for the progress of "The Race." One older resident recalled that Chicago's "Negroes" of the 1890s were few in number and "just about civilized and didn't make apes out of themselves like the ones who came here during 1918. We all suffer for what one fool will do."[9]

Though many Southern migrants had come from Southern cities, the "colored" sections of those cities, even the larger ones, were frequently quite rural in character, with livestock, unpaved streets, and no streetlights. Although many migrants made the journey North in their Sunday best and shared the older migrants' emphasis on propriety and respectability, Northerners viewed the lot of them as too "country" if not downright "uncivilized," pointing out when newcomers eschewed proper shoes and dress shirts during the summer months, returned home from jobs on streetcars in soiled work clothes, or sat on porches and stoops doing hair or chatting in an animated manner. It is not difficult to get people out of the South, the Black-owned *Chicago Whip* quipped, "but you have a job on your hands when you attempt to get the South out of them."[10] Even respectable Southerners with stable jobs found it difficult to win social acceptance from their Northern peers, but the migrants who labored as domestics and laborers received even more scornful and patronizing instructions on how to behave. Walter F. White of the NAACP wrote that many of the migrants were too often "care-free, at times irresponsible, and sometimes even boisterous," and that this "conduct caused complications difficult to adjust." Many Black newspapers published guides on manners and comportment, conducted cleanliness campaigns, tin can drives, and health promotion weeks, and gave out prizes for the most junk collected or cans salvaged. Chicago's chapter of the Urban League, which Northern Blacks and white allies founded in 1916 to help the new Southern migrants adjust to life in the North, issued a "Creed of Cleanliness" that proclaimed, "I AM AN AMERICAN CITIZEN," declared pride in the sacrifice of Negro soldiers' service, and extolled "NEW HABITS OF SELF-RESPECT AND CLEANLINESS" such as attending to the neatness of one's personal appearance on the street and refraining from wearing dust caps, bungalow aprons, house clothing, and bedroom slippers outdoors. "I WILL ARRANGE MY TOILET within doors," cleanliness pledgers proclaimed. "I WILL INSIST upon the use of rear entrances for coal dealers, hucksters, etc. . . . I WILL DO MY BEST to prevent defacement of property by children or adults."[11]

In his prior life as Walter Brister, when he lived in Chicago from near the turn of the century until 1913, Noble Drew Ali himself would have been considered an older settler if not properly an 1890s "Old Settler," and the emphasis on personal hygiene, patriotism, and public manners that became so characteristic of his Moorish Science Temple of America can be understood as part of a broader effort among the Black older residents of Northern cities to reform the morals and manners of Southern migrants.

Chicago's racial and racist struggles during the Great Migration were not just local skirmishes, but were also part of a global conversation about the fracturing of the Ottoman and British Empires and the insurgent national aspirations of colonized people of color around the world. In 1920, influential white racist Lothrop Stoddard published *The Rising Tide of Color against White World-Supremacy*. Seen from the perspective of the events of World War I, which Stoddard termed "the White Civil War," and the brewing anticolonial insurgencies in Africa, Asia, and the Middle East, the racist violence of Chicago was not just a skirmish over real estate values but was part of a global race war, the passing of the time when "uncounted myriads of dusky folk obeyed the white man's will."[12] Stoddard quoted a British-educated Afghan, Achmet Abdullah, who called racial prejudice "the cowardly, wretched caste-mark of the European and the American the world over," and predicted a coming global racial struggle. "You are heaping up material for a Jehad, a Pan-Islam, a Pan-Asia Holy War, a gigantic day of reckoning," Abdullah warned, calling for a modern Attila the Hun. "You are deaf to the voice of reason and fairness, and so you must be taught with the whirring swish of the sword when it is red."[13] In his 1921 *The New World of Islam*, Stoddard warned that "the world of Islam, mentally and spiritually quiescent for almost a thousand years, is once more astir, once more on the march."[14] For Stoddard and other white racists of the day, Islam was a key component of the anti-imperialist stirring of the darker races, one that had broader significance for a looming global race war. It was a message that not only reechoes in the racist apocalyptic thought of white nationalists today, but found a receptive audience among many "Negroes" in the North, whose daily existence, with discrimination at work, in housing, and in schools along with bombings, beatings, arsons, verbal assaults, and rioting, must have felt like something approaching warfare. Stoddard's books were sensations and widely debated in the press and the culture at large. The unsympathetic character Tom Buchanan in F. Scott Fitzgerald's *The Great Gatsby* praises "'The Rise of the Colored Empires' by this man Goddard," although Buchanan's effusive summary is undercut by his wife Daisy's winks and sarcastic comments. Even President Warren G. Harding, whose political opponents spread the rumor that he was one-eighth "Negro" himself, referred to Stoddard's book approvingly in his then-shockingly progressive address in Birmingham, Alabama, on October 26, 1921, in which he called for "full citizenship" and total political and economic equality for Blacks but rejected "social equality."

Harding's advocacy of civil rights and social separation was quite popular among Black Americans, many of whom had no desire to mix socially with whites, or suffer the threat of rape from the kind of white men who thought themselves sexually entitled to Black bodies, a brutal legacy of slavery and its violent aftermath. Eloquent Black Nationalist Marcus Garvey, who attracted between five thousand and seven thousand followers in Chicago, praised Stoddard's book as well.[15] In the aftermath of World War I, when race riots broke out across the country and several returning "colored" veterans of European combat were lynched for daring to wear a US military uniform in public, the question a lot of smart people were asking was not whether a global race war would break out, but when. For "Negroes" to convert to Islam in those years was not merely to change one's diet, alcohol consumption, and worship patterns, but to pick sides in the coming global racial conflagration, and to take a stand locally against non-Muslims who had pushed vice into Black neighborhoods and threw bombs through windows when Blacks attempted to escape high rent prices and substandard housing conditions.

Many "Negroes" wanted better housing and jobs but had no desire to escape the city-within-a-city that became known as the Black Belt. For them, Chicago's Black Metropolis was Mecca and Medina in one, a shrine and a refuge. Noble Drew Ali would advocate Islam, but he would also emphasize economic independence and self-sufficiency, by founding a string of successful businesses that employed and served his followers. In this he was not alone. By emphasizing political participation along with economic and social self-sufficiency, Black Chicagoans weathered economic downturns in 1921 and 1924 and made the remaining years of the 1920s the most prosperous Black people had ever experienced. Numerous migrant clubs encouraged social solidarity among former residents of states like Texas and Alabama or of specific cities such as New Orleans and Memphis, and also promoted economic solidarity by urging members to patronize businesses owned by fellow members. Many of Chicago's Black ministers urged race men and women to spend money with each other. From his Harlem headquarters, Marcus Garvey may have preached a vision of Black business activity and economic self-sufficiency, but Blacks owned very few Harlem businesses and the ones that Garvey founded soon foundered. Chicago's "New Negroes," in contrast, outstripped every other Black American community in business achievement, building as many as 1,800 businesses, including several banks, four magazines, and at least six newspapers. They also proudly supported their own politicians and professionals. In 1923, Chicago's two Black-owned banks had only $150,000 in deposits, a number that grew to $4 million by 1928. In that year, by one estimate, Chicago's two hundred thousand "colored" folks had $40 million in all banks, and controlled $4 billion in property.[16] In contrast, by 1921 Harlem's eighty-five thousand "race" men and women controlled only 584 businesses, and white-owned businesses, nightclubs, clothing stores, and drugstores dominated Harlem's commercial life long after Blacks predominated along its streets.[17]

Despite its frequent racial strife, persistent occupational struggles, and lack of decent housing, Chicago offered Southern-born "Negroes" vastly more freedom than they experienced in the South. For men relentlessly referred to as "boy" or "uncle" in the South, denied the respectful titles of "mister" or "sir," and hemmed into dead-end and backbreaking jobs, this new Northern freedom often provided an affirmation of manhood. As one migrant described Chicago, "I live better, save more, and feel more like a man."[18] It was a sensation that early Black converts to Islam would know well. Standing at the center of the Black Belt at Forty-Seventh Street and South Parkway, a person was surrounded by a swirl of "a continuous eddy of faces— black, brown, olive, yellow, and white."[19] There were Black-run newspaper dailies on the newsstands, stores with Black salespeople, and "colored" doctors, dentists, and lawyers, all overseen by uniformed "Negro" policemen and under the eyes of Black churchgoers, workers, beggars, prostitutes, and street urchins. On the famous State Street "Stroll" between Twenty-Sixth and Thirty-Ninth Streets, Black folks gathered in their finest to see and be seen, clustering outside of theaters like the Grand, where Walter Brister played trumpet in a Southern-themed musical revue in 1912, or the Pekin, the first Black-owned theater on the South Side, where former gambling kingpin Bob Motts created high-toned musicals for the South Side's "colored" elite.[20]

The conditions of comparatively poor job opportunities, substandard shelter, widespread educational delays caused by inferior schooling in the South, high rates of illness, the rapid exodus of teachers with the most seniority from schools on the South Side, and the concentration of vice in the Black Belt by the collusion of politicians, police, and organized crime also created the emergence of a ghetto, even if it was a ghetto with a vibrant and variegated internal life. Although Black Chicago boasted lively churches, fraternal organizations, Black-owned businesses, women's groups, educational groups, political advocacy groups, nightclubs, dance halls, saloons, and salons, the Black Belt soon led the city in poverty, percentage of women in domestic service, births to unmarried mothers, juvenile delinquency, tuberculosis, and infant mortality, in addition to being the city's center for prostitution and gambling.[21]

Hundreds of Black businesses hid slot machines or served as fronts for the lotteries known as "policy," and even respectable businesses in Chicago's Black community frequently had underworld ties to the gambling and policy businesses that coursed through the South Side. For example, famed banker Jesse Binga married the sister of Mushmouth Johnson, who had inherited 60 percent of his fortune and Binga used the funds to underwrite his bank; Mushmouth's underling Bob Motts plowed his gambling winnings into the tony Pekin Theater, "upcycling" lowlife profits into highbrow entertainment. Upon Motts's death, his sister Lucy Lindsey married gambling kingpin and political ward boss Daniel M. Jackson in 1925, and Jackson transformed the former Pekin Theater into the "Beaux Arts Club," a luxurious gambling resort and a kickback collection point for the South Side gambling syndicate.[22] After the city shut down the Pekin, Jackson turned an undertaking establishment on Michigan Avenue into the luxuriously appointed Dunbar Club, named for his old friend, the poet Paul Laurence Dunbar. According to historian Davarian Baldwin, "it was the underworld of policy gambling that stabilized the city's black economy and social world," underwriting a "vibrant urban culture of theaters, dance halls, and athletic and traditional business enterprises."[23] While that certainly was true, the unsavory aspects of brothels, nightclubs, and gambling resorts upset many Black observers, especially their facilitation of "immorality," graft, and political corruption in Black neighborhoods. Calling underworld establishments "influences of destruction," Junius Boyd Wood wrote in 1916 that "politically the Negro race is being exploited in Chicago by designing men." In exchange for political positions and jobs, "some individuals get a chance to make money through methods by which the race as a whole is held back and discredited."[24] That was the closest to a direct attack on Daniel M. Jackson as you could find during his lifetime. Robert Abbott's *Chicago Defender* never even called him a gambler while he was alive; for such frankness you would have to read Jackson's hometown *Pittsburgh Courier*.

Churches helped to address some of the hardships of life on the South Side. In 1900, only 28 percent of Chicago's still-modest Black population of forty-four thousand were regular churchgoers, according to historian Christopher Robert Reed.[25] But Chicago's Black churches greatly expanded their membership rolls during the Great Migration, when the Urban League distributed leaflets instructing migrants to "become an active member in some church."[26] Of course, many migrants needed little encouragement to join churches in Chicago, where there were so many more kinds of religious congregations than there were in their Southern places of origin. By 1928 there were 295 churches serving the Black Belt's more than two hundred thousand residents, and many had seats for thousands of worshippers. Partly in response to the dire needs of much of the Black population, Chicago's "race churches" were just as focused on "advancing the race" as in serving the Lord; most "Negro" worshippers would have seen no meaningful distinction between the two goals. In 1928, 45.1 percent of Chicago's "Negroes" belonged to large majority-Black denominations of Baptists, and 11.9 percent were Methodists. Predominantly white denominations like Roman Catholics, Presbyterians, and Seventh-Day Adventists claimed only 7.4 percent of total churches in Chicago's Black Metropolis.[27] But Noble Drew Ali had a lot of company in presenting alternatives to conventional "mainline" churches; smaller denominations and sects, which frequently met in storefronts rather than imposing edifices, also had many members. Nineteen percent of all South Side churches were "Spirit-filled"—meaning they were enthusiastic Holiness and Pentecostal churches—which featured up-tempo music, demonstrative "shouting," and call-and-response patterns between preacher and worshippers; among the Pentecostals, there was also the ecstatic holy babble of speaking in tongues. Black Spiritual churches, derived from nineteenth-century spiritualist communication with ghosts and other magical practices such as crystal-ball gazing and fortune-telling, made up another 5.8 percent of the total; their ranks in Detroit and New York included some "Mohammedan princes" who identified as Muslims. Even smaller Black sects composed a significant 9.8 percent of the total, encouraged by the city's ability to bring together seekers of arcane truths and to create a marketplace for magical services and occult beliefs. One Fred Starck ran the Aquarian School of Higher Thought and Church of Divine Science, while former "Hindu magician" Lauron William De Laurence's South Side interracial orgy cult was broken up by the cops in 1912, though he continued to influence occult enthusiasts through his many publications and his Brotherhood of Magic. The following year, the Wisconsin-born "colored" Chicago lunch counter operator Leafy Anderson founded her first Spiritual church in Chicago, long before she became the most prominent leader of Black Spiritual churches in New Orleans.[28]

Many Christian preachers attempted to better their communities and battled the underworld forces that held such sway on the South Side. Pioneering minister Reverend Reverdy C. Ransom courageously attacked the corrupt alliance of politicians, police, and policy kings in Chicago's Black community, and had his church bombed as thanks for his efforts in 1903, quitting the city for Boston two years later.[29] On the other hand, among the thousands of earnest church men and women who tended to the poor and built ministries predicated upon the Social Gospel of service to the needy in the spirit of Jesus Christ's teachings were some ministers who saw no conflict in preaching other-worldly salvation while enjoying an outsized percentage of this-worldly comforts. Black critics of the Great Migration–era churches often accused them of being rackets themselves, with hypocritical, greedy ministers and programs that did little for the people they were supposed to help.[30] Such dissatisfaction stoked interest in alternatives to Christianity, be they spiritualists with their body of esoteric beliefs and magical practices that built on migrants' familiarity with Southern systems of conjure, or the nascent Muslim groups who never had to look far for examples of philandering and fast-living Christian ministers with fancy suits and questionable morals. The pastor of Chicago's African Bethel Church made the newspapers in 1922 when he confessed to burglarizing $6,000 worth of lingerie and reselling it to women in his congregation, managing to become an exemplar of at least two of the seven deadly sins in one fell swoop.[31]

Examples of wasteful and ineffective spending among the hundreds of the Moors' Christian competitors were easy to spot. Black churches nationwide managed to spend 43.2 percent of their budgets on salaries and less than half as much on charitable works.[32] The Chicago chapter of the Urban League was the largest provider of social services on the South Side, and whites provided 83 to 90 percent of that organization's funding in the peak years of the Great Migration. Even when Black churches directed their efforts toward helping the indigent, those efforts were often poorly funded: Reverend Richard Wright's Trinity Mission in the Levee was perpetually cash-strapped and failed when Reverend Wright left the city in 1905, while the Institutional AME Church's program lasted only until 1915.[33] Ida B. Wells's Negro Fellowship League managed to operate its lodging house for only three years and expired altogether after ten. On the other hand, Olivet Baptist Church, led by the popular pastor Reverend Lacey Kirk Williams, boasted a membership ten thousand strong in the 1920s, and offered a full suite of social services, an employment bureau, and a daycare center.[34]

Black churches' plentiful musicales, fashion shows, concerts, plays, pageants, picnics, political rallies, and suppers provided entertainment and camaraderie for tens of thousands every week, and the preachers of the larger congregations became stars. The University of Chicago–educated Reverend Williams enthralled parishioners of all classes, and Pilgrim Baptist's dynamic Reverend Junius C. Austin was incredibly popular. In addition to those preachers who were well trained, erudite, earnest, and concerned with decorum and uplift of their brethren both in Chicago and Africa, there were some preachers who were consummate showmen and entertainers as much as men of faith, in some cases hamming their way through sermons that not only lacked book learning but even made a virtue of their preachers' lack of erudition. Perhaps even worse were the many Christian preachers who were known to be serial adulterers. "Minister Found Guilty of Too Much Lovemaking," the *Chicago Defender* headline blared on May 14, 1927, decrying the exposure of "another typical Elmer Gantry, the charlatan minister so ably depicted by Sinclair Lewis in his sensational novel."[35] Such tainted men of the cloth allowed critics to claim that the Black Church had lost its way. "I used to be active in the church," one migrant said. "I thought we could work out our salvation that way. But I found out better. These Negro preachers are not bothered about The Race—about all they think of is themselves." Nor was such criticism voiced only by backbenchers: in the 1930s, such eminent Black scholars as W. E. B. Du Bois, Benjamin Mays, and Carter G. Woodson offered critiques of the Black Church as an institution that had not lived up to its obligation to help the least fortunate.[36]

The massive influx of Southern migrants challenged Chicago's existing "Negro" churches, introduced more emotional forms of worship, and created disaffected worshippers who could have been drawn to Muslim worship precisely because Islam was reserved, dignified, contemplative, and beautifully austere in comparison to the catching the spirit, the "shouting," the enthusiastic call-and-response, and even the speaking in tongues that Southern migrants introduced into Black Chicago's religious world, a world that before the war had been dominated by Old Settler notions of decorum and respectability so reserved as to be almost staid. One Black West Indian religious seeker who came to reject Christianity and become a leading Black Israelite rabbi in New York referred to Southern emotionalism in worship with the damning phrase "niggerations."[37] Surely others felt the same way about histrionics from the pulpit or parishioners falling out in the aisles under the influence of ecstatic trance states.[38]

Not everybody in Chicago's Black community was on board with the common if hypocritical split between the hedonism of Saturday nights spent in resorts rife with gambling, booze, jazz, and prostitution, and the pious devotion of Sunday mornings. Some, like the followers of a new prophet, Noble Drew Ali, would sing "Moslem's That Old Time Religion" and mean it both in terms of their ancestral ties to Muslim Africa and the more recent loss of reserved forms of worship washed away by the demonstrative Southernisms of the recent flood of migrants. By 1925, many residents of the South Side had grown disaffected with Christianity and were looking for another path. For thousands who joined the Moorish Science Temple, Islam would be the answer.

CHAPTER ELEVEN

POWER BROKERS

Whenever in the pursuit of this objective the lone wolf, the un-
ethical competitor, the reckless promoter, the Ishmael or Insull
whose hand is against every man's, declines to join in achieving
an end recognized as being for the public welfare, and threatens
to drag the industry back to a state of anarchy, the Government
may properly be asked to apply restraint. Likewise, should the
group ever use its collective power contrary to the public welfare,
the Government must be swift to enter and protect the public in-
terest. The Government should assume the function of economic
regulation only as a last resort, to be tried only when private ini-
tiative, inspired by high responsibility, with such assistance and
balance as Government can give, has finally failed.

—PRESIDENT FRANKLIN DELANO ROOSEVELT, 1932[1]

Gamblers, pimps, madams, bootleggers, and other street level criminals were not the only source of illicit funds sloshing around Chicago's political swamp, as "colored" alderman Oscar De-Priest's opponents pointed out during his 1928 congressional campaign. A twisted tale of political intrigue, bribery, and vote-buying tied DePriest to utilities magnate Samuel Insull. The epicenter of this Gordian knot of racketeering was none other than the home of the Moorish Science Temple, the clubhouse at 3140 S. Indiana Avenue known as Unity Hall. Alderman DePriest and Mayor Thompson shared a powerful political benefactor in Insull, the public utilities czar of Chicago who controlled Commonwealth Edison, Peoples Gas, Chicago Rapid Transit's elevated railroads, and electric companies serving a hundred Chicago suburbs and dozens more communities across the Southeast and Midwest. Although he is not well remembered today, Insull was a titan of industry whose companies produced one-eighth of the nation's electricity in 1929, at which point his personal fortune was estimated at $150 million—more than $2.24 billion in 2020 dollars. Quite simply, in a decade famous for its pro-business ethos and meager protections for workers, "Emperor Insull" was America's most powerful businessman.[2] He was the president of eleven companies worth $3 billion (about $45 billion today) in the Roaring Twenties, the chairman of sixty-five more companies, and a director of another eighty-five. (Insull was not Jewish, despite his biblical first name, but after his downfall in 1934, rumors circulated that he was.) He came from London to be Thomas Edison's personal secretary in 1881 and rapidly rose up the ranks of Edison's companies, where he learned that kerosene companies, the hidebound competitors of newfangled electric illumination, had already bought off politicians across America, and the only way to get them to try electricity was to beat the grafters at their own corrupt game. Insull not only learned to play the bribery game, he excelled at it. He also helped organize the Edison General Electric Corporation and became a G.E. vice president. When the small local Chicago Edison power company needed a new president, he took a pay cut to take the job in 1892, then bought up the dynamos used to illuminate the 1893 World's Fair and used them to modernize electrical production in the Windy City, gradually buying out his competitors or driving them out of business. Insull, who was the largest patron of the Chicago City Opera, was the Babe Ruth of business and the Puccini of political corruption, in a class by himself in both interlocking endeavors.[3]

Insull controlled his companies through complex pyramid schemes of nested holding companies, and he controlled Illinois politicians through similarly opaque insider trading rackets by which he gave compliant politicians the opportunity to buy stock offerings before the general public at a steep 80 percent discount, then drove up the price of the stock through a flurry of purchases, allowing the insiders to cash out at grossly inflated prices before the stocks came back down to earth. But he also used less exotic methods, such as plain old cash bribes, distributed evenhandedly to both Republican and Democratic lawmaker-racketeers through lawyers such as Daniel J. Schuyler Jr. and Schuyler's partner Charles Weinfeld. When Insull's Commonwealth Edison seized the Peoples Gas Company in 1916, the headline in the *Day Book*, an ad-free newspaper, read: "Commonwealth Edison to Take Over Peoples Gas, and Also Take Over the Parties and City Government."[4] The prediction was perhaps intended to be facetious, but it turned out to be not far from the truth. Insull was no Svengali, pulling all the strings of local politics, but his influence was far greater than has been widely acknowledged, then or now. Because of Insull's many dealings with the city and the state, he needed votes on budgetary matters such as the price the City would pay for his elevated railroad lines in 1925—the City wanted to pay $80 million, but he insisted on $90 million.[5]

When Chicago's richest man, Sears, Roebuck and Company co-founder Julius Rosenwald, joined a reform effort underwritten by Samuel Insull known as "the Secret Six" to drive organized crime out of local politics, attorney Donald Richberg wrote Rosenwald a furious letter decrying the corruption of government officials by men "of whom Mr. Samuel Insull is a shining example, who buy political control to protect their private interests and thereby destroy honest government." Richberg, who went on to become one of the architects of the New Deal, said he did not see how a believer in good government like Rosenwald could associate with men associated with Insull in the "year by year corruption of government." Political reform could never come from such alliances. "If the business men of Chicago want honest government, they can get it. They can't get it by helping support Insull-Ettelson-Thompson combinations," referring to Insull and his longtime attorney Samuel A. Ettelson, who became the City of Chicago's corporation counsel for corrupt mayor Big Bill Thompson. "If I were organizing a group to clean out the City Hall, I would not tolerate the presence of a single man in the committee associated in interest with Mr. Insull," Richberg wrote, adding, "If I have not been sufficiently plain, I will speak even more plainly upon request."[6]

Insull shied from the limelight, but his scheming to raise fares, suppress strikes, and orchestrate favorable purchase agreements for his utilities provided much of the behind-the-scenes drama in Chicago politics during the 1920s. When former mayor Thompson returned after a four-year hiatus to run for the office again in 1926, he created a demagogic campaign against the World Court and proclaimed that if he ever met (England's King) George he would punch him in the nose. Ironically, this ultimately successful campaign was underwritten by a $32,925 contribution from the English-born Samuel Insull, as well as a direct $35,000 campaign contribution from Insull to Thompson.[7] Insull's goal was not only to win permanently higher fares on his streetcar lines, but to win a perpetual franchise to use the city streets, and with the backing of City Hall. Insull sent "traction bills" to the state legislature, where they failed due to a groundswell of outrage at Insull's tampering with the democratic process. Despite such setbacks from outraged voters, Insull thoroughly captured the regulatory process by buying politicians through his fixers in the firm of Samuel Ettelson, Daniel J. Schuyler, and Charles Weinfeld, and by getting his preferred politicians appointed to the Illinois Commerce Commission, which oversaw public utilities. In 1928, Edward R. Litsinger, a candidate in the rival machine of Illinois senator Charles Deneen, called City Corporation Counsel Ettelson the "personal luggage" of Samuel Insull, and pointed out that when it came to negotiating with the city, Insull merely had his lawyer, Schuyler, negotiate with his other attorney, Ettelson, the "Insullated lawyer."[8] One observer called Ettelson's appointment the most brazen and disgraceful thing in the history of Chicago, which was saying a lot.

It was through his influence on Thompson and Governor Small that Insull had a series of Black politicians appointed to the Illinois Commerce Commission, starting with Ed Wright, and continuing with Aldermen Oscar DePriest and Louis Anderson. Wright bucked the Thompson machine and sided with Deneen in 1927, saying, "I'm no political slave, and I don't propose to sell out my people to satisfy the whims of the downtown bosses."[9] But when Thompson won back the mayor's office after a four-year hiatus, Wright lost his county and state patronage and was replaced on the Illinois Commerce Commission by Daniel Jackson, a man who officially was an undertaker but whose more lucrative business was running the tony Beaux Arts Club and then the Dunbar gambling resorts. The *Philadelphia Tribune* announced the appointment with the note that "many times 'Dan' Jackson has been accused of knowing about gambling enterprises and protected cabarets in the principal Negro district of the city."[10] Nevertheless, Jackson joined his rival Oscar DePriest on the Commerce Commission. Being corrupt was not a disqualifier for Prohibition-era politicians in Chicago; it was practically a prerequisite.[11]

The case of Frank L. Smith, the head of the Illinois Commerce Commission, demonstrated that belonging to that state regulatory board could be quite financially lucrative for those who took money from Insull and other public utility barons. Smith won a US Senate seat after Insull and other utility czars gave hundreds of thousands of

dollars to his campaign, during the time he was the head of the board
tasked with regulating their industries. Irate, Julius Rosenwald offered Smith half a million dollars to withdraw from the race. Smith
refused, but Rosenwald managed to trigger a US Senate investigation. The Senate refused to seat the newly elected senator from
Illinois for fear that he was in fact the senator from Insull. Insull
and Schuyler testified before the Reed Committee of the US Senate that they had contributed $237,925 in the 1926 election cycle to
Thompson and his ally state's attorney Robert E. Crowe, but they
would not specify who had received $40,000 in contributions to "lo-
cal officers." Those numbers were likely only a fraction of the real
amounts; Senator Thaddeus Caraway of Arkansas aired rumors that
Insull had contributed millions into election campaigns in the 1926
cycle, which seems entirely plausible since Insull admitted to giving
$125,000 in three envelopes stuffed with cash to Smith alone.[12]

Samuel Insull's philanthropy on the South Side was part of his
wider effort to buy politicians and elections. The official story was
that Insull was a kind-hearted philanthropist who took a humanitar-
ian interest in Chicago's "Negroes" and was second only to Rosenwald
as their benefactor. According to this view of the world, Insull's spon-
sorship of the South Side Boys' Club, the Black-directed Provident
Hospital, and other South Side ventures stemmed from his generous compassion for Black people. "Insull had a rather kindly spot in
his busy heart for the struggles of the black man," Lucius C. Harper
wrote in the Insull-friendly *Chicago Defender* in 1938. "He took time
out to listen to many sad situations confronting us as a race, and often
brought his check book into play to relieve the worthy."[13] Insull's official memoirs stated that he and Schuyler as his longtime political fixer
were very much interested in helping the "colored people" of the South
Side of Chicago, and so established both the South Side Boys' Club
and "a community center for the older Colored people."[14] But Black
critics were nonplussed. The novelist Richard Wright got a job at the
South Side Boys' Club and was engrossed by the "wild and homeless
lot" of Black boys who visited the club, just as he was disgusted by the
hypocrisy of wealthy white donors using charitable giving to protect
their property values. The experience inspired his novels *Black Boy*
and *Native Son*. He felt that the real purpose of his task of distracting
the "Bigger Thomases" of the South Side with ping-pong and check-
ers was to protect the valuable white property at the edges of the Black
Belt. "I am not condemning boys' clubs and ping-pong as such," he

reflected later, "but these little stopgaps were utterly inadequate to fill up the centuries-long chasm of emptiness which American civilization had created in these Biggers. I felt that I was doing a kind of dressed-up police work, and I hated it."[15] Wright was right; there was an ulterior motive to Insull's South Side philanthropy, in addition to the function of taking Black boys off the streets. Under the guise of charitable giving, Insull engaged in another longtime Chicago activity: buying votes.

Insull's "community center," Unity Hall, was not just the headquarters of the Moorish Science Temple. It was also the hub from which Insull's lawyers distributed thousands of dollars that DePriest used to buy votes on the South Side for machine candidates aligned with Cook County boss Robert Crowe, Mayor Thompson, and Governor Len Small, compliant pols who would support the interests of the public utilities. As Insull's lawyer, Charles Weinfeld, testified in 1920 when audited for tax evasion by the Bureau of Internal Revenue (the predecessor of the IRS), the law firm of Weinfeld and Schuyler had spent thousands of Insull's dollars in the 1915 elections supporting various candidates, but had not paid taxes on that money as income. "We gave Oscar DePriest a lot of money in connection with campaigns," Weinfeld testified. "He would line up the black vote in connection with some special candidate that we happened to be interested in." Weinfeld also exposed the political nature of Insull and DePriest's ostensibly charitable giving: "We gave him [DePriest] money in connection with the People's Movement that is run as charitable organizations for the advancing of the colored people and indirectly it was political." (The People's Movement was a South Side political club DePriest ran with secret kickbacks from vice operators and bribes from Samuel Insull.) Weinfeld estimated that his law firm had spent $10,000 or $15,000 on DePriest's political campaigns by 1920, or between $128,000 and $192,000 in 2020 dollars.[16] As the Baltimore *Afro-American* explained, Insull reached out to DePriest through his attorney Schuyler beginning in 1915, and purchased the old Unity Hall at 3140 S. Indiana Avenue not long thereafter with Insull, Schuyler, and DePriest as the owners of record.

Unity Hall was a magnificent building, formerly serving as a Jewish clubhouse that hosted lectures and social events. It would now serve as DePriest's political headquarters, a combined "political and social center," and the mechanism by which Insull and his lawyer Schuyler would funnel money into the South Side to buy votes.[17]

DePriest made Unity Hall the headquarters for a Property Owners' Association, and "for seven or eight years it flourished as a political and welfare center, although the hand of Insull was never shown, and Schuyler was only suspected of being in the background," as the *Afro-American* explained.[18]

But by 1926, Insull's secret was at least partially exposed when Senator Caraway aired rumors that Insull was using Schuyler to buy votes in Chicago's Black wards. The same year, Chandler Owen, publisher of the Black socialist newspaper the *Messenger*, denounced the arrangement even more explicitly. "There is no greater menace among Negroes than that of money bags wielded by white corporation lawyers. In some respects, Dan Schuyler is the most notorious illustration of this menace," Owen wrote. "He and the utility interest are so interested in Negroes that they have a Boys' Club, and a political ward healers club in Chicago's black belt," referring facetiously to DePriest's People's Movement. Owen thought Insull could have done more good by removing racist barriers to Black employment among his thousands of employees:

> But how many Negro employees has the Peoples' Gas Company of Chicago? How many has the Commonwealth Edison Company? How many does the Chicago Rapid Transit Company employ? And, pray tell us what do they do? Can a Negro become a motorman or a conductor on the Chicago Rapid Transit system of railways? Can a colored girl be a stenographer or anything other than a scrub woman in the Commonwealth Edison Company? Can a Negro get near enough the Peoples' Gas Company to do anything besides pay his bill, or read a meter?[19]

There were over 150,000 "colored men and women" in Chicago, Owen noted, all using public utilities, making telephone calls, burning gas for cooking, heat, and light, using electricity, and riding streetcars and elevated railroads every day. And yet Insull refused to give Black people anything but menial jobs.

Even Robert Abbott's *Defender* echoed Owen's complaint about Samuel Insull's racist hiring practices in 1927, when it editorialized that Black citizens ought to ask Insull for jobs. "Our men in the state legislature should refuse to vote for measures that come up in the house and senate favoring public corporations that discriminate against our Race in the matter of hiring labor," the *Defender* opined.

"Our men, who are real Americans, are hardly used as janitors by the companies which are under Mr. Insull's control."[20] It was a common complaint among Chicago's Black residents that European immigrants who could not even pronounce the names of the city's streets could get jobs as conductors in Samuel Insull's Chicago Rapid Transit company, but Black American men and women generally could not find even menial labor in the same company. And yet Insull had nothing to fear from Chicago's Black politicians, as they were essentially on his payroll. And that is how rackets work: the racketeers, in this case Black politicians, reaped financial rewards for themselves and their families rather than do their jobs of creating economic opportunity for their two hundred thousand constituents.

During the elections of 1928, the *Baltimore Afro-American* published an anonymous anti-DePriest screed that detailed how the Republican Crowe-Thompson machine had undermined the Republican candidate for mayor in 1923 by funneling $30,000 of Insull's money through Schuyler to DePriest and his People's Movement, based at Unity Hall, in order to get Democrat William Dever elected: "Barbers got $5 each, buffet flat madams got a similar amount. A few of the preachers who were for sale got from $25 to $100. Anderson and others got some and helped Crowe and Thompson defeat Arthur Leuder for mayor, electing Mr. Dever."[21] In return, DePriest got to distribute jobs to about two dozen supporters during the Dever administration, including twelve in the sheriff's office, seven on the Sanitary District payroll, and several librarians in the offices of the corporation counsel and the city attorney. If Big Bill could not be mayor, he was not about to let another Republican step in and take over his patronage machine.

But after a decade of funneling money through DePriest, Insull and his fixers felt they were not getting a very good return on their investment. It is possible that their failure to extract a king's ransom from Chicago's voters for their elevated transit lines in 1925 was what finally spurred them to shake things up, as well as the belief that DePriest was pocketing an inordinate amount of the bribes that passed through his office. DePriest had invited a brilliant man with an incredibly varied career named Melvin Chisum to help him run his rackets, and set Chisum up with an office in Schuyler's swank offices downtown. Among many other accomplishments, Chisum had been an actor, an elocution coach, a journalist, and a steel mill efficiency expert during World War I. As an entertainer, he had also been friends with legendary musical comedians Bert Williams, George Walker, Bob Cole, and J. Rosamond Johnson. In addition, he had also worked extremely closely with Booker T. Washington for twenty-five years, including for a time as his confidential secretary. But Chisum had his detractors. Chandler Owen once wrote that Chisum was an "unscrupulous, irresponsible, treacherous and submarine Negro," and Chisum certainly submarined DePriest when he got out a pad and a pencil and demonstrated to Samuel Insull and Dan Schuyler how certain purchases that DePriest had made coincided closely with sums of money DePriest had received from Insull for his People's Movement rackets.[22] So much for honor among thieves.

After this revelation, DePriest lost Insull's good graces and Melvin Chisum became one of Emperor Insull's closest advisers, an efficiency expert for his companies, and a man Insull now trusted to make purchasing decisions worth hundreds of thousands of dollars. Flush with cash, Chisum broke the residential color barrier and bought a house in an exclusive suburb. With Booker T. Washington dead and Marcus Garvey imprisoned, Melvin Chisum even became regarded for a time as "the most powerful Negro in America."[23] Thus in 1926, when Insull's candidate for Senate was Frank Smith, the head of the Illinois public utilities regulatory commission, Schuyler and his partner, Samuel Ettelson, bought out DePriest's interest in the Unity Club for $13,000, and assembled a South Side vote-buying operation without him. Bishop Archibald J. Carey became president of the Unity Civic Club and Frank Summers, DePriest's secretary, became its executive secretary. Smith got the Black vote and Insull's investment "would pay big dividends to Insull if the Senate had not been so fussy," an anonymous author wrote in the *Baltimore Afro-American*, referring to the fact that the Senate forced Insull and Schuyler to testify and refused to seat their candidate Frank Smith because he had accepted so much money from Insull and other public utility barons while head of the commission tasked with regulating their industries. In 1927, Thompson returned to the mayor's office for his third and most brazenly corrupt term, and DePriest repaired his relationship with the Insull machine. "Big Bill returned, DePriest was restored to royal favor and was again allowed to gather up the crumbs that fell from the Insull table and to lick the hand of Ettelson and Schuyler," the *Afro-American* wrote.[24] Insull's covert alliance with the South Side's Black politicians explains why its three most prominent figures all enjoyed service on the Illinois Commerce Commission, the board that oversaw public utility companies.

After South Side congressman Martin B. Madden won the Republican primary and then died at the end of April of 1928, and Governor Len Small nominated DePriest to be the Republican candidate in the November election, DePriest's Black Democratic challenger circulated a scandalous anonymous broadside detailing Insull's and DePriest's influence-buying machine operating out of Unity Hall. At the time, DePriest's supporters decried the accusations as both racist and politically motivated, and the charges slowed but did not stop his ascent. But Insull's house of cards of holding companies collapsed with the stock market plunge in October of 1929 and the Great Depression that followed. He fled the country in his yacht in 1934 and the truth about DePriest's Insull-funded operations came to light and corroborated the charges made by DePriest's opponents back in the twenties. DePriest lost to Black Democrat Arthur Mitchell in 1934 and historians usually point to DePriest's opposition to the New Deal to explain that narrow loss. But the crumbling of the Thompson-DePriest rackets, partially funded by Insull, and his now-forgotten linkage to Insull that was exposed in 1934 congressional investigations were also important factors in ending the first Northern Black congressman's career in Congress.

It is all the more incredible that historians have thus far missed the role that Unity Hall played in buying elections on the South Side given that at least three reporters of the day compared Unity Hall and DePriest's vote-buying operation to none other than Tammany Hall, the home of New York's notoriously corrupt Democratic political machine in the nineteenth and twentieth centuries. An assessment by *Pittsburgh Courier* political reporter Stephen Breszka in 1934, the year of Insull's inglorious flight from justice, made that same exact comparison. "Old Unity Hall," he wrote, was "the palatial center which Mr. Insull at one time chose as the headquarters for his activities among the colored people," and "as hoary a factor in South Side Republican politics as Tammany Hall to the Democrats of the nation."[25]

After Insull's empire collapsed, President Franklin Delano Roosevelt used him as a punching bag, fulminating in a famous address before the Commonwealth Club of San Francisco on September 23, 1932, against "the Ishmael or Insull whose hand is against every man's" and who opposed government regulation of the economy.[26] So it was particularly fitting that Insull once met the representatives of

Ishmael when he and Noble Drew Ali crossed paths in Unity Hall. The story goes that Insull sponsored the most elaborate banquet ever given at the famous Appomattox Club, for the visiting journalists of the Associated Negro Press. After the meal, everyone was invited to hear Mr. Insull speak at Unity Hall, a mile away. Insull showed up promptly at 8:00 p.m., the scheduled hour of his talk—he was fastidious about punctuality—but there were only about a half-dozen people milling around the large hall. Not wanting his boss to be embarrassed at the poor turnout, resourceful Melvin Chisum sprang into action. He went down into the basement hall, where a meeting of the Moorish Science Temple was in progress. Mr. Chisum approached "the chief bey and informed him that he had a big man upstairs for a meeting and he needed an audience."

> "Bring your crowd up!" he commanded the Bey.
> The Moorish leader balked.
> "How much will you charge to bring your members upstairs?" Chisum asked.
> "Fifty cents a man," replied the Moore [sic], now interested.
> Chisum counted, dug into his pocket, and produced the money.
> At nine o'clock, Mr. Insull and [prominent "colored" physician Dr. Algernon] Jackson, both resplendent in tuxedos, strode down the aisle between the crowd of uniformed and turbaned Moors.
> The meeting was a success, but Insull seized the opportunity to scold the "editors" for their tardiness. After describing how he arose at 6 a.m. every day and made punctuality a creed, Mr. Insull said, "If colored people are as late getting to Heaven making C.P.T. time as they frequently do elsewhere, the white people will all be inside and St. Peter will have closed the gate ere they arrive."[27]

At least two of the people Insull was likely addressing, Claude Greene and Noble Drew Ali, would be at the pearly gates before too long, and Dan Jackson would join them there as well. There was a lot going on in this exchange: on the one hand, of course, there was Chisum's trickster deceit, keeping the "big man," his white boss, happy even as he pulled the wool over his eyes. On the other hand, Samuel Insull had just enough cultural competence to use the term "CPT," or "Colored People's Time," yet the manner in which he used it was plainly offensive, and, ironically, underscored one of the very appeals of Islam to the Moors: Muslims decried racial segregation in either heaven or earth. Beyond that, Insull lacked the basic level of cultural sensitivity to tell the difference between a group of Moors, wearing fezzes and turbans, and a group of journalists. He obviously had no clue who the Moors were; maybe he thought they were members of the fourth estate wearing Shriner regalia. But equally telling is that neither they, nor the absent journalists, had any idea who Samuel Insull was, or, if they did, they did not care to meet him if not paid to do so.

That was Samuel Insull in a nutshell: interested in Black people and philanthropic yet also racist, footing the bill in an extravagant ges-ture of hospitality—or was it bribery? Insull was so cold, austere, and accustomed to working in the shadows that the man who lit up much of the country had the star power of a sputtering bulb. Even while standing in the very building he had secretly purchased, observing the birth of Islam as a mass movement on American shores, he had no idea what he was witnessing. On the other hand, Insull's lavish spend-ing on the press event, the allegation that he had promised $100,000 in advertising to foreign-language newspapers who backed his can-didate in the 1926 senatorial election, and the white-glove treatment he received in the pages of the *Chicago Defender* suggest that Insull likewise paid to influence coverage in the Black press as well.[28]

Samuel Insull visited Unity Hall many times, often early in the morning—he was an early riser, and must have fit in the visits before he went to the office at 7:30 a.m. to oversee his empire. Early-morning visits also decreased the likelihood that his presence would be noted. He liked to keep a low profile; if he had returned to Unity Hall in 1934, Breszka surmised, the current manager, William Levi Daw-son, might have asked, "'Who are you?'" But "Insull probably could tell Mr. Dawson something," Breszka wrote. "He could describe how he had put many, many thousands of dollars through the old Unity Hall and point out where his 'donations' had led him. "'Young man,'" Breszka imagined the utilities baron saying to the future congress-man, "'beware! This is an evil house, whether you call it Unity or Congressional Hall. In bygone days, my hopes were in it, but they were sadly, tragically blasted. I feel the evil spirits still abound here. If you would be wise, think upon these things.'"[29] Thousands of Blacks escaped disenfranchisement in the South only to find racketeers of many races in the Windy City who collected their votes and sold them down the sewage-choked Chicago River.

CHAPTER TWELVE

MOORISH SCIENCE

Chicago is going to be your new Mecca.[1]
—NOBLE DREW ALI

According to a writer employed for the Illinois Writers' Project, a program of the New Deal, one hot August day in 1925, a plump middle-aged matron named Lily Sloane set off to place a bet with her local policy syndicate. "From the cool recesses of pool halls the infrequent click of ivory balls floated out to hang suspended in the brilliant sunshine," according to the anonymous writer who reported the story and imagined the scene about a decade later.[2] She gazed down Thirty-Seventh Street where it crossed State Street, and on the west side, "in the center of a dusty, open patch between two buildings, a little man stood on a box. He stood in the full glare of the copper late-afternoon sun, and a red fez on his head set his whole face on fire." The man gesticulated to a skeptical crowd, a black streamer trailing from the top of his fez. "He was brown and slender and had a little black moustache and was not at all bad to look at," the author reported. Suddenly, the man with the fez called her by name in a soft, rich voice: "Lily Sloane, I, your Prophet command ye to come unto me and learn the truth and be free in the name of your Father God, Allah!" Startled, Lily looked all around her but there was no one else who could have called—it was the man with the fez. The woman stumbled into State Street, in a daze. She almost did not want to look across the street, but she had to. "There the sun was a huge disc of orange fire, and in front of the sun, small and slender and

straight on the empty box, the Man was standing. He was motion-
less, arms outstretched to each side, his body a cross on fire." He was
staring straight at Lily Sloane, while bystanders nudged each other
and made jokes at the expense of this "Hindu," a word that was in
scare quotes in the 1930s original. The spectators began to laugh,
but "the Prophet stayed with his arms wide and a burning light in his
face, a cross against the sun." There was something arresting about
his visage, "burning with something holy and at the same time wild
and full of a strange kind of passion."

Lily Sloane stood frozen in the summer heat so long that an angry
white streetcar motorman had to clang his bell to get her to move.
Half dazed by the sun and the vision of the diminutive man in the
brimless red hat, she wandered into the local policy outlet and played
the exorbitant sum of fifty-two cents, all she had, on the numbers
5–7–4. When her numbers hit at the policy wheel later that evening,
Lily Sloane invested her riches in renting a rooming house with the
top two floors occupied and space for herself on the ground floor. The
anonymous writer continued:

> But the vision of the man would not leave her. Who was the little
> man with the fez and the face on fire like an angel? Not long after,
> she saw him once again preaching on top of his box at 37th and
> State Street. Once again, the passing people known as "Negroes"
> were paying him little mind, and scoffed at his jeremiad. "Laugh!"
> The little man roared, "but the day will come when you will weep!
> When the wrath of my father God Allah is poured out upon the
> earth you will regret that you did not heed his Prophet! That is
> why you are so easy to trick; that is why the European—the man
> you call the white man—can keep you in bondage. Oh, you will
> listen to *him*! Anything he tells you is alright. He took you out of
> Asia and gave you slave names; he calls you Black Folks, Colored
> People, Ethiopians, and you believe him! I tell you, brothers and
> sisters, there ain't but one race on earth, and that's the human race.
> That has got two branches—the Europeans—the man you call the
> White man, and the Asiatics—*us*. But you don't know that 'cause
> the European don't want you to know it. He wanta call you by your
> slave name and keep you working for him. And you let him do it. It's
> your own fault, brothers!"
>
> He stopped, and the laughter was less confident now, less mock-
> ing. Lily Sloane edged closer into the crowd, unnoticed. Some of

the people were listening with rapt attention; some were uncomfortable. The little man opened his arms and again he was a cross on fire against the sun. "Come all ye Asiatics of America and learn the truth of your nationality and birthright, because you are not colored, you are not black folks, you are not Ethiopians. You must claim a free name . . . a Moorish name. Learn of your Forefathers' Divine and Ancient Creed that you will learn to love instead of hate."[3]

This time the Prophet was met with murmurs of approval, not jeers. As the hot summer sun sank slowly behind the stockyards to the west, the man finished, and the crowd dispersed, but Lily Sloane remained. As he mopped his brow, Lily picked up his black satchel. He asked her why she did not leave with the rest of the unbelievers, and she stammered, "'You don't remember me, I guess,' she faltered . . . 'Why of course, Sister. Of course I remember you. Have you a lodging for tonight, Sister?'" Triumphantly, Lily Sloane entered her new home, and with her came the Prophet Noble Drew Ali. As the New Deal writer reported:

> Lily Sloane worshipped her new-found prophet. She became Lily Sloane-Bey, and was no longer a Negro. She was black, but she was no longer black, she was olive-skinned. She wore a long dress, down to her ankles, and with sleeves covering her arms even in such hot weather. She was shy at first in a red turban, then proud. She stood, not on the outskirts now, but next to the Prophet while he preached to the ever-growing crowd in the vacant lot. . . . Day after day the Prophet preached his doctrine of escape.[4]

The tenants on the top floor of Sister Sloane's boardinghouse, Mr. and Mrs. Edward Mealy, joined the sect and became Mr. and Mrs. Mealy-El. Others moved out, and were replaced with followers of the Prophet with their distinctive red fezzes for the men and red turbans for the women. Drew Ali used the front room for his study, and held meetings in the basement around the furnace. At night he would draw the shades and close the doors of his room and spend hours filling notebooks and scraps of papers with speeches, consulting well-worn copies of the Bible and various magical books published by the De Laurence Company of Chicago. He also spent cold winter nights tinkering with small bottles of herbs, liquids, and oils that he hid under his bed during the daytime, along with pastes and lotions. One night, all night, he revealed his plans to Lily Sloane, and shared with her the notebooks and the medicines under the bed. She left his chamber that night as the first Grand Sheikess of the Moorish Temple of Science (the original name of the group), knowing more of the secrets of the sect than any other person save the Prophet himself.

That was the public story of the founding of the Moorish Science Temple of America, as reported a decade after the events in question. The real story is even more interesting. A Black "Lily Sloane" appears in no census; the name is actually a reference to a ragtime two-step march from 1900, "Ma Tiger Lily," by A. B. Sloane. It was a syncopated humdinger of a cakewalk tune and almost always appeared last or second from last in band programs of the time; it really "took the cake." A trumpeter like Walter Brister who played concerts at the turn of the century might have played the number countless times, and it always appeared in programs as "'Ma Tiger Lily' . . . Sloane." Twenty-five years later, when Walter Brister needed a new pseudonym for his first female follower, "Lily Sloane" came to mind as easily as "Billie Jean Jackson" or "Veronica Costello" might to a middle-aged person today. Just as "Noble Drew Ali" was a pastiche of various titles common among Black Hindu magicians, Brister repurposed a name from his past rather than create one anew. Quite likely bands did not reproduce the lyrics anyhow, but the words of the original song were as base as the music was inspired, composed in a bad parody of Black speech common to minstrel shows: "Fur she's ma Lily my Tiger Lily, / She draws de niggers like a crowd of flies, / A Queen in shape and size." Even Walter Brister set out to transform "Negro" identity by rejecting such racial epithets and replacing them with respectful Muslim and "Moorish" ones, the new pseudonym's reference to an old ragtime song shows that Brister was shaped by an older era of show business, a time when "Afro-Americans" played "Hindoos" and bands of all descriptions played ragtime. In the famous photograph of the Moors' First Annual Convention, in October 1928, the former Eva Brister, now Eva Allen, sat next to her former husband, Walter Brister, a.k.a. Armmah Sotanki, a.k.a. Timothy or Thomas Drew, a.k.a. Noble Drew Ali. He was still as slim as ever, but her jowls had thickened, as had her midsection, compared with the years when she was an ingénue who tamed lions and wrangled snakes. Her focused gaze was even more determined, and all those years making her way in show business as a woman of color in Jim Crow America had honed her business-savvy brain to a fine edge.[5]

In his prior life as a musician on the South Side, Walter Brister would have necessarily come into ample contact with gamblers and gangsters, and taking the extraordinary step of removing oneself from the land of the living might have been an effective way of erasing a debt that could not otherwise be paid. Whoever went into the ground in his place, and whatever Brister's reasons for leaving in such an extraordinary manner, when he returned to Chicago as Noble Drew Ali he presented himself as a healer and reformer in the city that had become the largest and wealthiest Black city in the world, a place where economic opportunity and cultural expression marched wide-shoulder-to-wide-shoulder with corruption, destitution, and venality. The former Walter Brister/Armmah Sotanki/ Professor Drew applied everything he had learned as a performer, magician, and healer to the new role of Noble Drew Ali, but also incorporated a strong new element of religious reform and economic solidarity, inveighing against the moral dissipation he must have witnessed firsthand in the gambling dens, bordellos, and theaters where Black musicians plied their trades in Chicago at the turn of the twentieth century. Drew Ali learned about Islam from Suleiman's version of Muslim Shrinerdom, from whom he borrowed the Shriner title "Noble," the fez, and the idea that Islam was secretly the true religion of Black people, and quite likely learned from north Indian Ahmadiyya missionaries as well, who were actively recruiting "Negroes" in the 1920s. With its abstemiousness and dignified, even severe, form of worship, Islam offered the perfect antidote both to the gin-soaked world of cabarets and also to the increasingly emotional forms of Southernized Christian worship. The Moors were notable among South Side religious groups in that they sang few hymns, and used an "Eastern" form of chanting throughout their services.[6] Yet at the same time as Prophet Noble Drew Ali was inveighing against the habits of the South and the underworld, he embedded himself in the shadowy political matrix of the South Side.

After the crucial encounter in Newark and New York with the Muslim Shriner Abdul Hamid Suleiman, who had taught that African Americans were properly Muslims, and Professor Drew's uneven experiment with establishing a mosque in Newark, Drew Ali started the Moorish Temple of Science on the East Coast where he had worked earlier as Professor Drew, the Egyptian Adept. In 1929, ace "Negro" private eye Sheridan Brusseaux testified in front of a grand jury that Noble Drew Ali had begun his sect in several South Carolina cities in 1923, and that Drew was then known as "Eli Drew, The Prophet of Allah." Brusseaux himself was well positioned to investigate the Moors: he had been born in Little Rock, Arkansas, served in the Secret Service during World War I, and then founded the Keystone National Detective Agency with dozens of Black informants around the country after the war. He used this network to investigate the South Side prophet, and learned that after establishing temples in South Carolina, Drew moved on to North Carolina and Virginia, then to Washington, DC. According to this version of the Moorish Science Temple's origins, Drew did not arrive in Chicago until 1925, after already establishing a network throughout the eastern United States. Brusseaux had better information than anyone outside the Moorish Science Temple, even if he himself was suspect: it was Brusseaux who was hired by *Chicago Defender* editor Robert Abbott to entrap Marcus Garvey into selling stock in the Black Star Line in violation of Illinois state law during a visit to Chicago, an action that led to Garvey's prosecution and imprisonment for securities fraud in 1923.[7]

According to multiple sources, in August of 1925, Walter Brister as "Noble Drew Ali" began preaching on street corners of the South Side and started attracting followers. "Come all ye Asiatics of America and hear the truth about your nationality and birthrights, because you are not negroes," he was reported to say by one woman who heard the call of the slight man with the exotic Eastern costume. "Learn of your forefathers' ancient and divine Creed. That you will learn to love and not hate." He opened Temple #1 on October 15, 1925, at 329 E. 36th Place, with Brother Lomax-Bey as the Grand Governor and Brother Rucker-Bey as the Assistant Grand Governor.[8] The Holy Prophet, as his followers knew him, drew on the metaphor of electricity to describe his mission, saying things such as, "I have mended the broken wires, and have connected them with the Higher powers."[9] The preternaturally gifted Eastern mystic healing man with the bevy of root cures for common ailments soon assembled a small group of followers, whom he impressed by accurately predicting that the star and crescent moon, the symbol of Islam, would soon appear in the night sky, as indeed the moon and Venus combined to do on December 18, 1925.[10]

The Prophet offered escape from the strictures of racism by demolishing the concept of race itself. The people known as "Negroes" were in fact Asiatics of Islamic Moorish descent, he preached. Their original names were Bey and El. Here in America they were still enslaved, because Europeans kept their minds in bondage. In truth they were not black, but various shades of olive, and the use of color labels for races was part of the Europeans' plan to maintain their supremacy and that of the Roman Catholic Church. (In an era when there was palpable anti-Catholic prejudice, it was not unusual to find fulminations against Rome in the thought of alternative Black religious practitioners.) Europeans called themselves "white" because white symbolized purity, while they called Moors "black" because black symbolized death. The Moors gave the name "Negro" to the Niger River because, he said, it contained black water; "Ethiopian" meant division, and "colored" meant stained or painted, which they were not. "Can a man be a Negro, Black, Colored or Ethiopian?" he asked rhetorically in the publication *Koran Questions for Moorish Children*, before answering with a resounding, "No."[11]

Like Prince Ishmael, the Black "Hindu" who appeared on the bill the very first time Brister performed as Armmah Sotanki, Noble Drew Ali revered Buddha. In fact, the Moorish Prophet accepted all true and divine prophets, including Jesus, Buddha, Confucius, and Muhammad, but taught that Jesus had been sent for the salvation of Europeans, not Asiatics. Noble Drew Ali would become the last prophet for the "fallen" Moors of North and South America, to redeem them, to teach them the truth of their nationality and birthright, and to teach them to love and not to hate. The South Side was no stranger to exotic sects, but these newcomers stood out with their distinctive red headgear and even more distinctive historical and theological teachings. Although many greeted the new sect with hostility and suspicion, and children were said to taunt the Moors or even to throw stones at them on the streets, their numbers steadily grew.[12]

By May of 1926, Prophet Noble Drew Ali and his helpmate the Grand Sheikess established the home office of what he initially called the "Moorish Temple of Science" two blocks north of his original location, at 3229 S. Indiana Avenue in the heart of the South Side, less than half a block north of Pilgrim Baptist Church's imposing Moorish Revival edifice, two blocks from Robert Abbott's

Chicago Defender offices at 3435 S. Indiana Avenue, and only two blocks from the Michigan Avenue mansion where Lauron William De Laurence had conducted his orgies and sold his books of Hindu magic and Orientalist arcana. Drew Ali impressed his acolytes with displays of supernatural powers, such as the escape magic that "Hindoo" magicians had been displaying in circuses and sideshows for decades. A flyer for a May 16, 1927, meeting promised that Drew Ali, "the Seventh Wonder of the World," would present the Great Moorish Drama, including being bound by several yards of rope, "as Jesus was Bound in the Temple of Jerusalem," and would escape in a few seconds. He would also heal members of the audience without touching them, "manifesting his divine power."[13] The Moors incorporated with the state of Illinois in the spring of 1927, and that year the organization continued to spread across Black communities in the eastern United States, landing in Charleston, West Virginia, in March; Milwaukee, Wisconsin, in August; Detroit in October; and Pittsburgh in November. In 1928 they crossed the Mason-Dixon Line with a temple in Richmond, Virginia, founded in January, followed by Cleveland in April, Pine Bluff, Arkansas, in May, a second Chicago temple in July, one in Drew's former home of Newark the same month, and another in the City of Brotherly Love in August.[14] Brister/Drew/Ali had finally hit on a formula that worked, and he wasted no time in franchising it, no doubt benefiting from the zeal and business acumen of his ex-wife, Eva.

On one tour through the South in October of 1927, the Prophet visited Marcus Garvey, the leader of the Universal Negro Improvement Association, who was then imprisoned in the Atlanta Federal Penitentiary. Even though Garvey had once denied any connection to the eccentric Muslim prophet, he now received Drew Ali amicably. The *Chicago Defender* reported that "Mr. Garvey was very much pleased with the splendid uplift work being done by the Moorish Divine Movement," and the paper helpfully announced the Moors' ongoing membership drive.[15] Drew Ali's followers understood the encounter to mean that Garvey was the contemporary equivalent of John the Baptist, heralding the return of the Messiah, and that Noble Drew Ali was the modern-day Jesus. With the devoted adulation of his Moors, the affirmation of the most famous and arguably still the most influential Black leader in the world, and the support of America's most important Black newspaper, Walter Brister as Noble Drew Ali had truly arrived.

As "Professor Drew," Walter Brister had suffered his last arrest for practicing medicine without a license in December of 1923. But a few years later, the man formerly known as the magician Armmah Sotanki had pulled off his greatest magic feat of all, with the assistance of his ex-wife and fellow magician, Eva: they created the first "Black Muslim" mass movement—a term that Drew Ali would have rejected out of hand. Historian Patrick Bowen discounts claims that the Moors numbered over one hundred thousand, but estimates from a meticulous analysis of primary sources that the Moors reached seven thousand members by late 1928 with temples from Milwaukee in the north to Pine Bluff, Arkansas, in the south, with chapters in Detroit, Newark, Pittsburgh, and Richmond, Virginia, among others. Bowen estimates that by this time Prophet Noble Drew Ali had 3,000 followers in Chicago, 1,500 Moors in Detroit, where Garvey mentor Duse Mohamed Ali had recently helped to found the Islamic Society, and 459 adherents in Pittsburgh, with the other temples averaging a more modest 159 members each. Combined, Drew Ali's members were almost five times more numerous than the US Ahmadiyya movement at its height, even after years of the Muslim Indians' tireless missionary efforts.[16]

Although his religion was Islamic in that it venerated Allah, honored the Prophet Muhammad, and incorporated elements of Arabic and Islam found in the rituals of the Nobles of the Mystic Shrine of North America that were the basis of his teacher Suleiman's understanding of Islam, Drew Ali's teachings were otherwise remarkable only for how conventional they were, so perfectly in tune with the zeitgeist. In September of 1928, Drew Ali defined his goals along lines that fell well within the economic and social solidarity advocated by so many of his contemporaries in Black Chicago in the press and the pulpit alike. As the Prophet explained, the purpose of his Moorish National movement was to dispense charity and provide mutual assistance in time of distress; to improve the health of members and allow them to own better-quality homes; to find employment for members; and to teach the fundamental principles of "civilization," including obedience to the law, loyalty to government, and virtues such as tolerance and unity. "We are friends and servants of humanity," Drew Ali declared. "We are dedicated to the purpose of elevating the moral, social and economic status of our people." It would all be accomplished through the cardinal virtues of "love, truth, peace, freedom and justice."[17]

Drew Ali was explicitly Muslim: he claimed to be directly guided by Allah, just as he did in his prior persona as Newark's Professor Drew when he called on Allah in the midst of healing rituals. It little mattered that other Muslims questioned Drew Ali's claim to prophecy as blasphemous, or that there were no quotations from the Prophet Muhammad's Qur'an in *The Holy Koran of the Moorish Science Temple of America*, published in 1927, which came to be called the "Circle Seven Koran" because of the image on its cover of a circled seven, a number that acquired mystical significance in Hebrew Scriptures and Jewish Kabbalah. There is no reason to doubt Drew Ali's sincerity in his many professions of faith in Islam or his extolling its virtues to his thousands of followers. And since anyone who professes faith in Allah and Muhammad as His Prophet with sincerity becomes a Muslim, the Moorish Science Temple was undoubtedly Islamic, even if it was unorthodox.

With the exception of its final section, which appears to be original, Noble Drew Ali's Circle Seven Koran was copied from two books of esoteric wisdom. Chapters I–XIX come from *The Aquarian Gospel of Jesus the Christ*. The work was published by white mystical Christian preacher Levi Dowling, who was heavily influenced by Theosophy, and transcribed the book, he claimed, from the "akashic record" of fine ethers surrounding the earth that he believed recorded humanity's every word and thought. His *Aquarian Gospel* appeared in 1908 and was republished by the De Laurence Company in 1923. It filled in the missing years in Jesus's New Testament biography between adolescence and age thirty, claiming that Jesus had traveled to India and learned the ancient secrets of the Vedic masters and the Egyptians before returning to Jerusalem and his Crucifixion at Calvary. Like Dowling, and many others, Drew Ali took "peace" as his byword. There is also a clear Masonic influence in the Dowling/Drew Ali text, particularly in chapter V: 12–21, which explains how to perfect the soul with metaphors referencing the tools of the building trade, including the square and compass, the plumb line, and the twelve-step ladder.

Dowling, who led a group of self-proclaimed Gnostics and created a Brotherhood of Universal Peace in a beachside community south of Los Angeles, was in turn inspired by the book *La vie inconnue de Jesus Christ*, published in 1894 by a Russian Jew who converted to Orthodox Christianity and took the name Nicolas Notovitch. Notovitch claimed to have learned about the journey of Saint Issa (the Arabic name of Jesus) in India by discovering an ancient manuscript in a Tibetan monastery, although the monks denied that he had ever been there and Notovitch himself confessed to fabricating the story and the manuscript. The mystical use of the number seven that gave Drew Ali's text its name "Circle Seven Koran" derived from the seven Elohim, or spirits of God mentioned in the Hebrew Bible and repeated in Notovitch and Drew's text. The only changes Drew Ali made to Notovitch's text were substituting "Allah" for "God" and removing the description of Jesus having blond hair and blue eyes. But these substitutions created many anachronisms; ancient Jews and the first Jewish followers of Jesus are depicted worshiping "Allah," and the heading of chapter VI describes the "Life and Work of Jesus in India Among the Moslems," although Jesus lived before the advent of Islam in the seventh century and the chapter itself mentions Brahmin priests but no Muslims. Even more incongruously, the work mentions the "Triune Allah" and the divinity of Jesus, when the Prophet Muhammad explicitly rejected the Christian concept of the Trinity or the divinity of Jesus. In the late nineteenth century, the Islam-admiring Black missionary Edward Wilmot Blyden had predicted that Islam could serve as a gateway form of monotheism, converting West African pagans to a "lower" form of monotheism on the way to the "higher" truths of Christianity. But Noble Drew Ali's transformation of the Christian text *La vie inconnue de Jesus Christ* into a putatively Islamic one demonstrates that just the opposite occurred: by applying Islamic labels to a Christian text about the divinity and prophecy of Jesus, Drew Ali would convert Christians into Muslims, not Muslims into Christians.[18]

The second half of Ali's Circle Seven Koran, chapters XX–XLIV, "Holy Instructions from the Prophet," comes from a text published by followers of one of the Rosicrucian traditions that claimed the mantle of the multiracial Black sex magician Paschal Beverly Randolph. *Unto Thee I Grant*, from 1925, claims to have been compiled by an editor named "Sri Ramatherio," from an English text dating back to 1760. Allegedly, an "English gentleman" working for British interests in China had the book translated in 1749 from a Chinese text, which itself was a translation of an ancient Tibetan work obtained from the Dalai Lama. The Chinese translator believed that the work was originally written by Confucius or Lao Tzu, but since it includes references to tulips, Arabian perfumes, and crocodiles, Ramatherio suggests without offering any evidence that the book could have been a translation of a work by Egyptian pharaoh Akhnaten. In one passage reminiscent of the Song of Solomon, which Noble Drew Ali chose *not* to excise the way he had removed the description of Jesus being blond from *The Aquarian Gospel*, the author wrote in praise of a beautiful woman, "The whiteness of her bosom transcendeth the lily; her smile is more delicious than a garden of roses" (*Holy Koran*, Chapter XX:7). As Moorish Science adherent Peter Lamborn Wilson notes, *Unto Thee* presents itself as a mystical text, but its striking feature is its practicality and even its conservatism. Wilson hypothesized that the book was written a little before 1760 in England "by someone who had the Bible open to Proverbs as he wrote," and that the creator of the Tibetan legend was probably a Rosicrucian or a member of a Masonic order. And so, incongruously, two Orientalist books associated with Western traditions of exploring the Mystic East and claiming dubious origins in ancient Tibet, books created most likely by an English Protestant and a Russian Christian of Jewish origins, formed the core of the "Holy Koran" of the first Islamic mass movement in American history.[19]

But there are portions of the text that appear to have been dictated by Noble Drew Ali himself, as no source materials have been found and they are written in a voice similar to Drew Ali's published pronouncements. Chapters XLV–XLVIII tell the story of Africa, or "Amexem," and how Moorish domination once stretched across the lost continent of Atlantis to America, connecting indigenous Africans and indigenous Americans in ancient times. The text says that the white Founding Fathers of America stripped Moors of their nationality in 1774, causing them to lose and forget their Moorish identity, which Noble Drew Ali came to restore. As Wilson puts it, these sections are "less grammatical but more poetic than all the rest," and since no one has uncovered another source, the best guess is that Drew Ali composed them himself.[20] In chapter XLV, "The Divine Origins of the Asiatic Nations," Drew Ali includes among Asiatics the Moors, Arabians, Japanese, Chinese, "Hindoos," Moorish Americans (mistakenly called "Negroes"), Mexicans, Brazilians, Argentinians and "Chilians," Colombians, Nicaraguans, and Salvadorans. "All of these are Moslems," Noble Drew Ali proclaimed. It was as if he transposed the peoples of color he encountered as a member of Pawnee Bill's Wild West Show into the circle of Islam. As Noble

Drew Ali, Walter Brister taught that the intercultural and interracial tolerance behind the scenes at Wild West and circus shows was intrinsically Islamic. Even "Europeans" could gain a Moorish passport as either "Celts" or "Persians." For Drew Ali, and his followers, Islam became the antidote to white racism.

So what did Prophet Drew Ali teach that found such a receptive audience from Americans then known as "Negroes"? One of Drew Ali's core teachings was that Americans of African descent were mislabeled and should adopt their true identity as Moors, according to legend the descendants of the ancient Moabites. His Divine Constitution and By-Laws proclaimed that he was teaching his members they were part of a government, and "are not Negroes, Colored Folks, Black People, or Ethiopians because these names were given to slaves by slave holders" in the period of slavery that ended in 1865, "but this is a new era of time now, and all men must proclaim their free national name to be recognized by the government in which they live and the nations of the earth."[21] This call to redefine "Negro" identity had unquestionable appeal for people who had been struggling to define and redefine themselves in the face of racist attacks for centuries. Drew Ali's contemporaries, especially after World War I, were proudly calling themselves "New Negroes," but Drew Ali's maxim capitalized on this eagerness for reinvention and went even further: people of African descent were not Negroes at all, nor were they Black: they were Moors and "Asiatics," the descendants of African Muslims. While the number of Americans who could trace their ancestry to enslaved African Muslims were few by the late 1920s, there was a lot more truth in Noble Drew Ali's claim of African Muslim ancestry than the racist calumny represented by sideshow "wild men" that depicted Black people as "missing links," or even by Brister's own first turn in show business that depicted "Negroes" as cheerful and talented buffoons. "If you have race pride and love your race, join the Moorish Science Temple of America and become a part of this divine movement," Noble Drew Ali declared in one Friday address from September 28, 1928. "Then you will have power to redeem your race because you will know who you are and who your forefathers were, because where there is unity there is strength."[22] Naming and misnaming others of various colors around the world was an act of European psychological trickery that underlay European political control, Drew Ali explained. In a passage later echoed and made famous by Malcolm X, Drew Ali wrote that Europeans defined white as a color of purity, while black represented everything evil. By returning so-called race men and women to their proper self-knowledge as Moors, Drew Ali was relinking them to their true and illustrious history as descendants of the founders of "the first civilization of the Old World."[23] Just as "Negroes" needed to be renamed "Moors," individual followers of Noble Drew Ali received new names signifying their new status: ordinary followers received the suffix "El" after their surname, members with greater standing received "Bey," and leaders acquired the last name "Ali."[24] Like the Reverend Edward Wilmot Blyden and many other participants in the 1893 Columbian Exposition's African Ethnological Congress, Drew Ali was excited by the ancient glories of African civilizations and the thought that the people who now served others, hectored and maligned by patronizing lectures on the "techniques of civilization," were, in fact, ironically, the direct descendants of the creators of the ancient and exalted civilization of Islam, the most tolerant and least racist religion in the world.

In a world that defined prostitution, drinking, and gambling as not just illegal but sinful, and then pushed all those vices into Black neighborhoods, recovery from sin played a key role in Drew Ali's faith. He proclaimed that "Allah the Great God of the Universe ordained Noble Drew Ali to redeem his people from their sinful ways."[25] But at the same time, he taught in contradistinction to Christianity that humanity's nature was not inherently debased but rather divine. Drew Ali rejected the intermediaries of saints and spirits. Instead he wrote that Allah, God, was "infinite, perfect, and Holy," that God worked "for us and in us," that nothing happened without his knowledge and will, and that he "neither begets nor is begotten."[26] That Drew Ali taught that God worked "in" and not just "for" us is noteworthy in that Lauron William De Laurence, various Black Israelites connected to the Garvey movement, Detroit's Father George W. Hurley of the largest Black Spiritual church denomination, and other esoteric practitioners of the time all believed that God dwelled within themselves, that people could actually become gods, a belief in divine immanence with deep roots in esoteric and magical traditions.

Drew Ali's moral teachings were conventional to the extreme, which no doubt helped pave the way for their rapid embrace. He

preached moral rectitude, respect for patriarchal duties, and obedience to patriarchal authority. Advising husbands to support their
families, and wives to obey husbands and attend to their household
duties, he also urged sons and daughters to obey their parents, "be
industrious and become a part of the uplifting of fallen humanity."
This message of industry and uplift was standard fare for the time,
and could be heard from the pulpits, and even newspaper columns
and leaflets, of numerous "colored" church, newspapers, and migrant
service organizations. This emphasis on patriarchy, on men earning
a living while women tended the domestic sphere, directly responded
to a world that commonly denied Black men as well as women respect, dignified forms of address, and basic physical safety. The
Moors disapproved of divorce but allowed it for couples who could
not live together harmoniously.[27]

Perhaps more unusual given the times, in a world awash in illegal
alcohol sold by the nationwide crime syndicate during Prohibition,
Drew Ali commanded all "Moorish Americans" to "keep their hearts
and minds pure with love, and their bodies clean with water."[28] He
instructed temple leaders to avoid profanity, alcohol, and anything
that would cause public embarrassment or dissension, and forbade
meat, smoking, shaving, cosmetics, and hair straighteners. Islam's
prohibition on consuming alcohol and pork helped Noble Drew Ali
to differentiate his faith from the fast ways of the speakeasies or the
Southern ways of the migrants who filled Black neighborhoods with
stands selling barbecued pork and pickled pigs' feet. The profitable
Moorish Manufacturing Company concocted and sold root tonics
that made numerous health claims, and Drew Ali's emphasis on a
healthful diet allowed his Moors to remake themselves as Muslims,
and to shed eating habits associated with the South that they considered unhealthy. It also facilitated the Moors' interest in opening
grocery stores, and, eventually, farms, to provide for the healthful
diets of members and to provide self-supporting businesses for the
benefit of the organization.

Repeatedly, Drew Ali emphasized that Islam was a religion of
peace that taught its followers how to live in harmony with their surroundings and fellow men. "Islam is a very simple faith," the Prophet
wrote, emphasizing duty to both Allah and one's fellow creatures.
"It teaches the supreme duty of living at peace with one's surroundings. It is preeminently the religion of peace. The very name, Islam,
means peace. The goal of a man's life, according to Islam, is peace with

everything. Peace with Allah and peace with man."[29] Noble Drew Ali, the Moors, and later groups like the Five Percenters would inject the word "peace" into the Black urban lexicon as an all-purpose greeting and farewell that reinforced the importance of peacefulness in Islamic teaching. It was, however, one thing in short supply in Chicago during the violent reign of Al Capone, Samuel Insull, and Mayor Big Bill Thompson.

Like Booker T. Washington, Marcus Garvey, and countless Black ministers before him, Noble Drew Ali also emphasized economic solidarity. More unusually, he started a string of successful businesses that put his followers to work, provided a place for his congregants to recycle their dollars within the organization, and created lucrative profit streams for the aggrandizement of the movement and its prophet. Calling for greater economic power and better employment opportunities, Drew Ali wrote, "We shall be secure in nothing until we have economic power. A beggar people cannot develop the highest in them, nor can they attain to a genuine enjoyment of the spiritualities of life." He extolled the business achievements and business capacity of people mislabeled "Negroes," and castigated those who withheld patronage, support, and encouragement from Black-owned businesses. "The problems of life are largely social and economic. In a profound sense, they are moral and spiritual," he wrote.[30] In addition to the profitable Moorish Manufacturing Company, whose profits helped to support the Chicago headquarters, there were several Moorish grocery stores in Chicago and a Moorish moving company, among other enterprises. Temples in other cities started their own businesses, including grocery stores and a butcher shop, but the manufacture of medicines remained centralized on the South Side.

The Moorish Science Temple undoubtedly developed a rich religious life and a compelling set of rituals, although little of them have been published or otherwise entered the public record. There were three basic categories of followers of the Moorish Science Temple of America. Regular members were distinguished from adepts, who were allowed to attend "adept chambers" if they were living moral lives and were paid up on their monthly dues and "taxes." Leaders, at various layers, made up the third category: the temple heads were known as Grand Sheiks, and were overseen by Governors. The headquarters had a Supreme Grand Council overseen by the Prophet himself, with a Supreme Business Manager and other officers.[31]

The organization Drew Ali first called the Moorish Temple of Science was undoubtedly religious and Islamic from the start, even though Drew Ali described it as a "civic organization" when he recounted registering the organization with the state of Illinois in 1926, language which some have interpreted to mean that the organization only became religious when it was reregistered as the Moorish Science Temple of America with the State of Illinois in 1928.[32] But to say that a temple is a civic organization does not mean that it is not also a religious one, and it seems unlikely that Drew Ali's temple only gained a religious dimension after its rapid spread, given his prior description of himself as a "Moslem," his healing with root medicine, and his sale of the De Laurence publication detailing Jesus's sojourn in the East while still operating as "Professor Drew" on the East Coast.

In Chicago as well, Brister as Drew Ali also explicitly taught about Islam and represented himself as a Muslim prophet. He reproduced without acknowledgment long flowery passages about the history of Islam from a 1921 publication originally delivered as a lecture by Alfred W. Martin at the Society for Ethical Culture in New York City. He reproduced entire paragraphs word for word—"The Mohammedan religion" is "the least appreciated and most misunderstood" of "all the great religions"—he copied, simply inverting the order of the first and third phrases, but when he relayed Martin's history of Islam's spread, from Arabia to Syria, Asia Minor, Turkey, Africa, India, the islands of Sumatra, Java, and Borneo, Drew Ali tellingly lopped off the last geographical reference: "and finally gained a foothold in Eastern Europe," thereby omitting the fact that there were European Muslims and preserving the appeal of the religion to his followers as a counter to white supremacy. "Incalculably great is the debt of the world to the early representatives of Mohammedanism," Drew Ali copied Martin, "for it was they who transmitted the treasures of Greek literature . . . they who contributed to the sciences of algebra and chemistry, astronomy and medicine."[33] It was time to return Christianity to the European nations, as Noble Drew Ali's *Holy Koran* stated.[34]

Completing Drew Ali's appeal was his refiguring of history to demonstrate that wrongs committed against the people he called Moors would soon be righted. Drew Ali claimed to have been many famous characters from history, including Noah. "I remember when I was on the soul-plane. I remember when I was Noah." When the flood came men swam out to the Ark and banged on the door to be let in, but an angel came and took the key, perhaps emphasizing the necessity of getting on the new Ark of the Moorish Science Temple before the next catastrophe struck.[35] Noble Drew Ali taught that Jesus was of African blood, and was crucified by Rome for trying to redeem his people from the "Roman yoke" and the "pressure of the pale skins of Europe."[36] The Prophet also claimed to be the reincarnation of the Prophet Muhammad and told stories about his past exploits:

> I am a General as well as a Prophet. I was Mohammed. Mohammed defeated the Roman Empire. When I conquered Rome, we went in with the sword. You could hear the swords swinging. I cut the head of Rome off; pulled down the flags; sent letters to the other European governments, and asked them was I right. They said, "Yes Mohamed, you are right. Just let us have a place to live." I went into Rome with 72,000 men. When I ran out of men, I reached down, and picked up a handful of sand, I threw it up in the air, and when it came down, there were soldiers seated on camels.[37]

It was an image worthy of the *Arabian Nights*. In Islam, and in the personality of the Prophet Muhammad, Drew Ali found powerful, mythic allies who would reverse the plight of people misidentified as "Negroes." He imagined a rising tide of color and the coming race war just like Lothrop Stoddard did, but he would make "Europeans" sue for peace.

Many of Drew Ali's history lessons refigured US history from a Moorish perspective. He taught that the colony of Virginia passed a law in 1682 exempting Moors from bondage. In fact, the 1682 statute he referenced permitted the enslavement of "negroes, moores, mollatoes and others borne of and in heathenish, idollatrous, pagan and mahometan parentage." It later declared that "all servants except Turkes and Moores" should be converted to Christianity, but in the same sentence says that "Negroes, Moores, Mollatoes or Indians" may be both converted and enslaved. The language was contradictory enough that one could interpret it the way Drew Ali did.[38] In any event, the Prophet taught that the Founding Fathers had met in Philadelphia in 1774 and ruled that only "Negroes" could be enslaved, an edict that became law when the United States declared its independence from Great Britain in 1776. The same year, he taught, George Washington cut down a red Moroccan flag and hid it in a safe in Independence Hall so that America's Moors would not figure out their true national identity. This, he said, was the origin of the apocryphal story of Washington chopping down the cherry tree. According to Moorish Science Temple legend, the Prophet paid a visit to President Woodrow Wilson in Washington, DC, in 1912 and asked the president to return the red Moorish flag that George Washington had taken. The Prophet asked the president for the right to teach the Divine Creed and true history of Moorish people. Wilson said that no one would follow Ali because he was dark-skinned, and challenged him to return with fifty followers. The Prophet returned with ten thousand and the American government authorized him to teach Islam and return the Moorish national identity to the descendants of slaves.[39] Wilson did not actually become president until 1913, but such legends do not lend themselves to literal fact-checking. Rather they speak to deeper themes—in this case, the Prophet's determination to win recognition for his followers as full American citizens in an era of racist Jim Crow policies.

There was also an apocalyptic strain to Noble Drew Ali's thought; in coming days, there would be a settling of accounts by which Moors would be exalted and Europeans would get their just deserts. In his *Holy Koran*, he wrote "I, the Prophet, Noble Drew Ali, was sent by the great God, Allah, to warn all Asiatics of America to repent from their sinful ways; before that great and awful day that is sure to come." The South would have to pay for lynching and murder, "and pay off in blood." As the Prophet Noble Drew Ali, Walter Brister created his own version of the Ghost Dance like that of the Sioux Indians with whom he served in Pawnee Bill's Wild West Show in 1899 and 1900. By some unspecified means, North America would reject Europeans and send them packing back to Europe. In Noble Drew Ali's hands, Allah would right the wrongs of American history, and redeem his lost-found people, the Moors.

Noble Drew Ali's claim to be the reincarnation of the Prophet Muhammad, as well as the fact that he did not use the Qur'an, angered some Muslims. A Sudanese cleric named Sāttī Mājid Muhammad al-Qādī had ventured to New York by way of London and Cairo in 1904, and founded four Islamic groups as well as a majority-Black Sunni group in Brooklyn either called the Islamic Mission of

America or, alternately, the State Street Mosque. A fellow Muslim brought a copy of the Circle Seven Koran to Sāttī Mājid's attention. He scoured it but could find no hadith from the Qur'an in its pages. Likewise, Noble Drew Ali's claim to prophecy outraged the Sudanese graduate of Cairo's Al-Azhar University. So when Sāttī Mājid returned to Egypt in 1929 and presented a formal request for a fatwa, or judicial opinion, against Drew Ali from his alma mater, the Islamic clerics in Egypt declared the Moorish leader to be a *mutanabbī*, or "would-be prophet." Though Sāttī Mājid corresponded with his associates in New York, he never returned to the States, and there is no indication that he ever confronted Drew Ali or the Moors with this religious condemnation.[40]

Islam appears differently wherever it is found, and always incorporates legends, myths, and magical practices that predate its own appearance in any particular locality. Because anyone can become a Muslim by simply stating the one-sentence *shahada* with conviction—"There is no true god but Allah, and Muhammad is the Messenger (Prophet) of God"—it is pointless to argue about who is or who isn't a Muslim. Indeed the fatwa against Drew Ali never said that he was not Muslim, but rather that he was not a prophet. The fatwa episode is interesting, but religions are not made by clerics and defenders of orthodoxy; they are made by innovators who piece their faiths together like a collage, by the frequently heretical innovations of the agents of what Drew Ali follower Peter Lamborn Wilson calls "sacred drift."

Noble Drew Ali, like so many other religious founders, cut and pasted his teachings and practices from a wealth of references. That it found so many followers so quickly indicates that he struck a chord. But it was not a basic chord based on mere imitation of any one person or program; the Moors' program was not a simple derivation of Garveyite nationalism, as some scholars have maintained, nor a derivative version of Spiritual churches or Black Shriners, as others have posited. Instead, over the course of several decades, Walter Brister went from trumpet-playing "pickaninny" to a Hindu magician to Professor Drew, to Eli Drew, to Noble Drew Ali, learning as he transitioned between each identity from a wealth of sources—the general fascination with the Islamic Orient in American popular culture; the fellowship of Moroccan acrobats named "Ali" with whom he experienced the Princeton Riot; the community of "colored" magicians who presented versions of the Orient and then became healers and root doctors during the Great Migration; the secret Islamic religious ritual of the Shriners and the version of Islam preached by advocates of another unorthodox Muslim prophet, Mirzā Ghulām Ahmad, and the community of esoteric visionaries who shared an interest in the books of the De Laurence Company. In addition, the efforts of Chicago's "Old Settlers" to reform the ways of Southern migrants provided a template for religious reform movements of morals and mores. Drew Ali's movement and his charismatic persona were not the simple products of any single one of these experiences and influences but the complex and polycultural creations of all of them. Prophet Noble Drew Ali was the maestro of this symphony, a cultural virtuoso who altered the faiths of thousands, and eventually millions, of people of "Moorish" descent in the United States of America.

{ CHAPTER THIRTEEN }

MACHINE POLITICS

Under Ettelson's direction, a traction ordinance has already been outlined. Insull has already petitioned for higher fares on the elevated. The money has been paid; the deal has been arranged. The voters can indorse its terms now or throw the whole mess, reeking of graft and corruption, into the drainage canal. Pineapples and Plunder. These are the issues.

—CHICAGO TRIBUNE, April 7, 1928[1]

W e cannot understand the audaciousness or the magnitude of Noble Drew Ali's accomplishments without understanding the governmental repression Black radicals faced and the endemic political corruption of Chicago's machine politics. At a time when the Bureau of Investigation (the predecessor of the FBI) had already begun spying on Marcus Garvey and other Black Nationalists, Noble Drew Ali always stressed his patriotism; in this he appears to have learned much from the debacle of Grover Cleveland Redding's Star Order of Ethiopia. Redding, who claimed to be a native Abyssinian, took an antagonistic stance against the government, plotting an insurrection in 1920. At a parade the same year, Redding rode a white horse through the streets of the South Side as his followers burned an American flag and shot a Black police officer and a white sailor who confronted them. Seven hundred police officers responded, and the participants were arrested within a week. Like Redding, Drew Ali also used an African nationality to claim civil rights, but in contrast emphasized law-abiding and fealty to the United States government, changing the name of his group from Moorish Temple of

Science to the Moorish Science Temple of America in 1928, and taking an active role in local and statewide politics. Drew Ali proclaimed that his members must be law-abiding because "by being a Moorish American you are a part and a partial of the government and must live the life accordingly."[2] The Moors' membership cards declared, in all caps, "I AM A CITIZEN OF THE U.S.A."[3] When Moors began brandishing their membership cards in defense of their rights, Drew Ali admonished them not to do so, saying that the cards were for purposes of salvation and that flashing them at "Europeans" caused "confusion." He likewise demanded that his followers "must end all radical agitating speeches while at work in their homes or on the streets. We are for peace not destruction."[4] Drew Ali's patriotism did not appear to be opportunistic; in multiple internal communications to his members, he called the US Constitution one of the greatest documents of all time because it enshrined religious freedom and hence the right to worship the Qur'an as the revealed word of Allah.[5] "This organization is playing a useful and definite part in advancing the sacred obligations of American citizenship," the Chicago Defender testified in July of 1928.[6]

But there was another reason to emphasize civic participation and Americanism: the Prophet needed his followers to vote in order to be able to use their collective voting power as a bargaining chip within the machine politics of Chicago and Illinois. In Chicago's long tradition of political patronage, those who could deliver votes could become political power brokers, and as his followers came to number in the thousands, Noble Drew Ali embraced the role of kingmaker. Following Drew Ali's directives, the Moors voted, and they did so in numbers large enough to swing local elections. For example, by 1928, Drew's followers in Chicago numbered between two and three thousand adults, mostly concentrated in the Second Ward, which encompassed most of the Black Belt. In the election of February 1929, after Moorish business manager Claude Green wrote an article extolling the virtues of Alderman Louis B. Anderson, one of Mayor Big Bill Thompson's key allies on the City Council, the alderman won his election by only 1,487 votes; the support of the Moorish Science Temple was decisive in that outcome.[7] As investigator Sheridan Brusseaux put it, at election time Drew Ali threw his support to the "colored" politicians who could do him the most good, and during the 1929 aldermanic election he supported Anderson from the Second Ward against two other candidates.[8] By emphasizing voter participation wherever his temples were located, Noble Drew Ali exercised political power in local races across the country, and supported Republican Herbert Hoover in the presidential election of 1928. The *Detroit Free Press* reported "a deluge of dusky men all claiming the surname of Sheik, Bey or El," registering to vote in August of that year, most giving Southern states as their birthplaces but insisting on being listed as of the "Moorish" and not the "Negro" race.[9] By marshaling the votes of his followers, Noble Drew Ali was simply practicing politics Chicago style; first Edward H. Wright and then Oscar DePriest had built the Black South Side political machine into a key part of Mayor Thompson's machine using the same techniques, earning appointments and patronage jobs on the strength of their ability to deliver the Black vote in the Second and Third Wards.

Noble Drew Ali insinuated himself into the very heart of the South Side's Black political machine and used the power of his followers' votes to gain status in both local and state politics, shielding himself from the kind of prosecution for petty crimes that had hounded his career as Professor Drew in the greater New York area. Unity Hall stood only a block and a half north of a former synagogue that was now the home of Pilgrim Baptist Church, and it shared that building's Moorish Revival architecture, with prominent use of heavy semicircular arches over each window and a very Moorish semicircular arch inside of a rectangle framing the main front doors. Claude D. Greene, who would later become the business manager of the Moorish Science Temple, had won the concession to manage Unity Hall from none other than Republican committeeman Dan Jackson, also known as "the Big Boss" or "the King of Gamblers" for the many large gambling resorts he ran in the Second Ward. Greene was also a prominent supporter of Alderman Anderson of the Second Ward. Aaron Payne, the Moorish Temple's attorney and Noble Drew Ali's choice to succeed him as Prophet, was a longtime assistant to Alderman Anderson and held a plumb patronage job as a city attorney for Mayor Thompson.

Noble Drew Ali put his political affiliations on display in a series of public demonstrations of his political prestige in the months leading up to the violent murder of his business manager. In April of 1928, a party headed by Drew Ali had a "brief but pleasant" audience with Chicago's postmaster general and then received a tour of the postal facility at a time when a job in the post office was one of the

best and most secure jobs available to "Negroes."[10] But Noble Drew
Ali's political power was never more obvious than at the first annual
convention of his movement, held October 14–16, 1928, when his
followers from around the country poured into Chicago and heard
addresses at Unity Hall from the Prophet, his top officials, and many
of Chicago's Black political elite. The Moors received a welcome address from Alderman Anderson and received speeches from Jesse
Binga of the Binga State Bank; Oscar DePriest, who was a Republican candidate for Congress; Third Ward alderman Robert R. Jackson; Second Ward Republican committeeman Daniel M. Jackson;
and Illinois state representative George W. Blackwell, who himself
was a strong member of the Moorish Science Temple of America
and was also known as Blackwell-Bey.[11] The *Moorish Guide* newspaper promised to get out the vote for the Black candidates allied with
the Thompson machine, writing the following January that the three
thousand Muslims of the Grand Temple and the West Side Temple were preparing to register every adult to vote for the candidates
"whom they have been instructed to vote for," naming Anderson, De-
Priest, Blackwell, and Robert Jackson as beneficiaries of the Moorish
get-out-the-vote effort, coordinated through the Republican organizations "of which The Hon. Daniel M. Jackson is our matchless
leader. . . . The Moslems will be ready."[12]

It was not simply that Prophet Noble Drew Ali was able to compel so many power brokers to pay him homage by appearing at the
convention; it was also significant that so many pledged him fealty in
their statements. Jesse Binga's representative read a statement from
Binga saying, "I am the closest man to your Temple outside. We don't
need but one leader and there he is, Prophet Noble Drew Ali[,] and
I am going to follow him too."[13] Among the official photographs of
the convention were one of Drew Ali in conference with Binga and
another of the Prophet seated on a kind of throne wearing a turban plumed with feathers between Louis B. Anderson and Oscar
DePriest, the politicians looking slightly ill at ease in their somber
three-piece suits. Whether these politicians were merely stumping
for votes or had a deeper interest in the Moors is unknown, but certainly Drew Ali's level of access to Chicago's political elite was extraordinary for an alternative religious practitioner. Indeed, Drew
Ali aspired to national and international relevance. The Prophet and
his close associate, Charles Kirkman-Bey, traveled to Havana, Cuba,
in January of 1928 to attend the Sixth Pan American Conference,

with Kirkman-Bey serving as translator. Though he gave no speech, Drew Ali liked to keep the company of statesmen, as the leader of what he viewed as his own national group.[14]

On January 14, 1929, Prophet Noble Drew Ali attended the inauguration of Governor Louis L. Emmerson in Springfield, Illinois, enjoying breakfast with other VIP's aboard a special excursion train from Chicago. He had conversations with many distinguished Chicagoans throughout the day, and pronounced himself highly pleased with the trip and the many courtesies extended him by both military and state officials.[15] Moors around the country celebrated the Prophet's birthday on the same day with a grand Moorish costume ball in the main auditorium of Unity Hall at 3140 S. Indiana Avenue, and Drew Ali received congratulatory telegrams from Governor Len Small, congressional candidate Oscar DePriest, Judge Louis H. Burke, and Alderman Louis B. Anderson, among others.[16] The future for the Moorish Science Temple of America looked bright.

However, Noble Drew Ali had not simply been embedding himself within the political machine of Big Bill Thompson and his ally, State's Attorney Robert E. Crowe, in the second half of 1928; he had joined the machine at the precise moment when it was beginning to collapse, rejected at the polls by "anti-crime" voters in the violent primaries of April 10, 1928, and then decisively smashed in the elections of November 8, 1929. One cannot understand the eagerness of politicians to associate with the Moorish Science Temple or the violence that consumed the temple itself without appreciating the instability of the Republican machine of State's Attorney Crowe, member of the Board of Review Charles V. Barrett, Mayor Thompson, and Governor Len Small in these months, and the wider wave of racketeering-related violence that was wreaking havoc in the Second City.

William Hale "Big Bill" Thompson served three scandal-plagued terms as mayor of Chicago that were remarkable for the brazenness of their corruption and the care he did *not* take to disguise his involvement in bootlegging, gambling, vice, and organized crime. A former football star and cowpuncher, Thompson was elected alderman from the Second Ward in 1900 with the backing of the gamblers of the Sportsmen's Club of America thanks to the "colored" vote, and won the mayoralty the first time in 1915. That year the majority-Black Second Ward gave him a plurality of 6,702 votes in a citywide contest decided by only 2,508 votes. The "Negro" political organization of Ed Wright and later Daniel M. Jackson, Louis Anderson, and Oscar DePriest played a critical part in Thompson's electoral victories. Black voters were a crucial part of Thompson's "America First" coalition, despite his many nonsensical and outright buffoonish statements in the William Lorimer tradition of crowd-pleasing demagoguery. As native-born Protestants, Blacks could make common cause with the declining numbers of white native-born Protestants who were arrayed against the growing numbers of Catholic and Jewish immigrants and children of immigrants who voted heavily for the Democrats in Chicago as in other big US cities. And Thompson remembered those who put him into office, placing so many Blacks in City Hall jobs that his racist opponents crudely called City Hall "Uncle Tom's Cabin." The Black community's unwavering support for Thompson despite his well-publicized corruption was one factor in the racial animosity that bubbled over in the riots of 1919, according to the commission formed to investigate its causes. When he finally left City Hall in 1931, racist opponents gleefully sang the show tune "Bye Bye Blackbird" from the latest hit Broadway musical starring "Afro-Americans" to follow in the steps of *In Old Kentucky*.[17]

In 1917 a grand jury indicted DePriest for conspiracy to protect the gambling operation of legendary Black gambler Henry "Teenan" Jones. Jones testified that DePriest received thousands of dollars a month to protect gambling clubs and that he had personally paid DePriest $2,800. The prosecution produced a canceled check from DePriest to a city prosecutor, but star defense attorney Clarence Darrow won the South Side political kingpin's acquittal—by admitting that DePriest was a conduit between gamblers and politicians but claiming that he thought the tens of thousands of dollars he collected from vice operators were merely campaign contributions. After a stern admonition to the jury not to let racial prejudice get in the way of their decision, the jury acquitted DePriest, a result that many in Chicago's Black population celebrated, not because they thought DePriest was innocent but because they believed that he had been only practicing a typical Chicago racket. Nonetheless, the reputational damage DePriest suffered having admitted in essence to graft caused him to temporarily withdraw from political office, and forever tainted his reputation.[18]

Mayor Thompson grew to be so unpopular thanks to the widespread bribery, racketeering, and corruption during his administration that he declined to run again in 1923. The unpopular Democratic reformer elected in his stead, Mayor William Dever, instituted a "beer war" at the same time the state's attorney began an investigation of vice on Chicago's South Side. The city ordered illegal cabarets and gambling resorts closed, and the crackdown sent many gamblers packing for Havana while severely crimping the rackets controlled by Jackson and DePriest. Nevertheless, Dan Jackson was the only one to defy Dever's order to close down; with the collusion of local police, he kept his Racetrack resort on South State Street operating.[19] But Thompson was back and more brazen than ever in 1927, when his enemies at the *Chicago Tribune* reported that his campaign received a donation of $250,000 and the use of a thousand thugs from Al Capone's Outfit. It was alleged that in exchange Capone received the exclusive right to run gambling houses and houses of prostitution, to operate slot machines, and to control the sale of booze and beer in all of Chicago south of Madison Street.[20] That territory included the majority-Black South Side. Jackson and DePriest also led a guerrilla campaign on Crowe-Thompson's behalf in the 1927 mayoral campaign, when their Second and Third Wards gave Thompson 46,400 votes of his 83,000-vote victory.[21]

If Thompson and his fellow racketeers ever had the support of the majority of Chicagoans, they had lost it by the primary of April 1928. With their popularity waning, forces allied with Thompson resorted to brazen violence instead. The mayor's support sagged 25 percent among Blacks, and there was open criticism directed at Thompson and his Black cronies for allowing so much crime into the South Side. Veteran activist Ida B. Wells said that Thompson had appointed Blacks, but "he has not appointed the right men. They are grafting our people. We have vice near our homes." Olivet Baptist Church minister the Reverend L. K. Williams denounced the mayor for "placing a gambler like Dan Jackson over the respectable colored people of our ward."[22] But facing a population fed up with vice and violence, the racketeers in the Thompson machine misplayed their hand, or perhaps they only had one hand to play. The 1928 primary came to be known as the "Pineapple Primary" because Thompson-Crowe–affiliated gangsters tossed so many bombs (named after hand grenades which looked like miniature pineapples) into polling places, homes, and rival businesses to intimidate their opponents. Such attacks usually began with a "rolling peanut," an explosive without shrapnel that would make a tremendous noise but cause little real damage. If the target failed to fall in line, attackers would use a real bomb, called either a "pineapple," "egg," or "football," made with either dynamite or black powder. Of course with Thompson-Crowe controlling the levers of justice, there was no investigation, but one brave or foolhardy bomb maker was arrested and told police that Al Capone strategically used bombs to intimidate commercial and political rivals.[23] Bombs exploded at the homes of Senator Charles S. Deneen and Judge John A. Swanson two weeks before the primary, and dozens of Deneen supporters received letters threatening bombings. Deneen ally County Recorder Joseph Haas died on March 15 during the 1928 primary campaign, allegedly after a four-day illness of pneumonia, gifting six hundred jobs to the rival Thompson-Crowe faction when they installed the wife of Crowe ally County Commissioner John W. Jaranowski to the vacant post. Joseph Haas's widow, Minnie McKenzie Haas, took ill the day after her husband's death and died on March 21, allegedly of a broken heart. The following day, Deneen ward leader and gangster "Diamond Joe" Esposito was gunned down by assailants from a passing vehicle on March 22, less than a month before the 1928 primary.[24] Whether or not Joseph and Minnie Haas died of naturally induced natural causes, Deneen and his allies were quite literally under assault in the weeks before the election.

Election-related violence was especially bad in the Twentieth Ward, ruled by Thompson allies Morris Eller and his son, Judge Emanuel Eller. As the center of Al Capone's distilling operation, conducted in the homes of many of the ward's Italian immigrants, the Twentieth Ward was a neighborhood where the sweet smell of mash from alcohol production wafted out of so many apartments that its aroma filled the air.[25] Capone's Eller-affiliated gangsters punched, roughed up, and otherwise intimidated voters they suspected of supporting his opponents. But their most outrageous deed came on the day of the primary, when gangsters driving a car adorned with Eller banners pulled up next to a vehicle carrying Octavius C. Granady, an "Afro-American" who was challenging Morris Eller for the job of Republican committeeman for the Twentieth Ward. Granady tried to escape, but the gangsters pursued him for two and a half miles, catching up to him finally after he crashed and then gunning him down in broad daylight. Even by Chicago standards, it was a violent act so brazen that it demanded a response. The violence of the "America First" Crowe-Thompson gangsters backfired when the outraged public voted against the machine of Attorney General Crowe and Mayor Thompson in such great numbers that the election could not be stolen by the usual means. With the loss and the deposing of Crowe, new Illinois attorney general Oscar E. Carlstrom authorized a special grand jury to investigate "the Bloody Twentieth," in particular, and political corruption in Chicago more generally.[26]

It was this investigation through the summer and fall of 1928 that would ensnare DePriest in a corruption indictment once again, along with his political rival Second Ward Republican Party committeeman Dan Jackson, the "King of Gamblers."[27] The investigation came at a particularly inopportune time for DePriest, since the death of Congressman Martin B. Madden just after the primary had opened up a Republican slot on the ballot that would be filled by appointment. There was immediate speculation that the nod would go to a "Negro" since the First Congressional District included the South Side, and DePriest held the inside track thanks to his many years of service to the Crowe-Thompson machine. The committee that made the selection was made up of Daniel Jackson, Oscar DePriest, and their other Republican committeemen in the wards of the First Congressional District, but a petition on DePriest's behalf addressed to Mayor Thompson made it clear that "Big Bill" was the one who held the cards behind the scenes.

Jackson opposed DePriest's attempt to win the nomination, favoring either Alderman Anderson or former state senator Adelbert H. Roberts, a trespass that DePriest surely remembered. Some Black folks were disappointed but not surprised when the Republican nomination went to Oscar DePriest, thinking that there were many more qualified and less corrupt candidates available. But Thompson chose DePriest not despite the fact that he was corrupt, but *because* he was corrupt; he had labored for years to shake down vice operators and turn out Black voters for Thompson and other machine candidates and had therefore played the crooked rules of Chicago politics fair and square. Dan Jackson was an old face on the South Side but a newcomer to electoral politics, even though he had of course been paying tribute to political racketeers for years. DePriest won the battle, but he did not forgive easily—"His opponents may find out that he sends back as well as he receives," the *Baltimore Afro-American* wrote ominously.[28]

Jackson had other worries relating to his core business of gambling resorts and the wildly popular form of small-stakes gambling known as "policy." Chicago's "King of Gamblers" was fast friends and former running buddies with Casper Holstein, the debonair, sophisticated gambling czar born in St. Croix who controlled the betting on "the numbers" that was wildly popular in Harlem. On September 21, 1928, a white gang led by Dutch Schultz, a notoriously homicidal Jewish American gangster and bootlegger born Arthur Flegenheimer, kidnapped Holstein and demanded a $50,000 ransom. It was fellow gambler Dan Jackson who hurried from Chicago with a bag full of cash to pay off the kidnappers. The event not only led to Holstein stepping back from running the numbers in Harlem, but allowed white mobsters to take over as the ultimate bosses of vice in Black New York.[29] Chicago's King of Gamblers had to have been concerned that if Holstein could be kidnapped and held for ransom, the same thing could happen to him.

On October 4, 1928, the special grand jury charged DePriest, Jackson, police lieutenant Patrick Brady, and six other men with "aiding, abetting, and inducing" more than ten others to operate gambling flats and houses of prostitution and protecting them from the police. The rings allegedly used the downtown offices of two white "cashiers," John Coats and Francis Marian, where South Side racketeers were made to pay tribute. Jackson also had a "fixer" in his ring named Benjamin "Bennie" Herzberg, a 1922 graduate of the University of Chicago Law School who worked with the tony downtown firm of Rosenthal, Hamill & Wormser, a firm whose clients included Sears cofounder Julius Rosenwald and was, by 1933, counsel for the trustee of the bankrupt Insull Utility Investments, Inc.[30] The indictment also called the office of the city's "Insull-ated" Corporation Counsel, attorney Samuel A. Ettelson, "a perfect picture of spoils politics."[31] Investigators charged that Jackson was the boss of the Second Ward who had "assumed dictatorial powers over the police in the district, and allowed policy wheels, slot machines, and vice resorts to flourish unmolested."[32] The indictment likewise asserted that DePriest controlled the police in the Third Ward, and had once had a policeman removed from a polling place for interfering with a thug who was there to intimidate voters. The grand jury investigating the primaries found that on top of numerous irregularities throughout the city, there were more than four thousand "floaters"—voters paid to vote twice—in Jackson's Second Ward and DePriest's Third Ward.[33] The grand jury alleged that there were more than one thousand "resorts" in the Second Ward alone, and almost every store on the South Side had a slot machine. Graft payments from gambling operators in the form of campaign contributions were estimated at close to a million dollars in the 1928 election cycle alone. The Second Ward was the largest Black-dominated political machine in the country, and Republican committeeman Dan Jackson and Alderman Louis Anderson ran it with a ruthless efficiency that would have made Stalin proud. In a ward of twenty-four thousand voters, only six officially cast ballots for the Deneen candidate Edward R. Litsinger in 1926.[34]

Although DePriest and Jackson worked in neighboring wards and were indicted together, historian Robert Lombardo is likely correct: DePriest and Jackson were not merely rivals, they were enemies.[35] Jackson, after all, was an undertaker and gambling kingpin long before he was a politician, and DePriest's political graft ring preyed on gamblers. DePriest had founded his People's Movement and started collecting "campaign contributions" from gamblers in 1915, while Jackson did not hold political office until Ed Wright's downfall in 1926, when Jackson received the appointments of Second Ward Republican committeeman and Illinois state commerce commissioner, important positions that controlled patronage and put him in line for kickbacks from Illinois public utilities. The antagonism that made DePriest and Jackson enemies was in large part ecological: it was the antagonism between the hunter and the hunted, the person who charged rents and the person who had to pay them. As historian Michael Woodiwiss writes, during Prohibition in Chicago, gangsters took the risks, while public officials took the money.[36]

But a mere indictment or two were not enough to shake DePriest and the Thompson machine's quest to place DePriest in Congress. An indictment is not the same thing as a conviction, prominent NAACP member William Pickens wrote in a full-throated defense of DePriest published in the Black newspapers of Philadelphia and New York. When a group of party elders called on DePriest to end the campaign for Congress, DePriest responded: "I'll stay in till Hell freezes over for the benefit of my wife and children. I'll fight. Nothing but death will stop me." His determination not to let anything besides death stop him is notable in that it implied there was nothing he would not do to become a congressman. The venerable *Baltimore Afro-American* cheekily reported: "Hell hasn't frozen over yet, so he's still running."[37]

So when Noble Drew Ali invited DePriest, Jackson, Anderson, and other politicians from the Crowe-Thompson machine to share the dais with him and to address the assembled Moors at their first annual convention, he was embracing not merely Chicago machine politicians, but officials who were under indictment for corruption and busily trying to stem the tide of outraged citizens of all races who had come to associate the Thompson machine with bomb-throwing and machine-gun-toting gangsters. "It is a pitiable thing that the Negro race should be asked by men of supposed patriotic ideals, to support for congress a creature so odiferous as Oscar DePriest," wrote one critic who knew better than to give his or her name.[38] In the election of November, DePriest, as candidate for "the dirties," could manage only a plurality of 48 percent in an overwhelmingly Republican district; the support of the exotically dressed Islamic prophet and his fez- and turban-clad followers was therefore crucial in pushing the machine's candidate over the top and into Congress. It was an open question whether the US House of Representatives would seat such a compromised candidate, especially one still under indictment pending trial for political corruption.

CHAPTER FOURTEEN

MOORISH FACTIONS

*It takes finance to Uplift a down trodden people, and place
it among the other prosperous Nations of the world.*

—NOBLE DREW ALI, 1929[1]

Trouble was brewing just below the surface of the Moorish Science
Temple as Chicago politicians paid tribute to Noble Drew Ali at
the first annual convention in October 1928. Unbeknownst to his
new followers, the forty-four-year-old woman at his side at the most
famous photograph of the Moors, taken on the steps of Unity Hall
at that convention, was his ex-wife, Eva Allen. Now Eva, who had received second billing to her husband, "Armmah Sotanki," at the turn
of the century before making a name for herself as a star performer
in Black vaudeville, must have slid back into the role of the magician's
assistant, as her ex-husband wowed new followers with feats of magic
learned from their days together in circus sideshows. And what an
assistant she must have been, with her business acumen sharpened
by decades as a performer and talent booker in vaudeville, where she
had gained a reputation for organization and honesty in her dealings
with performers, whom she always paid on time. Since magicians
customarily worked with confederates planted in the audience, pretending to be hypnotized or volunteering to disappear into a basket,
as in the "Hindoo Basket Mystery" that the Sotankis performed,
what better plant could there have been than a master illusionist herself, a woman who already listed her profession as "magician" as a
young woman of nineteen when they were married in 1900?

The thing was, ever since the Islam-admiring Reverend Edward Wilmot Blyden left his wife for a younger student and then defended polygamy as not only faithful to Islam but as part of what he called "the African personality," Black men interested in sanctifying extra-marital relationships could turn to Islam to do so. Drew Ali "created a personal 'harem,' took in the money from all over the country and proceeded to live in Oriental style," in the jaundiced view of Detective Brusseaux, by taking three brides in the first years of the Moorish Science Temple, ranging from his secretary, Pearl, who was in her early twenties, to Christina, who was sixteen in 1929, to Mary Lou, who was fourteen that year and had been married to Drew Ali for two years with her parents' blessing. According to the *Chicago Defender*, the youngest wife was pregnant in the spring of 1929.[2] Drew performed all of these marriages without the blessing of the state of Illinois, which never would have sanctioned his practice of polygamy. What the Prophet's first wife thought of her husband's marital arrangements we can only imagine; after so many years on the road, during many of which he was based in Chicago and she was based in Cincinnati, perhaps exclusivity was not an important feature of their marriage. On the other hand, for a woman whose performance career was predicated in part on being perceived as sexually alluring, it might have rankled that her husband gave these three girlish beauties positions of public prominence, their pictures reproduced in Moorish Science newspapers, at the very moment when she was becoming more matronly than maidenly, while her own business acumen and role as the family's headliner for two decades was never publicly acknowledged by her husband's thousands of new followers.[3]

There are no extant records to document whether anyone recognized Drew Ali from his prior life, but with the huge and newsworthy success of Noble Drew Ali's Moorish Science Temple of America, it was likely that some of Walter Brister's former associates recognized him and spread the word, undermining his claim to divine prophethood among those followers who sought to split from him. After all, George Barrett said hello to Drew in Princess Sotanki's troupe in the pages of the *Indianapolis Freeman* in 1915, only a decade before Brister founded the Moorish Science Temple as "Noble Drew Ali," and Brister was part of professional circles of musicians and magicians who communicated with each other regularly through the "Negro" press that also carried their advertisements and reviews of their performances. Brister had been working professionally and quite

Hassan Ben Ali's Moorish Caravan, which performed in 1893 with the Sells Brothers Circus and outside the Chicago World's Fair. Such displays not only commodified Moorish Muslim identities with performers who would have been considered Black in the US but also made a show of Muslim religious acts, in this case the *hajj*.

William Henry Johnson, c. 1842–1926, a microcephalic New Jerseyan whom P. T. Barnum employed to portray "Zip, What Is It?," allegedly the "missing link" between lower apes and humans. This deeply racist performance reached more audience members than that of any other Black performer in his lifetime.

PRINCESS SOTANKI
Hindo ı Lion Tamer

Princess Sotanki, from the 1902 route book of the John Robinson Circus. The picture is the same as the one that ran in the 1900 Pawnee Bill Wild West Show route book, which identified her as E. Brister. This one is notable in that the book identifies her as a "Hindoo lion tamer."

Walter Brister as Armmah Sotanki, leader of the Sotankis' troupe of "Hindoo" fakirs starting in 1898. He took a backseat to his wife, Princess Sotanki, beginning in 1907.

Eva Brister in 1900 as Princess Sotanki and as she appeared seated next to Noble Drew Ali in the 1928 Moorish Science Temple photo—see the last photo in the insert for the full image.

Maud Allan dressed as Salome. Allan was a feminist and modern dance pioneer who created a shocking dance in 1908 to accompany the 1905 Richard Strauss operatic version of the 1896 Oscar Wilde play, *Salomé*.

Princess Sotanki in a 1913 publicity photo. Note the similarity to Maud Allan's costume, as well as the giant snake winding its way up her abdomen.

A collage of some of the dozens of advertisements for healers during the Harlem Renaissance, when Professor Drew was active, featuring Black men wearing turbans or fezzes.

Illustrations from the Islam Temple of (white) Shrine of the Ancient Arabic Order of the Nobles of the Mystic Shrine, 1906. The partying Shriner on the left carries liquor bottles marked Zem Zem for the sacred well in the holy city of Mecca, and Uncle Sam's top hat has been replaced with a fez labeled "Islam."

Prophet Noble Drew Ali (standing center) and temple members, at a religious service of the Moorish Science Temple of America, late 1920s.

Prophet Noble Drew Ali (back row) seated between leading South Side politicians Louis B. Anderson (left) and Oscar DePriest (right). Aaron Payne is seated at bottom right. First Annual Convention, October 1928.

Chicago's colorful mayor William Hale "Big Bill" Thompson, whose three terms in office were widely decried for their corruption.

Jack Guzik, the pimp turned criminal mastermind and the brains behind the Al Capone syndicate.

Samuel Insull, president of Commonwealth Edison and a slew of other public utility companies such as People's Gas, became infamous for buying political favors and opposing public ownership of public utilities.

Oscar Stanton DePriest, longtime Chicago alderman and the first Black congressman from a northern state, who was twice indicted for corruption but never convicted.

Members of the Moorish Science Temple of America posing before Unity Hall during their first annual convention, October 1928. Note Prophet Noble Drew Ali, founder of the MSTA (first row, standing, fifth from left), and Eva Allen, the former Eva Brister, a.k.a. Princess Sotanki, seated next to him.

"Do as I tell you and these dollars are yours." A cartoon from the front page of the *Chicago Defender*'s local edition next to a story about Noble Drew Ali's funeral, makes the case that some Black politicians were growing rich by taking bribes from Commonwealth Edison and other Samuel Insull companies.

publicly for thirty-two years by the time he founded the Moorish Temple of Science, and was a distinctive-looking, attractive, diminutive man.[4] Brister had faked his death in Chicago as well, only a decade before he returned as the Prophet, so there could have been plenty of former South Side associates who saw his picture in the newspaper in the late 1920s and recognized the former trumpeter, magician, and onetime child star of what was by then the most popular American play of all time. Drew Ali must have had a strategy to deal with this problem, whether by charm, money, or even coercion, since the team of enforcers sent to deal with Greene preexisted the Greene episode.[5] By choosing a different identity than the one he lived with until 1914, Noble Drew Ali created a highly brittle social identity; the slightest rumor or discrepancy in his self-presentation could create a crack that would destroy the entire façade, shuttering his profitable business empire.

🐦 🐦 🐦

There were severe tensions brewing in the Moorish Science Temple of America, principally over its lucrative business affairs. Prophet Noble Drew Ali stressed "peace" as his byword and as the central message of Islam, but keeping the peace even among his followers grew increasingly difficult as the organization grew, and the sums collected from membership dues, "taxation" of members, and the growing empire of herbal remedies and business enterprises increased as well. In addition to the membership dues of one dollar a month for women and two dollars a month for men, and the fee of one dollar for a membership button and card, Drew Ali instituted a system of taxation of his followers at the 1928 convention. An investigation by the private eye Sheridan Brusseaux estimated that the Moorish Science Temple was generating profits for the leaders of between $15,000 and $18,000 every month, principally from its Moorish Manufacturing Company, the Chicago-based concern that manufactured the healing oils and root medicines at industrial scale that Professor Drew had once retailed from his Newark apartment. That amounted to $216,000 a year in 1929, or $3.2 million in 2020 dollars after inflation. But accounting for inflation on its own does not do justice to what a large sum of money this was in 1929, when a typical Black male worker in Chicago might earn $24 a week, or $1,250 a year, and a Black woman might earn considerably less: $12 to $18 a week for factory work in Chicago, or about $800 a year.[6] And Brusseaux's estimate was only a guess at the funds coming into the central headquarters' coffers, one that did not include all the funds diverted by the branch temples, which numbered twenty-one by the autumn of 1929 and had anywhere from the seven thousand members that historian Patrick Bowen estimates to the twelve thousand to fifteen thousand members by Detective Brusseaux's count. Like any group, the number of partial members and others influenced by the teachings of the Moorish Science Temple of America (MSTA) might have been much larger than the number of paid-up members at any particular time. The true revenues could have been substantially higher than Detective Brusseaux's estimate, accounting for membership dues, buttons, cards, and profits from the sales of Moorish medicines, healing oils, and the operation of the sect's several groceries, butcher shops, and trucking companies.

Samuel Insull pioneered economies of scale and central manufacturing practices in the generation of electricity, building massive power plants and driving down consumer costs while funneling thousands of dollars into the pockets of politicians to facilitate the growth of his public utilities empire. In his own way, Noble Drew Ali did something similar for "Afro-American" folk religion, applying modern methods of centralized manufacture and advertising to the sale of herbal medicines that heretofore had been retailed laboriously and at considerable danger of arrest. Whereas before, as Professor Drew, he was subjected to three humiliating arrests, his new operation allowed him to go from being a small-time retailer to a large-scale wholesaler, with a fraction of the risk. If Drew Ali paid bribes to police and politicians, that was simply the cost of doing business in the Black Metropolises of the 1920s.

According to the *Chicago Defender*, arguments over financial matters bore the largest share of the blame for the deadly split within the MSTA that would lead to the murder of Claude D. Greene. But historians within the Moorish movement today report that politicians, recognizing the power and the profits at Noble Drew Ali's command, were trying to take over his movement by backing Greene's attempt to seize control of the Moorish Science Temple.[7] In the five months between the first annual convention in the middle of October 1928 and the Greene murder on March 14, Noble Drew Ali increasingly emphasized finances in his communications with temple heads. In January of 1929 the Prophet instituted an Emergency

Fund and required all members to contribute between one and two dollars monthly on top of their normal dues. He also declared that all of the organization's real estate be held in his name or in the name of the MSTA, and barred temple leaders from borrowing from their members, hinting at the existence of financial indiscretions within the organization. "Some of you have slipped and slipped drastically, so you had better lace up your shoes before I get there," Drew Ali declared in January of 1929.[8] His insistence on being the only one entitled to hold property or make significant financial decisions, his public dressing down of his temple officers and those who slipped in paying their increasingly burdensome dues, taxes, and other levies, and his almost hectoring tone might have as easily repulsed dissidents as drawn them closer to him.

The Prophet took tours of his seventeen temples in fifteen states in November of 1928 and again the following February to try and put their financial houses in order, but closer to home, trouble was brewing with his own Supreme Business Manager at the Chicago headquarters.[9] Noble Drew Ali's lack of formal education and low level of literacy, especially in contrast to the college-educated officers with whom he surrounded himself in the Moorish Science Temple, might help to explain some of the problems he encountered, and makes his achievement of creating the MSTA all the more remarkable. Drew Ali's pronouncements demonstrate the kind of tell-tale flaws that one would expect of someone whose formal education ended no later than his early teenage years when he first started working on Broadway in 1893. His published proclamations have the flavor of transcribed speech as opposed to written language, with numerous extended clauses, parenthetical remarks, and run-on sentences. He relied on secretaries, particularly his wife, Pearl, to do his writing for him; the smooth and even writing on the back of a postcard he sent from Atlanta after visiting the imprisoned Marcus Garvey does not match his only known signature signed in front of witnesses. That signature, made when he signed his name on the group's 1926 incorporation papers, was extremely disjointed, each letter going off at a different angle. On top of which, he actually misspelled his own name, adding an *n* to the end of "Ali," although some followers claim that Ali was intentionally trying to mask his identity by writing his name "Alin."[10] The *Defender* once wrote that Drew was "almost totally ignorant and can scarcely write his name," and another source wrote, "Though semi-literate, he possessed an eloquent tongue, a persuasive manner, and a native shrewdness which enabled him to sway the poor and un-lettered people who listened to him."[11] While he certainly was not ignorant, the archival evidence supports the conclusion that Drew Ali had limited literacy and most likely could not write very well.

Ali's struggles with the written word were in marked contrast to the expert penmanship and manifold educational achievements of his business manager, Claude Greene, forty-five years old, who was a graduate of the St. Paul Episcopal Church Day School of Shreve-port, Louisiana, and the famous Tuskegee Institute of Tuskegee, Alabama. Tuskegee was created and led by Booker T. Washington (1856–1915), the most influential Black man in America in his day, and its graduates carried with them the social networks, reputation for industry, and prestige that the Tuskegee name conveyed. Greene's wife, Agnes, was the daughter of Luke Ateman, who owned his own home in Chicago and was the owner of the largest moving and ex-press company in New Orleans as well as an investor in the country's largest Black-owned bank, the Binga State Bank. Greene came to Chicago around 1909, a decade before the Great Migration, and was a chauffeur and an interior decorator by trade before getting involved in buying and selling real estate. He once worked as a butler in the home of Sears, Roebuck chief executive Julius Rosenwald.[12]

Greene was also active in local politics. He not only held several positions in local government, but was captain of the Fifty-Ninth Precinct in the Second Ward. He was elected the head of the Chicago Boosters Civic Club in January of 1929, an organization that planned summertime excursions to the South for successful migrants like him and his family. He attested in the pages of the *Chicago Defender* that Alderman Louis B. Anderson was a man of ability, intelligence, and experience, and that "the Race needs able and purely representative men in public office if it is to be credited with being a factor in municipal affairs." The same article noted that he was "a close personal friend of the distinguished Moorish leader, Noble Drew Ali."[13] Greene also had an idealistic streak, if his own words are to be believed at face value. In his testimony for Alderman Anderson, Greene wrote, "As a progressive race we recognize abil-ity, intelligence and efficiency in the business man, the professional man, and in the public representative." He continued: "We honor men and women who have demonstrated their intelligence, ability and constructive leadership in their chosen fields of endeavour; we point with pride to their records and teach our children to emulate their noble qualifications."[14] In other words, not only was Greene well educated, he was socially prominent, a "Race man" of impeccable refinement, education, achievement, and professional credentials, and a well-networked leader at many levels of Chicago's Black Metropolis.

Greene was not the only well-educated, socially prominent, and politically well-connected member of the Moorish Science Temple's inner circle. Drew Ali's confidant, and according to the *Defender* his dying choice to lead the organization, was Aaron Payne, who graduated from Howard University, one of the nation's most prestigious Black universities, and was a "Negro All American" member of the Howard football team of 1920–21, which not only went undefeated, but never surrendered a single score the entire season. In a society with precious few "Negro" college graduates, let alone attorneys, Payne trained in law at the University of Chicago and passed the bar in the state of Illinois before becoming a prosecutor with the city; he was also a close supporter of alderman Louis B. Anderson. Like Greene, Payne was married to a socially prominent woman, in his case Evelyn Scott Payne, the daughter of Emmett J. Scott, who was formerly Booker T. Washington's closest adviser at the Tuskegee Institute, was the highest-ranking "Negro" official in the administration of Woodrow Wilson, and by 1928 served as the secretary-treasurer of Howard University. Scott was also a warm personal friend of Melvin Chisum, Samuel Insull's most powerful Black adviser.[15]

Noble Drew Ali's ability to attract politically well-connected, college-educated men and women of great ability not just as followers but as key officers in his organization separated him from every other Black alternative religious practitioner; it also stood in marked contrast to Marcus Garvey's failure to attract the college-educated Black elite as members of the United Negro Improvement Association. His foes ridiculed Garvey for selecting George Tobias, a clerk in the shipping department of the Pennsylvania Railroad, as UNIA treasurer, but he did not have a lot of college graduates to choose from for leadership positions. In contrast, the Moorish Science Temple of America's many college-educated members were major assets for Noble Drew Ali, as they would be for any organization engaged in enterprises as complex as the MSTA's manufacturing plant, mail-order business, and many local businesses. But it could not have taken the college-educated close associates of the Prophet very long to figure out that he was not very literate, or to understand the vast sums of money that he was arrogating to himself through his claim of divine election. The knowledge that he could not compose his own correspondence, let alone the text of his *Koran*, could have undermined his claim to prophethood in their eyes, and sown the seeds of dissension within the temple.

But no matter his literacy level, Noble Drew Ali was unwilling to let others capitalize on the formula he had painstakingly developed and the life's work he had accomplished as Armmah Sotanki, Professor Drew, and Noble Drew Ali. His business manager Claude D. Greene made an alliance with James Lomax-Bey, head of the Detroit temple and an original signee on the MSTA's 1926 certificate of incorporation, and planned to split off from Noble Drew Ali's temple and form a rival organization. Greene and Drew Ali might have also quarreled over a woman, as the *Defender* reported that Greene was rumored to have attracted the attention of Pearl Drew Ali, the first woman Drew Ali married during his reign as Prophet, a talented stenographer and secretary who, along with enjoying a prominent position as the cultured and beautiful twenty-two-year-old wife of the Prophet, was the leader of the Young People's Moorish League.[16]

The earliest public record of the factions tearing apart the Moorish Science Temple came in a proclamation from the Prophet dated January 18, 1929, a few days after he returned from the Illinois governor's inauguration. Addressing himself to "Dear Brother: Islam," the Prophet wrote that he was glad to know that he had "a few faithful Moors among you all," and that he wished them to know "the truth and the Divine Truth." He continued in one of his typically long, clause-laden, run-on sentences that resembled transcribed speech more than written language:

> There is a host of "jealousy" about me and the movement, now, by the same people of our side of the nation that claim it was only a joke, and unreal—but now, since they have found out from the Government Officials and the Nations of the earth that this is the only Soul-foundation that all Asiatics must depend on for their earthly salvation as an American citizen. They are working every scheme that they can to disqualify me so they themselves may take charge of the situation.[17]

The Prophet promised that everyone who paid his or her "divine respect to me and the Movement will be remembered," and asked for all his followers to "increase their faithfulness," saying "I need FINANCE and I need it bad. Never before have I needed finance as badly as I do at present, that I may shove aside the discord that is facing the Nation." It was, he wrote, all caused by jealousy at the Prophet's "fame and nobility" illustrated by his presence at the recent governor's inauguration and his plans to attend the inauguration of President Hoover on March 4.[18] On February 5 he issued another proclamation, asking for more "Uplifting Funds" and saying that he had sacrificed his "life, finance, and labor to place the Nation on an intelligent and financial footing. . . . The greater the sacrifice and loyalty to the Prophet—the greater your reward from Allah."[19] The many strained calls for extra finances, along with the rumor that business manager Claude Greene had grown close to the Prophet's wife and stenographer, suggests that Drew Ali may have lost control of some of the organization's revenue streams. The Prophet wrote a supporter on February 9, 1929, saying that he had uncovered a "game to be played on the 11 of this month" at his Detroit Temple Number Four, where he had discovered "unloyalty to our Moorish Law and Obligation" on the part of Grand Sheik James Lomax-Bey. Ominously, the Prophet said he "would like to know some good decent places to stay, because I am not going to stop at the former address [. . .] I do not think it safe."[20]

Drew Ali's onetime ally Jesse Binga opened the imposing, five-story, richly appointed Tudor Gothic "Binga Arcade" on the South Side on Saturday, February 12, with a ribbon-cutting ceremony featuring many of Chicago's most prominent citizens, but not the Moorish prophet. Located at Thirty-Fifth and State Street, the building featured stores on either side of an arcade, a gorgeous fifth floor assembly hall, and three floors of modern and well-equipped offices for professionals. The ballroom featured twenty glass chandeliers, each with twenty incandescent light bulbs, which created a dazzling display of Samuel Insull's electricity when lit. On April 27, Insull's Commonwealth Edison became the anchor tenant of the Binga Arcade when the company opened one of its stores displaying modern electrical appliances, a technique it commonly used to drive demand for its electricity. With the move into the Binga Arcade, Insull signaled that he did not just want South Siders' votes; he wanted more of their dollars as well. Commonwealth Edison may have been sensitive to critiques of its hiring practices lobbed by the *Messenger* and the *Defender*, because its representatives made sure to mention that the company then employed two hundred "Race employees" in its eight branch offices.[21]

Meanwhile, the power struggle for control of the Moorish Science Temple accelerated when the Prophet's rival and business manager Claude Greene resigned from the Moorish Science Temple after the regular meeting on Sunday, February 10, a day before the "game" that Drew Ali predicted Detroit rival James Lomax-Bey would play. The Prophet began another tour of his temples on Friday, February 15, traveling from Chicago to spend a week with the large and rebellious temple in Detroit. At the Holy Day meeting of that Friday, Grand Sheik Lomax-Bey denounced the Prophet in front of a gathering of fifteen hundred Moors in Detroit's Temple Number Four and revealed his plan to take control of the Moorish Science Temple of America. What the Prophet said or did in response was not recorded, but his letter just before the incident promised to involve his attorney, Aaron Payne, to "care for the situation according to the LAW."[22] The Prophet then moved on to briefer visits to Moorish Science communities in Newark, Philadelphia, Baltimore, and Richmond, ending in Pittsburgh. The fourth of March came and went without a hoped-for invitation to President Herbert Hoover's inauguration, so the Prophet toured his temples in Ohio and Arkansas in the first week of March.[23] Governor T. Thompson El of the Philadelphia congregation alluded to "the great test that the Temples all over, underwent a few days ago," and wrote that the Prophet "proved to all here that he is the most powerful man in the land." The Prophet's visit to Philadelphia began with a fish fry on Saturday night, during which Noble Drew Ali demonstrated his divine healing powers. "Many Moors rose from the dead Sunday night and are telling the story that the Prophet is truly in the land."[24] In Richmond, the halfway point of the tour, the local Moors reported that "Moors, unconscious Moors, Europeans and all, gave a welcome to the Prophet Noble Drew Ali, Founder of the Moorish Science Temple of America, that will be remembered for years." The writer claimed that the Prophet's tour was swelling the ranks of his movement, and predicted with millennial fervor that "the time is near when prophesies made awhile back will come to light." In the meantime, Moors should "remain firm, convince others, and all the while that only through our founder's doctrine of Love, Truth, Peace, Freedom and Justice can we advance in a manner in which all the peoples of the earth will respect and admire those of the Islamic faith."[25]

The Prophet returned from his grand tour of temples in March to an eviction notice from Unity Hall served by Claude Greene, demonstrating that although Greene was only the business manager, it was he and not the Prophet who controlled use of Unity Hall, as Dan Jackson, the "King of Gamblers" and "Big Boss" of Republican Second Ward politics, had selected Greene to run the building in 1925.[26] According to former member John Small Bey, the week of Monday, March 4, Noble Drew Ali approached him and asked him to kill Greene, offering to pay $1,000 plus his court expenses if there was a trial, and assuring him that he would win his freedom in the event he was arrested. According to a subsequent coroner's investigation, Drew "flashed" a thousand dollars, which he said he would give to anyone who would stop anyone trying to break up the sect.[27] Both Drew Ali's camp and Greene's faction held separate meetings on Sunday, March 10, 1929, that were intended to be secret but were infiltrated by the other side's spies. Greene's clique held its meeting at Unity Hall, and the Prophet's spies relayed that Greene had some of the strongest temples in the organization ready to follow him, alarming the Prophet. The following day, Detroit police arrested Lomax-Bey on a charge of embezzling $8,000 from the Moorish Science Temple. According to the *Defender's* interviews with members, Drew Ali brought his loyalist Cumby-Bey from Pittsburgh and some members of the Detroit temple and the secondary Chicago temple to attend his meeting, during which the assembled allegedly carefully planned Greene's murder and selected a crew to carry out the deed. Reportedly, they also planned to kill Greene's ally James Lomax-Bey, head of the Detroit temple.[28]

The following day Drew Ali issued a decree appointing Brothers Cumby-Bey of Pittsburgh and Childs-Bey of Cleveland "to investigate business etc." of Temple Number Four in Detroit because "Lomax-Bey has violated all DIVINE LAWS of the PROPHET. . . . I, THE PROPHET, declare his office vacant and the name of Grand Governor discharged." Declaring that each temple was under the supreme guidance of the Prophet, he proclaimed that when any temple head violated the Divine Laws and constitution, "he is a traitor and enemy to the Divine Creed and Unloyal to the National Government U.S.A. to which the movement is to make men and women better citizens."[29] The same day, Drew Ali moved the MSTA's office equipment out of Unity Hall, forced out by Greene.[30] Greene told his wife, Agnes, that he expected there would be trouble to come. On Wednesday night, March 13, the factions within the Detroit temple fought, and two Moors and two police officers were shot and wounded.[31]

The crew of assassins—some accounts say they numbered four or five, others say six, and still others say eight—confronted Greene at his office on the first floor of Unity Hall at 8:00 p.m. the next day, Thursday, March 14, where he was waiting for a weekly dance in the basement to begin. The group reportedly included gunmen from Detroit and Pittsburgh, and one of the triggermen was allegedly William Johnson-Bey.[32] Member Small Bey tagged Ira Johnson-Bey as the key member of the "slaying crew," and Unity Hall's janitor, Arthur Scott, confirmed that Ira Johnson-Bey was among the group who came into Greene's office on the first floor and requested that he speak with them in a room on the second floor. The group had been upstairs for five minutes when the janitor heard two shots and saw the assassins run downstairs and into the street. Scott rushed upstairs along with another witness, Clarke Ellis, and found Greene on his knees in a pool of blood, stabbed four times and shot twice, with his bowels protruding from the deep gash in his abdomen.

When the police showed up at Noble Drew Ali's home that night, they found a celebratory feast in progress. Sam Jackson, whom an eyewitness confirmed was in the "slaying crew," was taking part in the feast at the Prophet's home and ran away when the police arrived; he was collared by Attorney George W. Blackwell, state representative and MSTA member, as Jackson attempted to escape in the Prophet's high-powered automobile.[33] The Chicago police arrested forty members of the MSTA in response to the Greene killing, including Noble Drew Ali, although the Prophet was soon released. A mass meeting between the Drew Ali faction and the Lomax-Bey faction in Detroit the night of Tuesday, March 19, resulted in someone firing a shot while Lomax-Bey was speaking, triggering a brawl between the two warring sides. Two members of the Detroit riot police who responded to the melee were wounded along with Detroit temple members Stand Stone Bey and Zack Lowe Bey. The following day, the Prophet was back in Detroit to attempt to quell the uprising there and to accuse Lomax-Bey of pilfering $8,000 from the temple's coffers. He also issued a new proclamation dismissing Lomax-Bey from the order, signed by Drew Ali loyalists Cumby-Bey of Pittsburgh, Mealy-El of Chicago, and Chiles Bey of Cleveland, Ohio. Ira Johnson-Bey traveled from Chicago to Detroit, apparently intent on killing Lomax-Bey, who had fled the Motor City for his own safety.[34]

The Chicago police did little to investigate the Greene murder. Their response was so lackadaisical, in fact, that it gave credence to rumors that Drew Ali had spent thousands of dollars in bribes among the Second Ward's political and police channels, and that he was, as he claimed, effectively immune from prosecution. Coroner Herman Bundesen, who had defeated the Thompson machine's candidate in the recent elections and was part of the "anti-crime" forces opposed to the racket of politicians and criminals in the Thompson cabal, took control of the inquiry into Claude Greene's murder in May, taking the investigation out of the hands of the Stanton Avenue police station and assigning men from his own office to collect evidence. But there was not much evidence to collect two months after the incident. "Rumors of graft crept into the case when it was learned that no attempt had been made to arrest Johnson, who had appeared at Unity Hall, the scene of the murder, on two occasions within the past month," as the *Chicago Defender* reported in May.[35] The police had withheld evidence from the coroner, and did not notify material witnesses to be present at the coroner's inquiry.[36] Attorneys for the dead man's family repeatedly charged that prosecution of the murder had been blocked; the *Defender* reported the following winter that the MSTA had spent $7,000 (or $104,610 in 2020 dollars) in various channels to prevent a complete investigation and prosecution of the killing.[37]

What Drew Ali may not have counted on was that even if he could pay off the police, there were deeper layers and deeper pockets in the South Side's political rackets. The staging of a spectacular, gangland-style murder in the place from which Samuel Insull exerted covert influence on the South Side political machine threatened to unravel that poorly guarded secret and call unwanted attention to the unsavory alliance between the South Side's most prominent politicians, the Crowe-Thompson machine, organized crime, the police, and Chicago's greatest utilities magnate, all at the worst possible time: while Congressman-elect DePriest's legitimacy hung in the balance. Insull could not have been pleased by the desecration of his sumptuous South Side political clubhouse, particularly since his covert funding of the space and DePriest's political machine had become an issue in the recent congressional campaign and it was unclear whether DePriest's connections to Insull's money would sink the aspiring congressman's chances of being seated, as similar entanglements had already taken down Senator-elect Frank Smith.

Despite the prominent role of gory violence in the public's memory of Chicago's gangland wars of the Prohibition era and later, historian Mark Haller has argued that participants in illegal enterprises generally do not want to be in business with people who are prone to violence. For one thing, it calls too much attention to activities that they would prefer to remain secret, whether bootlegging, gambling, or vote-buying. For another, anyone in business with a violent person wonders if that person's violence will be turned on himself or herself next time.[38] The gory slaying of Claude Greene, longtime manager of Unity Hall and member of Chicago's Black political elite, meant that Noble Drew Ali could no longer be trusted, if he ever was. The parade of telegrams and speeches from politicians praising the Prophet came to an abrupt halt, but Chicago power brokers' umbrage must have gone deeper than that.

It was not easy to separate the corporate racketeers from the gangsters in 1920s Chicago. Indeed, Samuel Insull gave $100,000 to Mayor Thompson's 1927 election campaign, less than half of Capone's alleged contribution, and he once met with the infamous Capone to discuss using the gangster's thugs as his private security force. It was a harebrained scheme that Insull later rejected, but the fact that he even entertained the idea illustrates the natural kinship between the two.[39] Capone may have been more famous, but many critics and Capone himself claimed that Insull was actually Chicago's biggest racketeer. Emperor Insull's systematic corrupting of aldermen, state legislators, and state regulators was not only more far-reaching than Capone's crimes; it actually facilitated them. As the *Chicago Journal* wrote in 1922, Samuel Insull's elevated streetcar lines flagrantly broke their contracts with the city by charging higher fares than they had agreed to, and he litigated every negative judgment against them for years in the courts while "debauching" public officials. "What wonder if some underprivileged boys of the street make the motto their own, and start out to practice it in under-world fashion, with jimmy and gun?"[40] Insull and his fellow utility barons had labored for thirty years to establish the concept that no city or citizen had any rights that a corporation was bound to respect, as the *Journal* put it.

The Guzik-Capone gang loomed large over Chicago, and especially the South Side, where they controlled vice, and where the famous white-owned "black and tans" paid them tribute and bought their booze. By 1928, the Guzik-Capone combine was estimated to gross $105 million a year, or 1.57 billion in 2020 dollars—not as much as Insull's companies, but real money nonetheless. Biographer Laurence Bergreen claimed that Capone was the most influential man in Illinois and owned Governor Small, Mayor Thompson, and State's Attorney Crowe, although in truth those public servants had sold themselves so many times to so many buyers that it was hard to say who if anyone owned them most of all. Unlike Samuel Insull, everyone knew who Al Capone was, not just because of his wealth, but because of the reign of terror linked to prostitution, bootlegging, and gambling hiding behind his smiling, scarred face.

There was a very thin line between licit and illicit power in Prohibition-era Chicago, with its many bordellos, resorts, cabarets, and integrated "black and tans." The Insull lawyer-turned-city corporation counsel Samuel Ettelson brokered a deal that Capone would allow Blacks under the syndicate run by Dan Jackson to control their own nightclubs, gambling resorts, and places of prostitution in the Second Ward, so long as they allowed the Guzik-Capone Outfit to supply the booze. Capone started using a cleaning and pressing shop on the South Side as a distribution point to personally pay off police officers five dollars each Saturday, and struck a deal to supply Black rent parties with booze.[41]

The Moors were operating a profitable string of businesses in an environment dominated by racketeers, who would have had any number of reasons to be interested in the Moors' trucking company, cash businesses, and a profitable mail-order medicine business bringing in at least $15,000 a month. Racketeers might have tried to extract tribute or protection money from the Moorish Science Temple, as they commonly did with owners of all manner of commercial enterprises and trade associations in Prohibition Chicago. Indeed, members of the MSTA today recall that members at that time worked for Al Capone, and that Capone appreciated them because they never stole from him.[42] Quite likely that was because Moors were forbidden from using alcohol, and delivering alcohol for the Guzik-Capone syndicate was the primary way in which Capone employed Black people during Prohibition. We do not know the recipes for the Moorish Manufacturing Company's root tonics, but it was a common practice at that time for such medicinal concoctions to have high alcohol contents.[43] If the Moorish Manufacturing Company needed alcohol for its medicines, it was the Jack Guzik–Al Capone "Outfit" that controlled the illicit alcohol trade on the South

Side of Chicago. Without a question, operating lucrative businesses and infiltrating the South Side's underworld-connected political arena was a dangerous game with dangerous partners. The Prophet's catchphrase was "Love, Truth, Peace, Freedom and Justice," but he was about to learn how justice was served in the Chicago of Samuel Insull, Samuel Ettelson, Big Bill Thompson, Judge Eller, Jack Guzik, and the Capones.[44]

CHAPTER FIFTEEN

CHICAGO JUSTICE

If you pay a blackmailer, he asks for more blackmail. If you pay tribute to a crooked politician, he demands more tribute and when he sells out to you, he sells out also to the Al Capones.

—ATTORNEY DONALD RICHBERG
to Julius Rosenwald, 1930[1]

"They call your Mayor a circus man," Chicago mayor "Big Bill" Thompson once mused in a campaign speech. "Well I'd rather be a circus man than an undertaker." His audience laughed, but undertakers would be plenty busy on Thompson's watch as he turned Chicago into a circus of spoils politics and made alliances with Al Capone and other gangsters.[2] On Friday, April 13, 1929, two days before Thompson ally Oscar DePriest was to become a member of the US Congress, and after several unexplained postponements of his trial when the prosecutors asked for more time, First Assistant State's Attorney Frank J. Loesch made the astounding announcement that the state was dropping all charges against the twice-indicted candidate DePriest. Loesch, who had pursued DePriest for ten months, made the odd statement that he did not want to waste everyone's time with a trial. The state's attorney's office pushed ace detective and "race man" Sheridan Brusseaux in front of the press in an attempt to legitimize this strange turn of events, and Brusseaux gave the startling explanation that the prosecution of DePriest had begun the prior June because DePriest's own friends and fellow members of his People's Movement political organization had come to him telling of the candidate's crimes, and had brought witnesses as well to testify to the special grand jury. In other words, the indictment resulted from turncoats within DePriest's own organization, after he had engineered his own nomination to the vacant congressional seat. DePriest could not have been pleased with this revelation of back-stabbing, though it probably came as no revelation for a man who had battled the undertaker Dan Jackson and others for the right to represent the voters of the First Congressional District of Illinois. Brusseaux assured the press that he had found DePriest "absolutely clean and fully worthy of the confidence placed in him in his newly assigned duties," in one paper's report. It was an extraordinary statement about a man who had confessed to passing money between gamblers and politicians as part of Clarence Darrow's inspired 1915 defense, let alone coming from someone as knowledgeable about Chicago's rackets as Brusseaux.

But in January, between the indictment and the abrupt decision to drop charges, Brusseaux had received a plumb post with the Justice Department in Washington, DC. Officially, he got the job because he had done such a thorough job investigating criminal rackets on the Loesch special grand jury. But unofficially, his willingness to disavow the work that he and the state's attorneys had done must have helped him win the post with the Republican-controlled federal government.[3]

DePriest and Jackson did not invent their rackets; they had been going on in Chicago for decades, and every adult knew how things worked in the "wide-open town" that was Chicago. Nor was it unusual for cases to be summarily dropped "for lack of evidence" during Prohibition, when defendants were regularly able to bribe their way out of trouble. "Fixing cases became even more of an American institution during Prohibition," writes historian Michael Woodiwiss. "There were thousands of arrests, but when protected bootleggers stepped in front of judges, district attorneys suddenly found they had 'insufficient evidence,' or witnesses failed to turn up, or police officers admitted that they had overstepped themselves in the performance of their duties." US assistant attorney general Mabel Walker Willebrandt once complained she "spent more time prosecuting prosecutors than the people they were supposed to prosecute."[4] After the fall of Mayor Thompson in 1931 and the collapse of the Insull empire in 1934, when the full story of Insull's financing of DePriest's machine finally was revealed, corroborating the accusations that socialist gadfly Chandler Owen had been making since 1926, DePriest attempted a version of the defense that Clarence Darrow had used successfully in DePriest's corruption trial: he had taken money from Insull, but he did not know it was from him.[5] It was not a particulary persuasive defense for someone whose stock portfolio was larded with Insull companies stocks. Nevertheless, in 1929 the matrix of power rackets were still aligned, Chandler Owen was easy to ignore, and Oscar DePriest was allowed to slip out of the bonds of his indictment and into the chambers of the US House of Representatives. It was an escape worthy of the great Houdini himself.

Oscar Stanton DePriest became a national figure and hero to many when he became the first "Negro" member of the US Congress since 1901, and the first ever from a Northern state, when he took the oath of office on Monday, April 20, 1929. The *Defender*, which was firmly in his camp, obsequiously helped to airbrush the political racketeer with the gravitas of a "race" hero, as when it described him having "a thick mass of white hair . . . brushed back from a face stern to the point of grimness. A ruddy face, etched with deep lines of character and a pervading physical and mental strength made him readily the most conspicuous person in the house and certainly the focus of attention throughout the session."[6] Some hoped that having a Black man in Congress would improve life for all fifteen million American "Negroes." DePriest elicited a tremendous amount of pride, and helped to build Black political organizations in Boston and Harlem. The Black press devoted a lot of column inches to his efforts to break the barriers of Jim Crow in the US Capitol by eating in the House restaurant, or by his wife being admitted to a social club for wives of representatives, symbolic blows that many hoped would help broaden freedoms for all people of color.

And then there was the fact of the common misperception of the Black state and federal representatives who served during Reconstruction, which was that they were horrifically corrupt. Many people did not want to believe the truth about Oscar DePriest, that he was in fact corrupt, because it fit too perfectly into that old racist stereotype. When DePriest's Black opponent in the general election distributed an anonymous exposé of DePriest's indebtedness to Insull, the *Baltimore Afro-American* printed the charges but also said they sounded like Southern racism.[7] The popular and scholarly understanding of Black Reconstruction would not start to change until 1935, when W. E. B. Du Bois published his masterpiece, *Black*

Reconstruction in America: An Essay Toward a History of the Part Which Black Folk Played in the Attempt to Reconstruct Democracy in America, 1860–1880, and argued that Black voters and politicians were heroes of democracy, not villains.[8] Until that happened, to appraise DePriest for what he was fed too easily into the reigning racist interpretation of Black Reconstruction–era politicians.

Whereas the late representative Martin B. Madden had been one of the most powerful members of the House, DePriest received minor committee assignments, although his service on the US Postal Service was significant in that the post office employed the majority of Black federal employees. He introduced an anti-lynching bill that failed, but on the bill that created the New Deal's Civilian Conservation Corps he did manage to attach an anti-discrimination clause, though the provision failed to actually prevent discrimination in the CCC. But despite his modest legislative accomplishments, DePriest became a national figure, giving speeches in all sections of the country on civil rights and the importance of Black participation in American democracy, and nominating Black candidates to the officer training academies of West Point and Annapolis. He said his job was "to teach Negroes race pride," and he did what he could to bar discrimination in federal employment, to fight lynching, and to publicize racial discrimination from the floor of the Senate. In response, he received flattering press coverage in the "Negro" press and was acclaimed by some as "the greatest asset to the Negro race since the days of Frederick Douglass."[9] But as a Republican he also opposed Franklin Delano Roosevelt and the New Deal even though they were both popular among his constituents, and lost his seat in 1934 when Blacks had begun to shift toward the Democratic Party—and after the fall of Thompson and Insull in Chicago eroded the rickety scaffolding of purchased and coerced support that DePriest had done so much to build during his years collecting kickbacks and buying votes on the South Side.

DePriest's legitimacy was imperiled by two ongoing cases even after he took his seat in 1929: the investigation of Claude Greene's murder in Unity Hall and Daniel M. Jackson's looming trial on a similar indictment to the one that DePriest himself had so miraculously escaped. On May 14, 1929, the coroner's jury recommended William Johnson-Bey's arrest for murder and held Noble Drew Ali, Sam Jackson, and Joseph Darlington as accessories. In theory, coroner's juries were merely advisory and limited to determining the cause of death. Their findings were officially nonbinding on police, state's attorneys, or grand juries. But in practice, they determined whether a crime was committed and who committed it, and police and prosecutors usually accepted coroner's juries' findings as final.[10] But neither the police nor prosecutors were compelled to follow the advice of coroner's juries, and nothing came of the recommendation in the murder of Claude Greene.[11] With Coroner Bundesen poking around in the case, the police arrested the Prophet again in May, this time on a charge of statutory rape stemming from his marriage to Mary Lou Bey, whom the *Baltimore Afro-American* reported he had married with the consent of her parents, Foreman and Mozelle Bey, when she was thirteen and had impregnated when she was fourteen.[12] The Prophet himself called on his followers to appear at the grand jury hearing, and struck an upbeat tone: "Remember my laws and love ye one another," he wrote. "Prefer not a stranger to your brother. Love and truth and my peace I leave all."[13] The Prophet's defense lawyer, William Levi Dawson, a member of the Moorish Science Temple, replaced Claude Greene as manager of Unity Hall in the 1930s. Dawson would be instrumental in creating a Black wing of the Democratic Party and would serve in Congress from 1943 until 1970. The man who did as much as anyone besides Franklin Delano Roosevelt to bring Blacks from the Party of Abraham Lincoln to the Party of Andrew Jackson was once a member of the Moors.

If Dan Jackson had gone to trial, the proceedings could have at the very least embarrassed his old enemy, Congressman DePriest, and could have easily imperiled his seat in Congress. But then a fortunate turn ensured the longevity of DePriest's political career: Daniel M. Jackson, undertaker, burial society organizer, and Chicago's dapper "King of Gamblers," dropped dead on Friday, May 17, 1929, only days before his trial was to begin, allegedly of a flu that lasted six days—and by some accounts, only two. Jackson's last act before he fell ill was to reach out to the machine of Charles Deneen, whose South Side wing was now headed by veteran politico Ed Wright, indicating that he was chaffing at the control of the Thompson-DePriest machine and their allied vicelords. Political insider A. N. Fields, the secretary of Jackson's Second Ward machine, intimated that Jackson's death was the result of bad advice he received from "white friends," implying that his death was not a natural one but a murder. His "white friends" made a pretense of believing in Jackson, Fields wrote, but "their guidance and their advice were largely responsible for the unfortunate events which ultimately hurried him to an untimely grave. His reputation was destroyed in the house of his friends."[14] The label "white friends" could be a euphemism for white gangster business partners, as Jackson had necessarily cut deals with the Guzik-Capone Outfit, which controlled bootlegging and many vice hot spots on the South Side.

As Jackson was dying, his associates mobilized to wrest control of his business empire from his brother Charles, transferring the title of the Emanuel Jackson Funeral Home to themselves and taking over the Metropolitan Funeral Association. Although "the King of Gamblers" was rumored to be worth a million dollars and to keep $80,000 in cash in his safe at all times, most of that money vanished; the probate court valued his estate at $75,000, which Charles inherited along with control of Dan's gambling rackets. Jackson's old friend and running buddy Casper Holstein, whom he had once ransomed from white gangsters, attended the funeral, where six thousand mourners filed past the bier. Holstein was part of the group of black-clad mourners who boarded a special train and accompanied the body to its final resting place in the Jackson family plot in Pittsburgh's Allegheny Cemetery. With the DePriest investigation dropped and the undertaker Jackson six feet under, prosecution of the South Side political racketeering ring collapsed. DePriest, who had gained the opportunity to become a congressman by the death of former congressman Madden on April 27, 1928, now was cleared to remain in the House by the death of his rival Daniel M. Jackson one year later.[15]

Unfortunately, the bad luck and bad health among those who knew the inner workings of Unity Hall appeared to be spreading. Noble Drew Ali fell ill sometime in April—that is, a month after his first arrest for murder and a month before his second arrest for statutory rape. He began seeing a member of the sect, Aaron Payne's brother, Dr. Clarence H. Payne (or Payne-El), the chief intern at the South Side's Provident Hospital, on May 1, and his health worsened until he passed away on July 20, 1929, at 10:10 p.m. at his home at 3603 Indiana Avenue. He was surrounded on his deathbed by his attorney, Aaron Payne; his physician, Clarence Payne-El; and Foreman Bey, the father of his fourth and youngest wife. The cause of the Prophet's demise and death were unclear: Clarence Payne-El diagnosed the Prophet with tuberculosis and wrote that Noble Drew Ali died of "Tuberculosis Broncho Pneumonia" on the death certificate that he signed.[16] City Attorney Aaron Payne furnished the information for the death certificate, which his brother signed, yet in spite of this, there were reports within his organization that the Prophet had been poisoned.[17] According to contemporary members of the MSTA, the Prophet reportedly summoned one of his first Chicago followers, Edward Mealy-El, to his deathbed and stated, "I have my number, and my work of redeeming you people is finished, and I must now go, or I can't return, and if I don't return, I can't deliver you, and if I don't deliver you, then my coming was in vain."[18]

Thousands of mourners and the merely curious shuffled past the metal casket that held the Muslim Prophet, onetime Hindu magician, trumpeter, and former Broadway child star at Frank Edwards's undertaking parlor on the South Side, as the man born Walter Brister lay in state as Noble Drew Ali from Monday, July 29, through Friday, August 2, 1929. Male members of the Moorish Science Temple wearing their distinctive fezzes and sashes helped transport the heavy bier to the Pythian Temple at Thirty-Seventh Place and State Street where funeral services were held, complete with singing, an oration, and burial rituals. The "Eastern" part of the burial ritual was conducted by Charles Kirkman-Bey in a language that nonmembers did not understand: "Whatever he was saying in connection with this ceremony was as foreign to the audience as Caesar is to a fourth grade pupil, at least to that part of the audience not affiliated with the cult," wrote the *Chicago Defender*.[19]

Various historians and devotees have usually ascribed the Prophet's death either to a beating at the hands of the police or to tuberculosis. The *Defender*, long in the pocket of both Samuel Insull and Oscar DePriest, reported the possibility that Drew Ali had been injured while being interrogated by the police, while "the friends of Greene are beginning to wonder if the inevitable law of compensation, retribution of [or] just plain justice isn't being manifested in the sudden death of Drew."[20] The *Defender* repeated the story of a Drew Ali beating while in police custody several times, and the account has been amplified in many scholarly accounts of the Prophet's life, but the story has multiple flaws. For one thing there is a problem of timing: most deaths caused by beatings happen immediately. One exception would be a subdural hematoma—that is, bleeding between the brain and the skull—which can linger for weeks before being noticed, but when it presents, the victim dies quickly, not in a gradual, wasting illness of the kind that Drew experienced.[21]

But the beating theory also does not jibe with the *Defender*'s well-documented account, based on their reporting and the investigation of private detective Sheridan Bruseaux, that Noble Drew Ali had

paid thousands of dollars in protection money to local police and politicians. The police, after all, were so ineffectual in interviewing witnesses and investigating Greene's murder that Coroner Bundensen
took the case out of their hands. It simply does not compute that the
police would be both protecting Drew Ali to the extent of refusing
to investigate a gory homicide, and yet would have been so vigorous
in their interrogation of the same individual that they would have
beaten him severely enough to cause his death. Also, Drew Ali was
a public figure whose movements around Chicago in the year prior
to the slaying attracted flattering press comment. At a time when
even visits from out-of-town relatives drew press coverage in Chicago's many "Negro" newspapers, it is hard to imagine that if Drew Ali
had been badly beaten by the police that such an incident would not
have made it into the press or any of the records left by the MSTA
itself. The story of a police beating never had any corroborating evidence, which is not to say that some mystery does not remain about
the reasons for the Prophet's demise.

And then there was "Princess Sotanki," John Walter Brister's
former wife, Eva Allen. The last sighting we have of her was when
she was seated by her former husband's side wearing an Adept's rib-
bon in the famous photograph of the First Annual Convention in
October of 1928. Followers today often misidentify the mysterious
woman at the Prophet's side as either Pearl Drew Ali or the wife of
Michigan's Grand Governor, James Lomax Bey. But Pearl was still in
her twenties, and as of 1920, at least, James Lomax was married to
Eleanor Lomax, who was nine years younger than Eva. Census and
city directories also report that Eva lived in Cincinnati from 1920 to
1930.[22] Eva may have become "Sister Besharis," a conjure woman in
the Moorish movement remembered for always wearing a turban and
carrying a staff, with a wild look in her eyes. Sister Besharis was also
known as "the Moorish Princess," much like "Princess Sotanki," and
her name was also of Indian derivation.[23] As a woman reputed to be
a conjurer, not just a snake charmer and lion tamer, the one-time Eva
Brister might have had knowledge of the pharmacopeia of poisons
that were common parts of the hoodoo repertoire. Her latest husband, Adam Allen, had passed away by 1929; with one divorce, two
deaths, and one faked death among her first four spouses, Eva's husbands had a remarkably high mortality rate. But it is hard to imagine,
after fifteen years of marriage and eleven years apart, that Eva would

have reunited with her former husband in the Moorish Science Temple only to dispatch him, or that the charismatic prophet with a following of thousands and many lucrative income streams would have been worth more to her dead than alive. The former vaudeville star was supporting herself in 1930 with two lodgers as a self-employed express woman, at a time during Prohibition when making deliveries could be a lucrative trade.[24]

The mystery of Noble Drew Ali's death will probably never be solved, but neither can it be understood without appreciating the poorly guarded secret of how power worked in Prohibition-era Black Chicago. Noble Drew Ali was playing a dangerous game by insinuating himself into the South Side's shadowy power structure. The very brutality of the Greene killing, and its ham-fisted execution within the inner sanctum of Insull's secret South Side power hub, suggests that the perpetrators did not understand the matrix of power that such graphic violence disturbed. After all, it was not even worth the Moors' time to meet Samuel Insull until Melvin Chisum paid them fifty cents a head to trek upstairs that one night in Unity Hall, so Drew Ali must not have known who Insull was, let alone how Insull's money sloshed through the spigot of Unity Hall into the pockets of South Side barbers, hairdressers, and ministers. Even William Levi Dawson, Drew Ali's lawyer and a future congressman, would not have recognized Samuel Insull, according to reporter Stephen Breszka's account.[25] And though Noble Drew Ali was able to attract socially prominent, well-educated, and well-connected men like Claude Greene and Aaron Payne to his organization, in the end they undoubtedly understood Chicago's world of political rackets and power brokers better than he did. And so, in only four months, in the middle of a double indictment of two prominent Black politicians, three of the people connected to the Insull-owned Unity Hall were dead: Claude Greene, who was hired to manage Unity Hall by the "King of Gamblers," Dan Jackson; Jackson himself, the indicted politician and gambling titan who was one of DePriest's rivals on the South Side; and Noble Drew Ali, who allegedly ordered the murder of Greene, his business manager and rival, not long before his own death.

In the interlocking power matrixes of the South Side, everyone seemed to be only one degree of separation from everyone else. The *Defender* reported that the dying Prophet asked Aaron Payne to take his place as the Prophet of the Moorish Science Temple of America, but Payne judiciously demurred and instead moved into the role of business manager vacated by the murder of Claude Greene. City Attorney Payne held a city job and so was on the payroll of the Crowe-Thompson-DePriest machine. His father-in-law, Emmett Scott, was close friends with Melvin Chisum, Samuel Insull's chief Black adviser. Provident Hospital, the employer of Aaron's brother, Dr. Charles Payne-El, had been a recipient of the philanthropic largess of Samuel Insull and his companies since at least December of 1927, when Insull's companies donated state-of-the-art equipment for its operating rooms. The year after the Prophet's death, Insull spearheaded a $3 million fundraising drive for Provident Hospital with a banquet for Chicago's white and black moneyed power brokers at the famous Palmer House. Insull led the pledges with a commitment of $50,000, setting the pace for the white guests, and banker Jesse Binga led off with a commitment for $5,000, setting the benchmark for the Black ones.[26] But Insull's critics were not appeased by such acts of philanthropy. In 1929, socialist Norman Thomas debated Samuel Insull's brother Martin, and declared that "the strange adventures of the Insull holding companies illustrate the racketeering stage which capitalism has reached in its dying hour and the necessity for public ownership of public utilities." Only four years later, Samuel Insull would become a fugitive from justice, his many holding companies in ruins and thousands of investors left with worthless stock.[27]

The *Defender* produced no exposés on Insull, only once criticizing him in print, but it did create a damning cartoon, which it ran on the front page the same day that it announced the death of "the most Noble Drew Ali." The cartoon depicted a portly politician, listening to musical notes and money signs coming out of the horn of a Victrola phonograph like those sold by Samuel Insull's Commonwealth Edison stores. The caption read: "Do as I tell you and these dollars are yours." The meaning of the cartoon would have been clear to the readers of the *Defender*: "Emperor" Insull was holding an unhealthy sway over Chicago's Black politicians.[28] By 1934, after Insull's empire collapsed and the utility baron fled the country in disgrace, the hidden power he wielded had begun to be uncovered in certain newspapers—but not the *Defender*, which was steadfast in its support of both Insull and DePriest. When Democrat Arthur Mitchell successfully challenged DePriest in 1934, the Black newspaper the

Chicago World impugned both the congressman and Insull by writing of the challenger:

> He has never been indicted for grafting or in league with commercialized vice. He has never been removed from office and is not considered a disgrace to his people. He has never charged his people high rent when there was no necessity for doing so and he has never been accused of selling his people out to powerful interests and pocketing the money.[29]

In other words, by 1934 the official silence surrounding the misdeeds of both DePriest and Insull was breaking down. The same year, Stephen Breszka used a distinctive turn of phrase to describe DePriest's role at Unity Hall, given the violent nature of the Greene shooting: "When Insull was visiting, the big man with the gun around there was Oscar De Priest, and others who have either died or retired from public life."[30] Oscar DePriest had said that only death would stop him from reaching Congress. Instead, death undeniably helped him both to get to Congress and to remain there, whether or not the Grim Reaper had human assistance.

With Prophet Noble Drew Ali's death, his movement splintered. Members looted the organization's assets, and rivals fought over who would lead the Moorish Science Temple of America. His former chauffer fled with the Prophet's automobile, valued at $6,000 in 1929, or about $90,000 in 2020 dollars. One of his secretaries disappeared, as did the contents of Noble Drew Ali's bank account, containing between $60,000 and $100,000 (that's $900,000 to $1.5 million in 2020 dollars).[31] But the movement itself and its network of businesses, membership dues, "taxes," and other levies was producing income streams many times greater than the Prophet's individual wealth at the time of his passing, and Charles Kirkman-Bey vied among several others to become the next prophet of the Moorish movement. The factions in the organization at first split principally between Kirkman-Bey, Edward Mealy-El, and Ira Johnson, allegedly the leader of the slaying crew that killed Claude Greene, over who would become "Grand Vizier." Their dispute burst out into the open on the night of Monday, September 23, 1929, immediately following the Second Annual Convention of the MSTA, when four members of Ira Johnson's faction armed with revolvers visited the home of Supreme Business Manager Aaron Payne and demanded certain papers relating to the affairs of the organization that he had received at the recent convention. His wife, Mrs. Evelyn Scott Payne, grew suspicious and surreptitiously called the police as the men harangued her husband. When two officers responded to her call, Attorney Payne told them he was afraid the men were there to kill him. When the police officer demanded that the intruders throw up their hands and be searched, they refused. While one officer went to telephone for backup, the four men charged the remaining officer, who held them off by firing a shot into the floor, then passing a gun to former college football star Payne, telling him to shoot the first person who attempted to move. The officers and the city attorney held the men at bay until the patrol arrived, and the city placed a squad car at the Paynes' house in coming weeks in response to this incident and the five death threats Payne received from members of the Moorish Science Temple.[32]

The violence that crackled through Unity Hall in March would echo even more loudly two days later, when Grand Sheik and alleged Claude Greene killer Ira Johnson sent men to kidnap his rival Charles Kirkman-Bey. A group visited Kirkman-Bey's home at 442 West Elm Street and told him to come with them and bring his papers relating to the Moorish Science Temple. When they left, Kirkman-Bey's wife alerted the police, who rushed to the Moors' new headquarters in Drew Ali's old house at 3603 Indiana Avenue. A member of the group named Moe Jackson then led the police to 4139 South Parkway, where the Moors were holding Kirkman-Bey. But when they arrived Jackson double-crossed the cops and told the Moors inside that the law was at their door. The police then knocked Jackson down as they rushed into the flat and were met by a hail of gunfire. The police were using both sawed-off shotguns and revolvers, and the Moors fired with revolvers alone. The cops finally subdued the Moors with tear gas canisters, but only after one police officer and one Moor were dead; a second officer died of his wounds a few days later. The chaos of the shoot-out brought milling crowds of spectators to the scene. By one estimate, over half a million people visited the site to gawk, and city officials, fearing a massive riot like the ones that had broken out a decade earlier, turned the South Side into an armed camp with hundreds of police and National Guardsmen patrolling the streets. "Excitement following the outbreak was the greatest Chicago has known since the bloody riots of 1919," one paper reported.[33] Ira Johnson later confessed in court to being the one who killed officer William Gallagher, although with the aid of a lawyer he claimed somewhat implausibly that he did not know he was shooting at a police officer when the cops burst in. When the Moors were tried the following April of 1930, all the defendants pleaded guilty and received prison terms: Ira Johnson, fifty, received a sentence of life in prison, while Eugene Johnson, sixty-seven, and his son Mose Johnson, thirty, each got fourteen years.[34] In decades to come, the Moors would find prisons to be fertile recruiting grounds for new members.

Breaking with Mayor Thompson and aligning with Senator Charles Deneen was positively bad for one's health. A year after Dan Jackson made entreaties to the Deneen machine and dropped dead in days, Edward Wright collapsed after a surgery at the Mayo Clinic. He had been suffering from an unspecified illness ever since his break with Thompson in 1927. Meanwhile, the Deneen leanings of Jackson's camp and its opposition to DePriest became even clearer after Jackson's death. Robert Cole, a former Pullman porter whom Jackson had put in charge of the swanky gambling resort the Dunbar Club, became the head of the Metropolitan Funeral Association and used its coffers to support DePriest's opponent in 1930. It was alleged that Cole and other members of Dan Jackson's inner circle ran the association as a racket, controlling and operating the company "quite exclusively to their own benefit," and diverting its funds "to illegal and personal uses."[35] The political machine of Senator Charles Deneen recruited Cole, and for his troubles Jackson's successor was kidnapped by white gangsters, much as Jackson's buddy Casper Holstein had been. Cole raised a $5,000 (2020: $76,500) ransom and was released without being physically harmed. But no doubt "the white friends" who ran the South Side had extracted other financial concessions from Cole and sent a clear message: those who bucked the Crowe-Thompson-DePriest machine did not fare well in the age of "pineapples and plunder."[36]

In other words, Prophet Noble Drew Ali's death was not an isolated incident, but part of a string of deaths and a kidnapping among people who were associated with the Charles Deneen wing of the Illinois Republican Party and who opposed the machine of Attorney General Robert Crowe, Mayor William Hale Thompson, Governor Len Small—and their shadow partners in political racketeering in the underworld Outfit of Al Capone & Co. To review, Deneen ally County Recorder Joseph Haas died during the 1928 primary campaign, gifting six hundred jobs to the rival Thompson-Crowe faction. Deneen-affiliated racketeer Joe Esposito was gunned down less than a month before the 1928 primary. The murder of Octavius Granady on primary day by gangsters associated with Thompson ally Morris Eller demonstrated that the Thompson machine was not just willing to bomb its opponents' homes and polling places, but to shoot them down in cold blood in broad daylight. The death of longtime Deneen ally Martin Madden in April of 1928 gave Mayor Thompson the opportunity to select Oscar DePriest to run for Congress as the Republican candidate. The murder of Claude Greene, who had been hired by Dan Jackson, threatened to expose Samuel Insull's bribery ring run through Unity Hall.

The graphic Greene slaying, so soon after Drew Ali was pictured in a plumed turban between DePriest and Louis Anderson, also threatened the new congressman's legitimacy and turned the once-supportive *Chicago Defender* against the Moorish prophet. The Greene slaying made Noble Drew Ali a problem for the Thompson-DePriest machine, which his death allegedly from tuberculosis resolved. Dan Jackson's unnatural demise, blamed on the flu but explained by the secretary of his own political machine as the result of bad advice from duplicitous "white friends," removed a rival to DePriest just as Jackson made entreaties to the rival Deneen machine and immediately before he was to testify in a trial that could have unseated the new congressman DePriest. It was also dangerous to have a lot of assets lying around where underlings could get their hands on them; Jackson's associates looted his treasury, just as Noble Drew Ali's did. Any of these deaths aside from the Greene and Granady slayings could have indeed been from natural causes, but the likelihood that so many South Side political figures who either broke with the DePriest-Thompson-Crowe-Insull machine or transgressed against it all died of natural causes seems extremely small. The Thompson machine and its underworld allies had already proven that they would torture, bomb, kill, and kidnap to protect their prerogatives, and Dan Jackson's death showed that they were capable of employing the more subtle means of poisons and pathogens, not simply the staccato barking of tommy guns.

Walter Brister had begun life in Kentucky, entered show business through a fictionalized slave narrative in the hit show *In Old*

Kentucky, escaped the bounds of racism as a "Hindoo" magician with his lion-taming and snake-dancing wife, then threw off his mortal coil, assumed his brother's identity, and translated experience in business and magic to amaze and heal Southern migrants during the Harlem Renaissance. But Walter had his biggest impact when he founded the Moorish Temple of Science and then the Moorish Science Temple of America in Chicago, not only wholesaling root medicines but leading thousands of Americans of African descent, including a surprising number of Chicago's Black political elites, to new identities as Muslims and Moors, inspiring larger Muslim movements among Americans of African descent, not long after Walter Brister was finally committed to Chicago's soil as the revered Holy Prophet Noble Drew Ali.

THE BRIDGE

I come to set you free from that state of mental slavery that I found you in.

—NOBLE DREW ALI[1]

Chicago during Prohibition was a city transfixed by the spectacular staccato violence of gangsters' tommy guns, the rattle of Samuel Insull's electrified "El" trains, and the explosive pop of news photographers' magnesium-powder camera flashes. It was a city in which politicians, prosecutors, and even corporate titans were joined at the hip flask to the profitable rackets of the thugs, bootleggers, pimps, madams, and gamblers. It is easy to see how deaths that were not preceded by a blaze of gunfire slipped into the shadows in the spaces between so many Commonwealth Edison–powered electric lights.

In any event, Noble Drew Ali and the Moors suffered from a "first mover" problem common to innovators in many fields. The most successful companies are often not those who face the stiffest headwinds with a revolutionary product, but the imitators who draft off the leaders' success and then sprint past them when they falter. Around 1928, a diminutive migrant from Georgia named Elijah Poole, who worked at the Chevrolet Motors plant in Detroit, joined the Moorish Science Temple of America and a Black version of the Shriners. He saw Noble Drew Ali speak in Detroit and became a passionate advocate of the Moorish version of Islam. The Moors bestowed upon him a series of names: first Muhammad Ah, then Elim Ah Muhammad, and finally, Muhammad Ah Fahnu Bey.

The year after Prophet Noble Drew Ali's death, an ethnic Pash-tun from Afghanistan, who may have belonged to the Moorish Science Temple in Detroit, called himself Wallace Fard and started his own order, which he would call the "Allah Temple of Islam," with teachings very similar to Noble Drew Ali's. In fact, rumors circulated that Fard had joined the Moorish Science Temple under the name David Ford-El, and risen to the rank of Grand Sheik of the Chicago Temple in only a month, although there is no solid corroboration of that story.[2] It seems frankly impossible that an outsider could have climbed so fast in such a short period of time, particularly when Drew Ali was digging in and battling Greene and others within the movement, and there is no mention of Ford in any MSTA or newspaper accounts, which were quite clear about the personalities in leadership positions in the temple. In any case, Nation of Islam legend has it that when the police attacked Ira Johnson-Bey in September of 1929, Ford-El vowed to bring America to its knees in retribution, a prediction that was fulfilled, they say, by the stock market crash on October 29. Drawing on interviews with NOI members, Karl Evanzz reports that Ford-El claimed that "the crash proved that he was the reincarnation of Noble Drew Ali," and that he attracted thousands of Moors as a result.

Arriving in Detroit with his story of being the former Grand Sheik of the Moorish Science Temple of America and the reincarnation of its prophet, Ford renamed his Moorish organization the Allah Temple of Islam, and began using the names Wallace D. Fard and Wallace D. Fard Muhammad.[3] James Lomax, a.k.a. Ali Muhammad Bey, the head of the Detroit Moorish Science Temple who had battled Noble Drew Ali, feared for his life and fled to New York, then took the name Mehmed Bey and spent more than two months on a trip to Istanbul in the summer of 1930 in an unsuccessful attempt to gain permission to form a colony for American "Negro" Muslims in Turkey. In his absence, thousands of Moors in Detroit left the MSTA, many for Fard's new Allah Temple of Islam. Like the earlier group, Fard's sect used Moorish Science literature and fezzes. After Fard vanished in 1934, the former MSTA member Elijah Poole, now calling himself Elijah Muhammad, changed the name of Fard's organization to the Nation of Islam, and did not ban the use of fezzes until 1935. Elijah Muhammad's NOI used MSTA literature well into the 1940s.[4] When it recognized many of its first ministers decades later, many of them bore Moorish -El and -Bey names, testifying to the fact that America's largest and most famous "Black Muslim" religion had begun as a Moorish Science Temple splinter group.[5]

In fact, "the Messenger" Elijah Muhammad and the Nation of Islam benefited so much from Noble Drew Ali's demise that the rumor circulated for years in Chicago that Elijah Poole was responsible for the Moorish prophet's death.[6] While it is quite possible that Elijah Poole/Muhammad was part of the rebellious faction of the Detroit Moorish Science Temple, the rumor of his actual involvement in Drew Ali's demise is hard to square with the fact that he was not in Chicago in the crucial days in 1929 when the Moorish prophet sickened and died, and was not even a high-ranking member of the Detroit Moorish Science Temple at the time.

Scholar Patrick Bowen has demonstrated that Detroit MSTA dissident leader Lomax-Bey, now calling himself Muhammad Ez Al Deen, or Ezaldeen, traveled to Cairo and worked for fifty cents a day in a restaurant while he learned about Egypt, Arabic, and Sunni Islam. He returned to New York in December of 1936 as Muhammad Ezaldeen, preaching that Abraham's son Ishmael was descended from Ham, the biblical forefather of all Africans, and recruiting former members of the Moorish Science Temple with a version of Sunni Islam. His followers wore white turbans and red fezzes, and he taught that Jesus did not die on the cross, appealing to Moors familiar with Noble Drew Ali's emphasis on the life of Jesus. In 1938 Ezaldeen incorporated the Addeynu Allahe Universal Arabic Association (AAUAA), which spread within six years among many former members of the Moors in Rochester, Jacksonville, Newark, Philadelphia, Youngstown, Wilmington, Cleveland, and Detroit, and also formed farming communities outside of Philadelphia and in upstate New York. In the 1940s, other Muslim groups, many influenced by foreign-born Muslim immigrants, successfully recruited Black followers, taking names such as the Islamic Mission of America, the Moorish National Islamic Center, the Temple of Islam, and the Academy of Islam. The transformation from Noble Drew Ali's eccentric and polycultural version of Islam to a more orthodox variety hewing more closely to Sunni standards had begun.[7]

The fragmentation of Prophet Noble Drew Ali's Moorish Science Temple of America into dozens of factions and successor groups incubated a multiplicity of theologies, rituals, and political styles. As the Black Meccas of the 1920s turned into economically depressed ghettos in the 1930s, and as another wave of migrants arrived during the Second Great Migration of World War II, the socioeconomic conditions in Northern Black ghettos only worsened. As the suburbs exploded in amenities and popularity but walled themselves off from Blacks through the use of racist Federal Housing Authority guidelines and other forms of discrimination, the conditions in the older urban cores deteriorated, made worse in many cases by misguided "urban renewal" policies that destroyed inner-city neighborhoods for the sake of expressways, sports stadiums, concert halls, and the like. As racist discrimination in employment, education, and housing made the American dream appear to recede into the distance like a mirage on an Arabian desert, and as the nation dragged its feet in passing effective civil rights legislation, the mood in "colored" America soured. The next version of Islam to captivate the people still known as "Negroes" would not emphasize participation in the American political process, and its leaders would not expect or receive a seat at the table of corrupt but interracial municipal machines as they had during the more upbeat years of the Jazz Age. In the 1950s, a version of Islam that retained many of Noble Drew Ali's distinctive Black folk elements but emphasized militancy and separatism became newly popular.

Elijah Muhammad's Nation of Islam remained a small offshoot from the Moorish Science Temple until a young red-headed Black man from East Lansing, Michigan, the son of a Marcus Garvey organizer, converted to Islam while serving time for burglary in the late 1940s, changing his last name from Little to X. When Malcolm X was released from prison in 1952, the Nation of Islam had approximately five hundred members, far fewer than the members of the many branches of the Moorish Science Temple, or even the more orthodox Sunni groups. But Malcolm X was an electrifying speaker, a tireless and creative evangelist, and a dogged organizer, leading to the rapid expansion of the NOI in the 1950s. Journalists Mike Wallace and Louis Lomax produced a television documentary on Malcolm X and the NOI in 1959 called *The Hate That Hate Produced*, and scholar C. Eric Lincoln published a book on "the Black Muslims" in 1961, vaulting the NOI to national prominence, variously reviled and revered for its militant and uncompromising rhetoric, such as its teaching that whites were "devils." By 1963, thanks largely to Malcolm X's organizational brilliance, media celebrity, and electrifying oratory challenging US racism and Judeo-Christian hypocrisy, and due to exhaustion with violent attacks on the peaceful Black freedom struggle associated with the Reverend Martin Luther King Jr., the Nation of Islam boasted thirty thousand members, known for their discipline, their militancy, and their sharp conservative fashions. When Malcolm X split with the Messenger Elijah Muhammad over Muhammad's fathering of numerous children out of wedlock, and then was assassinated in 1965 by members of the Newark chapter of the Nation of Islam, actor Ossie Davis eulogized him as "our manhood, our living black manhood . . . our own black shining prince."[8] In death, Malcolm X became one of the most important inspirations for the Black Arts and Black Power movements, embraced for his love of Blackness and his rejection of the techniques of nonviolent resistance.

In Malcolm and Martin, two divergent Black American reinterpretations of "Hindu" anti-imperial traditions met, far from the Indian subcontinent: the Islamic "Hinduism" of the former Armmah Sotanki/Noble Drew Ali passed through the Moorish Science Temple to the more militant Nation of Islam and the eloquent Malcolm X, while the nonviolent resistance of white American Henry David Thoreau, reinterpreted in the fight against British colonialism and American racism by the Hindu ascetic Mahatma Gandhi, passed through the Reverend Howard Thurman, the Black Baptist minister who visited Gandhi in India in 1935, to Thurman's graduate student at Boston University, the spellbinding Reverend Martin Luther King Jr. In a sense both Malcolm and Martin were Orientalists, in that they were claiming messages from the Indian Orient, but they were doing so not to praise racism, but to bury it.

Upon Elijah Muhammad's death in 1975, leadership of the Nation of Islam passed to his son, Warith Deen Mohammed, who led the bulk of its members into orthodox Sunni worship, standardized their religion around the Five Pillars of Islam, and rejected the racialism of earlier phases of the NOI. Despite Minister Louis Farrakhan's actions in reviving the Nation of Islam in 1978, and the headline-grabbing statements he produced in the 1980s, today the NOI comprises only 3 percent of the country's Black American-born Muslims. Muslims who are Black and descended from Africans enslaved in the Americas make up 13 percent of the US' 3.45 million Muslims, and number approximately 448,500 in total, a figure many times larger than that of the religious pioneers who followed Noble Drew Ali or even Elijah Muhammad.[9] The Black Orientalist mystic scientists of the early twentieth century fused African American conjure practices with root medicine, Islam, the Shriners, occultism, and the *Arabian Nights* image of the Arab in popular culture, and thereby first established Islam as a mass religion in America. Yet almost all the descendants of those pioneering movements today practice their faith according to teachings of seventh-century Arabia's Prophet Muhammad.

Sometimes religious movements take a long time to develop, and we cannot really understand an actor or a movement until a century has passed and we can pry loose a few secrets by sifting through millions of newspaper pages and thousands of archival sources and catching small fragmentary clues emerging from patterns of light and shadow, even if other mysteries may never be solved. As Noble Drew Ali was once reported to have said, "The third and fourth generations will see the good of my work."[10]

In the end, no newspaper has ever been one hundred percent accurate, and the most severe allegations against Noble Drew Ali were never cross-examined in a court of law. Even if all the negative allegations about him were true, there was something noble about Noble Drew Ali. Despite the fact that Detective Sheridan Brusseaux testified that the Moorish Science Temple was run "as a racket," Noble Drew Ali's lasting legacy was as the creator of a religion, not a criminal conspiracy. The thousands of former "Negroes" he attracted to his religion acquired new identities as Moorish Muslims, new understandings of the historical rackets of slavery and racial oppression, new modes of dress, diet, and worship, and even new names. They believed the root tonics and healing oils they purchased to be efficacious, and perhaps they were, even if those claims were never vetted by any governmental body. Surely, Noble Drew Ali and many others made hundreds of thousands of dollars off the group's business ventures, but he also provided income streams for hundreds of employees. Noble Drew Ali fulfilled the dream that Booker T. Washington, Marcus Garvey, and just about every other "Negro" leader of the 1920s aspired to accomplish, which was to create successful Black-owned businesses, employing Black people and selling to Black customers, creating wealth for all in the process. That the Prophet worked with political racketeers like Dan Jackson, Oscar DePriest, and Louis B. Anderson and allegedly paid thousands of dollars in protection money to the police demonstrates that he understood how Chicago's political-police rackets worked: an organization on the South Side could not make profits of $18,000 a month, more than $3 million annually in today's dollars, without greasing the skids of Chicago's corrupt police and political machines.

Lest you think that it was routine for alternative religious figures to embed themselves into local political machines, it was not. Most Black alternative religious practitioners were socially marginal, tended to working-class clientele, and suffered frequent arrests as indeed Walter Brister did in his earlier guise as "Professor Drew." For the leader of a new religious movement like Noble Drew Ali to count among his members or close associates two aldermen, two future congressmen, a state representative, a city attorney, the chief intern of Provident Hospital, the leader of the largest Black political machine in the country, and the owner of America's largest Black-owned bank was extraordinary. For Brister to crack the code of access to the Black political and professional elite and their shadowy "white friends" was exceptional, but he may have flown too close to the sun.

Even as the numbers of Moors have dwindled in the twentieth and twenty-first centuries (their annual convention in 2007 attracted less than two hundred people), the image and ideas of Noble Drew Ali have spread through the affirmative testimonials of rappers such as Nas, Nick Cannon, Common, the Wu-Tang Clan, Rick Ross, Styles P, Black Thought, N.O.R.E., David Banner, Jay Electronica, ScienZe, Hell Razah, Sean Price, Waka Flocka Flame, Talib Kweli, and others. The artist formerly known as Mos Def now goes by a Moorish name, Yasiin Bey. He even put the famous photograph of the October 1928 First Annual Convention of the MSTA on the back of a 2009 album. Outkast's Andre 3000 was photographed wearing a fez in GQ magazine in 2017, and star quarterback Cam Newton started sporting the fez himself in December of that year—and also has a daughter named in reference to the sovereign citizen movement among some contemporary Moors who advocate that Moors are not bound by US law. In other words, people who have sold hundreds of millions of songs and have almost as many followers on social media are spreading awareness of Noble Drew Ali and the teachings of the Moorish Science Temple of America. Some of the readers of this book revere Noble Drew Ali as their Holy Prophet; for the rest of you, considering the fact that Moors and Muslims of African descent now make up 13 percent of the nation's 3.45 million Muslims, and include hundreds of rappers, athletes, comedians, doctors, lawyers, accountants, and congressmen and -women, and considering that the El is still clacking away, Edison is still powering Chicago's lights, and Peoples Gas is still heating its buildings, Noble Drew Ali and Samuel Insull might be the most influential Americans you had never heard of before picking up this book.[11]

🐦 🐦 🐦

If it is true, as Michael Gomez writes, that Noble Drew Ali was "necessarily the bridge over which the Muslim legacies of the eighteenth and nineteenth centuries crossed over into the Muslim communities of the twentieth and twenty-first,"[12] the question remains which Muslim legacies Ali conveyed. Although I have not presented the evidence and arguments in this volume regarding enslaved African Muslims in the Americas, I agree with other scholars that it is highly unlikely that those twentieth-century legacies were the cultural retention of memories, customs, and identities of antebellum enslaved African Muslims.[13] Noble Drew Ali was a bridge, then, but he was not a bridge between antebellum enslaved African Muslims and twentieth-century Black ones. Instead, he connected the twentieth century to ideas of Islam embedded within circuses, Shriners, Rosicrucians, Spiritualists, Theosophists, World's Fairs, and anti-imperial political activists. He is the bridge between Orientalist traditions of thinking about, representing, and embodying the Orient and twentieth-century Black American traditions of identifying as Muslims, but also the bridge between forms of Oriental anti-imperialism on the Indian subcontinent and forms of Orientalist anti-racism in America.

Black engagement with Islam in the late nineteenth and early twentieth centuries may have begun with images from the circus and the Shriners, from Rosicrucians, esoteric books, and Spiritual churches and merchants, but as the Age of Aquarius matured, and as immigration reform in 1965 permitted more foreign-born Muslims to bring their religions with them to the United States, these Orientalist tributaries flowed into the mighty *ummah* of global Islam. As in one of the Sotankis' "Hindoo" magic tricks in which they levitated a woman or made a person disappear from a woven basket, a transformation had occurred, not as other scholars have depicted through the "syncretic" mixture of pure ancestral inputs, or the maintenance of uninterrupted

African "retentions," but through the sincere exploration of diverse, heterodox, and frequently heretical worlds, patched together piecemeal through what might be called "polycultural bricolage."[14] As Noble Drew Ali himself said, "We have the blood of every nation flowing through our veins, thereby bringing about a cross spirit."[15]

🦅   🦅   🦅

Today Shriners of all races are aging and their numbers are dwindling. San Francisco's old majority-white Islam Shrine that once met in a splendid ersatz Oriental palace in the Tenderloin is no longer in San Francisco and is no longer called "Islam." The lodge moved to suburban San Mateo, twenty miles to the south, where they host the annual East-West Shrine college football all-star game, a fundraiser for the twenty-two Shriner children's hospitals, which offer free medical care for kids in need. After the attacks of September 11, 2001, when nineteen terrorists from Muslim-majority countries flew hijacked planes into the World Trade Center, the Pentagon, and a Pennsylvania field, American bigots, from a Christian-majority country, harassed and even murdered people they thought might be Muslims. Balbir Singh Sodhi, a Sikh gas station manager in Mesa, Arizona, donated seventy-four dollars to a fund for 9/11 victims four days after the attack, and an hour later was gunned down by an aircraft mechanic with Spanish and French surnames who told friends he was "going to go out and shoot some towel-heads." He yelled slogans at his court trial such as "I am a patriot!" and "I stand for America all the way!" The same day, a white man killed two people near Dallas, Texas: Waqar Hasan, a Pakistani Muslim, was shot in the face while cooking hamburgers in his grocery store the same day that Sodhi died, and Vasudev Patel, an Indian American, was shot in the chest while working with his wife behind the counter of a gas station they owned. The killer told a Dallas radio station he murdered Hasan and Patel to seek revenge for the World Trade Center attacks, "to retaliate on local Arab Americans or whatever you want to call them." On September 19, Ali Almansoop, a US citizen originally from Yemen, was shot in the back in Lincoln Park, Michigan, while fleeing his attacker, who threatened, "I'm going to kill you for what happened in New York and D.C." Hundreds of people who looked Indian, Afghan, or Arab suffered harassment, and the Federal Bureau of Investigation infiltrated and surveilled mosques around the country.[16]

In this tense climate, self-proclaimed patriots and racists some-times mistook Shriners sporting fezzes for Muslims and threat-ened them as well. Emphasizing the need to protect their members, two shrines changed their names: the Palestine Shrine became the Rhode Island Shrine, and San Mateo's Islam Temple became "Asiya," which members understood to be Arabic for "those who heal." Iron-ically, native Arabic speakers suggest it might be better translated as "cold-heartedness."[17]

It is worth heeding those scholars of Islamic Orientalism who blame it for creating a dehumanizing, dichotomous, and antago-nistic image of Muslims that could lead the US into war on flimsy evidence and faulty logic that would seem risible in a different part of the world. As comedian Dave Chappelle, who is both Black and Muslim, pointed out, we went to war because of aluminum tubes and yellow cake?[18] Neoconservative Orientalists assured us that the "Arab Street," shorthand for Arab political opinion, "respects strength" and would greet US troops "as liberators." *New York Times* columnist and Middle Eastern expert Thomas Friedman wrote pe-dantic columns about the "Arab street," and President George W. Bush said, "You can't distinguish between al-Qaida and Saddam," a statement that was true in that they were both Arab but false in almost every other way. Defense Secretary Donald Rumsfeld said there was "no question" that American troops would be "welcomed," while Vice President Dick Cheney said that "Iraqi streets" were "sure to erupt in joy," and the Israeli-Palestinian peace process would be enhanced. "I really do believe we will be greeted as liberators," he said. With the blessing of some US academics, the American mili-tary propagated this kind of misguided Orientalist indoctrination. "You have to understand the Arab mind," said a US infantry captain in Iraq. "The only thing they understand is force—force, pride and saving face." The war would be over in "weeks rather than months," Vice President Cheney assured the public. "It could last six days, six weeks. I doubt six months," said Rumsfeld.[19]

In reality, the US wars in Iraq and Afghanistan spilled over the borders into Pakistan and Syria and killed more than 480,000 people, including 244,000 civilians, over 14,750 US fighters (6,950 soldiers and at least 7,800 former servicemen turned mercenaries), while dis-placing 21 million Iraqi, Afghani, and Syrian refugees and leading to US counterterrorism operations in seventy-six countries, all at an estimated cost to US taxpayers of $5.9 trillion. As of this writing, there are still 8,400 US troops in Afghanistan and 5,200 in Iraq.[20]

Today, former president George W. Bush has turned from oil wars to oil paints, and most of the people in the United States and the world think it is criminal that he did not find his true vocation sooner. The United States of America has had a long romantic fascination with the Islamic Orient, as the story of Noble Drew Ali demonstrates. For some, it will be surprising to discover that there was actually less anti-Muslim hatred in this country a century ago than exists today. Perhaps this observation offers a sliver of hope for the future, shining like the crescent moon and the planet Venus that appeared in 1925 just as the Prophet Noble Drew Ali predicted they would: American Orientalist knowledge is seldom accurate, but neither is it always malicious. Oppressive discourses also contain liberating ones, submerged just below the surface of a myth or a mistranslation. The "cold-hearted" might just be trying to become "those who heal."

ACKNOWLEDGMENTS

Writing a book over the course of almost two decades necessarily creates more debts to more people than words can express, acknowledge, or adequately thank—not to mention the blessings of forces beyond any individual's control. As a friend of mine says, there are no atheists in a publishing foxhole. Nevertheless, I would like to attempt to acknowledge and thank a few of those who made this book possible, including all of my wonderful family and friends whose names I will not mention but without whom I would not be here. Patrick Bowen and Fathie Ali Abdat did foundational research that established the identity of Professor Drew as Thomas rather than Timothy Drew, providing a crucial point of connection for what I discovered of Walter Brister's early life and Noble Drew Ali's Chicago years. Christopher Robert Reed, William M. Tuttle Jr., Patrick Bowen, and Alan Deutschman read the manuscript in its entirety and offered valuable insights and encouragement, and, in Bill's case, precise, line-by-line copyediting. Kathryn Lofton read and commented on a portion of an early version of chapter 6, as did Bruce Moran and Paul Lovejoy for chapter 2. As I was completing the manuscript, I was privileged to share my discoveries with Ali's Men, a group of historians from various branches of the Moorish Science Temple of America, and I am deeply indebted to them not only for contributing key insights that improved the manuscript, but also for the gracious manner in which they received me and my findings. They are Lasana Tunica-El, Sharif Anael-Bey, Mahdi McCoy-El, Ash-Shaheed Snow-Bey, and Robert Webb-Bey. All the assertions and errors contained herein are my own, and not those of my generous readers and interlocutors.

No man is an island. My interest in allied topics began under the influence of professors Sylvia Wynter, Clayborne Carson, Arnold Eisen, and the late George Frederickson as an undergraduate at

Stanford University, as well as Tudor Parfitt, then of the School of Oriental and African Studies, the University of London, and the late Antony Kirk-Greene at St. Catherine's College, Oxford. My work continued at UCLA under the direction of my dissertation adviser, Brenda Stevenson, as well as Robert Hill, Gary Nash, the late Joyce Appleby, Henry Yu, Laura Edwards, Jessica Wang, Lynn Hunt, Margaret Jacob, David Sabean, Gabriel Piterburg, Donald Cosentino, and Carlo Ginzburg. I owe all of these professors a great debt for training me as a historian, although the vast majority of this book was written more than a decade after I earned my PhD in 2004.

Researching and writing this book over the last seventeen years has been a very long process that would have taken far longer without the generous support of numerous funders. I have been extremely fortunate to benefit from financial assistance from, in chronological order: the UCLA Department of History and its Carey McWilliams Fellowship; the Andrew W. Mellon Foundation, which generously funded a vital year at the Wesleyan University Center for the Humanities; Professor Victor Bailey and Kathy Porsch of the Hall Center for the Humanities of the University of Kansas, where I held a research fellowship and received and benefited from incredibly useful support and intellectual community; Vera L. Davis of the Black Metropolis Research Consortium Fellowship, housed at the University of Chicago; as well as James Grossman and Daniel Greene of the Newberry Library in Chicago and the National Endowment for the Humanities' yearlong fellowship at that institution. Finally, Cindy Mueller and the American Council of Learned Societies' Charles A. Ryskamp Research Fellowship have my enduring appreciation for funding a crucial year of research and writing toward the end of the process.

This project also benefited from the following monthlong research fellowships: the Donald C. Gallup Fellowship in American Literature at Yale University's Beinecke Rare Books and Manuscripts Library; the Research Fellowship at the Harry Ransom Center of the University of Texas at Austin; the Gilder Lehrman Scholarly Fellowship at the Columbia University Library; and the Friends of the Wisconsin Libraries fellowship at the University of Wisconsin at Madison. I would also like to thank Professor Henry Louis Gates Jr. and Abby Wolf of the Hutchins Center for African American Research at Harvard University, where I benefited from the monthlong NEH Summer Institute and through which I have enjoyed access to Harvard's libraries and online archival materials as a nonresidential fellow.

Many thanks to my agent, Don Fehr at Trident Media Group, who believed in this book and in my abilities as a writer. My editor at Beacon, Amy Caldwell, pored over every page and helped discipline my writing, and copyeditor Brian Baughan improved the text tremendously as well. The entire editorial, production, and marketing team at Beacon Press and the distribution team at Random House have been consummately professional and a joy to work with.

The National Endowment for the Humanities' budget in 2019 was $155 million, less than half of the real cost of a single F-35C fighter jet and approximately one five-thousandth of what this country spends on its military annually, not even counting spy agencies, the Coast Guard, and the Border Patrol. Nonetheless, the current administration has repeatedly attempted to eliminate the NEH altogether, which would be a decidedly unpatriotic act and a great loss for everyone who cares about American history. "Every tyranny in the world lives—and such systems have always lived—in a perpetual struggle against plain knowledge and illuminating discussion," as H. G. Wells wrote in 1937. Please do not throw out your old letters, diaries, and scrapbooks! Take them to a local archive where they can be preserved for future generations, and future historians, especially if we work together to expand the NEH's Division of Preservation and Access grant programs.

This book could not exist without the work of archivists over many generations at the following institutions: Austin, Texas: the Harry Ransom Center for the Humanities. Baraboo, Wisconsin: Circus World Museum and Archives. Cambridge, Massachusetts: the Harvard University Performing Arts Library. Chicago, Illinois: Loyola University of Chicago; Roosevelt University; the Art Institute of Chicago; the Chicago Historical Society; the Vivian G. Harsh Research Collection of the Chicago Public Library; the Newberry Library; the University of Chicago; the University of Illinois at Chicago; the Harold Washington Library of the Chicago Public Library. Detroit, Michigan: Archives of the Universal Hagar's Spiritual Church. London, England: the Victoria and Albert Museum Archives. Madison, Wisconsin: the University of Wisconsin Special Collections. Memphis, Tennessee: Archives of the Headquarters of the Ancient Egyptian Arabic Order of Nobles of the Mystic Shrine. New Haven, Connecticut: the Beinecke Rare Book and Manuscripts

Library, Yale University. New York, New York: the Schomburg Center for Research in Black Culture; the New York Public Library for the Performing Arts, the Dorothy and Lewis B. Cullman Center; the Special Collections of Columbia University Libraries; the Chancellor Robert R. Livingston Masonic Library. Normal, Illinois: the Circus and Allied Arts Collection of the Milner Library, Illinois State University. Princeton, New Jersey: the Special Collections of Princeton University. San Francisco, California: the San Francisco Public Library Special Collections. San Mateo, California: Archives of Asiya (formerly Islam) Shrine of the Ancient Arabic Order of the Nobles of the Mystic Shrine. Sarasota, Florida: the John and Mable Ringling Museum of Art and Archives of Florida State University.

Although there are still many sources that only exist on microfilm, this book could not have been written without others' collective efforts to digitize trillions of pages of newspapers, magazines, journal articles, and books, and I am grateful for the combined work of so many archivists in creating invaluable tools such as Google Books, FamilySearch.org, Ancestry.com, HathiTrust Digital Library, the California Digital Library, the California Digital Newspaper Collection, JSTOR, Project Muse, ProQuest Historical Newspapers, Readex America's Historical Newspapers, Newsbank African American Newspapers, the Library of Congress's Chronicling America, and Thomas Tryniski's incredible New York newspaper archive, FultonHistory.com. I was only able to keep track of 14,500 digital images thanks to a professional digital photography database program that I have followed through three different name changes: once called iView Media Pro, then Microsoft Expression Media, and then PhaseOne Media Pro. As someone who started taking notes in archives in pencil on scraps of paper, I fully appreciate how revolutionary these tools are. Digitization and digital tools ought to be generously supported and vigorously expanded, as we are all practicing digital humanities now.

I also want to acknowledge the tremendous service to scholarship performed by librarians everywhere, but especially the interlibrary loan staff of the University of Kansas, where I was fortunate to begin my career, and the interlibrary loan and LINK+ staffs of the University of Nevada, Reno, where I am lucky to continue it. Such crucial services combine the collections of regional universities and public libraries into the collective strength of a large research university.

I must thank the following presses for permission to republish content: part of chapter 3 appeared as "'Oriental Hieroglyphics Understood Only by the Priesthood and a Chosen Few': The Islamic Orientalism of White and Black Masons and Shriners," in *Islam and the Americas*, edited by Aisha Khan (Gainesville: University Press of Florida, 2015), 49–68. Part of chapter 8 appeared as "'A True Moslem Is a True Spiritualist': Black Orientalism and Black Gods of the Metropolis," in Edward E. Curtis IV and Danielle Brune Sigler, eds., *The New Black Gods: Arthur Huff Fauset and the Study of African American Religions* (Bloomington: Indiana University Press, 2009), 116–42. Thank you as well to all of the repositories that granted me permission to reproduce photographs, acknowledged individually in the photo credits.

Last but certainly not least, I want to thank the citizens of Berkeley, California, for their decision to desegregate their public schools in 1968, and for all the people of many races, classes, religions, genders, sexualities, and immigration statuses who pitched in to embrace integration, jazz, art, and academic excellence in the Berkeley Public Schools, which thereby produced not only Senator Kamala Harris, pianist Benny Green, guitarist Charlie Hunter, and saxophonist Joshua Redman, but decades of professionals, musicians, and scholars, including me.

IMAGE CREDITS

INSERT ONE
Photograph of Walter Brister as the Hindoo Magician Armmah Sotanki from the
    1900 Official Route Book of the Pawnee Bill Wild West Show, p. 81, Circus
    World Museum, Baraboo, WI.
Walter Brister as Prophet Noble Drew Ali, First Annual Convention of the Moorish
    Science Temple of America, 1928, Photographs and Prints Division, New York
    Public Library.
Circus World Museum, Baraboo, WI.
Barnum Circus 1886 Route Book, Circus World Museum, Baraboo, WI.
Strobridge Lithograph Co., *Barnum & Bailey: Fierce Onslaught by Moorish Warriors*,
    c. 1889. John and Mable Ringling Museum of Art.
Bridgeman Images.
Bridgeman Images.
Midway Types: A Book of Illustrated Lessons About the People of the Midway Plaisance,
    World's Fair 1893 (Chicago: American Engraving Co., 1894).
McManus-Young Collection, Library of Congress, Rare Book and Special Collec-
    tions Division, Washington, DC.
B. W. Kilburn, Alamy.
Alamy.
Alamy.
"The Pawnee Bill Riot," *Princeton Alumni Weekly* (Apr. 8, 1938): 605.
1900 Pawnee Bill Wild West Show Route Book.
Circus World Museum, Baraboo, WI.

INSERT TWO
John and Mable Ringling Museum of Art.
Matthew Brady Studio, National Portrait Gallery, Smithsonian Institution, Freder-
    ick Hill Meserve Collection.
Punch Wheeler, The John Robinson 10 Big Shows 1902 Route Book, Circus World
    Museum, Baraboo, WI.
Official Route Book of the Pawnee Bill Wild West Show, 80.
Left: Official Route Book of the Pawnee Bill Wild West Show, 83; right: First An-
    nual Convention of the Moorish Science Temple of America, 1928, Photographs
    and Prints Division, New York Public Library.

NOTES

INTRODUCTION: ORGANIC MOSAICS

1. James C. Scott, *Weapons of the Weak: Everyday Forms of Peasant Resistance* (New Haven, CT: Yale University Press, 1985), 331, 336.

2. Peter Lamborn Wilson, *Sacred Drift: Essays on the Margins of Islam* (San Francisco: City Lights Books, 1993), 22.

3. Emile Durkheim, *The Elementary Forms of Religious Life*, trans. Joseph Ward Swain (London: George Allen & Unwin, 1915), 3.

4. Jacob S. Dorman, "'Lifted Out of the Commonplace Grandeur of Modern Times:' Reappraising Edward Wilmot Blyden's Views of Islam and Afrocentrism in Light of His Scholarly Black Christian Orientalism," *Souls: A Critical Journal of Black Politics, Culture, and Society* 12, no. 4 (October 2010): 398–418.

5. Dusé Mohamed Ali, "Leaves from an Active Life," in *Comet* (June 12, 1937): 7; Ian Duffield, "Dusé Mohamed Ali and the Development of Pan-Africanism, 1866–1945," PhD diss., Edinburgh University, 1971; Ian Duffield, "Some American Influences on Dusé Mohamed Ali," in *Pan-African Biography*, ed. Robert A. Hill (Los Angeles: African Studies Center, UCLA and Crossroads Press/African Studies Association, 1987), 40–41; Ian Duffield, "Dusé Mohamed Ali, Afro-Asian Solidarity and Pan-Africanism in Early Twentieth-Century London," in *Essays on the History of Blacks in Britain: From Roman Times to the Mid-Twentieth Century*, ed. J. Gundara and I. Duffield (Aldershot, UK: Avebury, 1992).

6. Scott Trafton, *Egypt Land: Race and Nineteenth-Century American Egyptomania* (Durham, NC: Duke University Press, 2004); Claude McKay, *A Long Way from Home* (New York: L. Furman, 1937); Wayne F. Cooper, *Claude McKay: Rebel Sojourner in the Harlem Renaissance; a Biography* (New York: Knopf, 1990), 287–90.

7. Wilson, *Sacred Drift*, 6–7.

8. Steven Jay Gould, *The Mismeasure of Man* (New York: Norton, 1996); George M. Fredrickson, *Racism: A Short History* (Princeton, NJ: Princeton University Press, 2002).

9. Sylviane A. Diouf, *Servants of Allah: African Muslims Enslaved in the Americas* (New York: New York University Press, 1998), 170.

10. Jacob S. Dorman, *Chosen People: The Rise of American Black Israelite Religions* (New York: Oxford University Press, 2013).

11. Wilson, *Sacred Drift*, 22.

12. Associated Negro Press, "Murder Exposes Moorish Leader's Amours: 3 Women Named in Case," *Pittsburgh Courier*, March 23, 1929, p. 10.

13. Kambiz GhaneaBassiri, *A History of Islam in America: From the New World to the New Order* (New York: Cambridge University Press, 2010), 148–49.

14. "Ritual of the Shriners," in *Ritual of the Ancient Egyptian Arabic Order Nobles of the Mystic Shrine of North and South America and Jurisdictions, Inc.*, 10th ed. (1969; rev. ed., 1958), 62, http://www.phoenixmasonry.org/, accessed February 21, 2008.

CHAPTER ONE: OLD KENTUCKY

1. "Apocryphal Sayings of the Prophet Noble Drew Ali," https://hermetic.com /moorish/apocryphal-sayings-of-the-prophet-noble-drew-ali, accessed July 1, 2018.

2. "Theatres," *Morning Call* (San Francisco), September 23, 1894, p. 16.

3. "Theatres."

4. "In Old Kentucky," *Indianapolis Freeman* (September 24, 1910), cited in *Out of Sight: The Rise of African American Popular Music, 1889–1895*, ed. Lynn Abbott and Doug Seroff (Oxford: University Press of Mississippi, 2003), 407.

5. Abbott and Seroff, *Out of Sight*, 406.

6. "Pickaninny Band, in Old Ky Company," advertisement, *Indianapolis Freeman*, July 2, 1904, cited in Abbott and Seroff, *Out of Sight*, 408.

7. "In Old Kentucky."

8. "Dazey Play To Be Filmed 'In Old Kentucky,'" *Louisville Courier-Journal*, June 8, 1919, p. B5.

9. "Theaters and Music," *Brooklyn Daily Eagle*, September 3, 1893, p. 5.

10. "In Old Kentucky."

11. "Theatres."

12. *New York Clipper*, September 16, 1893, cited in Abbott and Seroff, *Out of Sight*, 407.

13. *Queens County Sentinel* (Hempstead, NY), September 19, 1894.

14. *Eastern State Journal* (White Plains, NY), December 30, 1893.

15. *Eastern State Journal*.

16. "The Busy Players," *New York Tribune*, January 14, 1894, p. 20.

17. *New York Clipper*, December 30, 1893, cited in Abbott and Seroff, *Out of Sight*, 409.

18. *Kansas City American Citizen*, November 22, 1895, cited in Abbott and Seroff, *Out of Sight*, 409.

19. *Leavenworth Herald*, December 14, 1895; "Amusements," *Yenowine's Illustrated News* (Milwaukee), August 4, 1894, p. 3.

20. "'In Old Kentucky' at the Theatre Royal," *Edinburgh Evening News* (Scotland), July 6, 1897, p. 2.

21. "'In Old Kentucky' at the Theatre Royal," *Edinburgh Evening News*, October 9, 1894, p. 2.

22. "The Playhouses," *Los Angeles Times*, November 9, 1897, p. 6.

23. Jessie Guzman, ed., Tuskegee University Archives, Box 132.020, database typed on paper, compiled at www.monroeworktoday.org/explore, accessed December 3, 2018.

24. Ida B. Wells, "Lynch Law in America," speech, January 1900; Patricia Ann Schechter, *Ida B. Wells-Barnett and American Reform, 1880–1930* (Chapel Hill: University of North Carolina Press, 2001).

25. "In Old Kentucky."

26. "The Pickaninny Band," *Bourbon News* (Paris, KY), August 2, 1898, p. 5.

27. June 4, 1880, US Census, State of Kentucky, Town of Carlisle, Precinct No. 4, County of Nicholas, Enumeration Dist. No. 92, Supervisor's District 5, Page 16, Lines 9–12.

CHAPTER TWO: ORIENTAL MAGIC

1. Sylvia Wynter, "The Pope Must Have Been Drunk, the King of Castile a Madman: Culture as Actuality, and the Caribbean Rethinking Modernity," in *Reordering of Culture: Latin America, the Caribbean and Canada in the Hood*, ed. Alvina Ruprecht and Cecilia Taiana (Ottawa: Carleton University Press, 1995), 17–41.

2. Karen Armstrong, *Islam: A Short History* (New York: Modern Library, 2000); Karen Armstrong, *Muhammad: A Prophet for Our Time*, Eminent Lives Series (New York: HarperCollins, 2006); Reza Aslan, *No god but God: The Origins, Evolution, and Future of Islam* (New York: Random House, 2005).

3. Edgar W. Francis, "Magic and Divination in the Medieval Islamic Middle East," *History Compass* 9, no. 8 (2011): 624.

4. Michael Muhammad Knight, *Magic in Islam* (New York: Tarcher Perigee, 2016), 30.

5. Knight, *Magic in Islam*, 16.

6. Francis, "Magic and Divination," 625.

7. Francis, "Magic and Divination," 624.

8. Edgar W. Francis, "Islamic Symbols and Sufi Rituals for Protection and Healing: Religion and Magic in the Writings of Ahmad ibn Ali al-Buni (d. 622/1225)," PhD diss., University of California, Los Angeles, 2005.

9. Mungo Park, *The Life and Travels of Mungo Park* (Edinburgh: Robert Chambers, 1838), 13.

10. Edward Said, *Orientalism* (New York: Pantheon, 1978), 2–3.

11. Said, *Orientalism*; Corrine J. Saunders, *Magic and the Supernatural in Medieval English Romance* (Cambridge, UK: D. S. Brewer, 2010), 16–17; Knight, *Magic in Islam*, 6.

12. Plato, *Alcibiades* and *Laws*, excerpts, trans. Marios Skempis, in *Defining Magic: A Reader*, ed. Bernd-Christian Otto and Michael Stausberg (Bristol, CT: Equinox Publishing, 2013), 19–22.

13. Augustine, *City of God* and *On Christian Doctrine*, excerpts, trans. Marcus Dods and William Benton, in Otto and Stausberg, *Defining Magic*, 33–40.

14. Thomas Aquinas, *Summa Theologica*, excerpt, trans. T. F. O'Meara and M. J. Duffy, in Otto and Stausberg, *Defining Magic*, 48–53.

15. Max Horkheimer and Theodor W. Adorno, *Dialectic of Enlightenment: Philosophical Fragments*, ed. Gunzelin Schmid Noerr, trans. Edmund Jephcott (Stanford, CA: Stanford University Press, 2002), xviii.

16. H. Floris Cohen, *The Scientific Revolution: A Historiographical Inquiry* (Chicago: University of Chicago Press, 1994), 286.

17. Mahmoud M. Ayoub, *Islam: Faith and History* (Oxford, UK: Oneworld Publications, 2004), 160.

18. Bruce T. Moran, *Distilling Knowledge: Alchemy, Chemistry, and the Scientific Revolution* (Cambridge, MA: Harvard University Press, 2006), 68, 71; Nicholas Goodrick-Clarke, *The Western Esoteric Traditions: A Historical Introduction* (New York: Oxford University Press, 2008), 41.

19. Simon During, *Modern Enchantments* (Cambridge, MA: Harvard University Press, 2002), 17; Moran, *Distilling Knowledge*, 69.

20. Goodrick-Clarke, *The Western Esoteric Traditions*, 41–63.

21. Frances A. Yates, *The Rosicrucian Enlightenment* (London: Routledge, 1972), 220–28; James Webb, *The Flight from Reason*, vol. 1, *Age of the Irrational* (London: Macdonald, 1971), 140–41.

22. Dorman, *Chosen People*, 168–74.

23. Keith Thomas, *Religion and the Decline of Magic: Studies in Popular Beliefs in Sixteenth- and Seventeenth-Century England* (New York: Oxford University Press, 1971), 54.

24. Charles Theodore Middleton, *A New and Complete System of Geography, Containing a Full, Accurate, Authentic and Interesting Account and Description of Europe, Asia, Africa, and America* (London: J. Cooke, 1777), 124.

25. Stanley Jeyaraja Tambiah, *Magic, Science, Religion, and the Scope of Rationality* (Cambridge, UK: Cambridge University Press, 1990), 18–20.

26. Middleton, *A New and Complete System of Geography*, 124.

27. Yates, *The Rosicrucian Enlightenment*; Brian Vickers, "Frances Yates and the Writing of History," *Journal of Modern History* 51, no. 2 (June 1979): 287–316; Wouter J. Hanegraaff, "Beyond the Yates Paradigm: The Study of Western Esotericism Between Counterculture and New Complexity," *Aries* 1, no. 1 (2001): 5–37.

28. David Stevenson, *The Origins of Freemasonry: Scotland's Century, 1590–1710* (Cambridge, UK: Cambridge University Press, 1990), 81, 84–86, 96–116, 126, 168.

29. Malcolm Gaskill, *Witchcraft: A Very Short Introduction* (New York: Oxford University Press, 2010), 76; William Monter, "Witch Trials in Continental Europe," in *Witchcraft and Magic in Europe*, ed. Bengt Ankarloo and Stuart Clark (Philadelphia: University of Pennsylvania Press, 2002), 12.

30. Thomas, *Religion and the Decline of Magic*; Philip Butterworth, *Magic on the Early English Stage* (Cambridge, UK: Cambridge University Press, 2005), xv–xvi; During, *Modern Enchantments*, 18–19.

31. Hildred Geertz, "An Anthropology of Religion and Magic, I," *Journal of Interdisciplinary History* 6, no. 1 (Summer 1975): 71–89.

32. Edward P. Thompson, "Anthropology and the Discipline of Historical Context," *Midland History* 3, no. 1 (April 1972): 41–55.

33. Murray Gordon, *Slavery in the Arab World* (New York: New Amsterdam Books, 1989).

34. Patrick Manning, *Slavery and African Life: Occidental, Oriental, and African Slave Trades* (New York: Cambridge University Press, 1990).

35. "Estimates," Trans-Atlantic Slave Trade Database, https://www.slavevoyages.org/assessment/estimates, accessed August 10, 2009; Neville A. T. Hall, *Slave Society in the Danish West Indies: St. Thomas, St. John, and St. Croix* (Kingston, Jamaica: University of the West Indies Press, 1992).

36. Allan D. Austin, *African Muslims in Antebellum America: A Sourcebook* (New York: Garland, 1984); Allan D. Austin, *African Muslims in Antebellum America: Transatlantic Struggles and Spiritual Struggles* (New York: Routledge, 1997); Diouf, *Servants of Allah*; Michael A. Gomez, *Black Crescent: The Experience and Legacy of African Muslims in the Americas* (New York: Cambridge University Press, 2005); Paul E. Lovejoy, *Jihād in West Africa During the Age of Revolutions* (Athens: Ohio University Press, 2016).

37. Sylviane A. Diouf, *Dreams of Africa in Alabama: The Slave Ship Clotilda and the Story of the Last Africans Brought to America* (New York: Oxford University Press, 2007); Walter Johnson, *River of Dark Dreams: Slavery, Capitalism, and Imperialism in the Mississippi Valley* (Cambridge, MA: Harvard University Press, 2013).

38. Diouf, *Servants of Allah*, 39–40.

39. Michael A. Gomez, *African Dominion: A New History of Empire in Early and Medieval West Africa* (Princeton, NJ: Princeton University Press, 2018), 240; Michael A. Gomez, *Pragmatism in the Age of Jihād: The Precolonial State of Bundu* (New York: Cambridge University Press, 1992); Diouf, *Servants of Allah*, 48, 61.

40. Lovejoy, *Jihād in West Africa*; Gomez, *Black Crescent*, 91–118.

41. Roman Loimeier, *Islamic Reform and Political Change in Northern Nigeria* (Evanston, IL: Northwestern University Press, 1997), 24–26.

42. Middleton, *A New and Complete System of Geography*, 1166.

43. Evans-Pritchard, *Witchcraft, Oracles and Magic Among the Azande* (Oxford, UK: Clarendon Press, 1937), 432.

44. Frederick Douglass, *Narrative of the Life of Frederick Douglass, an American Slave, Written by Himself* (Boston: Anti-Slavery Office, 1849), 72–73.

45. Theophus H. Smith, *Conjuring Culture: Biblical Formations of Black America* (New York: Oxford University Press, 1994), 159; Yvonne P. Chireau, *Black Magic: Religion and the African American Conjuring Tradition* (Berkeley: University of California Press, 2003), 63–67.

46. Paul Harvey, *Moses, Jesus, and the Trickster in the Evangelical South* (Athens: University of Georgia Press, 2012), 28–30.

47. This narrative of African backwardness was supported as much by Black Christians as their white coreligionists; see James T. Campbell, *Songs of Zion: The African Methodist Episcopal Church in the United States and South Africa* (New York: Oxford University Press, 1995), 66, 83, 84, 119, 266.

48. Chireau, *Black Magic*, 55.

49. Middleton, *A New and Complete System of Geography*, 80.

50. Alden T. Vaughan, *Roots of American Racism: Essays on the Colonial Experience* (New York: Oxford University Press, 1995), 27.

51. Paul Wolff Mitchell, "The Fault in His Seeds: Lost Notes to the Case of Bias in Samuel George Morton's Cranial Race Science," *PLoS Biology* 16, no. 10 (2018): e2007008, https://doi.org/10.1371/journal.pbio.2007008.

52. Evans-Pritchard, *Witchcraft, Oracles and Magic*, 476.

53. Karen E. Fields, "Witchcraft and Racecraft: An Invisible Ontology in Its Sensible Manifestations," in *Racecraft: The Soul of Inequality in American Life*, ed. Karen E. Fields and Barbara J. Fields (New York: Verso, 2012), 193–224.

54. Raymond Schwab, *The Oriental Renaissance: Europe's Discovery of India and the East, 1680–1880* (1950; repr., New York: Columbia University Press, 1984), 36; Said, *Orientalism*, 77–79.

55. Said, *Orientalism*, 76, 80–92; Todd Porterfield, *The Allure of Empire: Art in the Service of French Imperialism, 1798–1836* (Princeton, NJ: Princeton University Press, 1998); Trafton, *Egypt Land*, 3–4.

56. Frederick Engels and Karl Marx, *Manifesto of the Communist Party*, trans. Samuel Moore (Torfaen, UK: Merlin, 1998), 17.

57. Hugh Trevor-Roper, "The Invention of Tradition: The Highland Tradition of Scotland," in *The Invention of Tradition*, ed. Eric Hobsbawm and Terrance Ranger (1983; repr., Cambridge, UK: Canto/Cambridge University Press, 1992), 15–42.

58. Edward Burnett Tylor, *Primitive Culture: Researches into the Development of Mythology, Philosophy, Religion, Language, Art and Custom*, vol. 1 (London: John Murray, 1871), 101.

59. Tambiah, *Magic, Science, Religion, and the Scope of Rationality*, 67.

60. James George Frazer, *The Golden Bough: A Study in Magic and Religion*, vol. 1, abridged ed. (New York: Collier Books, 1922), 307.

61. Chris Goto-Jones, *Conjuring Asia: Magic, Orientalism and the Making of the Modern World* (Cambridge, UK: Cambridge University Press, 2016).

CHAPTER THREE: MUSLIM MASONS

1. F. Hopkinson Smith, "The Picturesque Side," *Scribner's Magazine* 12, no. 4 (October 1892): 604.

2. Joseph E. Ralph, "Exhibit L, Report of Joseph E. Ralph, Deputy Collector in Charge of Midway Plaisance, Jackson Park, Chicago, Ill. Midway Plaisance, Jackson Park, Chicago, January 29, 1894," in *Administration of Customs, World's Columbian Exposition, Letter from the Secretary of the Treasury, Transmitting Report of the Collector of Customs, at Chicago, Ill[.], Relating to the Administration of Customs Affairs at the World's Columbian Exposition* (Washington, DC: US Treasury Department, 1894), 34. Hereafter referred to as "Midway Customs Report."

3. John J. Flinn, *Official Guide to Plaisance, Otherwise Known as the Highway Through the Nations: Brought Down to August 10, 1893: With an Absolutely Correct Map and Numerous Illustrations* (Chicago: Columbian Guide Company, 1893), inside front cover; Ralph, "Midway Customs Report," 34. If admissions averaged fifteen cents, that sum represented more than forty-six million admission fees.

4. Frank H. Smith, *Midway Plaisance and World's Columbian Exposition* (Chicago: Foster Press, 1893), 2.

5. Christopher Reed has challenged Robert Rydell's claim that the Midway Plaisance itself reflected a hierarchical spatial ordering of various peoples, noting that the Dahomeyans occupied a central place next to the Ferris wheel and the Austrians. Christopher Robert Reed, *All the World Is Here! The Black Presence at White City* (Bloomington: Indiana University Press, 2000), 157; Robert W. Rydell, *All the World's a Fair: Visions of Empire at American International Expositions, 1876–1916* (Chicago: University of Chicago Press, 1984), 40, 41.

6. "The Story of the Midway Plaisance," *Daily Inter Ocean* (Chicago), November 1, 1893, p. 25.

7. Denton Jacques Snider, *World's Fair Studies: The Plaisance* (Chicago: Sigma Publishing, 1893).

8. Teresa Dean, *White City Chips* (Chicago: Warren Publishing Company, 1895), 25–26.

9. "Story of the Midway Plaisance."

10. J. Smith, "Within the Magic City," *Illustrated American* 13, no. 173 (June 10, 1893): 673–76.

11. Erik Larsen, *The Devil in the White City: Murder, Magic, and Madness at the Fair That Changed America* (New York: Crown, 2003), 208.

12. Cited in Robert W. Rydell, "A Cultural Frankenstein? The Chicago World's Columbian Exposition of 1893," in *Grand Illusions: Chicago's World's Fair of 1893*, ed. Claudia Lamm Wood, Patricia Bereck Weikersheimer, and Rosemary Adams (Chicago: Chicago Historical Society, 1993), 164.

13. Flinn, *Official Guide to Plaisance*, 20.

14. Ray Hanania, *Arabs of Chicagoland* (Charleston, SC: Arcadia, 2005), 10.

15. "Cairo Street Open," *Chicago Sunday Tribune*, May 28, 1893, pp. 1–2; Gertrude M. Scott, "Village Performance: Villages at the Chicago World's Columbian Exposition 1893," PhD diss., New York University, 1991, 162–63; Hanania, *Arabs of Chicagoland*, 10.

16. Snider, *World's Fair Studies*, 258.

17. Noble William Ross, Recorder and Historian, "Lu Lu" Temple, Philadelphia, "A History of the Ancient Arabic Order of the Nobles of the Mystic Shrine for North America," *A Library of Freemasonry*, vol. 5, ed. Robert Gould (London: John C. Yorston, 1906), 1–2, Harry A. Williamson Masonic Collection, Schomburg Center for Research in Black Culture, New York Public Library, Astor, Lenox, and Tilden Foundations (henceforth Williamson MSS).

18. William B. Mclish, *The History of the Imperial Council, 1872–1921*, 2nd ed. (Cincinnati: Abingdon Press, 1921), 12; Susan Nance, "Crossing Over: A Cultural History of American Engagement with the Muslim World, 1830–1940," PhD diss., University of California, Berkeley, 2003, 158.

19. International Shrine Clown Association, *Sahib Temple Clown Unit* (Nashville: Turner Publishing, 1989), 59.

20. Williamson MSS, 1.

21. Williamson MSS, 47.

22. Susan Nance, *How the Arabian Nights Inspired the American Dream, 1790–1935* (Chapel Hill: University of North Carolina Press, 2009).

23. Williamson MSS, 47.

24. Dale F. Eickelman and James P. Piscatori, eds., *Muslim Travellers: Pilgrimage, Migration, and the Religious Imagination* (Berkeley: University of California Press, 1990), 69; Jamil M. Abun-Nasr, *A History of the Maghrib in the Islamic Period* (Cambridge, UK: Cambridge University Press, 1987); Jonathan Riley-Smith, *The Oxford Illustrated History of the Crusades* (New York: Oxford University Press, 1995), 223.

25. Nance, "Crossing Over," 104–79; Timothy Marr, *The Cultural Roots of American Islamicism* (New York: Cambridge University Press, 2010), 178.

26. Names, dates, and locations of temples come from Mclish, *History of the Imperial Council*, 280–82.

27. Mclish, *History of the Imperial Council*, 105.

28. Mclish, *History of the Imperial Council*, 108.

29. Scott, "Village Performance," 220; "Dedication of the Turkish Mosque," *Sunday Inter Ocean*, April 16, 1893, p. 7; "Pilgrimage to the World's Fair," *Chicago Daily Tribune*, July 24, 1893, p. 7.

30. Dean, *White City Chips*, 37.

31. Scott, "Village Performance," 226–27; "Dedicated to Allah," *Daily Inter Ocean*, April 29, 1893, p. 9; "Shriners Dedicate Temple," *Chicago Daily Tribune*, April 29, 1893, p. 2; "Midway Plaisance Gets in Shape," *Chicago Daily Tribune*, May 1, 1893, p. 2; "Welcomed to Chicago," *Galveston Daily News*, April 30, 1893, p. 4; Barbara Kirshenblatt-Gimblett, "Making a Place in the World: Jews and the Holy Land at World's Fairs," in *Encounters with the "Holy Land": Place, Past, and Future in American Jewish Culture*, ed. Jeffrey Shandler and Beth Wenger (Philadelphia: National Museum of American Jewish History, 1997), 68, 70.

32. Dean, *White City Chips*, 38.

33. Dean, *White City Chips*, 19.

34. "Chicago Colored Society: Those Who Blazed the Way—An Old Timer Compares Past with Present," *Illinois Record* (Springfield), June 18, 1898, p. 1.

35. Allan H. Spear, *Black Chicago: The Making of a Negro Ghetto, 1890–1920* (Chicago: University of Chicago Press, 1967), 62–63.

36. Commission of Masonic Information, Prince Hall Grand Lodge, F. & A. M. of New York, *Freemasonry Among Men of Color in New York State* (New York: Prince Hall Grand Lodge Free and Accepted Masons, State of New York, 1954), 11, 14; Joseph A. Walkes, *History of the Shrine: Ancient Egyptian Arabic Order Nobles of the Mystic Shrine, Inc. (Prince Hall Affiliated): A Pillar Of Black Society, 1893–1993* (Detroit: Ancient Egyptian Arabic Order Nobles of the Mystic Shrine of North and South America and Its Jurisdictions, Inc. [P.H.A.], 1993), 23–40; Ezekiel M. Bey, "John G. Jones: The Father of Bogus Masonry," www.thephylaxis.org/bogus/john-jones.php, accessed June 15, 2008.

37. *The Secret Ritual of the Secret Work of the Ancient Arabic Order of the Nobles of the Mystic Shrine* (New York: Masonic Supply Company, n.d.), 7, cited in Yusuf Nuruddin, "The African American Experience," in *Muslims on the Americanization Path?*, ed. Yvonne Yazbeck Haddad and John L. Esposito (New York: Oxford University Press, 2000), 240; Charles W. Ferguson, *Fifty Million Brothers: A Panorama of American Lodges and Clubs* (New York: Farrar & Rinehart, 1937), 189.

38. Walkes, *History of the Shrine*, 58.

39. *Chicago Conservator*, June 11, 1893, cited in Walkes, *History of the Shrine*, 24–25; Ferguson, *Fifty Million Brothers*, 189; Yusuf Nuruddin, "African American Muslims and the Question of Identity: Between Traditional Islam, African Heritage, and the American Way," in Haddad and Esposito, *Muslims on the Americanization Path?*, 239.

40. *Proceedings of the Ninth Annual Session of the Imperial Council of the Ancient Arabic Order of Nobles of the Mystic Shrine of North and South America, Canada and Dependencies*, held at Buffalo, New York, Friday, August 1, 1901, 12–13, cited in Walkes, *History of the Shrine*, 45.

41. *Proceedings of the Ninth Annual Session*.

42. Imperial Council of the Ancient Egyptian Arabic Order of Nobles of the Mystic Shrine of North and South America, *Proceedings of Eleventh Annual Session Held at Newark, New Jersey* (Baltimore: Afro-American Co., 1909), 1, Archives of the Headquarters of the A.E.A.O.N.M.S., Memphis, Tennessee.

43. Walkes, *History of the Shrine*, 54.

44. Walkes, *History of the Shrine*, 23–39.

45. Imperial Council, *Proceedings*, 41.

46. Joanna Brooks, "Prince Hall, Freemasonry, and Genealogy," *African American Review* 34, part 2 (2000): 197–216.

47. Walkes, *History of the Shrine*, 429.

48. Walkes, *History of the Shrine*, 419.

49. Oriental Banquet Invitation, Islam Shrine, San Francisco, March 19, 1890, Archives of the Asiya Shrine Temple, San Mateo, CA.

50. Jacob F. Wright, "Imperial Potentate's Address," *Proceedings of the Twelfth Annual Session of the Imperial Council of the Ancient Egyptian Arabic Order of Nobles of the Mystic Shrine of North and South America, Detroit* (Baltimore: Afro-American Company, 1910), 22.

51. Eugene Phillips, "Imperial Potentate's Address," *Proceedings of the Thirteenth Annual Session of the Imperial Council of the Ancient Egyptian Arabic Order of Nobles of the Mystic Shrine of North and South America, Atlantic City, NJ* (Baltimore: Afro-American Company, 1911), 19, 22.

52. Eugene Phillips, "Imperial Potentate's Address," *Proceedings of the Fifteenth Annual Session of the Imperial Council of the Ancient Egyptian Arabic Order of Nobles of the Mystic Shrine of North and South America, Indianapolis* (Baltimore: Afro-American Company, 1913), 20.

53. Walkes, *History of the Shrine*, 41.

54. The Shrine rituals, while intended to be secret, are readily available in Masonic libraries and used booksellers and on a number of websites. They are also sometimes discussed or reprinted in annual proceedings of the Shriners, which are public records. The Prince Hall Shrine ritual has been published online: "Ritual of the Shriners," http://www.phoenixmasonry.org/masonicmuseum/History_of_the_Shrine.htm, accessed June 15 2008. The version quoted is from 1973, but it corresponds word for word with earlier versions of the ritual.

55. "Mystic Shrine Ceremonial Lectures," www.phoenixmasonry.org, accessed June 15, 2008.

56. "Shrine Lecture on Initiation," *Mystic Shrine Ceremonial Lectures*, 1, www.phoenixmasonry.org, accessed June 16, 2008.

57. "Shrine Lecture on Initiation," 6–7.

58. "Ritual of the Shriners," *Ritual of the Ancient Egyptian Arabic Order*, 62.

59. "Shrine Lecture on Initiation," 3.

60. "Shrine Lecture on Initiation," 1–2.

61. Walkes, *History of the Shrine*, 64.

62. Beverly Smith, "Harlem—The Negro City: Scores of Churches, Led by Pastors of Intelligence and Wide Training, Prove Great Factor in Spiritual and Social Life of Colony," *New York Herald Tribune* (February 13, 1930): 8; Harry A. Williamson, "Bogus Masonic Organizations," Williamson MSS.

63. Smith, "Harlem—The Negro City."

64. Lawrence W. Levine, *Black Culture and Black Consciousness: Afro-American Folk Thought from Slavery to Freedom* (New York: Oxford University Press, 1977), 268; see also Margaret C. Jacob, *Living the Enlightenment: Freemasonry and Politics in Eighteenth-Century Europe* (New York: Oxford University Press, 1991).

65. See, for example, Williamson, "Bogus Masonic Organizations," Williamson MSS; Commission of Masonic Information, *Freemasonry among Men of Color*.

66. "Negro Masons Eager to Aid in Fight on Frauds: Prince Hall Grand Lodge Favors Move of White Body to Rout Spurious Foreign Lodges," *New York World*, June 13, 1925.

67. Commission of Masonic Information, *Freemasonry among Men of Color*, 11, 14.

68. Commission of Masonic Information, *Freemasonry among Men of Color*, 15.

69. Harry A. Williamson, *Unrecognized Negro Masonic Bodies* (New York, c. 1954), 2/3339, Williamson MSS.

70. Williamson, *Unrecognized Negro Masonic Bodies*.

71. Williamson, *Unrecognized Negro Masonic Bodies*.

72. Commission of Masonic Information, *Freemasonry among Men of Color*, 11, 14; Williamson, *Unrecognized Negro Masonic Bodies*, unnumbered page between pp. 127 and 128; Williamson, *Index of Bogus Masonic Bodies*, vol. 1, last page, unnumbered, Williamson MSS.

73. Nance, "Crossing Over," 227–35.

74. *Transactions of the Sixteenth Annual Session of the Ancient Egyptian Arabic Order Nobles of the Mystic Shrine*, Pittsburgh, August 1914 (Baltimore: Afro-American Company, 1914), 7.

CHAPTER FOUR: IMPERIAL INFERNO

1. Thomas J. Morgan quoted in "Stead Has an Anarchy Show: Two Extraordinary Meetings in Music Hall, Chicago," *New York Times*, November 13, 1893, p. 1.

2. Donald L. Miller, *City of the Century: The Epic of Chicago and the Making of America* (New York: Touchstone, 1996), 534–35.

3. Miller, *City of the Century*, 535–36.

4. "Stead Has an Anarchy Show."

5. Henry M. Littlefield, "The Wizard of Oz: Parable on Populism," *American Quarterly* 16, no. 1 (1964): 47–58.

6. Miller, *City of the Century*, 550.

7. Quoted in Nancy Cohen, *The Reconstruction of American Liberalism, 1865–1914* (Chapel Hill: University of North Carolina Press, 2002), 194.

8. Daniel Bell, "Crime as an American Way of Life," *Antioch Review* 13 (1953): 131.

9. James Karst, "Our Times: The Louis Armstrong Childhood Arrest That No One Knew About," *New Orleans Times-Picayune*, December 21, 2014.

CHAPTER FIVE: HINDOO MAGIC

1. Rudyard Kipling, *The Ballad of East and West* (London: John Marshall & Company, 1900).

2. John (Fire) Lame Deer and Richard Erdoes, *Lame Deer, Seeker of Visions: The Life of a Sioux Medicine Man* (New York: Simon & Schuster, 1972), 228.

3. H. G. Wilson, *Season 1899, Official Route Book of the Pawnee Bill Wild West Show, Presenting a Complete Chronicle of Interesting Events, Happenings and Valuable Data for the Season of 1899* (Newport, KY: Donaldson Lithograph Co., 1899), frontispiece, 42. Circus World Museum, Baraboo, Wisconsin (henceforth CWM).

4. Associated Press, "Princeton Students Make Forcible Objection to a Circus Parade: Pawnee Bill's Men Parade," *Los Angeles Herald*, May 16, 1899, p. 1; Wilson, *Season 1899*, 43–44.

5. Wilson, *Season 1899 of the Pawnee Bill Wild West Show*, 44.

6. Sanborn insurance maps from 1895 reveals grocers at 36, 58, 98, 108, 118, and 134 Nassau Street; http://libweb5.princeton.edu/visual_materials/maps/sanborn /mercer/princeton.html, accessed November 4, 2014.

7. "Princeton Students Riot: They Attack Pawnee Bill's Wild West Combination," *New York Times*, May 15, 1899, p. 3.

8. Associated Press, "Princeton Students Make Forcible Objection," p. 1.

9. "Princeton Students Riot," p. 3.

10. Wilson, *Season 1899 of the Pawnee Bill Wild West Show*, 45.

11. "Students Battled Indians on Nassau Street in 1899," *Daily Princetonian*, May 25, 1920, p. 2.

12. Wilson, *Season 1899*, 46. Pawnee Bill's route book numbered the crowd at 1,400; the Associated Press at half that many.

13. Associated Press, "Princeton Students Make Forcible Objection to a Circus Parade," 1.

14. Harry Wilson and Lloyd F. Nicodemus, *Season 1900, Official Route Book of the Pawnee Bill Wild West Show Presenting a Complete Chronicle of Interesting Events, Happenings and Valuable Data for the Season 1900. Being the Official Record of the Devious Wanderings of the Troupers En Route with Pawnee Bill's Historic Wild West* (Newport, KY: Donaldson Lithograph Co., 1900), 80, CWM.

CHAPTER SIX: WHITE TOPS

1. Cited in Orrin C. King, *The Circus World of Willie Sells: With an Account of Circus Performances in Topeka, Kansas, 1858–1908* (Topeka: Shawnee County Historical Society, 1983), 67.

2. Sells Brothers Circus, "Just Returned from Australia . . . Hassan Ben Ali's Moorish Caravan" (Cincinnati, OH: Strobridge Lithograph Co., 1893), in *American Circus Posters in Full Color*, ed. Charles Philip Fox (New York: Dover, 1978), 13.

3. These posters and many others with Orientalist themes are included in the John & Mable Ringling Museum's online collection of circus posters, available at http://emuseum.ringling.org. Hereafter referred to as "JMRM Collection." In addition to the thirty posters featuring Hassan Ben Ali, there are twenty-two of Egypt, seventeen of Africa, fifteen of Arabs or Arabia, nine of Persia, and four of India, with seven others featuring Moors and five featuring Aladdin.

4. Helen Stoddart, *Rings of Desire: Circus History and Representation* (Manchester, UK: Manchester University Press, 2000), 13–21.

5. Welch, Delavan & Natham's National Circus Advertisement, in *Xenia Torchlight* (Ohio), June 29, 1848, reproduced in Charles Philip Fox, *Circus Parades: A Pictorial History of America's Greatest Pageant* (Watkins Glen, NY: Century House, 1953), 15.

6. See, for example, the representations of men from Borneo, Tibet, and Persia riding an "Asia Wagon" in Fox, *Circus Parades*, 81. In *Circus Parades* are also representations of "Orientals," 100, 111, 113, 115, 142, 147, and the "Africa Wagon," 151.

7. Fox, *Circus Parades*, 9–11.

8. Strobridge lithographs, JMRM Collection. P. T. Barnum's circus also advertised "Charming Illustrations of Arabian Nights' Stories, Nursery Rhymes and Children's Fables," in 1891. See Fox, *Circus Parades*, 91.

9. Fox, *Circus Parades*, 84–86, 91, 98–99, 100, 113, 147, 166.

10. Quoted in Robert M. Lewis, *From Tented Show to Vaudeville: Theatrical Spectacle in America, 1830–1910* (Baltimore: Johns Hopkins University Press, 2003), 112–13.

11. Segregation at circuses was common before the Civil War. Lewis, *From Tented Show to Vaudeville*, 112; Howard N. Rabinowitz, *Race, Ethnicity, and Urbanization: Selected Essays* (Columbia: University of Missouri Press, 1994), 213.

12. Coy Herndon, "Coy Cogitates," *Chicago Defender*, October 10, 1925, reproduced in Abbott and Seroff, *Out of Sight*, 217.

13. Abbott and Seroff, *Out of Sight*, 312–14.

14. There was also a "Prof. Ulato Monszaro, the South African Prince," who played more than sixty instruments, sang, and lectured on African custom in "native garb." *Richmond Planet*, July 22, 1893. On Oskazuma, see Abbott and Seroff, *Out of Sight*, 314–15.

15. For more on Johnson and the theme of the "missing link" in circus freak shows, see Bernth Lindfors, "Circus Africans," *Journal of American Culture* 6, no. 2 (1983): 9–14; Robert Bogdan, *Freak Show: Presenting Human Oddities for Amusement and Profit* (Chicago: University of Chicago Press, 1990), 12, 33, 42, 56, 66, 121, 133–44; Rosemarie Garland Thomson, *Freakery: Cultural Spectacles of the Extraordinary Body* (New York: New York University Press, 1996), 5, 33, 44–45, 140–46.

16. Bogdan, *Freak Show*, 271–72, citing Arthur Lewis, *Carnival* (New York: Trident, 1970), 74.

17. "Circus at Garden Is Full of Thrills," *New York Times*, March 22, 1914, p. 13.

18. "Barnum & Bailey: The Wizard Prince of Arabia," 1914, ink on paper, Strobridge Lithograph Co., TR2004.2722.490, JMRM Collection.

19. Lynne Abbott and Doug Seroff, *Ragged but Right: Black Traveling Shows, "Coon Songs," and the Dark Pathway to Blues and Jazz* (Jackson: University Press of Mississippi, 2007), 57–63.

20. The Field troupe toured until 1898, when they became known as Oliver Scott's Refined Negro Minstrels. Abbott and Seroff, *Out of Sight*, 331–35.

21. Abbott and Seroff, *Out of Sight*, 330–31.

22. Abbott and Seroff, *Ragged but Right*, 82. For more on Henry "Hen" Wise, see Bernard L. Peterson Jr., *The African American Theatre Directory, 1816–1960: A Comprehensive Guide to Early Black Theatre Organizations, Companies, Theatres, and Performing Groups* (Westport, CT: Greenwood Press, 1997), 32.

23. Abbott and Seroff, *Ragged but Right*, 5–15, 23–27, 34–38, 43–56; Peterson, *African American Theatre Directory*, 24–53, 71, 78–79, 97, 101, 158–59, 219.

24. Reed, *All the World Is Here!*, 51–53.

25. Abbott and Seroff, *Ragged but Right*, 231, 239.

26. Edward Wolf, "Negro 'Jews': A Social Study," *Jewish Social Service Quarterly* 9 (June 1933): 314–19; Ruth Landes, "The Negro Jews of Harlem," *Jewish Journal of Sociology* 9, no. 2 (December 1967): 178–80.

27. Abbott and Seroff, *Ragged but Right*, 224.

28. "All Races Found in Cairo City: Great Metropolis on River Nile Is Now Very Cultured," *Chicago Defender*, national ed., May 13, 1922, p. 13.

29. "All Races Found in Cairo City," p. 13.

CHAPTER SEVEN: DEATH DANCE

1. Sigmund Freud, *Civilization and Its Discontents*, trans. James Strachey (1930; repr. New York: Norton, 2010), 111.

2. "What Have Become of the Old Masters of Magic? How One of the Modern Magicians Who Came to Brooklyn Recalled the Days of the World Famous Herrmann and Kellar," *Brooklyn Daily Eagle*, April 23, 1916, 6.

3. "Grand Opera House—In Old Kentucky," *New York Dramatic Mirror* (January 9, 1897): 14; "New York State," *New York Clipper*, May 14, 1898, p. 176; "Down in Dixie," *Cincinnati Enquirer*, November 21, 1898, p. 3; "Thirty-Six Hundred: Active Singers Already Promised for the Jubilee Saengerfest," *Cincinnati Enquirer*, November 22, 1898, p. 3; "Heck's Wonder World Theater," *Cincinnati Enquirer*, November 29, 1898, p. 3; Wilson, *Season 1899*, 46.

4. Marriage Certificate, James Hammond, Eva Alexander, August 26, 1898, City of New York, Certificate no. 13220, New York, New York Extracted Marriage Index, Ancestry.com, from indices prepared by the Italian Genealogical Group and the German Genealogical Group, New York City Department of Records/Municipal Archives.

5. Wilson and Nicodemus, *Pawnee Bill Season 1900*, 81, 83.

6. "The Clipper Post Office," *New York Clipper*, December 12, 1903, p. 997.

7. "Plays and Players," *Sunday Herald* (Boston), March 11, 1900, pp. 14, 20.

8. Samri S. Baldwin, *The Secrets of Mahatma Land Explained: Teaching and Explaining the Performances of the Most Celebrated Oriental Mystery Makers and Magicians in All Parts of the World* (Hartford, CT: Calhoun Printing, 1895), 55–63.

9. Baldwin, *The Secrets of Mahatma Land Explained*, cover, 2.

10. Baldwin, *The Secrets of Mahatma Land Explained*, 55–58.

11. Baldwin, *The Secrets of Mahatma Land Explained*, 39.

12. Wilson and Nicodemus, *Pawnee Bill Season 1900*, 124.

13. "Heck's Wonder World" (Cincinnati); *New York Clipper*, April 27, 1901, p. 163.

14. "Plays and Players," *Sunday Herald* (Boston), March 11, 1900, pp. 14, 20.

15. Punch Wheeler, *The John Robinson 10 Big Shows 1902 Route Book* (n.p., n.d.), 17, 20, 47.

16. Wheeler, *The John Robinson 10 Big Shows 1902 Route Book*, 23.

17. Wheeler, *The John Robinson 10 Big Shows 1902 Route Book*, 23.

18. "Letter Box Mail," *Billboard* (Nov 4, 1905): 11; Advertisement, "Austin and Stone's Museum," *Boston Herald*, published as the *Sunday Herald*, December 31, 1905, p. 19; "Sotanki Princess Troupe—Pawnee Bill," *New York Clipper*, July 6, 1907, p. 533; "Ladies' List Princess Sotanki," *Billboard*, December 7, 1907, p. 78; "Lubin's Theatre, Baltimore, MD," *Billboard*, January 11, 1908, p. 26.

19. Princess Sotanki appeared with a female snake-handler named Serpenta at Chicago's Premier Theater in January 1909 and again in April 2010. "Premier [Theater, Chicago]," *Variety*, January 1, 1909, p. 21; "Chicago Variety Bills," *Billboard*, April 9, 1910, p. 40.

20. "'Paducah, Kentucky' Princess Sotanki, Messrs. Lee and Clark Entertain the Smart Set Company," *Indianapolis Freeman*, September 13, 1913, p. 6.

21. "Princess Sotanki at the Crown Garden Theatre, Indianapolis," *Indianapolis Freeman*, January 2, 1915, p. 5.

22. Sigmund Freud, *Beyond the Pleasure Principle* (1920; repr., New York: Norton, 1961).

23. There were male snake-handlers at both the 1876 and 1893 US World's Fairs. Bogdan, *Freak Show*, 256.

24. "Star Theatre," advertisement, *Savannah Tribune*, May 10, 1913, p. 5.

25. "Crown Garden, Paducah, Kentucky," *Indianapolis Freeman*, September 20, 1913, p. 5; "'Paducah, Kentucky' Princess Sotanki, Messrs. Lee and Clark Entertain the Smart Set Company."

26. Tim Owsley, "Princess Sotanki at the Crown Garden Theater, Indianapolis," *Indianapolis Freeman*, October 26, 1912, p. 5.

27. Owsley, "Princess Sotanki"; "Advertisement," *Cleveland Gazette*, September 21, 1912, p. 2.

28. "With Robbins Bros. Circus," *Indianapolis Freeman*, December 29, 1906, p. 5.

29. John W. Brister, April 8, 1914, Death Index, Illinois, "Cook County Deaths 1878–1922"; "Birth and Death Records, 1916–Present," index, Illinois Department of Public Health, Division of Vital Records, Springfield, Illinois.

30. "Southland," *New York Clipper*, April 20, 1912, p. 6.

31. George Slaughter, "Louisville, Kentucky," *Indianapolis Freeman*, November 30, 1912, p. 4.

32. "Chicago Weekly Review Stage Notes and Stroll Notes," *Indianapolis Freeman*, April 25, 1914, p. 5.

33. "Notes from the Victor Theatre, Brunswick, GA," *Indianapolis Freeman*, January 2, 1915, p. 5.

34. Hamilton County, Ohio, Marriage Certificate no. 290, 1919, Adam Allen and Eva Brister: Probate Court, Cincinnati; "The Present Situation of the Colored Performer," *Billboard*, December 10, 1921, p. 223.

35. "Notes from the J. C. O'Brien's Famous Georgia Minstrels," *Indianapolis Freeman*, March 14, 1914, p. 6.

36. "Notes from J. C. O'Brien's Georgia Minstrels," *Indianapolis Freeman*, June 27, 1914, p. 6.

37. "Notes from J. C. O'Brien's Famous Georgia Minstrels No. 1," *Indianapolis Freeman*, April 24, 1915, p. 5.

38. Haze Ali K. Ally was based at 620 Luciell [Lucille] Place, Memphis; advertisement, *Billboard*, January 16, 1915, p. 37.

39. "Notes from the Victor Theatre."

40. "Notes from the Victor Theatre."

41. E. Alfred Drew, "Where Will We Go?," *Indianapolis Freeman*, December 26, 1914, p. 11; "Gossip of the Stage," *Indianapolis Freeman*, July 1, 1909; "Notes from the J. C. O'Brien's Famous Georgia Minstrels," *Indianapolis Freeman*, March 14, 1914, p. 6; "Notes from J. C. O'Brien's Georgia Minstrels," *Indianapolis Freeman*, June 27, 1914, p. 6.

42. "S. B. Mancuso's Famous Southern Fun Makers," *Indianapolis Freeman*, February 22, 1913, p. 6.

43. "The Stage," *Indianapolis Freeman*, September 17, 1910, p. 6.

44. "Gossip of the Stage," *Indianapolis Freeman*, January 2, 1915, p. 5.

45. "The Present Situation of the Colored Performer," *Billboard*.

46. Drew, "Where Will We Go?"

47. "The Present Situation of the Colored Performer."

48. Peter Lee, *Opium Culture: The Art and Ritual of the Chinese Tradition* (Rochester, VT: Park Street Press, 2006), 2.

CHAPTER EIGHT: PROFESSOR DREW

1. Noble Drew Ali, *The Holy Koran of the Moorish Science Temple of America* (Chicago: Moorish Science Temple of America, 1927), chapter XLVII, verse 9.

2. Cincinnati, OH, City Directory, 1895, p. 249; Covington, KY, City Directory, 1897, p. 270; Cincinnati, OH, City Directory, 1898, p. 245; Cincinnati, OH, City Directory, 1898, Music Teachers, p. 2021; Cincinnati, OH, City Directory, 1903, p. 266; Cincinnati, OH, City Directory, 1905, pp. 260, 273; Cincinnati, OH, City Directory, 1909, p. 272; John W. Brister in the Cook County, IL, Deaths Index, 1878–1922.

3. James Walker, interview with C. Ellis-El, Grand Sheik of Temple #10 in Newark, NJ, 1981, reproduced in Azeem Hopkins-Bey, *Prophet Noble Drew Ali: Saviour of Humanity* (Morrisville, NC: Lulu.com for Ali's Men Publishing and Azeem Hopkins-Bey, 2014), 25.

4. "Dixon, Samuel," Newark, New Jersey City Directory, 1917, p. 623; Samuel Dixon was also listed as a charter member of the Canaanite Temple when it incorporated in 1924. Patrick D. Bowen, *A History of Conversion to Islam in the United States*, vol. 2, *The African American Islamic Renaissance, 1920–1975* (Leiden, Netherlands: Brill, 2017), 167–168. Bowen does not put much stock in the Walker account, but I find the corroborating city directory evidence convincing.

5. "Prof. Drew, the Egyptian Adept Student," card. Reproduced in Hopkins-Bey, *Prophet Noble Drew Ali*, 22; also in Fathie Ali Abdat, "Before the Fez: The Life and Times of Drew Ali, 1886–1924," *Journal of Race, Ethnicity, and Religion* 5, no. 8 (August 2014): 4; Kevin Mumford, *Newark: A History of Race, Rights, and Riots in America* (New York: New York University Press, 2007), 20. In the 1920s, Noble Drew Ali would acquire a large following in Newark's Central Ward (Mumford, *Newark*, 26).

6. Walker, interview with C. Ellis-El, reproduced in Hopkins-Bey, *Prophet Noble Drew Ali*, 25.

7. Thomas Drew, World War I Draft Registration Card Serial No. 2967, Order No. A0123, September 12, 1918. Cited in Abdat, "Before the Fez," 3.

8. Edward M. Coffman, *The War to End All Wars: The American Military Experience in World War I* (Lexington: The University Press of Kentucky, 1998), 24–29.

9. Thomas Drew, *Fourteenth Census of the United States, 1920*, line 35, State of New Jersey, Essex County, Newark Township, Supervisor's District No. 8, Enumeration District No. 161, Seventh Ward of City, Sheet No: 5A, enumerated January 6, 1920. See Abdat, "Before the Fez," 4.

10. Drew, World War I Draft Registration Card, cited in Abdat, "Before the Fez," 25.

11. "Stern Faced White Men Answer 'Call to Allah,'" *Newark Evening News*, August 24, 1920, p. 2; George Edmund Haynes, "Report: Impressions from a Preliminary Study of Negroes of Harlem, 1921," unpublished report produced for the National Urban League, 22, George Edmund Haynes Papers, box 1, folder: 1921 Report, Schomburg Center for Research in Black Culture, Astor, Lenox and Tilden Foundations; "'Egyptian Adept' Fails to Win Trust of Jury," *Newark Evening News*,

November 16, 1920; "Newark 'Healer' Accused of Doctoring Without a License," *Newark Evening News*, December 5, 1923.

12. J. A. Jackson, "J. A. Jackson's Page: In the Interest of the Colored Actor, Actress and Musician of America," *Billboard*, August 19, 1922, p. 85.

13. Ken Jessamy, "Harlem's Fakers: Streets Full of Turbaned 'Wise Men,'" *New York Amsterdam News*, August 28, 1937, p. 11.

14. "Oriental Costume Ball," advertisement, *New York Amsterdam News*, February 10, 1926, p. 7; "Sheik of Harlem," advertisement, *New York Amsterdam News*, August 1, 1923, p. 5.

15. Gaylyn Studlar, "'Out Salomeing Salome': Dance, the New Woman, and Fan Magazine Orientalism," in *Visions of the East*, ed. Matthew Bernstein and Gaylyn Studlar (New Brunswick, NJ: Rutgers University Press, 1997), 100; song titles and quotations, Chicago Public Library, Harold Washington Library Center, Music Information Center, Balaban & Katz Collection.

16. Vijay Prashad, *The Karma of Brown Folk* (Minneapolis: University of Minnesota Press, 2001), 39.

17. Winthrop D. Lane, "The Making of Harlem," *Survey Graphic*, March 1925, quoted in Jerome Dowd, *The Negro in American Life* (New York: Century Co., 1926), 27.

18. Vijay Prashad, *Everybody Was Kung Fu Fighting: Afro-Asian Connections and the Myth of Cultural Purity* (Boston: Beacon Press, 2001), 90–91.

19. Various newspaper advertisements, *New York Amsterdam News*, 1920–29; Herman Rucker [Black Herman, pseud.], *Secrets of Magic-Mystery & Legerdemain: The Missing Key to Success, Health and Happiness*, 15th ed. (1925; repr., NY: Empire Publishing, 1938).

20. Patrick A. Polk, "Other Books, Other Powers: The 6th and 7th Books of Moses in Afro-Atlantic Folk Belief," *Southern Folklore* 56, no. 2 (1999): 115–34.

21. "Use Pearse Health Builder," advertisement, *New York Amsterdam News*, May 5, 1926, p. 3.

22. "Spiritualism," *Negro Times*, February 26, 1923, Aubrey Browser Collection, box 2, folder "The Negro Times," Schomburg Center for Research in Black Culture, Astor, Lenox, and Tilden Foundations; T. J. Jackson Lears, *No Place of Grace: Antimodernism and the Transformation Of American Culture, 1880–1920* (New York: Pantheon, 1981), xv–xx, 3–58.

23. Chireau, *Black Magic*, 35–57.

24. Carolyn Morrow Long, *Spiritual Merchants: Religion, Magic, and Commerce* (Knoxville: University of Tennessee Press, 2001), 117–18.

25. Akpan Aga et al., advertisements, *New York Amsterdam News*, December 13, 1922, p. 2; and the following dates in 1923: January 24; January 31, pp. 3, 8; February 7, p. 8; February 14, p. 3; February 28, p. 3; March 7, p. 3; March 21, p. 3; March 28, p. 2; April 18, p. 2; April 25, p. 2; May 2, p. 2; May 9, p. 2; May 23, p. 2; May 30, p. 3; June 6, p. 6; August 15, p. 3; September 5, p. 3; October 13, p. 14; October 24, p. 3; October 31, p. 3; November 7, p. 3; "Effiong in Toils; Waits U.S. Action," *New York Amsterdam News*, February 6, 1929, p. 1.

26. On hoodoo and a discussion of conjure men and women in Northern cities in this period, see Chireau, *Black Magic*, 138–49.

27. "Divine Healer Jailed," *New York Amsterdam News*, August 29, 1923, p. 2.

28. Akpan Aga, advertisement, *New York Amsterdam News*, January 24, 1923, p. 3.

29. Professor Akpandanc, "Prof. Akpandac," advertisement, *New York Amsterdam News*, April 11, 1923, p. 2; Amadu, "The Mohammedan Scientist Dealing in Religious Incense," *New York Amsterdam News*, March 9, 1927, p. 3.

30. Patrick D. Bowen, "Prince D. Solomon and the Birth of African-American Islam," *Journal of Theta Alpha Kappa* 38, no. 1 (Spring 2014): 1–19.

31. "Colored Baptists," *Sun* (Baltimore), June 10, 1906, p. 7.

32. Dorman, *Chosen People*.

33. "Dr. Abdul Hamid of Egypt Guest of Harlem Masons," *Negro World* (April 8, 1922): 2.

34. "New Jersey," *Smart Set* 72 (October 1923): 10.

35. Bowen, "Prince D. Solomon and the Birth of African-American Islam"; Bowen, *A History of Conversion to Islam in the United States*, vol. 2, 133; FBI Subject File 62-576, "Sufi Abdul Hamid," Federal Bureau of Investigation, Washington DC; "N.Y. to Have Mohammedan Mosque," *Baltimore Afro-American*, July 28, 1923, p. 2.

36. Bowen, *A History of Conversion to Islam*, vol. 2, 120, 145.

37. Bowen, *A History of Conversion to Islam*, vol. 2, 108, 109, 115.

38. J. A. O'Meally, "Crescent or Cross? A Negro May Aspire to Any Position under Islam Without Discrimination," originally printed in *Negro World*, August 4, 1923, reprinted in *Moslem Sunrise* 2, no. 4 (1923): 263–64.

39. O'Meally, "Crescent or Cross?"; "True Salvation of the American Negroes: The Real Solution of the Negro Question," *Moslem Sunrise* 2, nos. 2 & 3 (1923): 184; Bowen, *A History of Conversion to Islam*, vol. 2, 107, 135–36; Abbie G. Whyte, "Christian Elements in American Negro Muslim Cults," master's thesis, Wayne State University, 1963, 22.

CHAPTER NINE: CHICAGO RACKETS

1. Claud Cockburn, "Rackets Strictly on American Lines," in *Faber Book of America*, ed. Christopher Ricks and William L. Vance (London: Faber and Faber, 1990), 378–79.

2. "Hold Moorish Temple Prophet in Murder Plot: Blame Split in Cult for Brutal Crime," *Chicago Defender*, city ed., March 23, 1929, p. 1.

3. "Love Cult Thot [*sic*] Responsible for Slaying," *Baltimore Afro-American*, March 23, 1929, p. 2.

4. "Murder for Profit," *Chicago Defender*, national ed. March 23, 1929, p. A2.

5. "Moorish Leader Is Postmaster's Guest," *Chicago Defender*, city ed., June 30, 1928, pp. 1–9; "Moorish Head Makes Plans for Conclave," *Chicago Defender*, national ed., July 21, 1928, p. A4.

6. "Stamp Out This Tribe!," editorial, *Chicago Defender*, city ed., September 28, 1929, p. 1; "6 Held to Grand Jury for Cult Battle Murders: Detective Bares Rise of the 'Moor Temple' Racket," *Chicago Daily Tribune*, September 28, 1929, p. 4.

7. St. Clair Drake and Horace R. Cayton, *Black Metropolis: A Study of Negro Life in a Northern City* (1945; Chicago: University of Chicago Press, 1970), 19.

8. Quoted in William Thomas Stead, *If Christ Came to Chicago! A Plea for the Union of All Who Love in the Service of All Who Suffer* (Chicago: Laird & Lee, 1894), 247.

9. Drake and Cayton, *Black Metropolis*, 55.

10. Mark H. Haller, "Illegal Enterprise: A Theoretical and Historical Interpretation," *Criminology* 29, no. 2 (1990): 212.

11. Thomas Bauman, *The Pekin: The Rise and Fall of Chicago's First Black-Owned Theater* (Urbana: University of Illinois Press, 2014), 9.

12. Christopher Robert Reed, *The Rise of Chicago's Black Metropolis, 1920–1929* (Urbana: University of Illinois Press, 2011), 160.

13. Junius Boyd Wood, *The Negro in Chicago: How He and His Race Kindred Came to Dwell in Great Numbers in a Northern City, How He Lives and Works, His Successes and Failures, His Political Outlook: A First-Hand Study* (Chicago: Chicago Daily News, 1916), 6.

14. Bauman, *The Pekin*, 6.

15. Bauman, *The Pekin*, 24–25.

16. Bauman, *The Pekin*, 10–11.

17. Bauman, *The Pekin*, 143.

18. Drake and Cayton, *Black Metropolis*, 539.

19. Haller, "Illegal Enterprise," 218.

20. Michael Lesy, *Murder City: The Bloody History of Chicago in the Twenties* (New York: Norton, 2007), 305.

21. Lesy, *Murder City*, 306.

22. Lloyd Wendt and Herman Kogan, *Big Bill of Chicago* (Evanston, IL: Northwestern University Press, 2005), 144–45.

23. Gus Russo, *The Outfit: The Role of Chicago's Underworld in the Shaping of Modern America* (New York: Bloomsbury, 2001), 19, 38, 506; Drake and Cayton, *Black Metropolis*, 366. Douglas Bukowski disputes the allegation that Capone was a large contributor to Thompson's campaign, but ignores the presence of Capone associates and gangsters like Daniel A. Serritella, Jack Zuta, "Big Tim" Murphy, Abie Arends, and Vincent "the Schemer" Drucci in City Hall. Douglas Bukowski, *Big Bill Thompson, Chicago, and the Politics of Image* (Urbana: University of Illinois Press, 1998), 218–21.

24. Drake and Cayton, *Black Metropolis*, 360–70; Bauman, *The Pekin*, 146; Reed, *Rise of Chicago's Black Metropolis*, 160.

25. Wood, *The Negro in Chicago*, 28, 30.

26. Carroll Hill Wooddy, *The Case of Frank L. Smith: A Study in Representative Government* (Chicago: University of Chicago Press, 1931), 87, 150–55.

27. Carroll Hill Wooddy, *The Chicago Primary of 1926: A Study of Election Methods* (New York: Arno Press, 1974), 5–17.

28. Wooddy, *The Case of Frank L. Smith*, 7, 132, 159.

29. Wooddy, *The Chicago Primary of 1926*, 13–14.

CHAPTER TEN: BLACK MECCA

1. "The Negro in the North: Chicago Is the Mecca of Black Criminals," *Louisville Courier-Journal*, February 8, 1903, p. A5.

2. Drake and Cayton, *Black Metropolis*, xxv–xxvi.

3. Christopher Robert Reed, *Knock at the Door of Opportunity: Black Migration to Chicago, 1900–1919* (Carbondale: Southern Illinois University Press, 2014), 219; James R. Grossman, *Land of Hope: Chicago, Black Southerners, and the Great Migration* (Chicago: University of Chicago Press, 1989), 4.

4. Drake and Cayton, *Black Metropolis*, 64; William M. Tuttle Jr., *Race Riot: Chicago in the Red Summer of 1919* (New York: Atheneum, 1970), 159.

5. Tuttle, *Race Riot*, 165.

6. "The Negro in the North."

7. Langston Hughes, *The Big Sea: An Autobiography* (New York: Knopf, 1940), 33; Tuttle, *Race Riot*, 166.

8. Hughes, *The Big Sea*, 33.

9. Reed, *Knock at the Door of Opportunity*, 228.

10. Grossman, *Land of Hope*, 154.

11. Tuttle, *Race Riot*, 170–71.

12. Lothrop Stoddard, *The Rising Tide of Color against White World-Supremacy* (New York: Charles Scribner's Sons, 1921), 3.

13. Achmet Abdullah, "Seen Through Mohammedan Spectacles," *Forum*, October 1914, quoted in Stoddard, *Rising Tide of Color*, 13.

14. Lothrop Stoddard, *The New World of Islam* (London: Chapman and Hall, 1922), 300.

15. Grossman, *Land of Hope*, 264.

16. Reed, *Knock at the Door of Opportunity*, 53; Drake and Cayton, *Black Metropolis*, 82; Reed, *The Rise of Chicago's Black Metropolis*, 25, 106.

17. Haynes, "Report: Impressions from a Preliminary Study of Negroes of Harlem, 1921," 71.

18. Drake and Cayton, *Black Metropolis*, 100.

19. Drake and Cayton, *Black Metropolis*, 379.

20. Davarian L. Baldwin, *Chicago's New Negroes: Modernity, the Great Migration, and Black Urban Life* (Chapel Hill: University of North Carolina Press, 2007).

21. Drake and Cayton, *Black Metropolis*, 205.

22. Bauman, *The Pekin*, 146–49.

23. Baldwin, *Chicago's New Negroes*, 50.

24. Wood, *The Negro in Chicago*, 5.

25. Reed, *Knock at the Door of Opportunity*, 132.

26. Grossman, *Land of Hope*, 146.

27. Drake and Cayton, *Black Metropolis*, 415, 417.

28. "Anderson, Leafiy [sic], 3151 Rhodes Avenue," *Fourteenth Census of the United States: 1920*, State of Illinois, Cook County, City of Chicago, Ward 2, Enumeration District 78, Sheet 12, p. 541; Jason Berry, *The Spirit of Black Hawk: A Mystery of Africans and Indians* (Jackson: University Press of Mississippi, 1995), 56, 111.

29. Reed, *Knock at the Door of Opportunity*, 114; Milton C. Sernett, ed., *African American Religious History: A Documentary Witness* (Durham, NC: Duke University Press, 1999), 337.

30. Drake and Cayton, *Black Metropolis*, 419.

31. "Colored Minister Charged with the Sale of Stolen Goods," *Chicago Daily Tribune*, May 31, 1922.

32. Benjamin E. Mays and Joseph W. Nicholson, *The Negro's Church* (n.p.: Institute for Social and Religious Research, 1933).

33. Reed, *Knock at the Door of Opportunity*, 127; Grossman, *Land of Hope*, 140.

34. Grossman, *Land of Hope*, 142. Thanks to Dr. Reed for the information about Olivet Baptist Church.

35. "Brands Pastor 'Morally Unfit': Court Order Puts Check on Minister," *Chicago Defender*, city ed., May 14, 1927, p. 1.

36. "Brands Pastor 'Morally Unfit'"; Drake and Cayton, *Black Metropolis*, 429.

37. Howard Brotz, *The Black Jews of Harlem* (New York: Free Press of Glencoe, 1964).

38. Milton C. Sernett, *Bound for the Promised Land: African American Religion and the Great Migration* (Durham, NC: Duke University Press, 1997), 4, 29, 190; Wallace D. Best, *Passionately Human, No Less Divine: Religion and Culture in Black Chicago, 1915–1952* (Princeton, NJ: Princeton University Press, 2005), 57–59, 98–101.

CHAPTER ELEVEN: POWER BROKERS

1. Franklin D. Roosevelt, "Commonwealth Club Address," September 23, 1932, http://teachingamericanhistory.org/library/document/commonwealth-club-address, accessed February 6, 2019.

2. Bukowski, *Big Bill Thompson, Chicago, and the Politics of Image*, 167.

3. Forrest McDonald, *Insull: The Rise and Fall of a Billionaire Utility Tycoon* (Chicago: University of Chicago Press, 1962), 3; Laurence Bergreen, *Capone: The Man and the Era* (New York: Simon & Schuster Paperbacks, 1994), 225; John F. Wasik, *The Merchant of Power: Sam Insull, Thomas Edison, and the Creation of the Modern Metropolis* (New York: Palgrave MacMillan, 2006), 196.

4. "When Samuel Insull Blows Out the Gas," *Day Book* 5, no. 145 (March 17, 1916): 1.

5. "Traction Bill of Dever Gives City No Voice: Entrusts $700,000,000 to Board of 9 Men," *Daily Worker*, February 14, 1925, p. 4.

6. Correspondence, Donald R. Richberg to Julius Rosenwald, September 17, 1930, p. 1, Julius Rosenwald Papers, box 32, folder 5, University of Chicago Library, Special Collections Research Center.

7. "Campaign Fund Data Refused by Witnesses: Messrs. Insull and Schuyler Again Challenge Right of Senate Inquiry," *Christian Science Monitor* (Feb. 21, 1927): 1.

8. Arthur Evans, "Rakes 'America First' as Ally of King George: Litsinger Hits 'Deal' and Ettelson," *Chicago Tribune*, April 7, 1928.

9. Wendt and Kogan, *Big Bill of Chicago*, 249.

10. "Dan Jackson Appointed to Commerce Body," *Philadelphia Tribune*, August 30, 1928, p. 1.

11. "America's Open Confession," *Pittsburgh Courier*, October 6, 1928, p. A8; Bauman, *The Pekin*, 146–49.

12. Wooddy, *The Case of Frank L. Smith*, 25, 52–56.

13. Lucius C. Harper, "Dustin' Off the News: They Both Knew Us; One Better Than the Other," *Chicago Defender*, July 30, 1938, p. 16.

14. "Memoirs of Samuel Insull, Written 1934–35, Final Approved Copy 1961 by Samuel Insull, Jr.," Samuel Insull Papers, box 21, Loyola University Chicago Archives.

15. Richard Wright, "I Tried to Be a Communist," *Atlantic Monthly* 174, no. 2 (August 1944): 61–70.

16. "Charges Cash for DePriest," *Des Moines Tribune*, May 28, 1934, p. 4.

17. "Samuel Insull Was an Angel to Chicago," *Baltimore Afro-American*, March 31, 1934, p. 1.

18. "Samuel Insull Was an Angel to Chicago."

19. Chandler Owen, "The Neglected Truth," *Messenger: New Opinion of the Negro* 7, no. 2 (February 1, 1926): 48.

20. "Ask Insull for Jobs as Street Car Men," *Chicago Defender*, city ed., July 16, 1927, pp. 1–5.

21. "How Clean Are Our Dirty Politics?," *Baltimore Afro-American*, October 27, 1928, p. 17.

22. Owen, "The Neglected Truth," 49.

23. "Melvin Chisum Dies in Philly After Accident: Had Most Colorful Career," *New York Amsterdam News*, July 14, 1945, p. A6.

24. "How Clean Are Our Dirty Politics?," 17.

25. Stephen Breszka, "Insull to Meet New Leaders When He Returns to Chicago: New Faces of Negro Leaders Are Now Located in Centers Where Former Utilities King Once Held Forth—Political Pot Continues to Boil," *Pittsburgh Courier*, May 5, 1934, p. 3.

26. Roosevelt, "Commonwealth Club Address."

27. "Insull Was Friend of Negroes: Chicagoans Hold Tongues in Their Cheeks as Uncle Sam Chases Ex-Millionaire," *Atlanta Daily World*, March 30, 1934, p. 1.

28. James Doherty, "He Was Cold, Austere, Jim Doherty Recalls, but I Liked Interviewing Him," *Chicago Sunday Tribune*, April 13, 1952; Wooddy, *The Case of Frank L. Smith*, 26.

29. Breszka, "Insull to Meet New Leaders When He Returns to Chicago," 3.

CHAPTER TWELVE: MOORISH SCIENCE

1. Prophet Noble Drew Ali, *Quotes of the Prophet: Moorish Science Temple of America, Prophet Noble Drew Ali, Founder—Oral Statements of the Prophet* (n.p., n.d.), 41, https://bit.ly/2Slhd61, accessed February 22, 2019.

2. The extended quotes at the start of this chapter are from: Anonymous, "I Your Prophet," pp. 1–21, Illinois Writers' Project, 1942/01, Manuscripts Box 45, Folder 6, Vivian G. Harsh Research Collection, Chicago Public Library. The original says that Lily Sloane picked numbers for "the numbers," a gambling variation popular in New York; in Chicago the preferred game of chance was called "policy," with numbers picked from a hat, or more commonly, a drum or "wheel," so I have called it that here.

3. Anonymous, "I Your Prophet."

4. Anonymous, "I Your Prophet."

5. Peter Lamborn Wilson mistakenly identifies her as Pearl Drew Ali, one of the three wives Brister took as Noble Drew Ali, but press reports and a picture from the *Chicago Defender* and the *Pittsburgh Courier* makes it clear that Pearl Drew Ali was in her twenties and a different person.

6. There are no descriptions of the services from Drew Ali's lifetime, but this account is built on descriptions of worship from 1934 and 1947. "Allah Hovers Over Lombard Street: Thousands Flocking to Banner of Chicago Mystic Who Claims to Be Mohamed Reincarnated," *Philadelphia Tribune*, October 25, 1934, p. 20; Frank T. Simpson, "The Moorish Science Temple and Its 'Koran,'" *Moslem World* 37, no. 1 (1947): 57.

7. "6 Held to Grand Jury for Cult Battle Murders: Detective Bares Rise of 'Moor Temple' Racket," *Chicago Daily Tribune*, September 28, 1929, p. 4; Judith Stein, *The*

World of Marcus Garvey: Race and Class in Modern Society (Baton Rouge: Louisiana State University Press, 1986), 79.

8. Hopkins-Bey, *Prophet Noble Drew Ali*, 70, 112.

9. *Moorish Guide 1928*, cited in Hopkins-Bey, *Saviour of Humanity*, 28.

10. Bowen, *A History of Conversion to Islam in the United States*, vol. 2, 200.

11. Noble Drew Ali, "Koran Questions for Moorish Children," in *The Supreme Understanding: The Teachings of Islam in North America*, written and compiled by Abdul Noor (San Jose, CA: Writers Club Press, 2002), 47.

12. "I Your Prophet," 12–13.

13. "Don't Miss the Great Moorish Drama," May 16, 1927, in Hopkins-Bey, *Saviour of Humanity*, 37.

14. "The Divine Constitution and By-Laws, Moorish Holy Temple of Science," Moorish Science Temple of America, Certificates and Documents 1926–1960 Folder, Schomburg Center.

15. "Noble Drew Ali Returns After Long Visit South," *Chicago Defender*, national ed., November 19, 1927, p. 5.

16. Bowen, *A History of Conversion to Islam*, vol. 2, 201n7.

17. Azeem Hopkins-Bey, *Prophet Noble Drew Ali: Saviour of Humanity* (Morrisville, NC: Lulu.com for Ali's Men Publishing and Azeem Hopkins-Bey, 2014), 82.

18. Simpson, "The Moorish Science Temple and Its 'Koran,'" 56–61; Abbie Whyte, "Christian Elements in Negro American Muslim Religious Beliefs," *Phylon* 25, no. 4 (4th Qtr., 1964): 382–88; Wilson, *Sacred Drift*, 19; Douglas T. McGetchin, *Indology, Indomania, and Orientalism: Ancient India's Rebirth in Modern Germany* (Madison, NJ: Fairleigh Dickinson University Press, 2009); 133; H. Louis Fader, *The Issa Tale That Will Not Die: Nicolas Notovitch and His Fraudulent Gospel* (Lanham, MD: University Press of America, 2003); Dorman, "'Lifted Out of the Commonplace Grandeur of Modern Times,'" 398–418.

19. Arthur Huff Fauset, *Black Gods of the Metropolis: Negro Religious Cults of the Urban North* (Philadelphia: Publications of the Philadelphia Anthropological Society, 1945), 41; Wilson, *Sacred Drift*, 19. Wilson credited chapter I to Drew Ali as well, but that chapter comes from the introduction of *The Aquarian Gospel*.

20. Wilson, *Sacred Drift*, 23.

21. "Divine Constitution and By-Laws."

22. Noble Drew Ali, "Prophet Drew Ali Speaks to the Nations: Needs Strong Men and Women," September 28, 1928, in Prophet Noble Drew Ali, *Humanity* (n.p., 1928) in Pamphlets and Printed Materials Folder, Moorish Science Temple of America Collection, Schomburg Center.

23. Noble Drew Ali, "What Shall We Call Him?," in *Moorish Literature: Moorish Science Temple of America, Prophet Noble Drew Ali, Founder* (n.p., 1928), 5, Pamphlets and Printed Material, 1928–1967 Folder, Moorish Science Temple of America Collection, Schomburg Center.

24. "Moorish Science Temple Ends 6th Annual Meeting," *Norfolk Journal and Guide* (September 23, 1933): 20.

25. Noble Drew Ali, "Divine Constitution and By-Laws."

26. Noble Drew Ali, "Divine Constitution and By-Laws."

27. "Allah Hovers Over Lombard Street," 20.

28. Noble Drew Ali, "Divine Constitution and By-Laws."

29. Noble Drew Ali, "What Is Islam?," in *Moorish Literature*, 10.

30. Noble Drew Ali, "Moorish Leader's Historical Message to America," in *Moorish Literature*, 13–14.

31. Noble Drew Ali, "Think This Over You Moors," in *Humanity* (1928), 4, 5.

32. Moorish Temple of Science, State of Illinois Incorporation form, November 26, 1926, cited in Bowen, *A History of Conversion to Islam in the United States*, vol. 2, 200.

33. Noble Drew Ali, "Moorish Leader's Historical Message to America, 13–14; Alfred W. Martin, *The World's Great Religions and the Religion of the Future* (New York: D. Appleton and Company, 1921), 148; Bowen, *History of Conversion*, 193.

34. "Allah Hovers Over Lombard Street," 20.

35. Prophet Noble Drew Ali, *Quotes of the Prophet: Moorish Science Temple of America, Prophet Noble Drew Ali, Founder—Oral Statements of the Prophet* (n.p., n.d.), 7, https://bit.ly/2Slhd61, accessed February 22, 2019.

36. Noble Drew Ali, *Holy Koran of the Moorish Science Temple*, chapters XLV, XLVI.

37. Ali, *Quotes of the Prophet*, 28.

38. See "An Act to Repeale a Former Law Makeing Indians and Others Free," Colony of Virginia, 1682, https://bit.ly/2txQfhA, accessed February 22, 2019.

39. Timothy Dingle-El, *The Resurrection: Moorish Science Temple of America, Inc.; The Truth: Be Yourself and Not Somebody Else* (Baltimore: Gateway Press, 1978), 32–33.

40. Ahmed I. Abu Shouk, J. O. Hunwick, and R. S. O'Fahey, "A Sudanese Missionary to the United States: Sāttī Mājid, 'Shaykh Al-Islām in North America,' and His Encounter with Noble Drew Ali, Prophet of the Moorish Science Temple Movement," *Sudanic Africa* 8 (1997): 137–91.

CHAPTER THIRTEEN: MACHINE POLITICS

1. "Pineapples and Plunder," *Chicago Tribune*, April 7, 1928.

2. "Partial" not "parcel" is in the original. Ali, "What Is Islam?," 10.

3. "Nationality and Identification Card, Moorish Science Temple of America," Moorish Science Temple of America MSS collection, Folder Certificates and Documents, 1926–1966, Schomburg Center for Research in Black Culture, New York Public Library, Astor, Lenox and Tilden Foundations.

4. Noble Drew Ali, "Divine Warning by the Prophet Noble Drew Ali," in *Moorish Literature*, 18.

5. Ali, "Moorish Leader's Historical Message to America," 11–12.

6. "Moorish Head Makes Plans for Conclave," *Chicago Defender*, national ed., July 21, 1928, p. A4.

7. "Oust 6 Aldermen at Polls," *Chicago Daily Tribune*, February 27, 1929, p. 1.

8. "6 Held to Grand Jury for Cult Battle Murders," 4.

9. "Proves Right to Vote by Records of 1892: Woman's Birth Certificate Lost in Chicago Fire; 'Beys' and 'Sheiks' Strike Snag," *Detroit Free Press*, August 3, 1928, p. 7.

10. "Moorish Leader Is Postmaster's Guest," *Chicago Defender*, city ed., June 30, 1928, pp. 1–9.

11. "Moors to Hold National Conclave October 14," *Chicago Defender*, national ed., October 13, 1928, p. 3. On Blackwell Bey, see next note.

12. *The Moorish Guide* (January 15, 1929), quoted in Hopkins-Bey, *Saviour of Humanity*, 70, 112.

13. Hopkins-Bey, *Saviour of Humanity*, 60.

14. National Archives, Washington, DC, Series Title: *U.S. Citizen Passenger Lists of Vessels Arriving at Key West, Florida*, NAI Number: 2790482; Record Group Title: *Records of the Immigration and Naturalization Service, 1787–2004*, Record Group Number: 85.

15. "Moorish Leader Attends Inauguration of Governor," *Chicago Defender*, national ed., January 19, 1929, p. 2.

16. "Birthday of Moorish Leader Is Celebrated," *Chicago Defender*, national ed., January 12, 1929, p. 3.

17. Tuttle, *Race Riot*, 184–207; Robert M. Lombardo, "The Black Mafia: African-American Organized Crime in Chicago 1890–1960," *Crime, Law and Social Change* 38, no. 1 (July 2002): 43; Arvarh E. Strickland, *History of the Chicago Urban League* (Columbia: University of Missouri Press, 2001), 60.

18. Arthur Evans, "Rise and Fall of Thompson's Machine Told: End Regime Filled with Scandal," *Chicago Daily Tribune*, April 9, 1931, p. 1.

19. Lombardo, "The Black Mafia," 43.

20. "Charges Capone Put $260,000 to Aid Thompson: Loesch Avers Bargain," *Chicago Daily Tribune*, February 17, 1931, p. 3.

21. Arthur Evans, "Vote on Cleanup Tomorrow: Leaders Rally to Anti-Crime Candidates: Predict Defeat of City Hall Crowd," *Chicago Daily Tribune*, November 5, 1928, p. 1.

22. Philip Kinsley, "Negroes Turning Against Mayor, Observers Find: Report 25% Loss in Favorite Wards," *Chicago Daily Tribune*, April 5, 1928, p. 4.

23. "Connects Capone with Bomb Buying: Prisoner Lays Bare The 'Pineapple' Industry," *Daily Boston Globe*, August 2, 1929, p. 4.

24. "Joseph F. Haas Dead," *New York Times*, March 15, 1928, p. 25; "All Political Factions Mourn Joseph F. Haas: Veteran Leader Dies of Pneumonia," *Chicago Daily Tribune*, March 15, 1928, p. 11; "Joseph F. Haas' Widow Dies of a Broken Heart: Passes Away Week After Husband's Death," *Chicago Daily Tribune*, March 22, 1928, p. 11; James Doherty, "Slay Diamond Joe Esposito: Shotgun Volley Kills Chicago Italian Leader Assassins Fire from Mysterious Auto," *Chicago Daily Tribune*, March 22, 1928, p. 1.

25. James Doherty, "Bloody 20th's Past Written by Gun Play: Pacelli Name Still Power in Ward's Politics," *Chicago Daily Tribune*, February 3, 1946, p. W1.

26. "Carlstrom to Call Special Grand Jury," *Chicago Daily Tribune*, April 11, 1928, p. 1; Evans, "Rise and Fall of Thompson's Machine," 8; John Bright, *Hizzoner Big Bill Thompson: An Idyll of Chicago* (New York: Jonathan Cape and Harrison Smith, 1930), 291–93.

27. "DePriest, Jackson Indicted: Chicago Startled over Charges of Graft," *Pittsburgh Courier*, October 6, 1928, p. 1.

28. "Congressman DePriest," *Baltimore Afro-American*, April 20, 1929, p. 9.

29. David Levering Lewis, *When Harlem Was in Vogue* (New York: Oxford University Press, 1997), 220–21; "Caspar [sic] Holstein, Wealthy Club Owner, Kidnapping a Case of Mistaken Identity Freed Man Tells Police," *Philadelphia Tribune*, September 27, 1928, p. 1.

30. "News of the Classes and Associations," *University of Chicago Magazine*, vols. 15–16 (1922): 354; "L. F. Wormser, Lawyer, Dead in Car Crash: Personal Attorney

for Late Julius Rosenwald Is Victim of Michigan Accident," *New York Herald Tribune*, August 11, 1934, p. 11.

31. "DePriest, Jackson Indicted," 1.

32. "DePriest, Jackson Indicted," 1.

33. "Capture Slayer in Granady Case," *Chicago Defender*, city ed., October 12, 1928, pp. 1(1).

34. "'Dan' Jackson, Former Pittsburgher, Who Learned Value of Hard Work, Becomes an Imposing Figure in Chicago's Political Life," *Pittsburgh Courier*, April 23, 1927, p. A4.

35. Lombardo, "The Black Mafia," 39.

36. Michael Woodiwiss, *Organized Crime and American Power: A History* (Toronto: University of Toronto Press, 2001), 189.

37. "How Clean Are Our Dirty Politics?," 17.

38. "How Clean Are Our Dirty Politics?," 17.

CHAPTER FOURTEEN: MOORISH FACTIONS

1. The original uses this two-word spelling of "downtrodden." Noble Drew Ali to "Dear Brother," correspondence, February 5, 1929, p. 1, in Moorish Science Temple of America Collection, Letters, Box 1, Folder 2, Schomburg Center for Research in Black Culture, Astor, Lenox and Tilden Foundations, New York Public Library.

2. "6 Held to Grand Jury for Cult Battle Murders," 4; Associated Negro Press, "Murder Exposes Moorish Leader's Amours," 10.

3. For a contemporary look at a similar phenomenon, see Debra Majeed, *Polygyny: What It Means When African American Muslim Women Share Their Husbands* (Gainesville: University Press of Florida, 2016).

4. "Notes from the Victor Theatre," *Indianapolis Freeman*, January 2, 1915, p. 5.

5. "Hold Moorish Temple Prophet in Murder Plot," 1.

6. "6 Held to Grand Jury for Cult Battle Murders," 4; Spear, *Black Chicago*, 157.

7. Ali's Men (Lasana Tunica-El, Sharif Anael-Bey, Mahdi McCoy-El, Ash-Shaheed Snow-Bey, Robert Webb-Bey; hereafter referred to as "Ali's Men"), interview by Jacob S. Dorman, video call, March 5, 2019.

8. "Think This Over You Moors," in *Humanity* (1928): 17.

9. "Moorish Leader on Tour Visits Subordinate Bodies," *Chicago Defender*, national ed., November 24, 1928, p. 3.

10. Hopkins-Bey, *Saviour of Humanity*, 30.

11. "Hold Moorish Temple Prophet in Murder Plot," 3; Anonymous, "I Your Prophet," pp. 1–21, Illinois Writers' Project, 1942/01, Manuscripts Box 45, Folder 6, Vivian G. Harsh Research Collection, Chicago Public Library.

12. "Hold Moorish Temple Prophet in Murder Plot," 3.

13. "Greene Heads Chicago Boosters Civic Club," *Chicago Defender*, city ed., January 12, 1929, p. 1–10.

14. Claude D. Greene, "Why Voters in the 2D Ward Will Re-Elect Ald. Anderson," *Chicago Defender*, city ed., February 22, 1929, p. 1–3.

15. "Aaron Payne Marked for Death by Moors," *Chicago Defender*, city ed., September 28, 1929, pp. 1–8; "Melvin Chisum Dies in Philly After Accident: Had Most Colorful Career," *New York Amsterdam News*, July 14, 1945, p. A6.

16. "Mrs. Drew Ali Organizes Young Moorish People," *Chicago Defender*, national ed., December 1, 1928, p. 3; "6 Held to Grand Jury for Cult Battle Murders," 4.

17. Noble Drew Ali, "Proclamation" (January 18, 1929), in Hopkins-Bey, *Saviour of Humanity*, 99–100.

18. Hopkins-Bey, *Saviour of Humanity*, 100.

19. Noble Drew Ali, "Proclamation" (February 5, 1929), in Hopkins-Bey, *Saviour of Humanity*, 100–101.

20. Noble Drew Ali to Brother and Sister Wise-Bey, Detroit (February 9, 1929), in Hopkins-Bey, *Saviour of Humanity*, 103–4. "Unloyalty" is in the original.

21. "Jesse Binga Adds New Land Mark to City's South Side," *Chicago Defender*, city ed., February 16, 1929, pp. 1–3; "Business Men Greet Edison Co. Officials: Welcome New Store on South Side," *Chicago Defender*, city ed., April 27, 1929, pp. 2–9.

22. Hopkins-Bey, *Saviour of Humanity*, 104.

23. "Prophet Begins Second Tour: Will Visit All Temples in America," *Moorish Guide* (February 1929), in Hopkins-Bey, *Saviour of Humanity*, 101–2.

24. Governor T. Thompson El, "Great Feast Held in Philly—Prophet and Governor Thompson El Are Honored by Moslems," *Moorish Guide* (March 1, 1929), in Hopkins-Bey, *Saviour of Humanity*, 102.

25. "Moors Greet the Great Prophet: Temple Welcomes Founder as He Blesses Moors," *Moorish Guide* (March 1, 1929), in Hopkins-Bey, *Saviour of Humanity*, 103.

26. "Hold Moorish Temple Prophet in Murder Plot," 1, 3; Associated Negro Press, "Murder Exposes Moorish Leader's Amours," 10.

27. Case 10005, Victim: Green, Claude, Defendant: Johnson, William, Date of Decision: May 14, 1929, Type of Legal Decision: Coroner's Verdict and Grand Jury, http://homicide.northwestern.edu/database/9629/?page=Object%20id%20#28 Interactive Database, accessed July 16, 2018.

28. "Hold Moorish Temple Prophet in Murder Plot," p. 3.

29. Prophet Noble Drew Ali, "Proclamation" (March 11, 1929), 104–5.

30. "Hold Moorish Temple Prophet in Murder Plot," 3.

31. Associated Negro Press, "Murder Exposes Moorish Leader's Amours," 10.

32. "Aaron Payne Marked for Death by Moors," 1–8; Case 10005, Victim: Green, Claude, Defendant: Johnson, William.

33. "Hold Moorish Temple Prophet in Murder Plot," 3.

34. "Hold Moorish Temple Prophet in Murder Plot," 3; Bowen, *A History of Conversion to Islam*, vol. 2, 388–89.

35. "Bury Slain 'Moor,'" *Chicago Defender*, city ed., March 23, 1929, pp. 1–7; "Cult Leader Being Held in Murder Case," *Chicago Defender*, national ed., May 18, 1929, p. 2.

36. "Cult Leader Being Held in Murder Case," 2.

37. "Moors' Trial 'Blows Up': Sick Juror and Allah the Cause," *Chicago Defender*, national ed., February 15, 1930, pp. 1, 3.

38. John Landesco, *Organized Crime in Chicago* (Chicago: Chicago University Press, 1968), chaps. 4 and 5.

39. Bergreen, *Capone*, 225–26.

40. "Lawlessness in High Places," *Chicago Journal*, May 22, 1922, scrapbook, Oscar DePriest Papers, Chicago History Museum.

41. Bergreen, *Capone*, 245–49.

42. *Ali's Men*, interview by Jacob S. Dorman, video call, March 5, 2019.

43. J. Worth Estes, "The Pharmacology of Nineteenth-Century Patent Medicines," *Pharmacy in History* 30 no. 1 (1988): 3–18

44. National Archives, Washington, DC, Series Title: *U.S. Citizen Passenger Lists of Vessels Arriving at Key West, Florida*, NAI Number: 2790482; Record Group Title: *Records of the Immigration and Naturalization Service, 1787–2004*, Record Group Number: 85.

CHAPTER FIFTEEN: CHICAGO JUSTICE

1. Correspondence, Donald R. Richberg to Julius Rosenwald, September 17, 1930, p. 2, Julius Rosenwald Papers, Box 32, Folder 5, University of Chicago Library, Special Collections Research Center.

2. Barbara S. Spackman, "Bill Thompson—Circusman," in Harold F. Gosnell Papers, Box 3, Folder Thompson, Mayor Bill, Special Collections Research Center, University of Chicago Library.

3. "Drop Charges Against DePriest: State Admits Defeat; Says Case is Weak," *Chicago Defender*, city ed., April 13, 1929, pp. 1(1); "Political Pals 'Double-Crossed' DePriest, Brusseaux Declares," *Philadelphia Tribune*, April 18, 1929, p. 2; "Bruseaux [*sic*] to Get Post in Washington: Wanted in Justice Department," *Chicago Defender*, city ed., January 19, 1929, pp. 1–8.

4. Woodiwiss, *Organized Crime and American Power*, 192.

5. "DePriest Denies Being Insull 'Pay Off' Man," *Pittsburgh Courier*, June 9, 1934, p. 2; "Insull Gifts Not Identified Says DePriest," *Baltimore Afro-American*, June 2, 1934, p. 20.

6. "DePriest Sworn In as U.S. Lawmaker," *Chicago Defender*, city ed., April 20, 1929, pp. 1(1).

7. "How Clean Are Our Dirty Politics?," *Baltimore Afro-American*, October 27, 1928, p. 17.

8. Nancy Joan Weiss, *Farewell to the Party of Lincoln: Black Politics in the Age of FDR* (Princeton, NJ: Princeton University Press, 1983), 81–89.

9. Weiss, *Farewell to the Party of Lincoln*.

10. Arthur Lashly, "Homicide (In Cook County)," in *The 1929 Illinois Crime Survey*, ed. John H. Wigmore (Chicago: Illinois Association for Criminal Justice, 1929), 596–98.

11. Case 10005, Victim: Green, Claude, Defendant: Johnson, William.

12. "Love Cult Thot [*sic*] Responsible for Slaying," *Baltimore Afro-American*, March 23, 1929, p. 2. Many followers deny this story, but it is corroborated by the 1930 census, which reported that a fifteen-year-old "Mary Drew" was living with her parents Foreman and Mozelle Bey, and that she was a widow who was married at thirteen. See: *Fifteenth Census of the United States, 1930*, 3619 S. Indiana Avenue, Chicago, Cook County, Illinois, Second Ward, Block 106, Enumeration District 16–62 (Washington, DC: National Archives and Records Administration, 1930), T626.

13. Noble Drew Ali, "I, Your Prophet," March 15, 1929, Moorish American Science Temple Papers [*sic*], Vivian G. Harsh Research Collection, Chicago Public Library.

14. A. N. Fields, "Colorful History of Early Chicago," *Chicago Defender*, February 4, 1933, p. 11.

15. "Daniel M. Jackson, Chicago Leader in Politics, Friend of DePriest, Dies After Ten Days From Influenza," *New York Age*, May 25, 1929, p. 3; Nathan Thompson, *Kings: The True Story of Chicago's Policy Kings and Numbers Racketeers: An Informal History* (Chicago: Bronzeville Press, 2003), 39.

16. Hopkins-Bey, *Saviour of Humanity*, 67.

17. Wilson, *Sacred Drift*, 43.

18. Sheik Way-El, *Noble Drew Ali and the Moorish Science Temple of America: The Movement That Started It All* (Washington, DC: Moorish Science Temple of America, 2011), 117.

19. "Drew Ali, Prophet of Cult, Is Buried with Pomp by Members," *Chicago Defender*, national ed., August 3, 1929, p. 1.

20. "Drew Ali, 'Prophet' of Moorish Cult, Dies Suddenly," *Chicago Defender*, national ed., July 27, 1929, p. 1.

21. Yad R. Yadav, Vijay Parihar, Hemant Namdev, and Jitin Bajaj, "Chronic Subdural Hematoma," *Asian Journal of Neurosurgery* 11, no. 4 (2016): 330–42.

22. James Lomax, *Fourteenth Census of the United States, 1920*, State of Michigan, Wayne County, Detroit, Enumeration District No. 55, Eleventh Ward of the City, Sheet No. 2B, Line 62, enumerated January 5, 1920; see, also, "Allen, Adam," in *Williams' Cincinnati Directory* (Cincinnati), various years, 1920–28. The listing disappears in 1929, and Eva Allen is listed as a widow in the 1930 census (see note 24).

23. Ali's Men, interview by Jacob S. Dorman, video call, March 5, 2019.

24. Eva Allen, *Fourteenth Census of the United States, 1920*, State of Ohio, Hamilton County, Cincinnati, Enumeration District No. 274, Sixteenth Ward of the City, Sheet No. 6A, Line 49, enumerated January 6, 1920; Eva Allen, *Fifteenth Census of the United States, 1930*; State of Ohio, Hamilton County, Cincinnati, Enumeration District 0177, Sixteenth Ward of the City, Sheet No. 2A, Line 3, enumerated April 3, 1930.

25. Breszka, "Insull to Meet New Leaders When He Returns to Chicago," 3.

26. "Hospital Benefits from Corporation Interest and Generosity," *Light: America's News Magazine* 4 no. 2 (December 3, 1927): 7; "Samuel Insull Was an Angel to Chicago," *Baltimore Afro-American*, March 31, 1934, p. 1.

27. Fitzroy K. Davis typescript (MSS Alpha Davis, Fitzroy K., Chicago History Museum), "The Human Drama of the Insull Trial" (November 1934): 172, 294.

28. "Many Attend Last Rites for Mrs. Martha DePriest: Pneumonia Victim," *Chicago Defender*, February 11, 1928, p. 4; "A Wonderful Program—to Him," cartoon, *Chicago Defender*, August 31, 1929, pp. 1(1).

29. "Mitchell for Congress," *Chicago World* (August 11, 1934), in Arthur W. Mitchell Papers, Box 2, Folder: General, Clippings and Correspondence, Chicago History Museum.

30. Breszka, "Insull to Meet New Leaders When He Returns to Chicago," 3.

31. "6 Held to Grand Jury for Cult Battle Murders," 4.

32. "Aaron Payne Marked for Death by Moors," *Chicago Defender*, city ed., September 28, 1929, pp. 1–8.

33. "Score Are Held as Aftermath of Bloody Fight," *New Journal and Guide* (Norfolk, VA), October 5, 1929, p. 1.

34. "Religious Cult Head Sentenced for Murder," *Hartford Courant*, April 19, 1930, p. 20.

35. "Seek Receiver for Million Dollar Concern: Chi Concern and Officers Face Bankruptcy," *Pittsburgh Courier*, December 24, 1932, pp. 1, 4.

36. "Seek Receiver for Million Dollar Concern," 1, 4.

EPILOGUE: THE BRIDGE

1. Ali, *Quotes of the Prophet*, 37.

2. Karl Evanzz, *The Messenger: The Rise and Fall of Elijah Muhammad* (New York: Vintage Books, 1999), 62–70. It should be noted that Evanzz's claim that Rosenwald, not Insull, bought Unity Hall is incorrect. There is also no mention of Greene in the papers of Julius Rosenwald, even after Greene's murder, suggesting that Greene did not make much of an impression on his onetime employer. Finally, the FBI and oral histories of the Nation of Islam on which Evanzz bases his account of the Moorish Science Temple are frequently inaccurate and need to be approached skeptically.

3. Evanzz, *The Messenger*, 68–69.

4. "Cultists Riot in Court; One Death, 41 Hurt," *Chicago Daily Tribune*, March 6, 1935, p. 1; Whyte, "Christian Elements in Negro American Muslim Religious Beliefs," 383; John Andrew Morrow, *Finding W. D. Fard: Unveiling the Identity of the Founder of the Nation of Islam* (Newcastle on Tyne, UK: Cambridge Scholars Publishing, 2019), 43, 187–88, 215, 218.

5. Ali's Men, interview by Jacob S. Dorman, video call, February 26, 2019.

6. John H. Bracey Jr., professor of Afro-American studies, University of Massachusetts, Amherst, email with the author, April 7, 2019.

7. Bowen, *A History of Conversion to Islam in the United States*, vol. 2, 387–96.

8. Manning Marable, *Malcolm X: A Life of Reinvention* (New York: Penguin, 2011), 459.

9. Pew Research Center, *U.S. Muslims Concerned About Their Place in Society, but Continue to Believe in the American Dream: Findings from Pew Research Center's 2017 Survey of U.S. Muslims* (Washington, DC: Pew Research Center, 2017), https://pewrsr.ch/2qibnaG, accessed August 14, 2018.

10. "Excerpts from the Apocryphal Sayings of the Prophet Noble Drew Ali," https://bit.ly/2vQ6Qz2, accessed August 15, 2018.

11. Tasneem Paghdiwala, "Eighty Years Ago a Prophet Came to the South Side and Drew Thousands of Followers. Today the Remaining Few Face an Uncertain Future," *Chicago Reader*, November 15, 2007, https://bit.ly/2Ur2icq, accessed January 23, 2019.

12. Gomez, *Black Crescent*, 203.

13. Gomez, *Black Crescent*.

14. On bricolage, see Dorman, *Chosen People*, 16–21.

15. "Excerpts from the Apocryphal Sayings of the Prophet Noble Drew Ali."

16. US Commission on Civil Rights, "Fears and Concerns of Affected, At-Risk Communities," in *Civil Rights Concerns in the Metropolitan Washington, D.C., Area in the Aftermath of the September 11, 2001, Tragedies*, https://bit.ly/2TFATX0, accessed February 7, 2019.

17. Shawn Neidorf, "Harassed, Insulted, Shriners Pay Price for Islam Imagery," *San Jose Mercury News*, reprinted in the *Chicago Tribune*, October 21, 2002, https://bit.ly/2ELivmj, accessed May 10, 2012.

18. David Chappelle, "Black Bush," *Chappelle's Show*, season 2, episode 3, aired April 14, 2004, Comedy Central, https://on.cc.com/1orVBRK, accessed February 7, 2019.

19. Eliot Weinberger, *What I Heard About Iraq* (London: Verso, 2005), 13, 18, 19, 33.

20. "Costs of War," a project of the Watson Institute of International and Public Affairs, Brown University, https://watson.brown.edu/costsofwar/, accessed January 23, 2019.

INDEX

Abbott, Robert, 144, 164, 175, 186
Academy of Music (New York), *In Old Kentucky* at, 19
Addeynu Allahe Universal Arabic Association (AAUAA), 249
Adorno, Theodor, 29
Afghanistan, war in, 256–57
Africa, 7–8, 38–40, 90–91, 134, 192, 254–55
African Americans. *See* Blacks
African Bethel Church (Chicago), 165–66
Africans, 91, 93
African Times and Orient Review (journal), 4, 139
Afro-American (newspaper), 174, 175
Aga, Akpan, 134–36
Ahmad, Mirzā Ghulām, 11, 140, 201
Ahmadiyya Muslims, 140, 141, 185, 189
Akpandac, Professor, 134–36
Al-Andalus, 24
al-Din, Nasir, 37
Alexander, Arthur, 101
Alexander, Eva, 101. *See also* Sotanki, Eva "Princess"
Al. G. Barnes Circus, 88
"The Al. G. Field Real Negro Minstrels and Troupe of Arabs," 94
Ali, Christina, 216
Ali, Dusé Mohamed (Duse Mohamed), 4–5, 138, 139–40, 189
Ali, Hassan Ben, 85–86
Ali, Mary Lou, 216, 235
Ali, Noble Drew (Timothy Drew, previously Thomas Drew, previously Armmah Sotanki, previously John Walter Brister): anti-Catholicism of, 187; apocalypticism of, 199; beliefs of, 161; birthday celebrations for, 207; as bridge, 254–55; on Chicago, 181; death of, 236–39, 241–44; as escape artist, 8, 119, 187; on finances, importance of, 215; formal education, lack of, 219–20; on freedom, 247; Claude

Greene's murder and, 143–44, 228, 234; historical reconfigurations by, 197–98; identity as Brister, 11, 124, 216–17; Insull and, 179; Islam, sources of knowledge of, 8; legacy of, 252–55; machine politicians, embrace of, 213–14; mentioned, 64; Moorish Temple of Science, establishment of, 186, 187–88; MSTA finances, focus on, 218–19; multiple marriages, 216; as Muslim prophet, 197; on own birth, 15; political activities of, 185–86, 204–6; political corruption, understanding of, 252–53; as Professor Drew, 123–42; on race, 41, 123; Sloane and, 181–84; statutory rape charges against, 235; Suleiman, borrowings from, 185; teachings of, 193–201. *See also* Brister, John Walter; Drew, Professor "Thomas" (Brister as); Moorish Science Temple of America; Sotanki, Armmah
Ali, Pearl Drew, 216, 219, 222, 238, 287n5
Ali Brothers (Pawnee Bill Wild West Show), 81, 82
Ali Mona, Prince, 115, 117–19, 130, 131
Allah Temple of Islam, 248–49
Allan, Maud, 110–11
Allen, Adam, 115, 238
Alexander, Eva, 184, 215, 238–39. *See also* Sotanki, Eva "Princess"
Allen's Minstrels, 95
Almansoop, Ali, 255
Almohads (Moors, *al-Muwahhidūn*), 25
al-murābitūn (Almoravids), 25
Amadu (religious "scientist"), 137
American Colonization Society, 95
American Moors, use of term, 13–14
Amistad (slave ship), 35
'Amr ibn al-'As, 24
Ancient Arabic Order of the Nobles of the Mystic Shrine for North America. *See* Shriners

Evanzz, Karl, 248, 295n2
Evening Post (newspaper), 153–54
Ezaldeen (Ez Al Deen), Muhammad, 186, 222–26, 238, 248, 249

fakirs, 78, 83
family structures, impact of slave trade on, 35–36
Fard, Wallace (D.), 248
Farrakhan, Louis, 251
Fatima (wife of Alī ibn Abī Ṭālib), 24
fatwa, against Ali, 200
Federal Housing Authority, racism of, 250
Fez, Morocco, as Islamic center, 52–53
fezzes, 52, 55, 248, 253
Ficino, Marsilio, 30
Fiddler, Harry, 95
Field, Al. G., 94
Fields, A. N., 235–36
Fields, Karen E., 42
Fields, Milton F., 58
Fields, Vina, 146–47
Field troupe, 278n20
First World War. *See* World War I
Fitzgerald, F. Scott, 161
Five Percenters, 196
Fleming, Walter M., 51
floaters (double voters), 212
Florence, William J. "Billy," 51, 56
Florida Blossom Minstrels, 95
Ford-El, David, 248
Foster, Stephen, 18
France, Black entertainers in, 121
fraternal organizations, 62–66. *See also* Shriners
Frazer, James G., 44
freak shows, 88–89, 91–92
Frederick V of Heidelberg, 32
freemasonry, 32, 56–57, 63, 64, 190. *See also* Muslim Masons; Shriners
French Caribbean, slave trade and, 36
French Revolution, impact of, 86–87
Freud, Sigmund, 99, 109–10
Friedman, Thomas, 256
Fuller, Hiram, 89

Gallagher, William, 243
Gandhi, Mahatma, 251
Garrett, Rebecca, 101
Garvey, Marcus Mosiah, 4, 139–41, 161, 162, 186, 188, 221
Geertz, Hildred, 33
gender roles, Ali's teachings on, 195
Georgia Minstrels, 105, 116
Ghana (ancient), Islam in, 24

Ghost Dance, 76–77, 199
Gibson, Orlando (Boneo Moskego), 91
Gilded Age, 3–5, 11, 67
God, Ali's teachings on, 194
Goins, Charles, 105
Golden Age of Jewish history, 24
Golden Age of Magic, 33–34
Golden Gate Quartet, 105
Goldman, Emma, 69
Gomez, Michael, 36, 254
Granady, Octavius C., 210, 244
Grand Theater (Chicago), Brister at, 113
Grant, Dr. B., 134–36
The Great Gatsby (Fitzgerald), 161
Great Migrations, 5, 115–17, 156, 158–67, 250
Green, R. W., 124
Greene, Agnes, 220, 225
Greene, Claude D.: Louis B. Anderson, article on, 204, 220–21; Insull and, 179; Moorish Temple factional politics and, 220–22, 224–26; murder of, 143, 218, 226–27, 234–35, 239, 244; Rosenwald and, 295n2; as Unity Hall manager, 205, 225
Grey, Alphonso, 105
Guiana, slave trade and, 36
Gulf Coast, African religious practices in, 39
Gullah Jack (conjurer), 39
Guzik, Jack (a.k.a. Jake) "Greasy Thumb," 150, 228–30, 236

Haas, Joseph, 210, 244
Haas, Minnie McKenzie, 210
Haiti, 39
hajj (pilgrimage to Mecca), 23
Hakim Bey (Peter Lamborn Wilson), 1, 6–7, 8, 192, 200, 287n5
Hall, Prince, 56–57
Haller, Mark H., 147, 150, 228
Hamid, Sufi Abdul (Eugene Brown), 54, 139
Hammond, Eva. *See* Sotanki, Eva "Princess"
Hammond, James, 101
Harding, George, 151
Harding, Warren G., 161
Harlem, New York City, 63, 131, 133, 162
Harper, Lucius C., 173
Harrison, Carter, IV, 148, 149, 151
Harrison, Hubert, 139, 140
Hartman, Fred, 65
Harvey, Paul, 39
Hasan, Waqar, 255
Hassan Ben Ali troupe, 49, 85–86
The Hate That Hate Produced (documentary), 250
Hausaland, 34, 37